D1444376

STRESS AND ANXIETY

THE SERIES IN CLINICAL AND COMMUNITY PSYCHOLOGY

CONSULTING EDITORS
Charles D. Spielberger and Irwin G. Sarason

IN PREPARATION

STRESS AND ANXIETY

Volume 13

Edited by
Charles D. Spielberger
University of South Florida

Irwin G. Sarason
University of Washington

Guest Editors
Jan Strelau
University of Warsaw

John M. T. Brebner
University of Adelaide

⬤ **HEMISPHERE PUBLISHING CORPORATION**
A member of the Taylor & Francis Group

New York   Washington   Philadelphia   London

Midtown

STRESS AND ANXIETY: Volume 13

1 2 3 4 5 6 7 8 9 0   E B E B   9 8 7 6 5 4 3 2 1 0

This book was set in Times Roman by Hemisphere Publishing Corporation. The editors were Debbie Klenotic and Deena Williams Newman; the production supervisor was Peggy M. Rote; and the typesetter was Shirley J. McNett. Cover design by Sharon M. DePass. Printing and binding by Edwards Brothers, Inc.

A CIP catalog record for this book is available from the British Library.

Library of Congress Cataloging-in-Publication Data

Advanced Study Institute on Stress and Anxiety in Modern Life,
Murnau, Ger., 1973.

Stress and anxiety: [proceedings]/edited by Charles D. Spielberger,
Irwin G. Sarason. Washington: Hemisphere Publ. Corp.
   v. :ill.: 24 cm. (v. 1–2: The series in clinical psychology
   v. 3–5: The series in clinical and community psychology)
   Includes bibliographies and indexes.
   1. Stress (Psychology)—Congresses. 2. Anxiety—Congresses.
I. Sarason, Irwin G., ed. II. Spielberger, Charles Donald, date, ed.
III. North Atlantic Treaty Organization. Division of Scientific Affairs.
IV. Title. [DNLM: 1. Anxiety. 2. Stress, Psychological. WM 172 S755a]
BF575.S75A38   1973   616.8'522   74-28292
                                MARC

ISBN 1-56032-139-3
ISSN 0146-0846
ISSN 0364-1112

III
EMOTIONAL REACTIONS TO STRESS

Contributors

MICHAEL J. APTER, Purdue University, USA
NOLA BIDDLE, University of Melbourne, Australia
JOHN M. T. BREBNER, University of Adelaide, Australia
ANNE E. BYRNE, Australian National University, Canberra, Australia
DON G. BYRNE, Australian National University, Canberra, Australia
BARBARA J. CHISHOLM, University of Otago, New Zealand
SERGE CROES, University of Giessen, Germany
PETER B. DEFARES, University of Amsterdam, The Netherlands
DENNIS G. DYCK, University of Manitoba, Canada
ANDRZEJ ELIASZ, Polish Academy of Sciences, Poland
SUSAN C. ETLINGER, University of Vienna, Austria
JOACHIM FUCHS, Johannes Gutenberg University, Mainz, Germany
GISELHER GUTTMANN, University of Vienna, Austria
JOHN WALLACE HINTON, University of Glasgow, Scotland
RICK HOWARD, University of Otago, New Zealand
MICHEL PIERRE JANISSE, University of Manitoba, Canada
GRAHAM A. R. JOHNSTON, University of Sydney, Australia
DAVID I. B. KERR, University of Sydney, Australia
ROBERT G. KNIGHT, University of Otago, New Zealand
HEINZ WALTER KROHNE, Johannes Gutenberg University, Mainz, Germany
WOLF LAUTERBACH, J. W. Goethe University, Frankfurt, Germany
ANJA LEPPIN, Freie Universität, Berlin, Germany
PAUL McREYNOLDS, University of Nevada–Reno, USA
PETER MERZ, University of Giessen, Germany
CATHY G. MOSER, University of Manitoba, Canada
MATTHIAS MÜLLER, University of Giessen, Germany
PETRA NETTER, University of Giessen, Germany
JENNIFER ONG, University of Sydney, Australia
MICHAEL C. F. PAIN, Royal Melbourne Hospital, Australia
JUDITH M. PAULIN, Otago Medical School, New Zealand
DORIT RABINOVITZ, Shiba Hospital, Israel
YARON RABINOVITZ, Shiba Hospital, Israel
LESZEK RADOMSKI, University of Warsaw, Poland
RALF SCHWARZER, Freie Universität, Berlin, Germany
CHARLES D. SPIELBERGER, University of South Florida, Tampa, USA
JAN STRELAU, University of Warsaw, Poland
SVEN SVEBACK, University of Bergen, Norway
YONA TEICHMAN, Tel Aviv University, Israel
JOHN W. G. TILLER, University of Melbourne, Australia
CYNTHIA YERAMA, University of Manitoba, Canada
HENDRIKA J. WAAL-MANNING, Otago Medical School, New Zealand
KAZIMIERZ WRZESNIEWSKI, Warsaw Academy of Medicine, Poland
EMERALD YEH, University of Manitoba, Canada

Preface

The *Stress and Anxiety* series was created to disseminate research findings based on presentations at international scientific conferences. In keeping with this goal, the research reported in Volume 13 was conducted by investigators from four continents and eleven different countries. The individual chapters are based primarily on papers presented at the 24th International Congress of Psychology held in Sydney, Australia, August 28–September 3, 1988. Most of these papers were presented in two symposia on "Stress and Emotions" organized by C. D. Spielberger, J. M. T. Brebner, and J. Strelau. The evolution of theory and research on emotional reactions to stress required broadening the title of these symposia to encompass both anger and anxiety.

This volume is organized into five main parts, each with a major theme, but with considerable overlap in the topics considered in the individual chapters. The chapters in Part I examine research findings on stress and emotion from the perspective of diverse theoretical models, differing in their emphasis on phenomenological, behavioral, and psychophysiological variables. The role of intrapsychic conflict and individual differences in personality as determinants of stress and emotion are examined in Part II. Research on anxiety and anger as the major emotional reactions to experimentally-induced and naturally-occurring stressors provides the focus for the chapters in Part III. The influence of a variety of stressors on neurophysiological reactions and hormone modulation are considered in Part IV. The chapters in Part V are concerned with complex interactions of Type A behavior with stressful circumstances to influence emotions, performance, achievement, and the risk for coronary disease.

The editors of this volume are indebted to the organizers of the 24th International Congress, and especially to Professor Sidney Lovibond, for inviting us to develop the symposia on Stress and Emotion and permitting us to arrange for the publication of this volume independently of the proceedings of the Congress. They were also most generous in allowing us to include several papers with relevant content that were presented at the Congress, but not included in our symposia.

In the division of labor associated with organizing the symposia and editing this volume, the major responsibility for reviewing the abstracts of the symposia papers, coordinating the scheduling arrangements with the Congress Secretariat, and editing the papers of the contributors from Australia and New Zealand resided with John M. T. Brebner. Jan Strelau encouraged and arranged the presentations by colleagues from Eastern Europe, and reviewed and edited their papers for publication. C. D. Spielberger assisted in organizing the symposia, assumed the major editing responsibility for papers from the U.S. and Western Europe, and coordinated the arrangements for the publication of the volume.

For her assistance in typing the abstracts and organizing the symposia on which this volume is based, the editors owe a special thanks to Sophie Tzamtzidis of the University of Adelaide. We would also like to express our appreciation to Veronica

Clement and Bob Arnold of the University of South Florida for their invaluable contributions in reviewing the manuscripts. Finally, we would like to acknowledge our gratitude to Virginia Berch for her expert assistance in preparing the manuscript for publication.

Charles D. Spielberger
Irwin G. Sarason
John M. T. Brebner
Jan Strelau

Attention

Please be advised that beginning with Volume 14 the STRESS AND ANXIETY series will change to STRESS AND EMOTION: Anger, Anxiety, and Curiosity. The series will continue to be based upon top notch international research, but its scope will be shifting as is reflected in the new title. Dr. Charles Spielberger will be expanding the reasoning for the broadening of the series in the upcoming Volume 14.

Also, please be aware that this will now be a series by itself and will be titled STRESS AND EMOTION: Anger, Anxiety, and Curiosity. It will no longer be a part of The Series in Clinical and Community Psychology.

Please join us at Hemisphere in our support of the expansion of this time-honored series.

I

STRESS AND EMOTION THEORY

1

Regulation of the Energetic Level of Behavior: Performance Under Stress Consisting of High Discrepancy Between Intensity of Stimulation and Level of Reactivity

Jan Strelau and Leszek Radomski
University of Warsaw, Poland

The energetic level of behavior (ELB), to which the regulative theory of temperament refers (Strelau, 1983, 1985), may be expressed in the intensity or magnitude of reactions (responses) to stimuli of given intensity or in the degree of effective functioning under stress, that is, under stimulation of extreme value: overstimulation or deprivation (Strelau, 1988). Relatively stable and characteristic for a given individual, intensities (magnitudes) of reactions are regarded, according to our theory, as an expression of a temperament trait called *reactivity* (Strelau, 1983).

Reactivity is, however, only one of the components on which the energetic characteristic of reactions or behavior depends. Among the many variables that contribute to the ELB characteristics, of special importance are (a) intensity of acting stimuli and (b) actual level of arousal. The stimulative value of a situation is determined by objective features of acting stimuli as well as by individual-specific subjective experience bound up with those stimuli. The subjective component of stimulation hardly undergoes experimental control because of difficulties in quantitative scoring.

The actual level of arousal is an outcome of the individual's psychophysiological state (e.g., fatigue, mood, anxiety, or self-consciousness), the stimuli operating prior to the behavior being measured, and individual differences in the chronic level of arousal characterized as arousability (Gray, 1964; Mehrabian, 1977). Reactivity, which is determined by physiological mechanisms regulating the level of arousal, recalls the concept of arousability as well as the Pavlovian notion "strength of the nervous system" (Nebylitsyn, 1972; Pavlov, 1951–1952; Strelau, 1983, 1985; Teplov, 1964). In distinction from arousability and strength of the nervous system, which, being related to each other (Gray, 1964), refer to physiological phenomena, reactivity pertains to psychological characteristics. Reactivity may be regarded as the behavioral component of arousability.

Preparation of this chapter was supported by the Minister of National Education (Grant RPBP III. 25).

Table 1   The stimulative value of situation (S) and level of arousability (A) as examples of Situation × Person interaction underlying the energetic level of behavior

Stimulative value of situation	Level of arousability		
	Low	Moderate	High
Low	$S \times A_1$	$S \times A_2$	$S \times A_3$
Moderate	$S \times A_4$	$S \times A_5$	$S \times A_6$
High	$S \times A_7$	$S \times A_8$	$S \times A_9$

Because the psychophysiological states as well as stimuli operating prior to the behavior to be measured do change over situations and time, the individual-specific chronic state of arousal (arousability, reactivity) and the stimulative value of the actual situation seem to be the most important determinants of the energetic level of behavior. On the basis of these two variables, both being further differentiated into three levels of intensity, a taxonomy of possible Situation × Person interactions underlying the energetic level of behavior is presented in Table 1.

Situations characterized by moderate stimulation seem to belong to the category of so-called normal situations. With few exceptions, they may be encountered most often in real life. This assumption holds true for all individuals, independent of their level of arousability. Thus the interaction of moderate stimulative value of situation with different levels of arousability ($S \times A_{4-6}$) should be regarded as most typical for behavior described from the energetic perspective.

In light of abundant evidence, we know that the best efficiency of performance, or, in general, optimal functioning, occurs when the energetic characteristics of behavior are based on the optimal level of arousal. Individuals differing in arousability (reactivity) need different intensity of stimulation to attain or maintain the optimal level of arousal (Strelau, 1983, 1987). The higher the level of arousability, the less intensive stimulation needed to reach that level. Thus we may assume that the following interactions of the stimulative value of situation with level of arousability ensure optimal functioning: Low Stimulation × High Arousability ($S \times A_3$), Moderate Stimulation × Moderate Arousability ($S \times A_5$), and High Stimulation × Low Arousability ($S \times A_7$).

Stress, when characterized from the point of view of ELB, has also its specificity. It consists of an unfavorable interaction between the intensity of stimulation and level of arousability. Stress is regarded here as a result of high discrepancy between the stimulative value of the situations (demands) the individual is confronted with, and his or her level of arousability (reactivity), the latter determining the capacity to cope with the demands. Taking into account our taxonomy, the following interactions will be the most unfavorable (stress generating): Low Stimulation × Low Arousability ($S \times A_1$) and High Stimulation × High Arousability ($S \times A_9$).

CHANGES IN REACTIVITY SCORES UNDER UNFAVORABLE INTERACTION: HIGH STIMULATION × HIGH AROUSABILITY

Many studies conducted in our laboratory examining the role of reactivity in the individual's functioning under extreme situations support the assumption derived from the taxonomy that the interactions $S \times A_1$ and $S \times A_9$ are highly stress generating. As a result of these unfavorable interactions, decrease of performance occurs or increase in the psychophysiological costs of the individual's functioning takes place (Eliasz, 1981; Klonowicz, 1985, 1987; Strelau, 1983, 1988). In these studies reactivity was mostly assessed by means of the Strength of Excitation (SE) scale from the Strelau Temperament Inventory (STI). The details regarding this questionnaire, as well as the arguments why the SE scale is a measure of reactivity, are described elsewhere (Strelau, 1983; Strelau, Angleitner, & Ruch, 1990). In these studies the behavior or reactions of individuals differing in reactivity were measured under stress (overstimulation or deprivation), whereas the STI was usually administered in normal situations.

It has been stated by one of us (Radomski, 1987) that the scores on the SE scale, aimed at measuring reactivity under threatening situations, change essentially as the measures of the SE scale under the normal situation. This regularity has been found in two independent studies, one conducted on 54 candidates of an aviation high school (male adolescents ages 14 to 16) and one conducted on 40 candidates for pilots (men ages 17 to 19). In both studies high-reactivity individuals scored under threat situations as if they were less reactive compared with SE scores obtained in normal situation. Furthermore, the results under threat did not correlate with the teacher's rating of reactivity, whereas the rating scores correlated significantly with SE measures when the STI was filled out in a normal situation. The threat used in both studies consisted of a very strong selection.

The obvious interpretation of these facts is that in both studies the social desirability (Edwards, 1957) effect occurred. Since it is known that resistance to stress and risky behavior are essential characteristics of pilots, the subjects, in spite of their high reactivity, responded in such a way as if they were less reactive, thus increasing the probability to succeed in tiding over the selection.

However, alternative interpretations are also probable. For example, we have to take into account that the selection pressure is a very stimulating situation, especially for high-reactivity individuals. This situation involves one of the most unfavorable interactions between the stimulative value of the situation and level of arousability/reactivity ($S \times A_9$). Because this type of interaction influences behavior, there is no reason to assume that behavior consisting of filling out the SE scale should not be influenced by the disadvantageous $S \times A$ interaction. If so, changes in responding to the SE scale under selection should be expected first of all in high reactivity subjects. In addition, because stress generates anxiety (Kendall, 1978; Wrzesniewski & Sosnowski, 1987) one may also assume that state anxiety of high reactivity individuals when confronted with stimulation of high intensity will be higher than that of low-reactivity individuals. This relationship has been supported by data obtained in our laboratory (Strelau, 1983). In the present study we examined whether this alternative hypothesis, which does not refer to the social desirability effect, could be defended. Responding to the SE items was regarded in the present study as an example of performance that takes place in a situation of stress.

In order to examine whether situations of high stimulative value influence response to the SE scale items, subjects were investigated during several stages of surgical treatment, before and after administering morphine (Experiment 1).

Morphine, in interaction with the monoamine oxidase neurotransmitters, deactivates the cortex, thereby decreasing the actual level of arousal.

To verify whether state anxiety under strong stimulation is present, especially in high-reactivity individuals supposed to experience the surgical treatment as highly threatening, anxiety was measured in subjects differing in level of reactivity. Various stages of surgical treatment were under control (Experiment 2). In this study diazepam instead of morphine was administered. This drug decreases the level of arousal first in the limbic structures, thus influencing the state of anxiety.

EXPERIMENT 1

Method

Twenty-two men ages 22 to 30 were subjects. All of them underwent surgical operation that consisted of removing varicose veins on the feet. Before being operated on they received extrameningeal anesthesia that caused reversible disconnection of neural conductance in the regions being operated. This allowed operation without generally anesthetizing the patient. During the surgery patients were in a state of analgesia, that is, not feeling pain but fully conscious. The disease subject to surgical treatment was not life threatening, and the patients were informed that no pain would be felt during the operation. Prior to the operation 15 mg of morphine was administered. Reactivity was assessed by means of two equivalent subscales (A and B) of the SE scale from the STI. The subscales contained 22 items each. Reactivity was scored three times: (a) prior to administering morphine, (b) 45 min after administering morphine but before the patient was carried to the operating room, and (c) several days after the surgical operation was finished but before the patient left the hospital. It was assumed that situation c was the least threatening, representative of a normal situation. It must be noted that all of the patients were pilots, accustomed to staying in hospitals for periodic medical examination.

Results

The scores on the reactivity scales obtained several days after surgery in a situation assumed to be a normal one correlated with reactivity measured during the anticipation of surgical operation—before and after administering morphine: $rs = .36$ (*NS*) and .57 ($p < .05$), respectively.

In order to examine whether changes in reactivity scores under different states of arousal depended on the level of reactivity assessed in normal situation, the scores were analyzed separately for high-, medium-, and low-reactivity patients. The results are presented in Table 2.

As can be seen, the only individuals showing changes in their answers to the items of the SE scale in situations differing in level of arousal were the high-reactivity subjects. In both situations of anticipation (before and after administering morphine) the level of reactivity was significantly lower compared with reactivity in the normal situation. It was also found that level of reactivity under the treatment of morphine decreased significantly compared with level of reactivity before the drug was administered.

Table 2 Changes in strength of excitation scale scores under distinct arousal states in individuals differing in the level of reactivity

	Anticipation stage		
Reactivity level	Before morphine	After morphine	After surgery
High (n = 6)	27.50	24.50	18.25
Medium (n = 7)	25.29	26.43	28.42
Low (n = 9)	34.67	35.44	35.00

Note. ◄- - - - -► $p < .05$. ◄————► $p < .01$.

Discussion

The fact that there was no statistically significant correlation between reactivity measured during the anticipation of surgery prior to administering morphine and reactivity assessed after surgery is not surprising if we assume that waiting for surgery that will take place several hours after examination is extremely stimulating. Because morphine decreases the level of arousal, the significant correlation between SE scores recorded after administering morphine and several days after operation seems to be understandable.

The statistically significant differences between SE scores in both anticipation stages compared with scores after surgery recorded in high-reactivity individuals only are in agreement with our hypothesis. Difficult to interpret, however, is the direction of changes. In both threatening situations, high-reactivity individuals scored as if they were less reactive. This result, being in accordance with data recorded in both selection studies mentioned previously, cannot be explained by the social desirability effect. Maybe it represents a kind of defense mechanism that consists of changes in self-perception under threat. Individuals who perceive themselves as less reactive than they usually are perhaps are using a strategy that allows in this situation more effective coping with stress. This interpretation needs to be verified. In fact, results obtained in both of the present experiments must be viewed with caution because of the small number of subjects investigated.

EXPERIMENT 2

Method

Forty men ages 18 to 35 were subjects. They were divided into two groups (A and B) of 20 subjects each. All of them underwent the same operation as in Experiment 1. The only difference was that instead of morphine, diazepam was administered. Reactivity was measured by means of the SE scale of the STI. The State–Trait Anxiety Inventory (Spielberger et al., 1970) (S-anxiety) was used to measure the state of anxiety in the following stages of the medical treatment: (a) during the day of operation, before diazepam was injected; (b) 45 min after the injection but before the patient was transported to the operating room; (c) while the patient was lying on the operating table but before anesthesia; (d) several minutes after the operation started; and (e) several days after the surgery but before the patient left the hospital. For technical reasons, in Group A level of anxiety was measured in Stage c but not Stage d, and in Group B anxiety in Stage d but not Stage c was measured.

Results

Taking into account the median for reactivity scores, individuals in Group A, in which anxiety was scored on the operating table but before anesthesia, were divided into high and low in reactivity, 10 subjects each. The groups differed significantly ($p < .001$) from each other. The results, illustrating the dynamics of state anxiety depending on the level of reactivity and measured in the different stages of medical treatment, are presented in Table 3.

As can be seen, for high-reactivity individuals level of anxiety before administering diazepam and while lying on the operating table was significantly higher as compared with the normal situation (i.e., after operation). In low-reactivity individuals the only significant increase in the level of state anxiety occurred when they were lying on the operating table. Contrary to the expectation that level of anxiety would be, in general, higher prior and during operation in low-reactivity individuals, this was not proved, however such a tendency occurs (see Table 3).

The results of Group B, for whom state anxiety was measured after the operation started, are presented in Table 4. There seems to have been a regularity as regards the increase of anxiety in high-reactivity individuals during anticipation of the operation before diazepam was administered because the results are similar to those for Group A. In low-reactivity individuals anxiety increased during the operation as well as after the administration of diazepam. The increase of anxiety after administration of the drug was not found in Group A. In Group B the differences in state anxiety depending on the level of reactivity are evident. In three of the four states of arousal state anxiety was significantly higher in high-reactivity individuals. It must be added that the differences in reactivity between high- and low-reactivity individuals was also highly significant ($p < .001$).

Discussion

The significantly higher level of anxiety in high-reactivity subjects as compared with low-reactivity subjects recorded in Group B in three of the four stages of surgical treatment is in agreement with our expectation. This tendency also occurred in Group A. One may conclude that, in general, the surgical treatment was

Table 3 Changes in state anxiety under different arousal states in high- and low-reactivity individuals: Group A

Subjects	Before diazepam	After diazepam	Operating table	After surgery
High reactivity	48.3	45.8	47.5 ◄------► 42.7	
Low reactivity	43.2	43.0	44.3	41.5
High/low reactivity				
t (18)	1.784	.654	.958	.375
p	.10	ns	ns	ns

Note. ◄----► $p < .05$. ◄——► $p < .01$.

Table 4 Changes in state anxiety under different arousal states in high- and low-reactivity individuals: Group B

Subjects	Before diazepam	After diazepam	Surgery	After surgery
High reactivity	44.4	42.2	47.1 ◄- - - ► 40.1	
Low reactivity	35.2	38.5	38.2 ◄- - - ► 30.7	
High/low reactivity				
t (18)	2.303	.957	2.116	2.589
p	.05	ns	.05	.02

Note. ◄- - - ► $p < .05$.

more threatening for high-reactivity individuals compared with low-reactivity individuals.

The results obtained in Groups A and B suggest that both situations—while lying on the operating table before anesthesia (stage c) and several minutes after the operation started (stage d)—did not differ in the generated level of anxiety. In both groups, high- and low-reactivity patients scored essentially higher in stage c or d compared with the normal situation (stage e). For both groups stage e was the one in which state anxiety was the lowest. This seems reasonable if we consider that several days after the surgery the threat disappeared. The fact that low-reactivity subjects scored essentially higher in state anxiety before and during the operation (Group A, stage c; Group B, stages b and d as compared with measures taken a few days after the surgery (stage e) suggests that the surgical treatment was threatening not only for high- but also for low-reactivity individuals.

The only result difficult to interpret may be found in Table 4. Namely, in stage b, after diazepam was injected, low-reactivity subjects in Group B gained—as compared with other states—the highest score in state anxiety, even though diazepam should reduce anxiety, especially in low-reactivity individuals. Such a reducing tendency (without statistically significance, however) was observed in high-reactivity individuals in both Groups A and B.

CONCLUSIONS

The results obtained in our experiments suggest that under conditions of surgical treatment changes in responses to the SE scale items occur; this is especially evident in high-reactivity individuals. A highly stimulating situation interacting with a high level of reactivity (arousability) should be regarded as an example of an unfavorable Situation × Person interaction that influences the individual's behavior. In our experiments the behavior consisted of responding to the SE items. Under the different stages of surgical treatment high-reactivity individuals scored as if they were less reactive compared with their reactivity assessment in normal situation. This result, difficult to explain, may have been due to the activation of some coping strategies used by high-reactivity subjects, for whom the various stages of surgical treatment were perceived as more threatening compared with the low-reactivity subjects. Evidence for this hypothesis stems from Experiment 2. The data obtained in this study show that high-reactivity individuals score higher in state anxiety than low-reactivity individuals. The data also indicate that the different stages of surgical treatment are more threatening for both high- and low-reactivity subjects compared with a normal situation.

Our study suggests that reliable responses to reactivity items can be obtained only under conditions characterized by proper interaction between the stimulative value of the situation and the individual's level of reactivity (arousability).

Further studies are needed to examine whether responses to inventory items, comprising different aspects of the arousability domain, change under unfavorable interactions and, if so, in what direction. Referring to our taxonomy of Stimulation × Arousability interactions, it is suggested that of special interest for these kinds of studies are the most unfavorable interactions: High Stimulation × High Arousabiity ($S \times A_1$) and Low Stimulation × Low Arousability ($S \times A_9$).

SUMMARY

We argue that the stimulative value of the situation and level of arousability (reactivity) are the most influential variables in determining the energetic level of behavior (ELB). Taking these two variables as a starting point, a taxonomy of possible Situation × Person interactions underlying the ELB is proposed. Attention is paid to stress-generating interactions that consist of high discrepancy between intensity of stimulation and level of arousability. Two experiments were conducted with the aim of examining the influence of a highly stimulating situation (surgical treatment) on performance in individuals differing in level of reactivity. The performance consisted of responding to reactivity items from the Strelau Temperament Inventory (STI) during different stages of surgical treatment. Because the situation was regarded as being threatening, especially for the high-reactivity subjects, state anxiety, as measured by the State–Trait Anxiety Inventory, was under control. The results show that the interaction of high stimulations with high level of reactivity generated the most stress; this was indicated by changes in responses to the inventory items and by high level of anxiety.

REFERENCES

Edwards, A. E. (1957). *The social desirability variable in personality assessment and research.* New York: Dryden Press.

Eliasz, A. (1981). *Temperament a system regulacji stymulacji* [Temperament and the stimulation regulating system]. Warsaw: Panstwowe Wydawnictwo Naukowe.

Gray, J. A. (Ed.). (1964). *Pavlov's typology.* Oxford, England: Pergamon Press.

Kendall, P. C. (1978). Anxiety: States, traits-situations? *Journal of Consulting and Clinical Psychology, 46,* 280–287.

Klonowicz, T. (1985). Temperament and performance. In J. Strelau (Ed.). *Temperamental bases of behavior: Warsaw studies on individual differences* (pp. 79–115). Lisse: Swets & Zeitlinger.

Klonowicz, T. (1987). *Reactivity, experience and capacity.* Warsaw: Wydawnictwa Uniwersytetu Warszawskiego.

Mehrabian, A. (1977). Individual differences in stimulus screening and arousability. *Journal of Personality, 45,* 237–250.

Nebylitsyn, V. D. (1972). *Fundamental properties of the human nervous system.* New York: Plenum Press.

Pavlov, I. P. (1951–1952). *Complete works* (2nd ed.). Moscow: U.S.S.R. Academy of Sciences. (In Russian)

Radomski, L. (1987). *Reaktywnosc a zmiany poziomu aktywacji pod wplywem sytuacji rozniacych sie wartoscia stymulacyjna: Regulacja poziomu energetycznego zachowania* [Reactivity and changes in arousal level under situations differing in stimulative value: The regulation of the energetic level of behavior]. Unpublished doctoral dissertation, University of Warsaw, Warsaw, Poland.

Spielberger, C. D., Gorsuch, R. L:, & Lushene, R. E. (1970). *Manual for the State-Trait Anxiety Inventory.* Palo Alto, CA: Consulting Psychologists Press.

Strelau, J. (1983). *Temperament-personality-activity.* London: Academic Press.

Strelau, J. (1985). Pavlov's typology and the regulative theory of temperament. In J. Strelau (Ed.), *Temperamental bases of behavior: Warsaw studies on individual differences* (pp. 7–40). Lisse: Swets & Zeitlinger.

Strelau, J. (1987). Personality dimensions based on arousal theories: Search for integration. In J. Strelau, & H. J. Eysenck (Eds.), *Personality dimensions and arousal* (pp. 269–286). New York: Plenum Press.

Strelau, J. (1988). Temperament dimensions as co-determinants of resistance to stress. In M. P. Janisse (Ed.), *Individual differences, stress, and health psychology* (pp. 146–169). New York: Springer Verlag.

Strelau, J., Angleitner, A., & Ruch, W. (1990). *Strelau Temperament Inventory (STI): General review and studies based on German samples.* In C. D. Spielberger & J. N. Butcher (Eds.), *Advances in personality assessment* (Vol. 8, pp. 187–241). Hillsdale, NJ: Erlbaum.

Teplov, B. M. (1964). Problems in the study of general types of higher nervous activity in man and animals. In J. A. Gray (Ed.), *Pavlov's typology* (pp. 3–153). Oxford, England: Pergamon Press.

Wrzesniewski, K., & Sosnowski, T. (1987). Anxiety and the perception of real and imagined stress situations. *Polish Psychological Bulletin, 18,* 149–158.

2

A Structural Phenomenology of Stress

Michael J. Apter
Purdue University, USA

The attempt is often made to define and study stress in entirely objective, especially physiological, terms. Yet in these terms it is impossible to make such distinctions as those between welcome challenge and unwelcome threat, desired risk and undesired danger, passionate interest and horrified attention, willing commitment and unwilling obligation. In other words, it is difficult in entirely physiological terms to distinguish between pleasant and unpleasant forms of emotion and exertion. Yet this distinction goes to the very heart of stress as we experience it in our everyday lives. Thus, anxiety is stressful, but excitement surely is not; unavoidable exertion may be stressful, but freely chosen exercise would not appear to be; strenuous play is not stressful, but hard work often is. Such differences may, of course, be reflected in the psychophysiological record; but they cannot in principle be made sense of without reference to the level of subjective experience.

In this chapter, an alternative approach to stress—and indeed to motivation, emotion, personality, and other psychological topics—will be presented, an approach that starts from experience and works outward to physiological, behavioral, and other objective variables. The approach has been referred to as "structural phenomenology" (Apter, 1981, 1982) and draws attention to the fact that the phenomological field has structure (over and above the structure and pattern of its contents) and that this structure at a given moment constitutes a kind of "internal climate" or "way of being" for an individual. Structural phenomenology is, then, the study of psychological processes in relation to phenomenal structure—both structure at a given moment of time and structure over time (i.e., both synchronic and diachronic structure).

More specifically, I shall examine stress from the perspective of a theory that was generated within the structural–phenomenological framework and is known as "reversal theory" (Apter, 1982). This theory is now a body of ideas and evidence to which contributions have been made by researchers working in a variety of fields (e.g., Apter, Fontana, & Murgatroyd, 1985; Apter, Kerr, & Cowles, 1988). In this chapter I sketch several of the basic ideas of the theory; considerably more detail can be found in Apter (1982) and Apter (1989), the latter reviewing all the evidence that bears on the theory to date as well as presenting the whole of the theory itself.

REVERSAL THEORY

Here, in brief, are a few of the pivotal ideas of reversal theory. (New technical terms appear in italics.)

1. Understanding the experience of motivation is essential to understanding both the full range of everyday behavior and also various types of psychopathology. Motivational experience has two levels: At the lower, or motivational, level various aspects of motivation are experienced such as arousal level, relation of means to ends, relation of the ongoing behavior to contextual rules, and so on. At the higher, or metamotivational, level the lower level is open to various alternative interpretations by the individual, so that the same motivational variable can, for example, give rise to different degrees of pleasant or unpleasant hedonic tone, depending on the interpretation and without the variable itself changing in value.

2. At the metamotivational level, such interpretations go in pairs of opposites so that the variable concerned is experienced in one way or the other at all times; however, switching from one to the other is also possible under different conditions. (The situation is not unlike that of perceptual reversals, as in perception of the Necker cube.) We may therefore refer to pairs of *metamotivational modes* and to *reversal* between these modes.

3. These modes are states, but they are states within which a range of emotions can be experienced depending on the values of the variables being interpreted. In other words, they are not single-value emotional states like anxiety. For example, one pair of modes is referred to as the *anxiety-avoidance* and *excitement-seeking* pair. In the former, arousal will be experienced as somewhere on the range from pleasant relaxation (if it is low) to unpleasant anxiety (if it is high). In the latter, it will be experienced as somewhere on the range from unpleasant boredom (if it is low) to pleasant excitement (if it is high). It should be noted that both modes extend over the whole arousal range so that this account of the relationship between arousal and hedonic tone is quite different from that of optimal arousal theory.

4. As the last example makes clear, reversal theory rejects simple homeostatic notions for those of *bistability*—high arousal is preferred under some conditions (i.e., when the excitement-seeking mode is in operations) and low arousal under other conditions (i.e., when the anxiety-avoidance mode is in operation). Arousal preference (which can change) is metamotivational and has to be distinguished from actual arousal level, and also from arousability. Each mode, then, not only interprets but also sets into action, and controls, activities designed to achieve the preferred level of the variable on which it operates.

5. Although metamotivational modes are states, people experience innate tendencies to be in one or the other mode, for each pair of modes, over time. Because this tendency is not a trait in the conventional sense—because everyone will be expected to spend at least some periods in the state that does not correspond to their bias, and to be as fully "in" that state as someone would be who has a bias toward it—it is referred to as *dominance*. We could thus speak of anxiety-avoidance dominance, or excitement-seeking dominance. In this way, tendencies in intraindividual differences are shown to underlie interindividual differences.

6. Reversals between modes are brought about by three factors in interaction:

   Environmental events and situations. A given event, when suitably cognitively interpreted, can induce a *contingent reversal*. For example, a sudden loud noise, interpreted as a threat, will be expected, other things being equal, to bring about a reversal to the anxiety-avoidance mode (in which the high arousal caused by the noise will be experienced as anxiety).

Frustration. If the preferred level of some experienced aspect of motivation is not achieved, then the resulting frustration is increasingly likely, other things being equal, to induce a reversal. For example, if one cannot experience excitement in the excitement-seeking mode, one will eventually "give up," a reversal to the anxiety-avoidance mode will take place, and the low level of arousal will be experienced as relaxation.

Satiation. As the individual remains in a given mode, so satiation of that mode builds up in such a way that it increasingly helps, in conjunction with other factors, to bring about a reversal; eventually it will become strong enough to induce a reversal on its own even in the absence of other facilitating factors. The effect of this is that there is a kind of internal rhythm of alternation between modes in a given pair of modes. This rhythm, however, can be overridden by environmental events or by frustration. It is the balance of this internal rhythm that is supposed to underlie dominance (see #5 above). An effect is that the individual may sometimes experience, and behave in reaction to, the same circumstances in opposite ways. In other words, inconsistency in this view is inherent to human nature and does not depend on different situations.

7. A discrepancy between the preferred and actual level of a motivational variable is referred to as *tension.* Thus if high arousal is experienced in the anxiety-avoidance mode, which prefers low arousal, it will be experienced as tension. Tension cannot be equated with arousal, however, because in the excitement-seeking mode, in which high arousal is preferred, it will be low arousal that will be experienced as tension. Tension can also be experienced in relation to other motivational variables (see below).

Tension is likely to give rise to *effort* on the part of the individual to overcome that tension. Whereas tension is experienced as a kind of unease or discomfort, effort is experienced as determination, or a willingness to invest energy to overcome the discomfort. Reversal theory therefore distinguishes among arousal, tension, and effort.

8. The other pairs of metamotivational modes postulated by reversal theory are as follows:

Negativism and conformity. In the negativistic mode one prefers to feel that one is defying rules, conventions, and expectations, whereas in the conformists mode one prefers to feel that one is respecting them.

Mastery and sympathy. In the mastery mode one's orientation to interpersonal transactions is one that construes them as having to do with power, that is, taking or yielding up. In the sympathy mode, in contrast, one construes interpersonal transactions as to do with caring or nurturing, that is, giving or being given.

Allocentric and autocentric. In the autocentric mode it is what happens to oneself that matters. In the allocentric mode one identifies with another person (or object or group) and what happens to this other is what matters most—even at one's own expense.

Telic and paratelic. In the telic mode one likes to see one's current activity as embedded in a hierarchy of goals extending into the future; that is, one is serious and likes to feel that what one is doing is important and has significance beyond itself. In the paratelic mode one likes to feel that what one is doing is encapsulated in such a way that it has no effect on anything beyond itself and can be enjoyed for itself and the immediate fun that it can provide.

From many points of view, the anxiety-avoidance mode can be seen as part of the telic mode: Anxiety is felt in the face of serious goals and is likely to increase as these goals increase in perceived importance or as movement toward such goals is frustrated; achieving goals is likely to be followed by the pleasant low arousal of relief and relaxation. Similarly, the excitement-seeking mode can be seen as a facet of the paratelic mode: In enjoying an activity one is likely to experience some measure of excitement, fascination, or *joie de vivre*, whereas failing to enjoy an activity is likely to be associated with boredom.

STRESS IN REVERSAL THEORY

From the reversal theory perspective, stress does not concern arousal as such. If we associate stress with unpleasant experiences, then in terms of this analysis it is *tension* that is stressful, especially if marked or prolonged. Thus boredom (low arousal) can in principle be as stressful as anxiety (high arousal).

But tension in relation to the variables acted on by any of the metamotivational modes can be stressful. Thus, if an individual is in the negativistic mode but cannot express defiance or rebelliousness, he or she will feel stressful tension, perhaps in the form of anger. If an individual is in the mastery mode and cannot achieve feelings of power he or she will experience the tension of humiliation. If an individual is in the allocentric mode but is doing better out of some transaction than the person the individual is interacting with, he or she will feel the tension of guilt. And so on. In other words, stress is polymorphic in experience, and we might expect to find that different types of stress have different somatic or behavioral effects.

Furthermore, according to this analysis, each type of stress has an opposite type of stress. The stress of anxiety contrasts with the stress of boredom. The stress of being unable to behave negativistically (e.g., as anger), contrasts with the stress of being unable to behave in a suitable conformist way (e.g., as embarrassment). The stress of humiliation in the mastery mode is counterbalanced by the stress of shame in the sympathy mode. The stress of guilt in the allocentric mode is set against the stress of resentment in the autocentric mode. (Actually, matters are more complex than this—see Apter, 1988, 1989—but this gives a good indication of the way in which stress comes in binary opposites.) Tension, therefore, can never be understood in terms of motivation alone—it is always about a *relationship* between motivation and metamotivation, that is, the actual and preferred levels of the variable concerned.

Stress is therefore associated with tension. But reversal theory also suggests that stress is associated with effort—that is, determination and the expenditure of effort are also stressful when they are imposed on the organism. We can therefore talk about, and need to distinguish, *tension-stress* and *effort-stress* (Apter & Svebak, 1989; Svebak, 1988a). Phenomenologically these two forms of stress are certainly distinct. The former, as already noted, is a form of unease; the latter, a feeling of working at things, not giving up, trying hard. The first is an unpleasant feeling; the second, the reaction to this feeling that may or may not be successful in overcoming the feeling. For example, anxiety may be experienced as tension-stress, and then effort expended to overcome the perceived causes of the anxiety. Or the tension-stress may be in the form of guilt, in which case effort may be experienced in the attempt to "make things up" with the injured party.

On the whole, it would appear that tension-stress is associated with the sort of unpleasant emotions that patients report to psychiatrists (or clients report to counselors)—feelings of guilt, acute or chronic anxiety, dammed-up anger, resentment toward loved ones, boredom with work, and so on. And effort, when it becomes stressful, would appear to result in such actual bodily reactions as tiredness, aching muscles, nausea, and, in the long-term, exhaustion, autoimmune deficiencies, and related problems. Looking at things in this way helps to explain these two different types of stress reaction, the psychiatric and psychosomatic. We should note straight away, though, that there is likely to be considerable overlap between them because effort-stress will be frequently associated with tension-stress, and in the worst case—when the effortful strategies used to overcome tension are ineffective—there will be high levels of both.

The stressors that bring about tension-stress include all those factors that play a part in producing, or maintaining, high levels of tension. These can include environmental events (e.g., anxiety-causing threats or resentment-causing unfairnesses), psychological events (e.g., anxiety-causing memories of previous traumas, anger-causing expectations of others' actions, or guilt-causing desires for selfish gain) and also feelings brought about by bodily symptoms (e.g., feelings of anxiety or anger)—the latter taking us into a vicious circle of stress in that these tensions may eventually have the effect of exacerbating these same bodily symptoms.

As well as particular events' being stressful, it is also possible for there to be an enduring and innate tendency to mismatch between the individual's arousability and preferred level of arousal. Thus, if a person is easily arousable but is anxiety-avoidance dominant, then he or she will be likely to experience anxiety frequently. If on the other hand, the individual is not arousable but is excitement-seeking dominant then he or she may need regularly to take extraordinary measures—such as taking risks, gambling, playing dangerous sports, or being disruptive—to gain the high level of arousal desired. Again this emphasizes the insistence of reversal theory that stress and pathology concern motivational/metamotivational mismatches and cannot be understood at the motivational level alone, as so many theories seem to imply. To take just one example, Eysenck (1988) suggested that the antiemotional characteristic identified by Grossarth-Maticek (e.g., Grossarth-Maticek, Bastiaans, & Kanazir, 1985) is the opposite of neuroticism. But the opposite of antiemotional would be proemotional, and no one would claim that the neurotic is proemotional, only unavoidably emotional. (In Eysenck's usage, this is the case by definition.) The confusion arises because Eysenck did not distinguish between the level of preferences (which is the level to which Grossarth-Maticek et al. appeared to be referring) and the level of tendencies, to which neuroticism applies.

This also reminds us again that mismatches can occur for opposite reasons and that for each type of tension-stress there is an opposite type. This would not, however, appear to be true of effort-stress. Effort, especially if intense and prolonged, may become extremely unpleasant and produce various types of somatic effect irrespective of the exact nature of the tension. It is, however, very possible that when the effort is expended playfully, for its own sake, and in response to challenges rather than threats, it remains pleasant and unstressful. In other words, where the paratelic mode is in operation, it may well be the case that effort-stress is minimal or nonexistent.

One final point in this analysis is that the distinction between tension-stress and effort-stress helps us to understand the difference between depression and burnout. Both may be said to occur when the individual gives up hope of overcoming tension-stress and becomes resigned to boredom, anxiety, humiliation, or some other form of tension. But depression occurs in relation to low effort-stress, little effort being expended because the individual feels it is unlikely to meet with success. In the burnout case, the giving up occurs following a long period of high effort-stress and determination to succeed.

RELEVANT RESEARCH

This is not the place to review all the experimental, psychometric, and other research that has been carried out to test hypotheses derived from reversal theory. As mentioned earlier, a recent and extensive survey has been conducted (Apter, in press). However, several lines of research that bear closely on the reversal theory account of stress, and were in fact generated by it, deserve mention here.

First, Martin and his colleagues at the University of Western Ontario have carried out a number of studies of the telic/paratelic modes in relation to stress (Dobbin & Martin, 1988; Martin, 1985; Martin, Kuiper, & Olinger, 1988; Martin, Kuiper, Olinger, & Dobbin, 1987). The results of these can be summarized as follows:

1. High-telic-dominant and high-paratelic-dominant subjects showed a different pattern of relationship between level of stress (measured by a life event scale) and mood disturbance (measured by a mood scale). Telic-dominant subjects reported increased disturbance as a function of increased stress; paratelic-dominant subjects, however, showed an opposite relationship, at least over low and moderate levels of stress—as stress increased, so did an *improvement* in mood. As stress levels became high, however, paratelic-dominant subjects reverted to the telic pattern. This would seem to suggest for the latter that as levels of arousal increased in response to stress, so did the pleasure experienced, as predicted by reversal theory. But above a certain level of stress, increasing numbers of the paratelic-dominant subjects reversed to the telic state and displayed the telic pattern. (The same overall pattern of result was also found when a daily "hassles" scale was used instead of the life event scale.)
2. In another study, it was found that for subjects who reported that the main stressor in their lives was resolved (implying a relative lack of ongoing stress), the more paratelic dominant the subject, the more disturbed he or she was as measured by a depression inventory. For subjects whose main stressor was unresolved, however, the more telic dominant the subject, the more disturbed he or she reported him- or herself to be; or, to put it the other way round, the more paratelic dominant the subject, the less disturbed he or she was by the presence of such a continuing unresolved form of stress.
3. When the same procedure was followed, but using an objective biochemical index of stress responses in the form of amount of cortisol in a standard volume

of saliva, a similar pattern was found in relation to resolved stressful events. (In this case, however, no relationship was found between telic dominance and cortisol levels for unresolved stressors.)

Taken overall, these results provide strong support for the reversal theory contention that not only are paratelic-dominant people able to resist the effects of stress to a greater degree than telic-dominant people, but they positively relish and thrive on stress, at least up to certain levels.

Second, in a series of psychophysiological experiments, Svebak has explored the telic and paratelic modes, and mode dominance, as moderator variables in the effect of threat on a range of physiological variables. Some of the main findings are as follows:

1. Tonic electromyographic (EMG) gradients during tasks under conditions of threat are significantly steeper in the telic than the paratelic mode, and this effect is amplified if hedonic tone is reported to be unpleasant (implying the presence of tension-stress). Svebak has suggested on the basis of this finding that muscular problems resulting from stress (e.g., backache, or migraine headaches) are most likely to occur when tension stress is experienced in the telic state.
2. Heart rate during tasks under conditions of threat is significantly accelerated in telic-dominant as compared with paratelic-dominant subjects. A particularly strong effect is found when telic Type A subjects are compared with other combinations of telic/paratelic dominance and Type A/B behavior. This led Svebak to suggest that proneness to heart attack may be predicted better by the Type A telic dominant combination than by the Type A behavior pattern alone.
3. Hyperventilation is more likely to occur during tasks under conditions of threat in telic-dominant as compared with paratelic-dominant subjects. Svebak suggests therefore that psychosomatic symptoms associated with hyperventilation (e.g., dizziness or nausea) are more likely to occur in telic-dominant than paratelic-dominant people as a reaction to stress.

Reviews of these and many other findings of Svebak and his colleagues can be found in Svebak (1983, 1985, 1988b, 1988c) and Apter (1989).

Third, three independent studies (Baker, 1988; Howard, 1988; Murgatroyd, 1985) of the strategies used by telic-dominant as compared with paratelic-dominant subjects in coping with crisis and stress have all come up with essentially the same main finding, namely, that telic-dominant subjects are more problem focused and paratelic-dominant subjects more emotion focused, using these terms in the sense of Lazarus (Lazarus & Folkman, 1984). In other words, telic-dominant subjects tend to expend effort more in ways that relate to external stressors and paratelic-dominant subjects do so in relation to psychological stressors.

Finally, it will have been noticed that all these lines of research have focused on the telic/paratelic distinction and on tension-stress rather than effort-stress (although some of Svebak's results could also be interpreted as showing the effects of effort-stress). This is largely because the telic/paratelic distinction was the first to be formulated in reversal theory, and the tension-stress idea developed earlier than that of effort-stress. Furthermore, psychometric instruments were developed first for measuring telic/paratelic dominance (Murgatroyd, Rushton, Apter, & Ray,

1978). However, the situation is beginning to change, and, among other developments, Svebak has now constructed a test that gives an indication of degrees of both tension-stress and effort-stress and, in relation to tension-stress, of such stress as it relates to all metamotivational modes. Preliminary data using the measure show the somatic effect of tension-stress to be related to the particular form of tension being experienced.

THE INEVITABILITY OF STRESS

Even in the space of this brief chapter it can be seen that structural phenomenology, in relation to stress (as to other topics in psychology), provides an approach that is both coherent and distinctive. Starting from the idea that experience itself has structure and a number of universal states of mind can be identified in structural terms, it works its way out toward those physiological and behavioral variables that most approaches take as their starting point. In doing so, it discloses some previously unsuspected patterns.

At the same time, in the specific form of reversal theory, it takes issue with a number of widespread assumptions about the psychological processes that underlie the generation of stress. In particular, it challenges the widespread "feeling" that emerges in different forms in most theories of personality, motivation, psychopathology, and stress that psychological functions and dysfunctions can be explained entirely in terms of balance, equilibrium, or homeostasis. Instead it suggests that matters need to be understood by reference to matches and mismatches between preferred and actual levels of certain variables, with the preferred levels changing in discrete jumps under certain conditions. In cybernetic terms, most theories are about the "regulation" of variables, whereas reversal theory is about both regulation and "control," "control" being concerned with the setting of preferred levels. (Analogously, a thermostatically controlled room has its temperature *regulated* in accordance with a preferred range of temperature values; these values are themselves *controlled* by the individual who chooses them.) Reversal theory suggests that whereas changes at the level of regulation are continuous, those at the level of control are discontinuous and even dramatic because they involve switches between opposite ends of the dimensions concerned.

Reversal theory also takes exception to certain views that are often expressed in the popular, and supposedly scientifically based, literature on stress. For example, it is often implied that if one thinks positively, or acts decisively, or follows some set of relaxation or other exercise, stress can be altogether avoided. Reversal theory implies that this is unlikely, indeed that the discomforts that underlie at least one type of stress (tension-stress) are an integral part of the cybernetic guidance of behavior. Furthermore, reversal theory suggests that the avoidance of one type of stress makes an individual more vulnerable to another. Thus maintaining low levels of arousal may help an individual to avoid the stress of anxiety but not that of boredom; effortful action may overcome tension-stress of any kind, but only at the expense of effort-stress. This does not mean that an individual must be stressed at all times—far from it. Rather it means that stress is always waiting in the wings, and will inevitably in a normal healthy life come on stage from time to time. The aim is not to suppress it entirely but to prevent it from becoming the leading character.

There is also an increasingly popular view that a little stress is good for a person. This is based on the optimal arousal idea that a moderate amount of arousal is pleasant. Reversal theory, of course, argues that this is too simple, that it all depends on what you mean by stress. If challenge, and problems and hassles, is meant, then an individual can certainly enjoy these in the paratelic state (as demonstrated in the work by Martin and his colleagues). But such stress, however mild, will be genuinely stressful in the telic state. And every type of tension stress, telic or paratelic (or of any kind related to any metamotivational mode), will be unpleasant and in this respect also will be stressful, even in small amounts.

In reversal theory, motivational/emotional systems are complex and hierarchical and, as conscious agents, we have only precarious control over them. This may seem less than optimistic as a basic for prevention and therapy; however, the study of these systems in a way that recognizes their full complexity and lability holds more hope for the future than some of the simplistic ideas that are being widely promulgated at the present time, at least in the burgeoning popular literature on stress avoidance.

SUMMARY

Stress is examined from the point of view of a general structural phenomenological theory known as "reversal theory." A number of central ideas from this theory are introduced, including the concepts of metamotivational state, reversal, bistability, dominance, tension, and effort. It is then argued that there are two fundamentally different types of stress: (a) tension-stress, which is the experience of a discrepancy between the actual and preferred level of some salient motivational variable, and (b) effort-stress, which is the experience of effort devoted to overcoming tension-stress. Because metamotivational states go in pairs of opposites, the specific form of tension-stress that can arise in relation to a given state will be structurally related to an opposite form of tension-stress that can arise in the opposite state (e.g., anxiety tension-stress is opposed by boredom tension-stress). A number of types of research supporting these ideas are reviewed, and it is concluded that structural phenomenology in the form of reversal theory provides a coherent and distinctive approach to stress, and one that challenges a number of accepted ideas in this area. It also holds out promise for future research and practice.

REFERENCES

Apter, M. J. (1981). The possibility of a structural phenomenology: The case of reversal theory. *Journal of Phenomenological Psychology, 12*(2), 173–187.

Apter, M. J. (1982). *The experience of motivation: The theory of psychological reversals.* New York: Academic Press.

Apter, M. J. (1988). Reversal theory as a theory of the emotions. In M. J. Apter, J. Kerr, & M. Cowles (Eds.), *Progress in reversal theory* (pp. 43–62). Amsterdam: North-Holland.

Apter, M. J. (1989). *Reversal theory: Motivation, emotion and personality.* London: Routledge.

Apter, M. J., Fontana, D., & Murgatroyd, S. (Eds.). (1985). *Reversal theory: Application and developments.* Cardiff, Wales: University College Press; and Hillsdale, NJ: Erlbaum.

Apter, M. J., Kerr, J. H., & Cowles, M. (Eds.). (1988). *Progress in reversal theory.* Amsterdam: North-Holland.

Apter, M. J., & Svebak, S. (1989). Stress from the reversal theory perspective. In C. D. Spielberger,

I. G. Sarason, & J. Strelau (Eds.), *Stress and anxiety, volume 12* (pp. 39–52). Washington, DC: Hemisphere.

Baker, J. (1988). Stress appraisals and coping with everyday hassles. In M. J. Apter, J. Kerr, & M. Cowles (Eds.), *Progress in reversal theory* (pp. 117–128). Amsterdam: North-Holland.

Dobbin, J. P., & Martin, R. A. (1988). Telic versus paratelic dominance: Moderator of biochemical response to stress. In M. J. Apter, J. Kerr, & M. Cowles (Eds.), *Progress in reversal theory* (pp. 107–116). Amsterdam: North-Holland.

Eysenck, H. J. (1988). Personality, stress and cancer: Prediction and prophylaxis. *British Journal of Medical Psychology, 61,* 57–75.

Grossarth-Maticek, R., Bastiaans, J., & Kanazir, D. T. (1985). Psychosocial risk factors as strong predictors of mortality from cancer, ischemic heart disease and stroke: The Yugoslav prospective study. *Journal of Psychosomatic Research, 29,* 167–176.

Howard, R. (1988). Telic dominance, personality and coping. In M. J. Apter, J. Kerr & M. Cowles (Eds.), *Progress in reversal theory* (pp. 129–142). Amsterdam: North-Holland.

Lazarus, R. S., & Folkman, S. (1984). *Stress, appraisal and coping.* New York: Springer.

Martin, R. (1985). Telic dominance, stress and moods. In M. J. Apter, D. Fontana, & S. Murgatroyd (Eds.), *Reversal theory: Applications and developments* (pp. 59–71). Cardiff, Wales: University College Press; and Hillsdale, NJ: Erlbaum.

Martin, R. A., Kuiper, N. A., & Olinger, L. J. (1988). Telic versus paratelic dominance as a moderator of stress. In M. J. Apter, J. Kerr, & M. Cowles (Eds.), *Progress in reversal theory* (pp. 91–106). Amsterdam: North-Holland.

Martin, R. A., Kuiper, N. A., Olinger, L. J., & Dobbin, J. (1987). Is stress always bad? Telic versus paratelic dominance as a stress moderating variable. *Journal of Personality and Social Psychology, 53,* 970–982.

Murgatroyd, S. (1985). The nature of telic dominance. In M. J. Apter, D. Fontana, & S. Murgatroyd (Eds.), *Reversal theory: Applications and developments* (pp. 20–41). Cardiff, Wales: University College Press; and Hillsdale, NJ: Erlbaum.

Murgatroyd, S., Rushton, C., Apter, M. J., & Ray, C. (1978). The development of the Telic Dominance Scale. *Journal of Personality Assessment, 42,* 519–528.

Svebak, S. (1983). The effect of information load, emotional load and motivational state upon tonic physiological activation. In H. Ursin & R. Murison (Eds.), *Biological and psychological basis of psychosomatic disease: Advances in the biosciences* (Vol. 42, pp. 61–73). Oxford, England: Pergamon Press.

Svebak, S. (1985). Psychophysiology and the paradoxes of felt arousal. In M. J. Apter, D. Fontana, & S. Murgatroyd (Eds.), *Reversal theory: Applications and developments* (pp. 42–58). Cardiff, Wales: University College Press; and Hillsdale, NJ: Erlbaum.

Svebak, S. (1988a). A state-based approach to the role of effort in experience of emotions. In V. Hamilton, G. H. Bower, & N. Frijda (Eds.), *Cognitive perspectives on emotion and motivation* (pp. 145–172). Dordrecht: Martinus Nijhoff.

Svebak, S. (1988b). Personality, stress and cardiovascular risk. In M. J. Apter, J. Kerr, & M. Cowles (Eds.), *Progress in reversal theory* (pp. 163–172). Amsterdam: North-Holland.

Svebak, S. (1988c). Psychogenic muscle tension. In M. J. Apter, J. Kerr, & M. Cowles (Eds.), *Progress in reversal theory* (pp. 143–162). Amsterdam: North-Holland.

3

Susceptibility to Stress and Anxiety in Relation to Performance, Emotion, and Personality: The Ergopsychometric Approach

Giselher Guttmann and Susan C. Etlinger
Institute for Psychology, University of Vienna, Austria

Conventional psychological testing methods have traditionally called for special ambient conditions: a neutral, disturbance-free, if not to say "sterile," environment. This type of environment best facilitates obtaining data about a person's potential for performance and is the classical setting for the measurement of the intelligence complex as well as related, more isolated, experimentally circumscribed motoric, cognitive, or perceptive acts (e.g., Anastasi, 1968; Meili, 1937).

But the very same field of science, namely psychology, tells us that the measured potential for performance only roughly indicates the level of performance in the real-life situation. Despite this, psychologists have shown little inclination to move beyond measuring "unadulterated" abilities. The one dual study demonstrating a budding realization of other test purposes, e.g., performance under load, was soon relegated to oblivion and, for all practical purposes, essentially unheeded (Ewig & Wohlfeil, 1926a, 1926b). Although there are many underlying psychological factors such as concentration, recognition, motivation, attribution, temperament, affect, and so on that intervene to influence the quality of actualized performance, such factors are largely ignored.

And everyday behavior is not normally, in fact is rarely, carried out in a setting such as that provided by the traditional psychological test laboratory. On the contrary, the individual is hardly ever granted this ideal while functioning in the real situation. Therefore, it is no wonder that the consequence is often a large discrepancy between psychological test results and performance observed, e.g., at work, in competition, and in school. Measuring capabilities in a "silent chamber," so to speak, will not aptly serve accurate prognosis.

More than a decade ago we initiated a novel approach to arrive at a realistic diagnosis of stress experience under real-life conditions, pairing these findings with those of objectified performance. We moved the sport psychological diagnostic setting out into a natural one, in this case, the mountains, adding an authentic aspect to paper-and-pencil testing and the use of elaborate indoor, stationary de-

Studies in ergopsychometry were supported by the Ludwig-Boltzmann-Institute für angewandte Sportpsychologie und Freizeitpädagogik, Vienna, Austria.

vices. These initial studies (Heitzlhofer, 1978; Lackner, 1979) looked into the dynamics of appetence–avoidance behavior over five measurement periods from the early pre- to the late postperiod of novices' rock-climbing experience. The results led to a new way of thinking regarding our testing modus: There was no one pattern in the dynamics of the reaction to this stressful situation. The reaction pattern of some beginners began as eustress and deteriorated to a feeling of distress either during or following the actual climbing experience. But there were those who reacted quite oppositely to the novel risk situation, and others who rated their feelings of attraction to the task equally during and just after the accomplished ascent, but the one group's recollection of the event was diametrically opposed to that of the other (see Figure 1).

We (Lackner, 1979) had coupled subjective experience with (objectified) performance. In a supplementary laboratory test session, these tyro climbers were subjected to pursuit-rotor tasks (dominant hand). The association under ordinary test conditions between performance in the pursuit-rotor task and performance during rock climbing was negligible. In the repetition of this task under load (pulling an expander with the free, nondominant hand) predictability rose dramatically (Wilks's λ = 0.8; agreement in allotments according to discriminant analysis).

NASCENT STAGES OF ERGOPSYCHOMETRY

Testing for Competitive Competence Under Load

These results were the midwife to a new way of thinking about psychological testing procedures. They clearly showed that there is no interindividual unilinear relationship between performance under neutral versus load conditions. Neutral testing may reveal the potential for performance, but without data gathered from a reasonable facsimile of the real-life load situation, there will be no reliable basis for a serviceable prediction of actual performance on the scene.

Such was the genesis of *ergopsychometry*, a dualized program allowing for comparison of neutral versus load performance (see Guttmann, 1982, 1984, 1986; Guttmann, Bauer, & Trimmel, 1982; Guttmann, Bauer, & Vanecek, 1982; Guttmann, Thuri, & Weingarten, 1981). In its pure form, the psychological variables under question are measured twice: once under neutral conditions and once during a load condition chosen for its relevance to the type of performance under study.

Judo and Table Tennis

In 1979 we embarked on studies using this method to contrast talented, experienced judoists and table-tennis players with nonathletes (Weingarten, 1981, 1985). Physical load defined as pedaling on a bicycle ergometer at 150–200 watts for about 10 min (inducing an average pulse rate of 120–130/min) served as ergopsychometric model. Weingarten chose "channel capacity" (locating one particular dot randomly placed within a 5 × 5 autotypy field presented at 10 different tachistoscopic rates; exposure time, .01 s; approximately 25 trials), "visual search speed" (six different slides displaying an array of differently sized and shaped geometric figures, each numbered; the task was to name the number of the target figure; score consisted of time required and number of mistakes), and "proneness to risk taking" (pokerlike gambling for stakes up to about $1; score consisted of

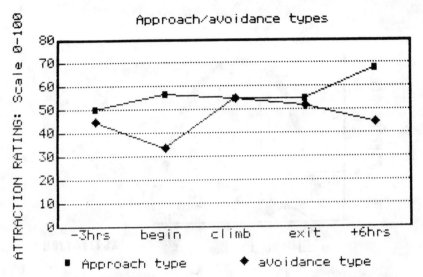

Figure 1   Conflict of decision: The two personality types observed as they face and then
reflect on their initiation into rock climbing. −3hrs = novices' ratings of their
stress experience (attraction vs. aversion) in relation to the climb 3 hr before
beginning the ascent; begin = ratings at the bottom of the ascent; climb = ratings
halfway up the rock; exit = ratings upon arrival at the top; +6hrs = ratings 6 hr
after having completed the climb. Scale: Each participant rated his feelings of
"attraction" and of "aversion" on a scale from 0 (*no such feelings*) to 100 (*only
such feelings*); the instructions were explicit that the sum of both ratings must not
be 100.

size of bet and sum of latency time until each bet was actually placed) as dependent
variables. They not only separated the high-performance athletes from the nonathletes, but also, at a more subtle level, separated the more successful from the
less successful among the athletes themselves (parallelized with regard to age,
length of the period, scope of and personal dedication to training, and so on). The
less successful of the athletes, whose performance did not meet expectations during competition, we named "training champions" (TCs).

These results confirmed our theoretical frame of reference. The relationship
between activation and performance as a ∩-shaped curve has been observed under
many different experimental conditions (e.g., Child & Waterhouse, 1953; Easterbrook, 1959; Lindsley, 1951; Yerkes & Dodson, 1908). And if maladjusted
activation indeed is a cause of decline in performance, then a method designed to
elicit optimization in the level of activation should lead to an improvement of that
performance. In its simplest, most likely form, it can be illustrated by the examples in Figure 2.

In Figure 2, Subject A is habitually less activated. Under stressful conditions,
his or her level rises, thus enabling or even facilitating better performance. Subject
B, on the contrary, is habitually highly activated. The addition of a load condition
leads to "overload," in the form of added stress-induced activation, in this case
synonymous with a decline in performance. For Subject B, learning to control
activation should lead to an improvement, the extent of which will depend on the

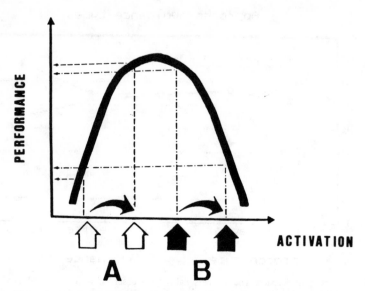

Figure 2   Relationship between performance and activation. A represents a
typical candidate for consistent performer; B represents a typical
candidate for training champion (see text).

person's starting position on the activation curve and his or her mastery of the
technique.

STUDIES CONFIRMING ERGOPSYCHOMETRY'S PROGNOSTIC VALUE

Orienteering

We therefore proceeded with studies in this direction, initially keeping to sports
as a model of a stress-loaded performance situation. One sport requiring the aforementioned discriminating qualities is orienteering. The runner seeking the personally best-suited, fastest passage through pathless, open terrain must process many
visual stimuli and messages simultaneously and the faster, the better.

These initial investigations (Beiglböck, 1983; Bischof, 1983) in combination
were conceived to answer questions pertaining to the discriminative, in ergopsychometric terms, prognostic value of different indices of levels of activation, measures of anxiety and aggression, and the therapeutic merit of self-control techniques for beneficial regulation of activation.

The same independent variables were used in both studies. The 31 subjects
were all members of the Austrian male orienteering elite (ages 17 to 35). For the
physical load condition, the bicycle ergometer was set at an initial load of 2.5
watts/kg (2.2 lbs) body weight at 60 rpm. As far as coaches' calculations allow,
this represents a proper estimation of the average load for an orienteerer in the
competitive situation. The load was increased (steps: 150 kg/min) in a continuous

series with a steady state (4 min) at each level up to about 75% of each participant's aerobic capacity. The external criterion for the classification of TC was the trainers' assessment.

A critical performance-related dependent variable was tailored to reflect actual demands encountered during orienteering (see Beiglböck, 1983): Parallel forms of photographs depicting natural field scenes were taken for single locations from each major point of the compass, that is, facing east, west, south, and north. The subjects were then required to match each set of four photographs, respectively, to single, isarithmic contour field map sections corresponding to each correct set, in random, mixed presentation, under each test condition (neutral vs. load)—see Figure 3.

An essential part of Beiglböck's (1983) customized test program for orienteers was also discriminative reaction time to complex tasks (combinations of acoustic and optical signals, reactions via button-press and pedal) presented on the Vienna Reaction Timer[1] (Dr. G. Schuhfried, Vienna, Austria).

Beiglböck sought a conclusive answer to the question whether TCs can be identified on the basis of the metabolic indices pulse and blood pressure. His study (1983) continued in this vein by adding the crucial therapeutic element: Can the practice of self-control techniques (progressive relaxation according to Jacobson, 1934) influence TCs' capability under load?

Bischof's (1983) study focused on other activation parameters and investigated a possible relationship between anxiety and/or attributional style, as one variable, and performance, as the other. It included the following questions:

1. Is the general level of activation characteristic of orienteerers higher than that of the normal population?
2. Are significant deviations from an "optimal" activation level in the sense of hyper- or hypoactivation observed for TCs versus consistent athletes (CAs) (those runners whose performance stays constant or even improves under load)?
3. Do the TCs rate the way they feel momentarily more negatively than the CAs?
4. Is there a relationship between the level of activation and that of anxiety-coping mechanisms?
5. Are there differences in attributional style between TCs and CAs?

The parameters Bischof (1983) chose to objectify level of activation were critical flicker frequency (CFF) regarding nonspecific physiological activation (see Schmidtke, 1951) and duration of the spiral aftereffect (SAE), index for cortical saturation (see Holland, 1965). Data objectifying personality factors regarding attributional style (questionnaire developed by Lester, 1986) and coping mechanisms related to anxiety (Krohne's [1974] German translation of Byrne's [1961] Repression-Sensitization [RS] Scale) were also collected.

On the basis of the test instruments described, the authors came to the following conclusions:

---

[1]This device and all others cited, including the test material they present, were designed and constructed by companies or individuals specializing in manufacturing apparative psychological testing equipment. The companies or individuals are identified in parentheses in the text.

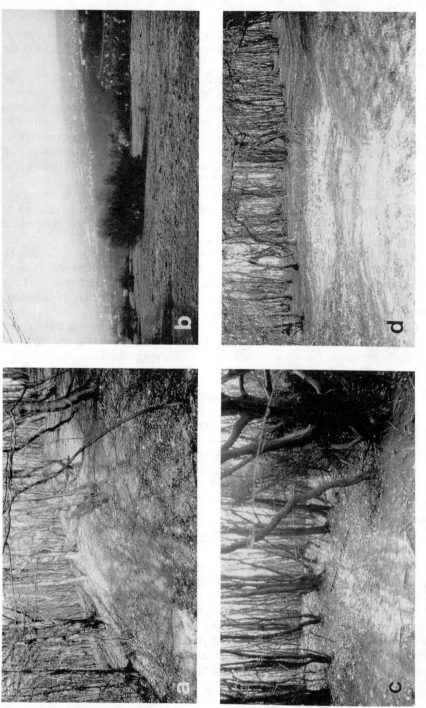

Figure 3 Example of a performance-tailored task for orienteerers. All four photographs of the landscapes (a–d) were taken from one vantage point, but in 90°-angle rotation, capturing the view from each major point of the compass. The five isarithmic contour, topographical excerpts (e) constitute a multiple-choice cognitive task: Only one is the correct match to the four snapshots. (Answer: #5)

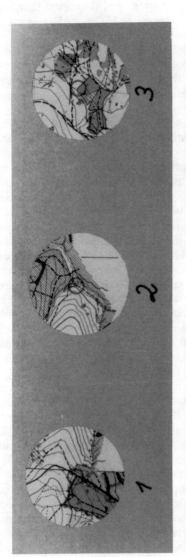

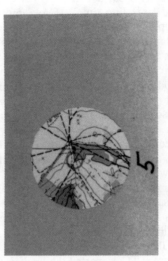

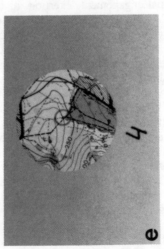

Figure 3 Example of a performance-tailored task for orienteerers. All four photographs of the landscapes (a-d) were taken from one vantage point, but in 90°-angle rotation, capturing the view from each major point of the compass. The five isarithmic contour, topographical excerpts (e) constitute a multiple-choice cognitive task: Only one is the correct match to the four snapshots. (Answer: #5)

Whereas neutral testing revealed no differences, the combined load-condition scores of Beiglböck's data stemming from the parameters "specific orienteering test" (CAs, stable; TCs, decline; t (4) = -2.93, $p < .05$, dependent samples, one-tailed) and "reaction time" (CAs, improvement, t (25) = 2.85, $p < .01$, dependent samples, one-tailed; TCs, decline, t (4) = -2.93, $p < .05$, dependent samples, one-tailed) reliably separated the CAs from the TCs, highly in agreement with their own trainers' separate evaluation (one ambiguous case of disagreement from the group of 31 athletes). In contrast to these findings, the physical indices pulse and blood pressure were found to be unsuitable for discriminating between these different types of performers.

Further, Bischof's (1983) data testified to subtle differences in the following parameters: A generally higher level of activation, in the form of "mental alertness" (nonspecific activation) as measured by a higher CFF, characterized the orienteerers as a whole versus the norm population. To our surprise, she found no difference between TCs and CAs. However, the CAs alone showed significantly enhanced nonspecific activation (CFF: $n = 25$, $p = .001$, $\alpha = 1\%$) and diminished cortical saturation (SAE: $n = 25$, $p = .027$, $\alpha = 5\%$) after the load condition, indicating a greater dynamic range of activation and a postload heightened awareness of the outer world (extraversion; see Eysenck & Rachmann, 1968). According to their verbal reports, the CAs also felt a "high" at the postload interview, whereas TCs reported the load as having been "strenuous," "relatively difficult," and so on. These latter attributions conformed to the Lester attribution questionnaire data, which showed TCs to attribute "success" (and "failure") to (lack of) personal engagement, exertion, or industry, that is, to internal unstable factors. The CAs, in contrast, attributed the outcome of performance to their "own capability" (internal, stable attributional style), in harmony with their postrun testimony. Both groups were characterized as "repressors" (signifying anxiety denial as defense mechanism) on the basis of the RS Scale.

No relationship between raters' evaluations of the orienteerers' general level of anxiety (audio-video films of participants' behavior in the field) and cortical saturation among the successful group was found (CAs: $n = 25$, $r = -.07$). However, the negative correlation among TCs was remarkable ($n = 6$, $r = -.72$; $\alpha \leq .05$). A high degree of cortical saturation was observed in combination with raters' significantly low judgments of TCs' anxiety. This statistical discrepancy between CAs and TCs lies in the CAs' lower postload SAE values.

Psychological parameters in load conditions tailored to the actual load situation—here visual transformations ("specific orienteering test") and sensomotor speed ("discriminative reaction time")—could classify the orienteerers into reliable, actual performance-predictive categories. The physiological dynamics of activation (CFF and SAE) were also shown to differentiate between these two groups during the load condition. The TCs stayed within the same range on both measures. The profile of those orienteerers whose performance was stable or improved (CAs) stands in contrast: increased nonspecific activation (CFF) under load while cortical saturation (SAE) was decreasing. These CA characteristics are observed in combination with higher scores on complex-reaction-time and visual information transformation tasks, not to mention favorable competitive performance. A higher CFF indicates "enhanced awareness of the outer world," certainly a condition conducive to peak orienteering across unfamiliar country. Further, CAs attributed success to their own ability. This indicates stability at the cognitive, attributional level. A decrease in cortical saturation (SAE) could be an expression of a clearinghouse effect, allowing the successful orienteerer to concentrate on optimally suited decisions regarding mastery of the terrain to his specific strengths. Both types of athlete showed an inclination to repress anxiety (RS Scale), translated into "head-on attack" coping strategy expressed as increased performance under anxiety. Something else must have been responsible for the differences in competitive performance, because after the TCs had undergone 6 weeks of training in a relaxation technique, they were no longer separable from the CAs: The data gathered during follow-up load testing showed a 20% to 25% improvement in the TCs' performance!

In sum, the orienteerers' overall performance leads to a picture of the athlete as being typically higher strung than a comparable sample of nonathletes ("nonspecific activation" as well as "anxiety"). Orienteerer CAs are even manifesting enhanced load-dependent levels of nonspecific activation (CFF). But load is seen to induce a reduction in the CAs' level of cortical saturation not observed in the TCs, whose load performance is not commensurate with that of the CAs. We must view this finding in the light of the favorable relationship for TCs between relaxation training and (improved) performance under load. Two questions follow: First, is the presumably more cognitive component ("cortical saturation") the crucial variable differentiating between CAs and TCs? Second, if so, did relaxation training directly or indirectly have a beneficial, direct effect on the level of cortical saturation?

Regatta Sailing

Ergopsychometric testing now proceeded on a complementary track, the next subjects being regatta sailors. Visual imagery had played an eminent role in discriminating between skilled and less skilled orienteerers. And it is reasonable to assume that the decisive capability factors separating success from failure in regatta competition include prospective visual imagination allowing the contestant to project the positioning complex beyond the next buoy. Mayrhofer (1986) thus ratiocinated that such dependent variables as "clarity of imagery," "clarity of kinetoimagery," "imagery speed," and "body scheme" (in consideration of such nautical maneuvers as "coming about," which requires the crew to act out rapid, smooth shifts of position while handling the running rigging optimally) be critical indices.

Her subjects were 44 18 to 28-year-old male pilots of dinghy sailboats (Laser, Finn, 470, 420). The sample was divided evenly into "successful" sailors (members of the Austrian National team, all having consistently placed respectably in international competition and met fixed qualification criteria) and TCs (total of annual placings in regattas yielded a rank below the best third of all national colleagues for the relevant boat class). Much dinghy sailing is performed in an awkward, tiring posture, hanging abeam outboard, windward. For training purposes, an apparatus has been constructed, called the "outrider," which simulates this position (see Figure 4). This device served to implement the load condition with allowance for minor concessions (intermittent holding on to the seat) to compensate for the disadvantageous discrepancy between (motional) regatta and

Figure 4 Photograph of the performance-tailored load condition for regatta sailors: the
"outrider." (With kind permission of Gottfried Paurnfried and the ORAC Verlag,
Vienna, Austria.)

(static) experimental "hanging" and, in some cases, the absence of tight mainsheet
as support.

The dependent measures included an abbreviated form of the Body Image
Screening Scale (BISS; Fichter & Meermann, 1981), relevantly adapted to the four
following values: point of maximum width of head and of shoulders plus (inside)
length of each leg and arm. "Clarity of imagery" and "kinetoimagery" were
examined with parallel forms (Gittler, 1984; Jirasko, 1985) of the Visueller Vor-
stellungs Test (VVT; Visual Imagery Test), each consisting of 20 mixed items (3
warm-up items, 5 geometric–schematic items, 5 recollective items, 5 imaginative
items, and 5 items involving mental dice rotation). Each item is rated on a 5-point
scale for "clarity and distinctness" as well as "motions." These ratings refer to
the quality of the image produced. The Imagery Speed test items (12 per parallel
form) were provided by the author upon request (e.g., Steiner, 1980). They are so
conceived that the dimensions imagery and speed are in fact the capabilities employed in solving the problems and not other, in this context, cognitive "crutches."

Surprisingly, "body scheme" could not distinguish between the two groups of
sailors. Both groups overestimated head and shoulder width and correctly estimated or underestimated the arm and leg long measures, that is, projected onto the
real-life regatta situation (avoiding the swinging boom, hooking in the feet for
hanging, and so forth), and both groups seem to have left a margin for error in
both dimensions (width and length). However plausible "body scheme" seemed as
critical variable, with hindsight we conclude that a measure of kinesis is probably
more relevant as index for this sport. However, the results of the visual (kineto-)
imagery tests confirmed this choice: Under load, only the TCs' values sunk significantly (Wilcoxon matched-pairs signed-ranks test: "clarity of image," $n = 22$,
$z = -2.931$, $p < .01$, two-tailed; "clarity of kinetoimagery," $n = 22$,
$z = -2.159$, $p < .05$, two-tailed). Whereas neutral testing could not discriminate (TCs $\approx$ CAs), the load condition did: Not only had the TCs' performance

deteriorated per se, but in a measure separating them clearly from the CAs (Mann-Whitney U test: "clarity of image," $n = 22$, $z = 2.56$, $p < .02$, two-tailed, corrected for ties; "clarity of kinetoimagery," $n = 22$, $z = 2.17$, $p < .03$, two-tailed, corrected for ties). "Visual speed" reflected differences between the TCs and successful sailors under both testing conditions. The more successful sailors functioned consistently, (χ^2 $(1, N = 22) = NS$, dependent samples, and moreover better, under both conditions (U test: $p < .001$ for differences between CAs and TCs under neutral and load testing). The diminution of TCs' performance from neutral to load condition was, by strong contrast, dramatic (Wilcoxon test: $n = 22$, $z = -3.263$, $p < .001$, dependent samples, two-tailed).

These results demonstrate how important it is to pinpoint the correct prognostic variables, regarding the test battery as well as the load condition. Moreover, they substantiate differences in cognitive processing capacity, although these data leave open the question of the activation contribution to these differences.

Ice Hockey

The prospects of gaining access to all members of a team for testing in the locker room immediately prior to any league game are conceivably dim for any outsider. As a respected member of a national league team and goalie for the national team in Austria, Philipp (1988) was even able to conduct a longitudinal study spanning a whole league season among his team colleagues under these experimentally conducive conditions.

Identifying TCs and measuring the individual dynamics of prematch anxiety were the primary aims of his study. At the outset, the following tests were presented with the intention of gathering psychological background material: the Freiburg Aggression Questionnaire (FAF; Hampel & Selg, 1975), which takes several forms of aggression into account (spontaneous, reactive, and angry/explosive, under which three forms are the categories "aggressivity," "self-directed/depressive," and "inhibited aggression"); the German version (Krampen, 1981) of the Questionnaire on Locus of Control (IPC; Levenson, 1973), which assesses "locus of control" according to the categories "internality/self-control," "powerful others orientation/control exercised over oneself by others/externality," and "chance control orientation"; and the *Gruppenbewertungsverfahren* (Group Evaluation Method) (GBV; Schellenberger, 1973), which objectifies the group's structure from a social psychological standpoint (each team member rates on a 7-point scale the desirability of each other team member's presence in various anticipated situations).

The continuous measurement of "prestart state" (Eigenzustandsskala [Own-State Scale; EZ]; Nitsch, 1974) and "state and trait anxiety" (State–Trait Anxiety Inventory [STAI]; Spielberger, 1972; Spielberger, Gorsuch, & Lushene, 1970) stood at the heart of this unique investigation. Philipp's teammates completed both questionnaires sitting in the locker room during the last 10 min prior to each of the season's 14 championship matches, balanced with respect to home and away games.

Ergopsychometric testing began subsequent to the season's final game. Both the STAI and EZ were included in this test battery. In order to take the special demands of the sport into account, a speed form of the Culture Fair Test Scale-3

(CFT-3; Cattell, 1972) (German version, Weiß, 1971), Visual–Acoustic Reaction (power as number of errors and speed in milliseconds using the Vienna Reaction Timer [Dr. G. Schuhfried, Vienna, Austria]) as well as the subtests Tracing Lines (dominant hand) and Aiming (each hand separately) of the *Motorleistungsserie* (Motor Performance Test) (MLS; Dr. G. Schuhfried, Vienna, Austria) were added to the ergopsychometric test set. The load condition was carried out prior to each single test on the bicycle ergometer (model "Tunturi," Steyr-Daimler-Puch, Graz, Austria) set at 80 rpm with an individually measured resistance resulting in a constant pulse of 180 beats/min, roughly corresponding to the players' actual rate during matches.

To give an exact example of the ergopsychometric design for reference purposes, we include this portion of the investigative schedule in meticulous detail and chronological order:

Neutral Condition: measurement of pulse, visual–acoustic reaction test, pulse, EZ
   Scale, pulse, MLS, pulse, STAI State Scale, pulse, (ice hockey logic test),[2]
   pulse, CFT-3 speed test, pulse.
Intermission: setting the bicycle ergometer correctly for each subject (seat height,
   pedaling resistance factor).
Load Condition: pulse, bicycle load, load pulse measurement, reaction test, pulse,
   bicycle load, pulse, EZ Scale, pulse, bicycle load, pulse, MLS, pulse, bicycle
   load, pulse, STAI State Scale, pulse, (ice hockey logic test plus simultaneous
   bicycle load),[2] pulse, CFT-3 speed test.

The sample included all field players of Philipp's own national league team. One literally fell out of the sample midway, as a result of injury during play and subsequent convalescence (final $N = 17$). This particular team is of rare homogeneity, no imported players being on the roster presently. These men have come up through the younger ranks and played together for many years. The same holds for the trainer, who has worked with this group (average age = 23) over many seasons.

To substantiate the validity of the test-dependent categorization as TC, the trainer was enlisted as external criterion. In the course of the season, he rated each player on a 7-point scale (from *outstanding*[1] to *unsatisfactory* [7]) at three different times on the following items: general capability, technical–tactical performance, physical capability (fitness), mental concept of the run of play (in simple words, "Is he 'with it' or not?"). Those whose ratings worsened over time were designated as TCs. On the basis of the trainer's ratings, 5 of the 17 players were classified as TCs.

The first primary result of Philipp's (1988) study was that neutral testing could not differentiate between the subgroups. Ergopsychometric testing, by contrast, could: The major results of the discriminative reaction-test clearly separate the TCs from the CAs. Whereas the CAs committed fewer errors under load than under neutral conditions ($n = 12$, $t (11) = 2.93$, $p < .02$, dependent samples, two-tailed), the corresponding performance of TCs deteriorated ($n = 5$,

---

[2]This test is not described here because it was conceived and included solely with postinvestigative hockey-specific counseling in mind. It should be noted, however, that it did discriminate between TCs and CAs, in the expected direction.

t (4) = −3.14, p < .04, dependent samples, two-tailed). The difference in this performance between TCs and CAs was reliable, F (11, 4) = 1.09, t (15) = −5.14, p ≪ .00, homogenous, independent samples, two-tailed. The CAs' reaction-test completion time under load versus neutral condition diminished, t (11) = 2.81, p < .02, dependent samples, two-tailed, whereas the TCs' claimed more time: midway through the test, NS; at completion of load test, t (4) = −4.07, p < .02, dependent samples, two-tailed. The difference between CA and TC load performance completion time was confirmed (for CAs, M = 5,138.08 ms, SD = 691.64; for TCs, M = 6,851.00 ms, SD = 642.39; F (11, 4) = 1.16, t (15) = −4.74, p ≪ .000; homogenous, independent samples). In short, under load the CAs made fewer errors and reacted faster, whereas the TCs response to load was quite the opposite.

By discriminant analysis on the basis of these three parameters for power and speed ("number of errors," "duration of test: Midway through the tasks," and "completion time for test"), 91.7% (11 of 12) of the CAs and 100% of the TCs (n = 5) were allotted in agreement with their coach's own ratings. This agreement in allotment was highly reliable, Wilks's λ = .25468, χ^2 (3, N = xx) = 18.465, p < .001.

According to the factor Mood of the Own-State Scale, the CAs' values lay equably and inconspicuously below the norm under both conditions, whereas the TCs' mood under neutral conditions was above norm. Their mood then sunk significantly into the below-norm domain under load, t (4) = 3.46, p < .03, dependent samples, two-tailed.

Motor performance (the Tracing Lines subtest of the MLS in both cases, i.e., from left to right and right to left) was interesting in that the CAs made more mistakes in absolute numbers under all conditions than the TCs, but the only significant statistic was the TCs' apparent greater sensitivity to load: They made more mistakes in load testing than during neutral testing, t (4) = −3.94, p < .02, dependent samples, two-tailed. In the parameters "duration of erroneous tracing" and "completion time" the CAs were also better, in absolute numbers, but no difference was reliable. And both groups were seen to shorten these times under load (NS). We conclude that the laboratory-suited test of fine-motor coordination does not apprehend the type of precision capabilities whose (dis)integration finely discriminates between these ice hockey players' performance on the field.

The question regarding possible interaction of these factors with the variable "anxiety," measured by Spielberger's STAI, brought forth an unexpected, albeit plausible explanation. On the one hand, according to the basic, preergopsychometric assessment of "trait anxiety," the values for the group of CAs are reliably higher than those of the TCs (for CAs, M = 36.5, SD = 6; for TCs, M = 29.6, SD = 4.1; F (11, 4) = 2.19 [homogenous]; t (15) = 2.31, p < .04, independent samples, two-tailed: see Figure 5). It was the CAs who were habitually more anxious! Whereas the TCs' state anxiety values lay clearly below the norm (below the 32nd percentile), those of the CAs were even above average (above the 61st percentile).

This finding made us all the more curious to examine the data from the STAI state anxiety measurements. We found that the CAs reacted to load with a decrement in state anxiety, their load value being somewhat below that of the TCs' neutral value (raw scores: CA load = 33.9 vs. TC neutral = 35.6, NS). In another form, the CAs began ergopsychometric testing at the 65th percentile and decreased in state

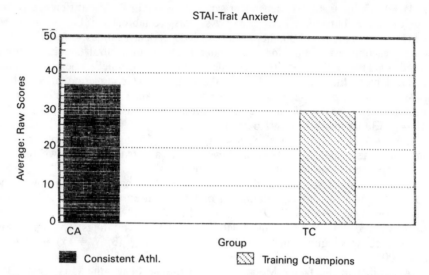

Figure 5   Trait anxiety difference on the Spielberger State–Trait Anxiety Inventory between consistent athletes and training champions under neutral testing conditions (*p* < .05).

anxiety to the 51st percentile under load: For neutral testing, *M* = 37.0, *SD* = 3.19; for load testing *M* = 33.9, *SD* = 4.42; *t* (11) = 2.94, *p* < .02; dependent samples, two-tailed. In contrast to the CAs, the TCs' neutral values put them at the 58th percentile, with state anxiety "exploding" up to the 96th percentile of the norm population (albeit, the latter's values relate to neutral conditions): For neutral testing, *M* = 35.6, *SD* = 5.77; for load testing, *M* = 52.4, *SD* = 4.39; *t* (4) = −4.23, *p* < .02, dependent samples, two-tailed. The difference in state anxiety between the CAs and TCs under load was highly significant, *F* (11, 4) = 1.01, *t* (15) = −7.87, *p* < .000, homogenous, independent samples.

It is noteworthy that both the CAs' and the TCs' values even under neutral conditions lay above the norm (50%). This finding coincides with Bischof's (1983) finding that the group of high-performance athletes measured at higher levels of habitual activation than a representative group defined as the norm population. Further, the TCs arrived at a level of state anxiety commensurate with that surpassed by merely 4% in the distribution of the norm group. Their raw scores illustrate this relationship (see Figure 6).

The ice hockey training champion is also susceptible in other aspects. Again, the diagnosis according to traditional testing would be quite the contrary to that mandated by ergopsychometric data. Under the neutral condition, the CAs scored lower on the speed-adapted CFT-3 than the TCs. Given the additional load information, the CAs were shown to have improved their performance, *t* (11) = −2.70, *p* < .03, dependent samples, two-tailed, where the TCs' achievements decreased, *t* (4) = 3.16, *p* < 0.04, dependent samples, two-tailed.

The findings concerning attributional style (IPC), that is, "locus of control," again harmonize with those of Bischof (see above). Both groups (CAs and TCs) of both populations (ice hockey players and orienteerers) were rated as below average on the externality dimension of success-rated attributions (IPC "powerful others orientation"). Although they can be called "self-reliant," the Philipp data left open the question whether they relied more on their own capability or more on their own efforts. Bischof's data suggested the latter (internal instable control) for TCs, and the former for CAs, that is, internal stable control. Whereas "self-reliance" in relation to the individual sport orienteering is nearly self-explanatory, the trait is not so obvious for a team athlete. One could, however, easily understand the attribution in the light of peer responsibility: Team players perceive an obligation to give their best. And attributing success to one's own efforts could also be a (volatile) component contributing to the enhanced level of state anxiety observed in TCs under load.

ERGOPSYCHOMETRY BRANCHES OUT

Testing for Vocational Qualification

The ergopsychometric setting now moved from the sports arena into the barracks (Krehàn-Riemer, 1986). Candidates for the rank of noncommissioned officer (NCO) were tested ergopsychometrically for possible stress-induced changes in personality. The rationale for such a study is easily conceivable, because the NCO's duty is to execute and exercise command over and keep cohesion among cohorts in stressful situations, whether these be limited to peacetime forms such as potential criticism from superiors or insubordinance from the enlisted ranks, or, according to the worst possible scenario, pressures at the battlefront. Thus, more than mere academic interest underlies such a search for reliable prediction regard-

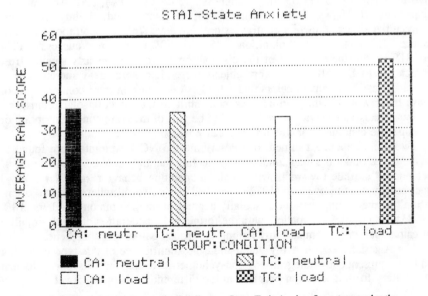

Figure 6 State anxiety scores on the Spielberger State–Trait Anxiety Inventory under the neutral and load conditions, respectively (see text).

ing the load-dependent dynamics of various factors in these men's personality profile.

The aspirants ($N = 109$ men ages 18 to 25) answered three personality questionnaires: the Freiburger Personlichkeilsinventar (Fahrenberg, Selg, & Hampel, 1973) (FPI; Freiberger Personality Inventory), the German version (Krampen, 1981) of the IPC (Levenson, 1973), and the *Fragebogen zur direktiven Einstellung* (Questionnaire of Attitudes Toward and Uses of Authority) (FDE; Bastine, 1977). On the first day of the applicants' testing procedures, these candidates were presented the three tests under the neutral condition. They repeated the tests on the third and last day of the NCO assessment examinations. This time they were subjected to a relevant physical load condition. Under the direction of a military superior, they first underwent a preliminary "pulse-priming" procedure to increase activation: a 400-m race followed by 15 fast knee-bends and 10 brisk push-ups. They thereupon immediately commenced work with the questionnaires. The load continued in the form of interruptions every 60 s: Over the first 10 min 15 knee-bends were performed every 60 s; over the second 10 min, 10 knee-bends were performed every 60 s; and over the rest of the testing period, 5 knee-bends were performed every 60 s. The questionnaires were completed during the breaks interrupting the exercise regimen.

On this basis, we found some dimensions of the NCO candidates' personality tests to be modified in varying percentages of the group by the addition of load. The following percent statistics refer to percentage of candidates whose load responses (vis-à-vis neutral condition) fell into the relevant extreme (chi-square tail versus percentage unchanged under load). The chi-square values (two-tailed) were calculated taking the standard error in measurement of each scale into account according to $\sigma_x = z(\sigma\sqrt{1 - r_{tt}})$, whereby $p \leq .05$ and $z = 1.96$.

For about a fourth of the group, a significant diminution ($p \leq .01$) in "depressive feelings" (31% vs. 65%), "frankness" (25% vs. 70%), and "spontaneous aggression" (22% vs. 70%) was measured; the same trend, slightly tempered, characterized the parameters "extraversion" (18% vs. 76%), "aspirations to dominance" (17% vs. 73%), "inhibition" (15% vs. 80%), and "nervousness" (12% vs. 81%), with the other tail of the distribution curve being clearly smaller (rest percentage to $\Sigma = 100\%$: Fewer subjects were characterized by increased, extreme values in these parameters under load). A decrease in most combinations of these traits would signify an advantageous shift in the direction of circumspect, rational, decisive behavior were it found to be part of the compound description of one specific candidate for this professional position.

Two other dependent dimensions describing the NCO aspirants were found to be *enhanced* under the load condition: the feeling that they could determine others' behavior ("attitude toward instructional/commanding behavior": 16% vs. 74%) and the dimension Levenson (1972) described as "powerful others external orientation" or the feeling that one is socially dependent on the opinion of others (18% vs. 83%)—a finding compatible with the former in consideration of the desirability of camaraderie and compatibility among the troops paired with obedience.

The Austrian Federal Army understood the significance of this type of testing and has subsequently integrated ergopsychometric testing into its psychological test battery for the selection program at the differential diagnostic level.

ERGOPSYCHOMETRY IN THE CLINIC

Primary Raynaud's Syndrome

Concomitantly with the Krehan-Riemer (1986) study, a clinical study, necessitating a different type of experimental design, was underway. Schwarz (1986) took the primary Raynaud's syndrome as model for the physical expression of stress-liability. Manifestation of the idiopathic Raynaud is expressed in painful vasospastic attacks as circulatory disorders in the tips of the fingers, not attributable to any organic cause. These attacks are triggered by coldness or by emotional stress and are often brief (about 30 min).

Twenty-five morbus Raynaud patients (ages 17 to 78, $M = 42$; 19 women) were compared with 25 healthy controls (ages 20 to 76, $M = 41$; 17 women), parallelized for profession and level of education. In this study, the following load condition was carried out under the supervision of the attending physician: The stricken hand was placed into a bowl containing cool water (12° Celsius) for 3 min. During this time, the subject checked off the questionnaires with the free hand. (Subjects were free to discontinue the testing at will, but none did; nor were any attacks elicited by this design). Following the douse, the questionnaires were completed (total time = 4 to 8 min). The controls dunked their nondominant hand; otherwise, the objective conditions for both groups were commensurate. This psychological test was carried out within the framework of a thermographic control examination. Therefore, it was possible to objectify the effects of the load on the basis of the thermographs, as well as via the temperature measure of the middle finger and the ball of the thumb for all patients and for 5 of the controls.

There were differences registered as physiological reaction to the load condition: The manual "cold shock" also elicited vascular constriction in the controls. The difference was one of degree and scope—the controls' hands, better supplied with blood at preload measuring, showed a more widespread reaction to the treatment, in reference to area as well as drop in temperature. Likewise, their recovery was more widespread and faster.

The other dependent variables were defined by the FPI, FDE, and IPC as well as an additional questionnaire for the test group, (the Social Readjustment Rating Scale [SRRS]; Holmes & Rahe, 1967), to estimate the influence of psychosocial factors (life events) in inciting Raynaud attacks. For both groups, during the neutral test session biographical data were collected using the *Biographisches Inventar zur Diagnose von Verhaltensstörungen* (Biographic Inventory for the Diagnosis of Behavior Disorders) (BIV; Jäger, Lischer, Münster, & Ritz, 1976) and the Gießen Test of Self-Image (Beckmann & Richter, 1975).

The results of the biographical inventory confirm that, at the time of testing, the subjective description of the family situation (parents' style of upbringing, parental interaction) was the same for both the test group (TG) and the control group (CG). Despite this, the TG had an infinitely higher disposition toward somaticizing stress ("psychophysical constitution": For TG, $M = 5.32$, $SD = 2.70$; for CG, $M = 1.96$, $SD = 1.17$; $t (48) = 5.7$, $p \ll .00$). The TG was also measured as experiencing more stressful factors in private and social situtations than the CG: For TG, $M = 1.92$, $SD = 1.631$; for CG, $M = 1.00$, $SD = 1.00$; $t (48) = .021$, $t (48) = 2.40$, respectively, $p < .03$. Furthermore, higher scores in the dimension "ego strength" testified to the TG's weaker feelings of self-assuredness and assertiveness, separating them from the CG (for TG, $M = 4.48$, $SD = 2.52$; for CG, $M = 2.92$, $SD = 2.12$; $t (48) = 2.37, p < .03$). The TG also reported weaker habits regarding "sociability" (for TG, $M = 4.72$, $SD = 2.32$; for CG, M = 2.44, SD = 1.96; $t (48) = 3.76, p \ll .00$) and was more reserved and withdrawn (for TG, $M = 24.56$, $SD = 4.14$; for CG, $M = 17.88, SD = 6.79$; $t (48) = 4.20, p \ll .00$). The TG subjects were moreover described by much higher values in the dimensions "anxiousness," "neuroticism," "generally depressive psychic tenor," and "social compliance and inhibition" ($p \le .01$). (All t test data were normally. distributed according to the Kolmogorov-Smirnov test.)

In short, the Raynaud patients' personality profile prior to ergopsychometric test—like that of the controls, still within the confines of the "normal" range—outlined a quite different psychogram from that of the controls, characterized by tendencies to obsessive neuroticism; heightened tendencies toward inhibition, socially and emotionally; and an aggravated awareness of real as well as potential, hypothetical threats to valued personal relationships.

In ergopsychometric terms (neutral [M_n] vs. load [M_l]), the cold-water test condition elicited no shifts along personality dimensions among the controls (results of all subtests were nonsignificant). But among the patients (TG), pronounced, *tempering* modifications in the dimensions "aggressivity" ($M_n = 3.04$, $SD = 1.86$ vs. $M_l = 1.96$, $SD = 1.06$; $t (48) = 3.42, p < .00$), "generally depressive psychic mood" ($M_n = 6.48$, $SD = 2.76$ vs. $M_l = 5.44$, $SD = 3.00$; $t (48) = 2.34, p < .03$), "dominance" ($M_n = 2.96$, $SD = 1.81$ vs. $M_l = 2.20$, $SD = 1.58$; $t (48) = 3.61, p \ll .00$) and a very pronounced enhancement of "directive attitude toward and use of authority" ($M_n = -11.20$, $SD = 11.59$ vs. $M_l = -6.96$, $SD\ 11.09$; $t (48) = -3.07, p < .00$) were observed (see Figure 7).

Schwarz (1986) interpreted these ergopsychometrically measured data in the following context: The better balanced personality profile of the primary Raynaud syndrome patients under load conditions, drawn on the strength of paper-and-pencil test reactions, could be the consequence of their somatization of any psychic

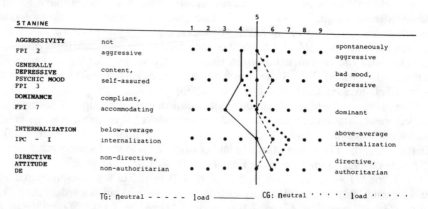

Figure 7 The effects of load on various personality factors in a psychosomatic clinical population (Raynaud syndrome). Vertical indices: the factor (in boldface) and the test instrument.

and/or physiological stress. Stress is not articulated at the emotional level but rather organically. The addition of minor, "subthreshold" stress seems to mobilize tried and true psychological coping mechanisms, whereby one would have to presume that more intense, "suprathreshold" stress would be articulated as an acute outbreak of the physiological symptoms. Ergopsychometric testing avails the therapist of a viable dynamic reference profile of the patient.

Organic Psychosyndrome and Monopolar Depressives

Kryspin-Exner (1987) combined the basic temporally spaced test sessions with a one-test-session/interpopulation comparison. This design provided for four temporally separated measurements of "state," "neurological arousal," and "general fatigue," interspersed with two tests of "perceptual power" and one of "perceptual speed." Kryspin-Exner compared the performance under load of informed and consenting patients whose disorder had been clincially diagnosed as "organic psychosyndrome" (n = 16) and "monopolar depressive" (n = 11) with that of two control subgroups: "personnel" (n = 17), consisting of nurses and orderlies following their night shift at the clinic, that is, at a time when they were under the influence of sleep deprivation; and "kindred" (n = 12), consisting of volunteers from the clinical administrative staff, their healthy relatives, or friends.

Objective stress induction was introduced in the form of task-relevant, self-paced, and set-paced load, respectively. The data stemming from these load conditions were placed in reference to known, clincially relevant parameters, such as mood, perseveration, and fatigue (see below). These test instruments and conditions were as follows:

State of well-being. The *Klinische Selbstbeurteilungs-Skalen* (Clinical Self-Evaluation Scales) (KSb-S; Zerssen, 1976), including parallel forms allowing repeated measures, was designed to yield an overall picture of changes over time in the subject's momentary feelings regarding well-being. Twenty-eight adjectives and their antonyms were presented at each of four temporally equally spaced runs, furnishing four separate evaluations on a 3-point scale including *corresponds best to my momentary mood/state* for either end of the scale and *neither/nor* in cases of absolute indecision.

Perseveration tendency. Perseveration tendency is considered a form of ontogenetically and phylogenetically understood regression to more primitive forms of neurological coping with excess cognitive or emotional processing demands (Breidt, 1973; Guttmann, 1967; Remschmidt, 1971). The *Perseverationstestgerät* (PTG) (Perseveration Test Unit; Kurt Zickler, Pfaffstätten, Austria) provides a 3 min test program and consists of pressing one of nine buttons in random order according to a metronomically defined rhythm. It was also included in the test block the subjects completed four separate times. The perseveration coefficients yielded four temporally separate measures of redundancy ("perseveration") for the subject's respective current button-pressing patterns.

Critical flicker frequency. The CFF is a measurement of the frequency threshold (in hertz) at which discrete light impulses fuse into one subjectively experienced homogeneous stream of light, and vice verse, as an indication of general activation or fatigue; in other words, it is a vigilance index (Schmidtke, 1965).

The threshold is ascertained in a series of forced-choice decisions indicating the placing of flashes displayed electronically (Flicker Fusion Unit, Bruno Zak, Simbach am Inn, West Germany) in ascending and descending (hertz) order. The procedure lasts 10 min or less and was run as third in the block repeated four times.

Power. The Drive and Concentration Test Unit (Bruno Zak, Simbach am Inn, West Germany), an electronic form of the Pauli test (Pauli & Arnold, 1970) of visual and mental attention span (i.e., tenacity and drive), was used. Subjects are presented pairs of single digits for addition via monitor. The digit in the unit's place of the first sum is typed into the system as the answer and serves likewise as reaction-dependent pacer and first numeral for the next pair of digits to be added. The duration of this task is a half-hour for each of the two sessions, and the task was interspersed between the first and second and between the third and fourth KSb-S, PTG, CFF tests.

Speed. Stimulus-paced, complex, randomly ordered tasks were presented via determination unit (DET; Bruno Zak, Simbach am Inn, West Germany) allowing for a clear identification (button and/or pedal) of each component out of a reaction

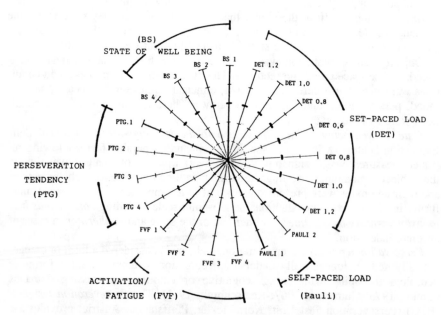

Figure 8 Skeleton of the stars depicting the changes in the respective values across test sessions. Beginning at "noon" and progressing counterclockwise: BS represents state of well-being; "spokes" (radii) 1 through 4 = rating at each of the four measurement periods. PTG represents perseveration tendency (readiness to perform); spokes 5 through 8 = rating at each of the four measurement periods. FVF represents critical flicker frequency (nonspecific activation/fatigue); spokes 9 through 12 = rating at each of the four measurement periods. Pauli represents reaction-dependent "power" load, spokes 13 and 14. DET represents determination unit (fixed-interval "speed" load), spokes 15 through 21 = each pace setting separately. Radii: apex = 0, first concentric divider = 1 SD, second = 2 SDs, third = the middle of the normal range, fourth = 4 SDs, and fifth = 5 SDs.

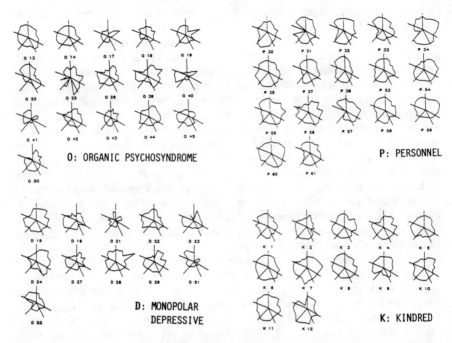

Figure 9 Top row: Left, stars for the organic psychosyndrome patient group; right, stars for the personnel control subgroup. Bottom row: Left, stars for the monopolar depressive patient group; right, stars for the kindred control subgroup.

complex to chains of acoustic and optical signals. This device was programmed in seven presentation frequency stages, with the stimuli (50/stage) being on display every 1.2 (first stage), 1.0, 0.8, 0.6, 0.8, 1.0, and 1.2 (seventh stage) s. The descending/ascending order took into account that the patient population should not be left with a feeling of failure! (The O.6-s pace maximum load had been established in a pretest as the border of just-tolerable overload for the patients and served to ensure predicative data regarding brain organic functioning under load.) This multilevel task was presented once, between the second and third administration of the KSb-S, PTG, and CFF test block.

All subjects were screened on the basis of other routine tests for measuring such psychologial variables as memory, attention, and so forth. The criterion for inclusion in the sample was that the neutral-condition values all fall within the range of the norm, to allow for revelation of dynamic reaction patterns in obviously not clinically impaired population samples and to provide for homogenous subgroups. These groups were further parallelized according to gender and age.

The results are shown in Figures 8 and 9. For the very reason that they were clincially interpreted in the single-case method, Figure 9 illustrates each individual's dynamics. Further reference values for these individual "stars" are the screening data (KSb-S, DET, and CFF within the range of the norm: third stanine or center of each radius).

Interesting inter- as well as intragroup differences were ascertained. For example, those professionally accustomed to working under load (the personnel group, i.e., the sleep deprivation condition) improved under increasing speed demands ("consistent performers"), despite signs of fatigue (e.g., a slowing of the rate of improvement) and slightly enhanced tendencies to perseveration. The data for the monopolor depressives suggest a load-approach to therapy: Their performance under time load remained adequate, they rated their state of well-being higher, and they were more highly motivated (as judged on the basis of the PTG values) immediately following these demands. The organic psychosyndrome group could be distinguished from the monopolar depressives on the basis of (their poorer) quality of performance rather than its quantity. In general, one can speak of an impaired tolerance for load, expression of disruption of the integration of cognitive functions. There were however, subtle differences among the patients of the organic psychosyndrome group: Some were simply not able to perform correctly under speed conditions per se (poor performance at all speeds), and the performance of others at the outset (moderate stimulus presentation speed) was comparable to that of the three other groups but deteriorated rapidly with gathering presentation speed and was accompanied by a concomitant decline in the companion load-dependent values (Pauli, PTG). In the ensuing, decreasing-speed phase of the DET test, the organic psychosyndrome patients resembled the personnel group in that their restitution was also delayed, but the phenomenon was more generalized (KSb-S, PTG, and CFF). This observation stood in contrast to that of the kindred group and the depressive group both of whom recovered more rapidly.

These results confirm the effectiveness of the ergopsychometric approach in clinical settings, not only in differential diagnosis, but as a potential support where decisions regarding reinstatement into the work force are concerned. Furthermore, the indispensability of the particular test design for the speed condition must be recognized: The return to patient control under the load performance demands, out of therapeutic–humanitarian reasons, yielded crucial supplementary, finely resolved insights into the specific nature of the different disorders.

Alcohol Abuse

The first study in this category (Beiglböck, Feselmayer, & Bischof, 1989) kept to the "simple" ergopsychometric test/retest design and undertook to distinguish between the occurrence of TCs among alcohol dependents ($n = 20$; mean age $= 31$), psychosomatic patients ($n = 20$; mean age $= 26$), and a parallelized (by age and profession) inconspicuous control group ($n = 23$). The critial dependent variables were associative memory (Grünberger's [1977] parallel form of the Arnold and Kohlmann Demenztest [Test of Dementia], 1953), concentration (Pauli test, paper-and-pencil form), choice reaction time to two visual stimuli (Vienna Reaction Timer, Dr. G. Schuhfried, Vienna, Austria), perceptual–motor coordination of reaction to complex stimuli presented at a moderately set, constant pace (Vienna Determination Unit, Dr. G. Schuhfried, Vienna, Austria), and self-rated state (four-item questionnaire presented prior to neutral testing, between neutral and load conditions, and as postload follow-up). Load was defined by white noise (subpain threshold, i.e., 75 dB or less).

The criterion for inclusion in the TC group was "significant decrease in performance in at least one of the tests." On the basis of this classification, 70% of the psychosomatic and 75% of the alcohol-dependent patients were allotted to the TC group. In contrast, twice as many of the controls (56.5%) belonged to the group of consistent performers (CPs; same or improved performance in all tests), versus 43.5% control TCs. The questionnaire designed to quantify momentary state brought the following insights: The TCs did not show any changes over the total test period, consistently reporting high levels of activation and alertness. The CPs self-rated their "level of activation" as well as their "alertness" as significantly ($p < .05$) enhanced under load. Once again, the association between arousal and performance was observed, paired with a greater dynamic range characterizing the CPs. But it was not the sensomotor component of activation that revealed differences in performance among this clinical population. These data also point to a need to break the activation dimension down into its putative component parts.

A continuation of this work was conducted by Hauk (1989). Her population was composed of 147 alcohol abusers (85 female, 62 male) of normal intelligence (median age = 39). The primary dependent variables were associative memory (Grünberger's [1977] parallel form of the Arnold and Kohlmann Demenztest [Test of Dementia], 1953), attention and the power and speed dimensions of memory (*Syndrom-Kurztest* [Syndrome Short Test]; SKT, Erzigkeit, 1977), visuomotor co-ordination set at a pace of 56 signals per minute (Vienna Determination Unit, Dr. G. Schuhfried, Vienna, Austria), and CFF. The load condition—white noise over head phones (75 dB or less)—necessitated foregoing acoustic signals on the determination unit. Both phases of ergopsychometric testing were carried out on 1 day, 3 weeks after the patients had been admitted to the clinic. (Parallel forms for neutral and load testing were available.) The criterion for classification as TC was a decline in performance in one of the above achievement tests (associative memory, SKT, or work at the determination unit). On the basis of this selection standard, 120 TCs (82%) were identified versus 27 (18%) CPs in this clinical population. The latter were not included in further testing.

The underlying purpose of Hauk's (1989) study was to identify the TCs and then test the efficacy of the progressive relaxation technique. Thus, the TCs determined on the basis of the first test series and still in stationary care were randomly assigned to treatment ($n = 53$) or nontreatment/control ($n = 56$) groups (note that 11 of the TCs left the clinic prematurely and thus eliminated themselves from the evaluation. Those in the control group were promised treatment following the investigation.) The treatment group underwent instruction three times weekly over the next 3 weeks.

At the end of 3 weeks ergopsychometric testing was repeated. One must keep in mind that we are now dealing with a randomly divided population of TCs, the treatment TCs having already undergone relaxation training and the control TCs not yet treated. The results of this second test series left only 15 of the treated TCs (28% of all treated) remaining in the TC category (according to the original TC criterion), whereas 52 of the control TCs (93% of that group), by whatever means, were still unable (or unwilling) to carry their particular level of performance in the neutral condition over to the load condition. The difference between the numbers of improved performers between treatment group and controls was extreme: χ^2 (1, $N = 109$) = 45.2235, $p \ll .000$.

The discriminating variables were observed to be those demanding cognitive performance. Regarding associative memory there had been no differences between those TCs comprising the treatment group and those comprising the control group prior to treatment, but there were significantly fewer numbers of TCs among the treatment group after they received relaxation training than among the controls on the basis of ergopsychometric comparisons of test results, χ^2 (1, $N = 109$) = 10.35, $p \ll .00$. Attention and power and speed of reproduction, tested by the SKT, discriminated similarly: Again, no pretreatment differences between the groups, but significantly fewer numbers of TCs remaining in the treatment group after they received relaxation training than among the controls on the basis of ergopsychometric comparison, χ^2 (1, $N = 109$) = 29.94, $p \ll .000$. A sensomotor task (the Vienna Determination Unit) could not separate the treated patients from the control group still awaiting relaxation therapy. Both groups' performance improved under load commensurately.

At this point it is necessary to backtrack to the initial ergopsychometric test session, on the strength of which the TCs were selected from the entire clinical population. The physiological data regarding nonspecific activation or fatigue had not distinguished the TCs from the CPs immediately prior to this first, pre-sample-selection ergopsychometric neutral test condition (CFF median: 39.5 for TCs vs. 38.5 for CPs; $p = .28$, Mann-Whitney U test for nonnormal distribution and nonhomogenous variances). The corresponding values following right after neutral testing (actual second CFF measurement of nonspecific activation) in this initial test set were 40.10 for TCs, 38.10 for CPs ($p \approx .06$).

Thus we observe the first leg of an interesting phenomenon: The TCs were already revealing a tendency to reach their activation maximum immediately following testing under neutral conditions, whereas the activation of the CPs was actually starting to ease off at this measurement. The CFF postload values offer an interesting and plausible insight into the profile separating the TCs from the CPs: The former's activation remained at this higher level previously primed by testing per se. But the CPs, having realized a dip in activation under neutral conditions, seemed to rev up under load. Such results are in principal conformance with the picture (see Figure 2) portrayed on the Yerkes-Dodson ∩ curve representing the relationship between performance and activation and with Bischof's (1983) data.

After the TCs were divided into treatment versus control groups, the CFF performance of the treatment TCs showed a notable tendency. Although, in absolute values, their median CFF values for each of the analogous measurements (i.e., preneutral, postneutral, and postload) remained higher than those of the original CPs in the ergopsychometric sample pretest, the curves now ran nearly parallel to each other. The median values of the entire TC group prior to subdivision into treatment and control groups, respectively, described a ∩ curve ("1": 39.5, "2": 40.1, and "3": 39.9; see Figure 10). Following relaxation training, the median values of the treatment TCs inverted the curve by 180° to U form ("1": 40.0, "2": 39.9, and "3": 40.6; see Figure 10). Those who received treatment were now more prone to relax during neutral testing. They began to emulate the CPs' processing, thus apparently gaining some leeway for themselves, in anticipation of the impending load condition (corresponding median values for CPs: "1": 38.5, "2": 38.1, and "3": 38.3; see Figure 10).

DISCUSSION AND CONCLUSIONS

From the present vantage point, we observe that tests of cognitive speed and power functions have been best suited to discriminate between TCs and CPs:

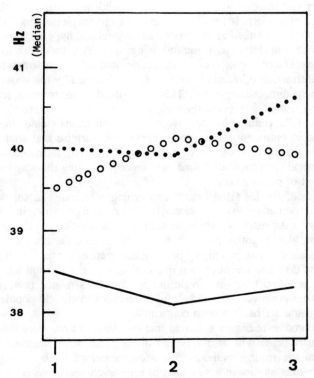

Figure 10 Treatment training champions' (TCs') emulation of
consistent performers' (CPs') load processing behavior:
TCs' prerelaxation-training ∩ curve (O O O) becomes,
after training, a U curve (■ ■ ■) parallel, at higher
levels, in absolute terms, to CPs' dynamics (———).
CFF = critical flicker frequency;
1 = pre-neutral-condition measurement;
2 = post-neutral-condition measurement;
3 = post-load-condition measurement (see text). Test
Group (treatment TCs, *n* = 53): Those who received
relaxation training after preselection testing (values refer
to second test session, after training). TCs (*n* = 120):
Entire population as determined by the preselection
testing (values refer to the preselection test session).
CPs (*n* = 27): The CPs as determined by preselection
testing (values refer to preselection test session). All are
median frequency values in hertz.

channel capacity, visual search speed, visual transformation dexterity, reaction
time, clarity of imagery, sport-specific logic, speed CFT-3, associative memory,
attention, and power and speed of reproduction. Differential duration of spiral
aftereffect as a measure of cortical saturation indicates a critical component of the
activation parameter. The dynamics of state anxiety, exploding for TCs and deflat-

ing for CPs under load, reveal a very promising target for therapeutic intervention. The picture furnished by the STAI evaluations points to the group of CAs as having better (inherent or learned) situation-dependent control over their heightened feelings of anxiety. It further substantiates our suspicion that TCs could be helped by a program aimed at harnessing anxiety-related hyperactivation and contributes to such considerations as the following: Anxiety corresponds to undefined, nonexplicit hyperactivation, so to speak, accelerated activation without additional, definitive information (Guttmann, in press), as witnessed by the above-norm values along both dimensions among TCs in postload measurements (cf. Bischof, 1983; Philipp, 1988). In view of the weight of the cognitive differential separating TCs from the CPs, training in cognitive coping mechanisms would conceivably be a fruitful aid in optimizing TCs' performance. We surmise that some CPs were labeling their anxiety in a positive way, relaxing their mind, as manifested in lower levels of cortical saturation after load, and thereby clearing the way for maintaining their level of performance.

The results of Hauk's (1989) study concerning accelerated motor performance of a clinical group under load coincide with observations by Kryspin-Exner (1987) with monopolar depressives, whose motor performance also improved under load testing. Here, also, ergopsychometric testing points to a therapeutic approach including physical exercise promising positive experiences for the target population. But one must take into consideration that our data do not warrant labeling sensomotor tasks as all-purpose prognostic indices for stress-related performance. Although they deliver revealing and helpful differences in clinical populations, their value among athletes has not been confirmed.

It has become increasingly apparent that the trend to ever more sensitive measurement instruments will also serve to allow predicative statements based on ergopsychometric testing methods in a wide variety of fields. The preliminary results of ongoing studies in a new area of ergopsychometric research—the grade school classroom—corroborate Kryspin-Exner's (1987) conclusion that quantity *and* quality of performance discriminate between TCs and CPs. Attention to both parameters on the basis of an appropriate choice of tests can bring fruitful insights for therapeutic intervention.

Those studies including measurements toward a personality profile (Krehan-Riemer, 1986; Schwarz, 1986) revealed unanimously that the stress-prone TCs experience, under load conditions, a decrease in the dimensions "aggressivity," "generally depressive psychic mood," and "dominance" while on the other hand reporting an enhancement of "directive attitude toward and use of authority" and "extroversion/externality." This pertains to the populations of candidates for NCO (Krehan-Riemer) and primary Raynaud syndrome patients (Schwarz). Philipp's (1988) and Bischof's (1983) data show that the CP (competitive athlete) is characterized by below-average "externality" and hyperactivation, as measured either in the form of trait anxiety or as physiological index (nonspecific activation). The ergopsychometric approach to personality diagnosis demonstrates that the load-dependent modifications are often quite unexpected, and indeed enlightening.

It is also becoming increasingly clear that "activation," in this respect, is a crucial index that will benefit by resolution into its component parts. The picture evolving testifies to the validity of the ∩ Yerkes-Dodson activation–performance function, which itself also delivers an explanation for the double-pronged observations collected via the aforementioned studies: One type of TC is generally described by the dynamics illustrated in Figure 2. The other type registers activation measures at about the level of Subject B under neutral conditions (left-hand solid arrow) and *decreases* critical components (apparently cognitive) of that level of activation, whereby he facilitates an increase or hinders a decrease in actual competitive (load) performance.

Hauk's (1989) curiosity led her to persevere at the level of TC identification to compare the data available, according to which she juxtaposed CAs, the inconspicuous norm population, and the clinical group of alcohol abusers. The proportion of TCs among CAs was, not surprisingly, lowest (20%)—their avocation calls for dependable performance under stress. The norm population was about evenly divided between CAs and TCs (57% vs. 42%). And more than four-fifths of the clinical population was susceptible to stress-reduced performance. Some critical questions concern the group of TCs among the norm population: How many among them remain inconspicuous because they are the very ones whose daily routine only rarely calls for maximum performance, and by virtue of this fact regularly function quite satisfactorily? How many comprise the anonymous number of unregistered, unknown cases who, though suffering in some way, shy away from the therapeutic or clinical setting? Furthermore, in view of the inverted proportions regarding athletes and patients, how viable would a light regimen of physical exercise of the individual's choice be as a therapeutic tool? Athletes by choice may be self-selecting by virtue of their quality of stress resistance. On the other hand, physical exercise could also have its own salutary psychological effects, in the direction of promoting coping.

Ergopsychometry has now expanded onto the international stage in the form of joint research and ergopsychometric applications in cooperation between the schools of medicine, education, physical education, and psychology at Tokai University in Japan and the Institute of Psychology in Vienna. This venture encompasses exchanges at the professorial level, computer compatability, seminars and laboratory setups. The Institute of Psychology in Vienna has also been honored by the award for the first Fulbright Research Scholarship in Sports Psychology to Professor D. V. Harris (Pennsylvania State University) to carry out ergopsychometric brain-wave studies in our neuropsychological laboratory. Ergopsychometry has reached its future.

SUMMARY

Ergopsychometry entails dualized psychological testing: comparing the results from testing first under neutral conditions followed by testing under performance-appropriate load. Its primary intention is to deliver viable prognoses of performance in the stressful, real-life situation. Its sensitivities and applications are discussed and the conclusions they allow presented, in "state of the art" form. Initially, sport psychological tool, it has now matured and successfully been introduced into the fields of professional counseling and clincial diagnosis.

REFERENCES

Anastasi, A. (1968). *Psychological testing.* New York: MacMillan.
Arnold, O. H., & Kohlmann, Th. (1953). *Leistungspsychologische Untersuchungen* [Performance

psychological studies of the problem of dementia]. Vienna, Austria: *Wiener Zeitschrift für Nervenheilkunde und deren Grenzgebiete VI* [Viennese Journal for Neurology and Related Fields], 91–122.

Bastine, R. (1977). *Fragebogen zur direktiven Einstellung* [Questionnaire of Attitudes Toward and Uses of Authority]. Göttingen, Federal Republic of Germany: Hogrefe.

Beckmann, D., & Richter, H. E. (1975). *Gießen-Test*. Bern, Switzerland: Huber Verlag.

Beiglböck, W. (1983). *Eropsychometrische Diagnostik in der Sportpsychologie. Aktivierungsmessung und der Versuch einer Beeinflussung durch Selbstkontrolltechniken* [Ergopsychometric diagnostics in sports psychology. The measurement of activation and the attempt to influence it by means of self-control techniques]. Unpublished doctoral dissertation, University of Vienna, Vienna, Austria.

Beiglböck, W., Feselmayer, S., & Bischof, B. (1989). Ergopsychometrie—Neue Wege der experimentellen Psychodiagnositk pathologischer Belastungsreaktionen [Ergopsychometry—a new approach to the experimental psychodiagnosis of pathological reactions to load]. *Zeitschrift für experimentelle und angewandte Psychologie, 36*(1), 16–30.

Bischof, B. (1983). *Psychologische und Psychophysiologische Moderatorvariablen in der Belastungsdiagnositk—eine sportpsychologische Untersuchung an Orientierungsläufern* [Psychological and psychophysiological moderator variables in load diagnostics—a sport psychological investigation of orienteering runners]. Unpublished doctoral dissertation, University of Vienna, Vienna, Austria.

Breidt, R. (1973). Lassen sich Perseverationen durch Hirnschädigungen erklären? [Can Perseverations Be Explained by Cerebral Damage?]. *Psychiatrica Clinica, 6,* 357–369.

Byrne, D. (1961). The repression-sensitization scale: Rationale, reliability, and validity. *Journal of Personality, 29,* 334–349.

Cattell, R. B. (1971). *Culture for test-scale 3.* Champaign, IL: Institute for Personality and Ability Testing.

Child, I. L., & Waterhouse, I. K. (1953). Frustration and the quality of performance: II. A theoretical statement. *Psychological Review, 60,* 127–139.

Easterbrook, J. A. (1959). The effect of emotion on cue utilization and the organization of behavior. *Psychological Review, 66,* 183–201.

Erzigkeit, H. (1977). *Der Syndrom-Kurztest zur Erfassung von Aufmerksamkeits- und Gedächtnisstörungen* [The syndrome short-test for measuring disturbances of attention and memory: The SKT]. Vaterstetten, Federal Republic of Germany: Vless Verlag.

Ewig, H., & Wohlfeil, H. (1926a). Psychologische Beiträge zur Ermüdungsforschung bei maximalen körperlichen Anstrengungen. I: Das Verhalten der Aufmerksamkeit [Psychologial contributions to fatigue research during maximal physical exertion. I: The course of attention]. *Archiv für Hygiene, 97,* 162 (abstract).

Ewig, H., & Wohlfeil, H. (1926b). Psychologische Beiträge zur Ermüdungsforschung bei maximalen körperlichen Anstrengungen. II: Das psychomotorische Verhalten [Psychological contributions to fatigue research during maximal physical exertion: II: Psychomotor behavior]. *Archiv für Hygiene, 97,* 251 (abstract).

Eysenck, H. J., & Rachmann, S. (1968). *Neurosen = Ursache und Heilmethoden* [The causes and cures of neurosis]. Berlin, German Democratic Republic: VEB-Deutscher Verlag. (original work published 1965.)

Fahrenberg, J., Selg, H., & Hampel, R. (1973). *Freiburg Persönlichkeitsinventar* [Freiburg Personality Inventory] Göttingen, Federal Republic of Germany: Hogrefe.

Fichtner, M. M., & Meermann, R. (1981). *Zur Psychopathometrie der Anorexia nervosa. Ursachen und Behandlungen* [On the psychopathometry of anorexia nervosa. Causes and treatments). Stuttgart, Federal Republic of Germany: Enke.

Gittler, G. (1984). Entwicklung und Erprobung eines neuen Testinstruments zur Messung des räumlichen Vorstellungsvermögens [Development and pilot test of a new test instrument for measuring spatial imagination]. *Zeitschrift für differentielle und diagnostische Psychologie, 5,* 141–165.

Grünberger, J. (1977). Psychodiagnostik de Alkoholkranken [Parallel form of the Arnold and Kohlmann Dementia Test of Memory]. In *Psychodiagnostik des Alkoholkranken* [Psychodiagnostics of the alcohol abuser] (pp. 137–145). Vienna, Austria: Maudrich.

Guttmann, G. (1967). Die Anwendung des Zeigeversuches in der Diagnostik [Application of the button-press test in diagnostics]. *Psychologie und Praxis, 2*(11), 49–60.

Guttmann, G. (1982). Ergopsychometry—testing under physical or psychological load. *German Journal of Psychology, 6,* 141–144.

Guttmann, G. (1984). Ergopsychometry. In R. Corsini (Ed.), *Encyclopedia of Psychology* (pp. 446–447). New York: John Wiley and Sons.

Guttmann, G. (1986). Ergopsychometric testing: Predicting and actualizing optimum performance under load. In M. H. Appley & R. Trumbull (Eds.), *Dynamics of stress: Physiological, psychological, and social perspectives* (pp. 141–155). New York: Plenum.

Guttmann, G. (1990). *Angst: eine neue psychologische Deutung und deren praktische Konsequenzen* [Anxiety: A new psychological interpretation and its practical consequences]. Vienna, Austria: Eigenverlag des Ministeriums.

Guttmann, G., Bauer, H., & Trimmel, M. (1982, July). *Ergopsychometry—testing under physiological or psychological load.* Presented at the 20th International Congress of Applied Psychology, Edinburgh, Scotland.

Guttmann, G., Bauer, H., & Vanecek, E. (1982, July). *Cortical DC—potentials and learning.* Presented at the 20th International Congress of Applied Psychology, Edinburgh, Scotland.

Guttmann, G., Thuri, T., & Weingarten, P. (1981, August). Ergopsychometry—testing under physiological and psychological stress. Presented at the Fifth World Sport Psychology Congress, Ottawa, Canada.

Hampel, R., & Selg, H. (1975). *Fragebogen zur Erfassung von Aggressivitätsfaktoren* [Questionnaire for measuring aggressivity factors]. Göttingen, Federal Republic of Germany: Hogrefe.

Hauk, E. (1989). *Ergopsychometrie bei klinischen Gruppen: Die Auswirkungen einer Selbstkontrolltechnik auf die Leistungen bei Alkoholikern* [Ergopsychometry for clinical groups: The effects of a self-control technique on alcohol-abusers' performance]. Unpublished master's thesis, University of Vienna, Vienna, Austria.

Heitzlhofer, K. (1978). *Der Appetenz–Aversions-Konfliktverlauf beim Klettern: Eine Typenanalyse* [The course of the appentency–aversion conflict during rock-climbing: An analysis of types]. Unpublished doctoral dissertation, University of Vienna, Vienna, Austria.

Holland, H. C. (1965). *The spiral aftereffect.* London: Pergamon Press.

Holmes, T. H., & Rahe, R. H. (1967). The Social Readjustment Rating Scale. *Journal of Psychosomatic Research, 11,* 213–218.

Jacobson, E. (1934). *You must relax.* New York: McGraw-Hill.

Jäger, R., Lischer, S., Münster, B., & Ritz, B. (1976). *Biographisches Inventar zur Diagnose von Verhaltensstörungen* [Biographic Inventory for the Diagnosis of Behavioral Disorders]. Göttingen, Federal Republic of Germany: Hogrefe.

Jirasko, M. (1985). *Mental Imagery: Visuelle Vorstellung und visuelle Vorstellungsfähigkeit* [Mental imagery: Visual imagery and visual imagination]. Unpublished doctoral dissertation, University of Vienna, Vienna, Austria.

Krampen, G. (1981). IPC—Fragebogen zu Kontrollüberzeugungen. [German version of Levenson's IPC Scales]. Göttingen, Federal Republic of Germany: Hogrefe.

Krehan-Riemer, A. (1986). *Ergopsychometrische Studie im Persönlichkeitsbereich—ein Vergleich der Persönlichkeitsvariablen unter ergopsychometrischer Belastung und unter neutralen Bedingungen* [Ergopsychometric investigation of personality—a comparison of personality characteristics under ergopsychometric load and under neutral conditions]. Unpublished doctoral dissertation, University of Vienna, Vienna, Austria.

Krohne, H. W. (1974). Repression–Sensitization Skala [Repressor–Sensitizer Scale]. *Zeitschrift für klinische Psychologie, 3,* 238–260.

Kryspin-Exner, I. (1987). Ergopsychometrie und Hirnleistungsdiagnostik [Ergopsychometry and the diagnosis of cerebral performance]. In H.-U. Wittchen (Ed.), *Beiträge zur klinischen Psychologie und Psychotherapie* [Contributions to clinical psychology and psychotherapy]. Regensburg, Federal Republic of Germany: Roderer Verlag.

Lackner, E. (1979). *Experimentelle Untersuchung über den Einfluß psychischer und motorischer Fähigkeiten auf die Kletterleistung von Anfängern* [Experimental investigation of the influence of psychic and motoric capabilities on novices' rock-climbing performance]. Unpublished doctoral dissertation, University of Vienna, Vienna, Austria.

Laux, L., Glanzmann, P., Schaffner, P., & Spielberger, C. D. (1981). *State-Trait Angstinventar* [German version of Spielberger, Gorsuch, and Luchene's (1970) State–Trait Anxiety Inventory]. Weinheim, West Germany: Beltz.

Lester, M. (1986). *Entwicklung eines Fragebogens zur Messung von Attribution im Zusammenhang mit Erfolg und Mißerfolg* [Development of a questionnaire for the measurement of attribution in relationship with success and failure]. Unpublished doctoral dissertation, University of Vienna, Vienna, Austria.

Levenson, H. (1972). Distinctions within the concept of internal–external control. Development of a new scale. *Proceedings of the 80th Annual Convention of the American Psychological Association, 7,* 261–262 (summary).

Levenson, H. (1973). Multidimensional locus of control in psychiatric patients. *Journal of Consulting and Clinical Psychology, 41*(3), 397–404.

Lindsley, D. B. (1951). Emotions. In S. S. Stevens (Ed.), *Handbook of Experimental Psychology* (pp. 473–516). New York: John Wiley.

Mayrhofer, J. (1986). *Die Bedeutung der Vorstellung im Segelsport: eine ergopsychometrische Untersuchung* [The significance of imagery in regatta-sailing: An ergopsychometric investigation]. Unpublished master's thesis, University of Vienna, Vienna, Austria.

Meili, R. (1937). *Psychologische Diagnostik* [Psychological diagnostics]. Munich, Federal Republic of Germany: E. Reinhardt.

Nitsch, J. R. (1974). Die hierarchische Strucktur des Eigenzustandes—ein Approximationsversuch mit Hilfe der Binärstrukturanalyse [The hierarchical structure of one's own state—an attempt at approximation with the aid of the binary structure analysis]. *Diagnostica, 20,* 142–164.

Pauli, R. & Arnold, W. (1970). Pauli-Test (PT). Test material. Munich, Federal Republic of Germany: Entress Verlag; Testhandbuch (Test manual). Munich, Federal Republic of Germany. Barth Verlag. (Both in German.)

Philipp, A. (1988). *Ergopsychometrie im Leistungssport: psychologische Aspekte der Leistungstestung unter Belastung* [Ergopsychometry in competitive sports: The psychological aspects of testing performance under load]. Unpublished doctoral dissertation, University of Vienna, Vienna, Austria.

Remschmidt, H. (1971). Redundanz und Regression. Informationstheoretische Gesichtspunkte zum Verständnis psychopathologischer Phänomene [Redundancy and regression. Information on theoretical aspects toward understanding psychopathological phenomena]. *Psychiatrica Clinica, 4,* 65–81.

Schellenberger, H. (1973). Das Gruppenbewertungsverfahren [Procedure for evaluating groups]. In *Theorie und Praxis der Körperkultur.* Berlin, German Democratic Republic: VEB Verlag.

Schmidtke, H. (1951). Über die Messung der psychischen Ermüdung mit Hilfe des Flimmertests [On the measurement of the course of psychic fatigue using the Flimmer test]. *Psychologische Forschung, 23.*

Schmidtke, H. (1965). *Die Ermüdung* [On fatigue]. Bern, Switzerland: Huber.

Schwarz, U. (1986). *Ergopsychometrische Testung von Patienten mit primärem Raynaud-Syndrom* [Ergopsychometric examination of patients with primary Raynaud syndrome]. Unpublished master's thesis, University of Vienna, Vienna, Austria.

Spielberger, C. D. (1972). Anxiety as an emotional state. In C. D. Spielberger (Ed.), *Anxiety—current trends in theory and research* (Vol. 1, pp. 24–49). New York: Academic Press.

Spielberger, C. D., Gorsuch, R. L., & Luchene, R. H. (1970). *State-Trait Anxiety Inventory.* Palo Alto, CA: Consulting Psychologists Press.

Steiner, G. (1980). *Visuelle Vorstellungen beim Lösen von elementaren Problemen* [Visual imagery while solving elementary problems]. Federal Republic of Germany: Klett-Cotta.

von Zerssen, D., in collaboration with Koeller, D. -M. (1976). Klinische Selbstbeurteilungs-Skalen (KSb-S) aus dem Münchner Psychiatrischen Informations-System [Clinical Self-Evaluation Scales from the Munich Psychiatric Information System]. Weinheim, Federal Republic of Germany: Beltz.

Weingarten, P. (1981, April). *Performance diagnosis with young sportsmen by means of ergopsychometry.* Paper presented at the First Sports Psychology Symposium, Munich, West Germany.

Weingarten, P. (1985). Applied ergopsychometry with references to table-tennis and judo. *Studia Psychologica, 27*(1), 47–51.

Weiß, R. H. (1971). Cattel-Weiß Testheft CFT 3 Skala 3 [German version of Cattell's (1971) CFT scale 3]. Braunschweig, Federal Republic of Germany: Westermann Verlag.

Yerkes, R. M., & Dodson, J. D. (1908). The relation of strength stimulus to rapidity of habit formation. *Journal of Comparative Neurology and Psychology, 18,* 459–482.

4

Stress Model Development and Testing by Group Psychometrics and One-Subject Psychophysiology

John Wallace Hinton
University of Glasgow, Scotland

The following are quotations from a chapter entitled "Stress—How Useful a Concept?" in a book on stress and occupational psychology in the United States (Krinsky, Kieffer, Carone, & Yolles, 1984). Different contributors made these observations:

> *I think that the word "stress" is a useless term and that it creates problems and does not promote understanding. (p. 123)*
> *Stress can be viewed as a composite consisting of a stressor, the vulnerability or the particular reaction of the individual, and the supportive context. (p. 124)*
> *I think that anxiety is a kind of stress. It is one kind of stress among many others. (p. 128)*
> *Stress is a set of cognitions prompted by environmental stimuli and possibly leading to anxiety or physical disability or nothing for that matter. (p. 128)*
> *I equate it [stress] with dis-ease, and that's the term that seems most important to me. (p. 128)*
> *To say there are good stresses, bad stresses, dis-stresses and so on is trivial. (p. 129)*
> *With too little stress you have boredom, indifference, total lack of productivity. But go over the "right" amount of stress and you decrease productivity. (p. 134)*
> *Short of ridding the English language of the word, we must make it less trivial, less of a dumping ground, more precise. (p. 140)*

Some time ago I naively waded into this morass and now, after 8 years of researching and theorizing at Glasgow University Stress Research Unit, we think we are beginning to "see the light." Our view of psychological stress is that neither the engineering model (stress seen as being environmental) nor the medical model (stress seen as a set of responses) is acceptable, for the reasons argued cogently elsewhere (Cox, 1978, Chapter 1). We define stress as a "self-inflicted" mental state resulting from the appraisal of perceived external demands being in excess of perceived capabilities, where satisfactory coping is regarded as important. This fits well with studies on animals (Weiss, 1970, 1972) that show that

Thanks are due to the Carnegie Trust, whose financial support promoted the author's presentation of papers and research discussions in Australia, which helped considerably in compiling this chapter. The support of the British Council must be acknowledged for the ongoing research link with the Work Science Section of the University of Dresden. In particular, discussions with Dr. Peter Richter, Professor Winfried Hacker, and Professor Klaus Scheuch have been most helpful. These individuals also provided new test materials that were further developed for the present research. Finally, for proofreading and advice on the manuscript, thanks are due to Elke Rotheiler, my co-worker.

53

extended lack of control over noxious stimuli leads to physiological stress responses and contributes to psychosomatic diseases.

Regarding stress as generated by perceived coping incapacity (PCI) avoids problems in trying to assess objective demands and objective capability in an attempt to get a demand/capacity ratio. The latter would be required by the approach of McGrath (1976) and Lazarus and Cohen (1978), who assumed that stress occurs when the individual's capacities are outstripped by the demands. In contrast, Schulz and Schönpflug (1982) argued that stress is greatest if capacities just match demands, or the latter are marginally greater. However, Harrison (1978) proposed that the lowest degree of stress occurs where capacities and demands just match: Both overload (demands exceeding capacities) and underload (capacities exceeding demands) can be regarded as stress inducing. Thus, PCI would be high in both underload and overload, and there could be marked individual differences relating to such personality factors as introversion and extroversion because extroverts are particularly intolerant of monotony (Davies, Shackleton, & Parasuraman, 1983).

By taking the view that stress results from a totally subjective cognitive appraisal of PCI, self-rating scales become potentially valid methods of measuring this aspect of stress generation. Furthermore, from this perspective, it does not matter whether stress is induced by underload, overload, or a balance between abilities and demands. Indeed which view is correct may depend on individual personality factors and specific environmental situations.

We are, of course, interested in subjective underload or overload when involved in job design, but such considerations are irrelevant to the problem dealt with in this chapter, namely, the development and testing of a general model of stress, where PCI leads to a range of stress responses and subsequent feedbacks.

Our study of stress began with the idea of Lazarus (1976) that stress results from a cognitive appraisal process and with the general theoretical model presented by Cox (1978). Our biocognitive model of stress was extended and modified on the basis of psychophysiological considerations and reasoning presented by Hinton (1989). On the output side of the model we felt there should be a link between physiological stress responses and emotional responses, which in turn would affect cognitive reappraisal.

A review of our ideas on the biocognitive model of stress and how psychophysiology contributes to measurement in the model was given by Hinton (1988). Stress is conceived of as an intervening variable—a brain function involving the hypothalamic, limbic, autonomic, and endocrine systems. The resulting mental state can be assessed only from measures of stress generation and its results. The measures of generation involve subjective cognitive criteria while the outputs can be assessed in terms of emotional–cognitive, physiological, and behavioral responses (Figure 1).

Many feedbacks from stress responses occur that affect both PCI and the perceived importance of coping and motivation. For simplification these feedbacks are not shown in Figure 1, but they are the subject of our future investigations. A multivariate correlational approach to the study of stress is therefore inevitable but, as argued by MacKay and Cox (1987), criterion contamination has been hard to eradicate. Consequently the question of causal relationships has been difficult to answer.

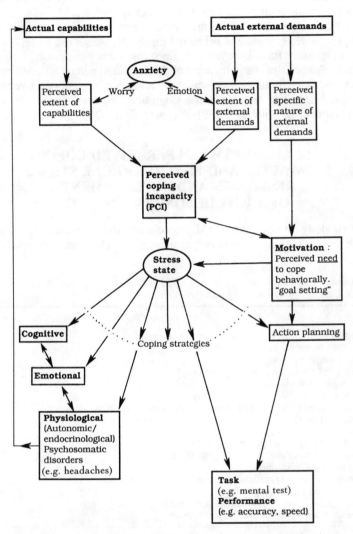

Figure 1 Theoretical stress model for task performance demand situation
with no feedback.

MEASUREMENT OF PERCEIVED COPING INCAPACITY

MacKay, Cox, Burrows, and Lazarini (1978) presented a "stress" scale that we used in our laboratory, together with Spielberger's State–Trait Anxiety Inventory (STAI; Spielberger, 1983) in a number of studies involving stress generation. We subsequently found a very high correlation ($r = .93$) between these two scales (with 83% similarity between items). Hence the "stress" scale was measuring state anxiety. We reasoned that although anxiety may be an important "feed-forward" in the stress model as proposed by Cox (1978), coping with perceived demands is central to the concept of stress. Furthermore, the fear component of anxiety is by no means the only emotional stress response.

Taking the view of Cox (1978) that stress depends in part on the discrepancy between perceived demands and perceived capability, we set out to design a questionnaire to measure this discrepancy. Sixteen questions were selected covering a wide range of aspects of the perception of demands and perceived abilities. These were arranged in a 10-point rating scale with a balance of eight negative and eight positive questions: The result was the Cognitive Appraisal Stress Test (CAST; Rotheiler, Hinton, & Mitchell, 1989) of general PCI (Table 1).

THE LINK BETWEEN PERCEIVED COPING INCAPACITY AND PHYSIOLOGICAL STRESS RESPONSES AND DEVELOPMENT OF A PSYCHOSOMATICS SCALE

Our first study investigated the validity of the CAST by examining its relationship with the physiological stress output, namely, psychosomatic complaints. The

Table 1   Items in and factor analysis of the original Cognitive Appraisal Stress Test (Hinton & Rotheiler, 1987) measuring perceived coping capacity (PCI)

Items[a]

1. I generally find myself under excessive time pressure.
2. I find many things too difficult to handle.
3. Usually I am able to concentrate.
4. Mostly, I feel I am able to make correct decisions.
5. I can usually think clearly.
6. Various demands which confront me I find confusing.
7. Generally I need to give a lot of attention to demands made on me.
8. I usually feel capable.
9. Much of my life is too complicated.
10. I feel that most situations are easy to deal with.
11. Usually I have no difficulty in sorting out ideas.
12. I am generally a quick thinker.
13. My abilities are usually sufficient for what I am expected to do.
14. Generally I feel I am coping well.
15. I often find my ability to pay attention disturbed.
16. Frequently I cannot reason as clearly as I should.

Factor analysis[b]

Principal component
General PCI scale: Items 2(+), 4(−), 5(−), 8(−), 10(−), 11(−), 13(−), 14(−), and 16(−)

Varimax rotation (for University Work)
Scale 1. Cognitive Slowness and Incapability: Items 8(−), 12(−), and 13(−)
Scale 2. Perceived Dithering in Decision Making: Items 4(−), 5(−), 6(+), and 11(−)
Scale 3. Perceived Attention and Concentration Problems: Items 3(−) and 15(+)
Scale 4. Excessive Demands: Items 1(+), 2(+), and 9(+)

[a]The items (eight "positive" and eight "negative") were rated on a 10-point scale from *disagree strongly* (1) to *agree strongly* (10).
[b]Item 7 was deleted because it proved to be essentially a motivation variable.

hypothesis was that PCI (as measured by the CAST) would predict the extent of psychosomatic ailments.

A Psychosomatic Ailments Questionnaire (PSYSOM) was developed by Hinton and Rotheiler (1987), based on an inventory by Scheuch and Vogel (personal communication, December 20, 1988; Vogel et al., 1987). Scheuch and Vogel selected the 30 most frequent psychosomatic complaints of more than 1,000 teachers who had ceased work, reportedly because of job stress or "burnout."

After translation into English, a scale of measurement was constructed that combined the aspects of intensity, frequency, and duration for each "symptom" (Table 2). This list of ailments, which has served us well, was derived on the presumed basis of work stress, but, unlike most other psychosomatic questionnaires, few "mental" problems were included so that the risk of criterion contamination was reduced.

Initially we used the PSYSOM scale to obtain an overall score, but we also used subscores based on grouping ailments into crude scales reflecting physiological considerations (e.g., cardiovascular and skeletal muscular). The PSYSOM raw scores (a product of frequency, duration, and annoyance) were unacceptably positively skewed, so a square root transformation was used to obtain reasonable normalizations (Hinton & Rotheiler, 1988; Hinton, Rotheiler, Mitchell, & Arthur, 1988; see Footnote b in Table 2).

The two self-rating scales of stress generation (CAST) and stress response (PSYSOM) were administered on separate days to a class of 75 second-year female students of average age 20. The forms were completed rapidly under time pressure. The PSYSOM scale correlated significantly with CAST ($r = .42$, $p < .001$). The correlation of CAST with the PSYSOM subscale Skeletal Muscle Tension was .67. The correlations with Skin Disorder ($r = .31$) and Cardiovascular Problems ($r = .37$) were also statistically significant. Questions concerning sleep quality and sensory oversensitivity did not correlate with PCI, indicating that the significant results were not simply due to a response bias to complain generally.

THE MEASUREMENT OF DIFFERENT ASPECTS OF PERCEIVED COPING INCAPACITY

Factor analysis was next conducted on the CAST. The CAST was administered to 108 students with instructions to respond with regard to (a) life in general, (b) the work situation, (c) home and domestic situation, and (d) social life outside the home. We discovered one principal-component factor that applied across all four factor analyses. A general PCI scale of 9 items was thus constructed. The items with the heaviest loadings on this factor were "I usually feel capable" and "Generally I feel that I am coping well" (scored negatively) (see Table 1).

Varimax rotation identified different factors that were specific to the situation for which PCI scores were obtained. Because we had a particular interest in predicting university examination performance, we constructed subscales from the identifiable varimax factors for "university work." As detailed in Table 1, these subscales were (a) Perceived Cognitive Slowness and Incapability, (b) Perceived Dithering in Decision Making, (c) Perceived Concentration and Attention Problems, and (d) Perceived Complicated and Time-Pressured Life (excessive demands).

Table 2   Items in the original Psychosomatic Ailments Questionnaire (Rotheiler, 1989) and factor
analysis of the short form of the Questionnaire

Items[a]

1. Difficulty in falling asleep
2. Bad dreams
3. Fatigue in spite of sound enough sleep
4. Exhaustion[b]
5. Getting tired quickly[b]
6. Disturbance in sleeping
7. Diarrhea, indigestion[b]
8. Feeling sick
9. Bad appetite or feeling full
10. Stomach upset[b]
11. Wind, bowel aches[b]
12. Itching without skin rash[b]
13. Irritation of skin (e.g, dryness)[b]
14. Irritation by noise
15. Irritation by light
16. Irritation by odors
17. Headaches[b]
18. Migraines
19. Heart pains—sharp or dull aches[b]
20. Heart pounding or palpitations[b]
21. Feeling giddy[b]
22. Breathlessness[b]
23. Perspiring (e.g., from palms, not from physical exertion)[b]
24. Dry mouth
25. Voice disturbances (hoarse, clearing throat)[b]
26. Numbness of hands/arms/legs[b]
27. Muscle tension, especially neck and shoulders[b]
28. Blinking, face tics[b]
29. Hands trembling[b]
30. Lower back pains[b]

Factor analysis of short form (Mitchell, 1989)

Principal component (main scale)
   Items 4, 5, 10, 12, 17, 20, 21, 22, 23, 25, 27, 39, 30, and AI[c]

Varimax rotation (for University Work)
   Scale 1. Skeletal Muscular: Items 27, 30, and AI[c]
   Scale 2. Fatigue: Tiredness, Exhaustion, and Headaches: Items 4, 5, and 17
   Scale 3. Cardiovascular: Items 19, 20, and 21
   Scale 4. Breathlessness and Perspiring: Items 22, 23, and 28
   Scale 5. Dermatological: Items 12, 13, and 26
   Scale 6. Digestive: Items 7, 10, and 11

[a]Self-ratings for each item were made for each item as follows: Frequency (F)—daily (6), weekly
(5), fortnightly (4), monthly (3), yearly (20), never (1); annoyance (A)—extremely (4), fairly (3), a
little (2), very little (1); and duration (D)—continuous or on and off all day (2), not so (1). A composite
score was computed for each item by multiplying and taking the square root of F.A.D.
[b]Item was included in short form.
[c]Additional item for short form, called "muscle aches (not associated with exercise)."

PREDICTION OF EXAMINATION PERFORMANCE: THE INFLUENCE OF MOTIVATION, PERCEIVED COPING INCAPACITY, ANXIETY STATE, AND PLANNING ORIENTATION

For our research on stress model development, we wanted to take into account motivation and state anxiety in predicting the effective coping response of examination performance. Finding no suitable available instrument, we produced a General Motivation Scale (GEMOS; Table 3) using the basic method described above for developing the CAST scale. We found a general principal component of motivation, applicable over home, social, and work situations. This resulted in a 10-item main scale of general motivation. As with CAST, the varimax subfactors were specific to the situation. The work motivation subscales were identified as (a) Perceived Need to Deal with External Demands, (b) Perceived Need to Achieve

Table 3 Items in and factor analysis of original General Motivation Scale (Hinton et al., 1989)

Items[a]

1. I feel the need to "get down to doing things."
2. I feel problems must be faced up to.
3. I think it is important to do my best at all times.
4. I tend to let things drift.
5. I find it difficult to feel motivated.
6. I take it easy.
7. It doesn't bother me much if I can't get on with activities.
8. I don't feel a need to cope.
9. I just can't be be bothered.
10. I feel like giving up when seeing difficulties.
11. It is important to me to cope very well.
12. It is important to me to take difficulties seriously.
13. I aim for perfection whatever I do.
14. I want to achieve something.
15. I feel pretty unmotivated.
16. I don't feel I have to face demands on me.
17. I don't see the need to make an effort.
18. It bothers me if duties pile up.
19. I find it unnecessary to attend to demands on me.
20. I see each difficulty in my life as a matter of importance.

Factor analysis

Principal component
General Motivation scale: Items 1(+), 7(−), 9(−), 11(+), 12(+), 13(+), 17(−), 18(+), 19(−), and 20(+)

Varimax rotation (for University Work)
Scale 1. Perceived Need to Deal with External Demands: Items 1(+), 2(+), 3(+), 16(−), and 17(−)
Scale 2. Perceived Need to Achieve Perfection: Items 11(+), 12(+), 13(+), 14(+), and 2(+)
Scale 3. Enterprise: Determination to Take Action: Items 4(−), 5(−), 6(−), 9(−), 10(−), and 15(−)
Scale 4. Perceived Need to Get on and Cope: Items 7(−) and 8(−)

[a]The items (10 negative and 10 positive) were rated in terms of the extent to which they were regarded as applying to the subject, using a 10-point equal-interval scale.

Perfection, (c) Enterprise: Determination to Take Action, and (d) Perceived Need to Get on and Cope.

In predicting examination performance, we were also concerned with the possible effects of state anxiety in the examination room. A particular interest was the "worry" aspect of anxiety, which, as Eysenck (1983) indicated, probably underlies performance deterioration. A number of studies, including that of Morris and Liebert (1970), have indicated a relationship between worry and final examination scores, while emotionality appears to be irrelevant. Hence we applied the Spielberger STAI state anxiety questionnaire. Students were asked to indicate how they normally felt when faced with an examination situation. A separation was then made into the worry and emotionality components (described below).

Finally, we considered that an orientation toward planning and organization of work would be important in affecting performance in examinations. Therefore, a preliminary questionnaire called Self-evaluating, Planning, Orientation, and Differentiation (SEPOD) devised by Hacker in 1987 (W. Hacker, personal communication, August 20, 1987) was also applied. This was factor analyzed to produce scales indicating different aspects of organization and goal planning, but the questions were multifaceted and it was difficult to interpret and label the factors clearly, except for one, Extreme Circumspection in Planning (see Table 4).

Thus we administered, over a period of several weeks, a series of self-rating scales to monitor factors affecting stress generation: PCI (CAST), motivation (GEMOS), work planning and organization (SEPOD), and examination anxiety state (STAI) to assess cognitive worry and emotional feeling associated with examinations. The stress generation and coping strategy measures were used to predict the mean percentage marks obtained by combining the results of two essay examinations: (a) an important final class examination and (b) the highly competitive university examination for admission to the honors psychology program. The class final examination was given 3 weeks after the last questionnaire had been administered, and the university examination occurred 5 weeks after the final questionnaire. The other dependent variable was the PSYSOM measure of stress-induced ailments—a shortened version (Mitchell 1989) (see Table 2) discussed later.

In predicting the behavioral stress-coping response of examination performance, scales from both GEMOS and CAST were relevant (Figure 2). The relevant CAST scale was Perceived Concentration and Attention Problems (Scale 3), the correlation with examination performance being −.35. The positive correlation value (.35) was found between motivation, GEMOS Scale 3 (Enterprise: Determination to Take Action), and examination performance. Other subscales of GEMOS correlated between .13 and .20 with examination performance, and the

Table 4 Planning scale (SEPOD) positive pole items loading on Scale 2, Extreme Circumspection in Planning

---

In general when doing something:

1. I find it necessary to think about previous mistakes.
2. I even plan for eventualities which other people would consider unlikely.
3. I tend to plan things which other people would tackle without planning.
4. I prefer to improve a plan several times rather than make a mistake later on.

Each item was rated using a 5-point scale to indicate the degree to which it applied.

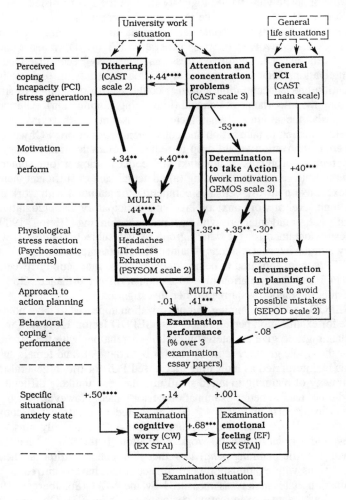

Figure 2 Intercorrelations between salient work stress generation and
response factors in university students (30 male and 75 female)
(Mitchell 1989; Hinton et al., 1989). Arrows indicate presumed
directions of influence. Thick lines indicate the predicted
significant correlations *p < .01, **p < .001, ***p < .0001,
****p < .00001, two-tailed.

GEMOS principal-component (General Motivation) scale correlated .29 (p <
.01).

A highly significant negative correlation (− .53) occurred between GEMOS
Scale 3 and CAST Scale 3: The interesting question here is whether perceived
attention and concentration problems affect determination to take action, or vice
versa. The correlations between GEMOS Scale 3 and the CAST subscales of PCI
were all negative and significant statistically. It could be argued that high motivation to take action causes a focus of attention on work and so effects a decrease in

PCI, but the opposite view would logically fit with the theory of learned helplessness (Seligman, 1975). Thus, if one perceives that coping is very difficult, then a way of reducing stress is to become demotivated; this is assuming that both motivation and PCI are involved in stress generation (Figure 1). When students perceive they cannot cope, cognitive stress reactions may occur that feed back to reduce motivation. That is, perceived difficulties in studying (especially due to poor attention and concentration abilities) could lead to the cognitive strategy of downgrading the importance of demand (impending examination). Alternatively or simultaneously, the attitude "what I can't get is not worth trying for" would reduce determination to take action and consequent work effort: PCI would remain high, whereas motivation would drop to reduce intolerable stress.

The perceived problems of attention and concentration in our students could have had multiple causation, including (a) an actual lack of sufficient mental abilities, (b) excessive nonwork demands competing for attention with work demands, and (c) a high level of work anxiety, involving anticipatory fears (cognitive worry/ ego threat) that would interfere with task-relevant thinking (Hinton, 1989).

The results obtained for the whole group of 105 subjects (Figure 2) were confirmed by similar intercorrelations obtained from separated male and female subsamples. Thus there appeared to be no doubt about the interaction between motivation and PCI and their relationships to examination performance. However, the nature of this interaction requires further investigation.

The SEPOD scales of planning and organization appeared to have no predictive relevance for examination performance. One SEPOD factor, Extreme Circumspection in Planning, did give an interesting set of correlations with the general CAST scores for the whole group (Figure 2) and for both the male and female subgroups. Could this be interpreted as indicating that raised PCI for life in general leads to a coping strategy of planning to avoid small mistakes and unlikely difficulties? This strategy did not lead to better examination performance. However, low but consistently significant correlations ($p < .02$), indicated that extreme circumspection related to generally increased psychosomatic ailments (especially muscle tension and aches) and a *reduced* general work motivation. If the SEPOD had been concerned with specific planning *behavior* rather than general attitudes, then significant correlations with examination performance might have occurred.

Examination state anxiety as measured by the STAI (Spielberger, 1983) was uncorrelated with actual examination performance ($r = .03$). On the basis of observations by Morris and Liebert (1970) and Eysenck (1983), it was decided to split state anxiety into "cognitive worry" (Items 3, 5, 6, 9, 12, 13, and 20) and "emotional feeling" (Items 2, 7, 8, 11, 14, 17, and 18). The prediction was that cognitive worry would relate to performance impairment, whereas emotional feeling would correlate with improved performance. If this occurred, it would explain the zero correlation of the total state anxiety score with examination performance. Unfortunately, this hypothesis was not supported by the evidence: The correlation of the emotional feeling component with examination performance remained at zero ($-.05$) and, although the trend was in the right direction, the correlation of examination cognitive worry with examination performance was only $-.14$. When emotional feeling was partialed out, the correlation of cognitive worry with examination performance ($-.18$) was still not statistically significant.

In an attempt to obtain an improved prediction of examination performance, the two best predictors—GEMOS Scale 3 (Enterprise: Determination to Take Action) and CAST Scale 3 (Perceived Concentration and Attention Difficulties)—were combined in a multiple correlation. The resulting R of .41, F (2, 82) = 8.2, p = .0006, represented an improvement over the individual work motivation and PCI predictors. Inclusion of the examination cognitive worry measurement in the R produced no change, and therefore a reduction in the predictive significance occurred.

The psychosomatic stress ailments as measured by the PSYSOM all had correlations of almost zero with examination performance. This suggests the independence of behavioral coping from physiological stress reactions, indicating that a student can feel "terrible" while studying, but it will not affect examination performance. Presumably fatigue, muscle tensions, and so forth dissipate when aroused by the examination per se and when the student is finally involved in the answering of questions.

SPECIFIC PERCEIVED COPING INCAPACITY FACTORS PREDICTING SETS OF PSYCHOSOMATIC COMPLAINTS

The PSYSOM items having highest correlations with PCI (CAST) were selected for a short form. PSYSOM scales (Table 2) are based on factor analysis of short form data from 108 students (70 female and 38 male, mean age = 20).

The correlation matrix, giving the interrelationships between all the main scales and subscales referred to above, was analyzed. The main results are shown in Figure 2. The finding reported earlier of a significant correlation between general PCI (CAST) and general psychosomatic ailments (PSYSOM) was confirmed. The correlation between the CAST main scale (General PCI) and the PSYSOM main scale (Overall Ailments) was .36 (p < .001). The most impressive relationship of the General PCI scale with psychosomatic subscales occurred with the PSYSOM Subscale 2 (Fatigue: Tiredness, Exhaustion, and Headaches); the correlation of .44 (p < .001) probably indicated the effect of work pressure during the weeks before the final examination, because this correlation was relatively low on the earlier study with no examination pending. The most significant relevant correlations between CAST and PSYSOM subscales were between PSYSOM Scale 2 and CAST Scales 2 (Dithering in Decision Making) (r = .34) and 3 (Perceived Concentration and Attention Problems) r = .40).

A rough check was made on the extent to which PCI depended on feedback effects of psychosomatic problems. Students were asked to rate on a 10-point scale the extent to which ailments affected how well they could cope with their work. The low and nonsignificant correlation obtained (.18) increases our confidence in the view that PCI *causes* the self-reported physiological stress reactions, rather than the reverse, in students.

In summary, the reader's attention is drawn again to Figure 2, which illustrates the significant intercorrelations between variables that have a bearing on the prediction of physiological stress reactions (psychosomatic ailments) and results of behavioral coping (examination performance). The direction of the arrows indicates only the presumed directions of influence. The results are highly significant statistically, given that the population size was quite large (N = 105). The correlations are remarkable, bearing in mind that (a) the scales of PCI, motivation, and psychosomatic ailments contained only a few items; (b) there was no apparent criterion contamination; and (c) there was no guarantee of full subject involvement or cooperation (i.e., a number of subjects could have been careless).

Follow-up research was conducted on an occupational group, namely, 55 university library employees (Bell, 1989). The CAST and the 19-item PSYSOM were applied to this group over a slack work period (in the summer) and during a high-pressure work period (the first 3 weeks of the university year). For the slack period, correlations between PCI and PSYSOM were found to be totally insignificant. However, at the time of maximum work pressure, the CAST scales correlated significantly with the PSYSOM scales. The relevant correlations were of the same degree as with the student sample.

Figure 3 shows that for the high-pressure period the most significant correlation ($r = .54$, $p < .0001$) was between the CAST General PCI scale and the PSYSOM Overall Ailments scale. As in the study on students, CAST Subscales 2 (Perceived Dithering in Decision Making) and 3 (Perceived Concentration and Attention Problems) correlated to the greatest extent with the total PSYSOM score ($r = .47$, $p < .001$, in each case). Regarding intercorrelations between CAST subscales and PSYSOM subscales (Figure 3), the outcome of the student study was

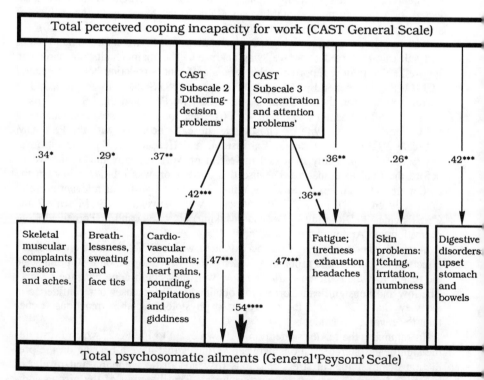

Figure 3 Relationship between perceived coping incapacity for work and psychosomatic ailments in a university library work group under maximum work loading ($N = 54$) (Bell, 1989; Rotheiler et al. 1989). Values are Pearson r correlations. $^*p < .05$, $^{**}p < .01$, $^{***}p < .005$, $^{****}p < .001$, two-tailed.

again replicated in that CAST Scale 3 related maximally to PSYSOM Scale 2 (Fatigue: Tiredness, Exhaustion, and Headaches) under high-pressure work conditions. However, dithering correlated most significantly with PSYSOM Scale 3 (Cardiovascular Complaints), and less so with PSYSOM Scale 2, as compared with the student groups. In general, the cross-validations are encouraging, and the fact that objective increase in work pressure in the employee groups produced the cross-validatory results supports the theory that stress due to PCI causes psychosomatic ailments.

ONE-SUBJECT PSYCHOPHYSIOLOGICAL STUDY OF STRESS GENERATION MEASURES AND PSYCHOPHYSIOLOGICAL STRESS RESPONSES

The CAST measure of PCI and the GEMOS measures of motivation have recently been converted to produce specific task or test versions. Studies are currently being carried out on single well-trained subjects (based on the research philosophies of Wundt and Skinner). The subject is extensively trained in the use of questionnaires, completely adapted to the laboratory situation, and thoroughly practiced in the performance of the test to be used. Varied types of task interference are selected in consultation with the subject on practice trials, to give differing levels of disruption of performance. Extended tests are then carried out in which repeated measures are obtained on batches of performance tests while psychophysiological responses are simultaneously recorded. Following each test batch, the subject is asked to complete the task versions of both CAST and GEMOS.

Figure 4 illustrates the results of our first experiment. The correlations are given to parallel the results presented for the large group study (Figure 2) already discussed. The predicted correlations were significant.

Although we measured finger pulse volume (FPV), it does not appear in Figure 4. (This study confirmed our previous experience that this index does not provide a reliable indication of stress response—some subjects showed massive vasodilation.) As can be seen from Figure 4, the physiological stress responses that correlated with PCI significantly ($p < .01$) were nonspecific skin conductance response rate, finger pulse fluctuation rate, and tonic heart rate. (The FPV fluctuation measure was the frequency of reductions in excess of 25% in the three-pulse running average. This novel index was considered to show the rate of bursts of sympathetic nervous activity.) PCI predicted the percent correct in the Düker (1963) mental arithmetic test ($r = -.44$, $p < .01$), which was done under constant *extreme* time pressure. Physiological stress responses appeared to be quite distinct from the behavioral performance. State anxiety correlated significantly with perceived coping incapacity, but had no significant relationship with psychophysiological variables. This arduous one-subject research is continuing, and it is hoped that over the coming years a series of confirmatory tests will emerge.

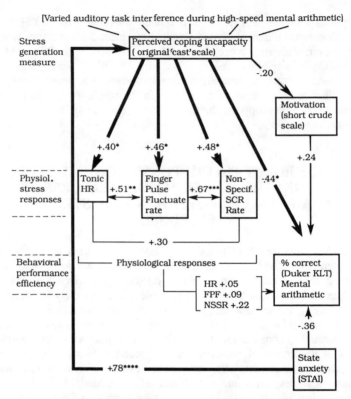

Figure 4 A psychophysiological study on one male subject: Correlations
between salient stress generation and response factors under
varied levels of work stressors (task interference) with no
feedback (Hinton, Bell, & Keenan, 1988). Arrows indicate
presumed direction of influence. Thick lines indicate predicted
significant correlations. Correlations were based on 40 data
points. Physiological data were sampled while carrying out a
mental arithmetic computer task (set to give an average 15%
correct over 40 repeated batches of 50 calculations).
Questionnaire data were collected immediately after each set of
calculations, with reference to the testing period. HR = heart
rate, SCR = skin conductance response, NSSR = nonspecific
SCR rate, STAI = State–Trait Anxiety Inventory. $^*p < .01$,
$^{**}p < .001$, $^{***}p < .0001$, $^{****}p < .00001$, two-tailed.

A SMALL-GROUP PSYCHOPHYSIOLOGICAL
STUDY ON STRESS AND PERFORMANCE

An experiment was carried out on 12 female subjects. This was a psychophysiological study in which nonspecific skin conductance response was recorded under
high stress induction conditions, in the course of assessing the efficacy of a purported antiperspirant (Rotheiler, Hinton, & Stewart, 1988). In this case, the task
itself was the stressor, together with instructions that the test related to intelligence. The computerized test entailed semantic identifications in which difficulty
of syntax was varied. This test was a modification of that used by Baddeley (1978)

as described by Hinton (1989). The response time was recorded for batches of sentences that were correctly identified as describing the relative position of two letters. The most significant results are illustrated in Figure 5. The task version of CAST was completed after testing.

Performance reaction speed on the relatively easy sentences was very significantly "predicted" by PCI ($r = -.83$). The cognitive worry aspect of the state anxiety scale also correlated significantly with response speed ($r = -.71$). However, as in our previous studies, under high-stress conditions involving active performance, we found that state anxiety did not correlate with the psychophysiological responses. The correlations of performance speed (on items correct) with psychophysiological measures were significant: High nonspecific skin conductance response rate and amplitude related to slower performance ($r = -.60$ and $-.87$, respectively). These results provide interesting evidence of links between stress generation and response factors.

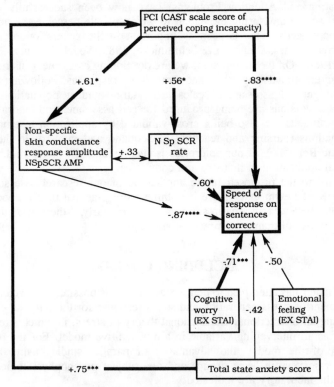

Figure 5 A psychophysiological study on 12 female students under high stress induction conditions: Correlations between salient stress generation and response factors during sentence interpretation tests (Rotheiler, Hinton, & Stewart, 1988). (Correlations of State–Trait Anxiety Inventory [STAI] with physiological responses were very low and statistically non-significant.) Arrows indicate presumed direction of influence. Thick lines indicate the predicted significant correlations. $^*p < .05$, $^{**}p < .02$, $^{***}p < .01$, $^{****}p < .0001$.

FUTURE DEVELOPMENTS IN RESEARCH
ON THE TESTING OF STRESS THEORY

Psychophysiological research on the theoretical model of stress is continuing in our department using single subjects, where the subject is a student with a vested interest in the success of the project. This has two major advantages, one of which is the elimination of psychophysiological response specificity factors and the other of which is that the subjects voluntarily are prepared to "endure" levels of stress induction probably comparable to that experienced in real-life situations (something that cannot ethically be achieved with normal subject volunteers). This clearly is a tedious and long-term approach to the research, but such studies, if replicated, could provide solid validation of the theoretical model of stress.

Large group studies are continuing in which we aim to develop further new assessment measures for the validation of the theoretical model of stress. The most relevant scales of PCI (Perceived Dithering in Decision Making and Perceived Concentration and Attention Problems) have now been successfully expanded. Currently we are measuring the extent to which people perceive the nonsatisfaction of their needs. This is seen as important in the generation of stress and psychosomatic illness (Scheuch & Schreinicke, 1983; Vogel, Scheuch, Naumann, & Koch, 1988). On the output side, we are developing assessment instruments for monitoring emotional, cognitive, and work stress responses. Following the development of general assessment scales using large student populations, parallel specific-task versions are being produced for self-assessment on laboratory tests. These instruments are also being cross-validated by application to employees in work situations (nursing and teaching in Scotland and industry in the German Democratic Republic). If our enterprise is successful, then there would be scope for general application in industry and commerce.

In regard to the proposed future application of our research, we support the dictum of Kurt Lewin that "there is nothing more practical than a good theory," but we also believe that, in stress research particularly, "there is nothing more theoretically useful than good practical application."

CONCLUDING COMMENT

This chapter has attempted to demonstrate that it is possible to develop methods of assessment of stress generation and stress response for the purpose of successfully testing an interactional–transactional theory of stress, in which stress is conceived of as an intervening variable in a biocognitive model. For the purpose of validation of the model, the advantages of parallel studies using both self-assessment surveys in large groups and one-subject psychophysiological experiments in the laboratory are indicated.

SUMMARY

The concept of stress is presented as a self-inflicted mental state, intervening between stress generation factors and stress responses. Subjective cognitive appraisal of perceived coping incapacity (PCI) is regarded as a primary stress generator. Personality traits and states (e.g., anxiety) are seen as influencing this process. Physiological, emotional, and cognitive stress responses are regarded as interrelated and affecting motivations and behavioral responses. "Stress" is conceptualized as being at the center of a complex in which actual ability, actual demands, PCI, and motivation are influenced by various stress responses and their consequences. An assessment is made of the possibilities for measurement of the relevant factors in stress generation and response. In the research reported in this chapter, psychometric measurement scales were constructed to assess PCI and general motivation and were applied in the prediction of examination performance and psychosomatic ailments. Our Cognitive Appraisal Stress Test (CAST) measure of PCI significantly predicted psychosomatic ailments in university students, and also in university librarians during a high-pressure work period but not during a steady work period. (Stress-related psychosomatic ailments were assessed by a newly developed scale called PSYSOM.) Poor examination performance (essay writing) was significantly predicted by the CAST Perceived Attention and Concentration Problems subscale and also by a low score on the General Motivation Scale (GEMOS) Enterprise: Determination to Take Action subscale. High PCI (CAST) related to low motivation (GEMOS). Psychosomatic and examination performance data were not related. A specific-task version of CAST is now being used in extended one-subject psychophysiological experiments: We are using varied levels of interference during repeated work tasks and repeated self-assessments using CAST. So far high correlations have been obtained between PCI and the measures of heart rate, nonspecific skin conductance response, and the rate of fluctuation in the amplitude of finger pulse volume. The results thus far illustrate the successful testing of a stress model that is still under development.

REFERENCES

Baddeley, A. D. (1978). A three-minute reasoning test based on grammatical transformation. *Psychonomic Science, 10,* 341–342.

Bell, N. (1989). *Stress and psychosomatic complaints in library work.* Honours psychology thesis, University of Glasgow, Glasgow, Scotland.

Cox, T. (1978). *Stress.* London: MacMillan.

Davies, D. R., Shackleton, V. J., & Parasuraman, R. (1983). Monotony and boredom. In G. R. Hockey (Ed.), *Stress and fatigue in human performance* (pp. 1–32). New York: Wiley.

Düker, H. (1963). Uber reaktive Anspannungssteigerung [On increase in reactive vigilance]. *Zeitschrift für experimentelle angewandte psychologie, 10,* 75–81.

Eysenck, M. W. (1983). Anxiety and individual differences. In G. R. Hockey (Ed.), *Stress and fatigue in human performance* (pp. 273–298). New York: Wiley.

Harrison, R. V. (1978). Person–environment fit and job stress. In C. L. Cooper & R. Payne (Eds.), *Stress at work* (pp. 175–205). New York: Wiley.

Hinton, J. W. (1989). The interaction between anxiety state and performance efficiency: Application of psychophysiology. In C. D. Spielberger, I. G. Sarason, & J. Strelau (Eds.), *Stress and anxiety, Volume 12* (pp. 199–216). Washington, DC: Hemisphere.

Hinton, J. W. (1988). The psychophysiology of stress and personal coping styles. In H. L. Wagner (Ed.), *Social psychophysiology and emotion: Theory and clinical applications* (pp. 175–195). Chichester, England: Wiley.

Hinton, J. W., Mitchell, E., & Rotheiler, E. (1989, July). *Academic performance as a function of specific aspects of motivation and perceived coping incapacity.* Paper presented at the 10th International Conference of the Society for Test Anxiety Research, Frie University, Amsterdam.

Hinton, J. W., Bell, N., & Keenan, F. (1988). *One-subject psychophysiological study of stress and mental test performance.* Unpublished report, Stress Research Unit, Glasgow University Psychology Department.

Hinton, J. W., & Rotheiler, E. (1987). *The development of the cognitive appraisal stress test (CAST) of* perceived coping incapacity (PCI). Unpublished report, Stress Research Unit, Glasgow University Psychology Department.

Hinton, J. W., & Rotheiler, E. (1988). *A scale for the assessment of the extent of psychosomatic ailments.* Unpublished report, Stress Research Unit, Glasgow University Psychology Department.

Hinton, J. W., Rotheiler, E., Mitchell, E., & Arthur, M. M. (1988). *Perceived coping incapacity and psychosomatic ailments in female students. Unpublished report, Stress Research Unit, Glasgow University Psychology Department.*

Krinsky, L. W., Kieffer, S. N., Carone, P. A., & Yolles, S. F. (Eds.). (1984). *Stress and productivity: Volume 9. Problems of Industrial Psychosomatic Medicine.* New York: Human Sciences Press.

Lazarus, R. S. (1976). *Patterns of adjustment.* New York: McGraw-Hill.

Lazarus, R. S., & Cohen, J. B. (1978). Environmental stress. In I. Altmann & J. F. Wohlwill (Eds.), *Human behavior and environment* (Vol. 1, pp. 89–127). New York: Plenum.

MacKay, C., & Cox, T. (1987). Self-report techniques. In A. Gale & B. Christie (Eds.), *Psychophysiology and the electronic workplace* (pp. 293–311). New York: Wiley.

MacKay, C., Cox, T., Burrows, G., & Lazarini, T. (1978). An inventory for the measurement of self-reported stress and arousal. *British Journal of Social and Clinical Psychology, 17,* 283–284.

McGrath, J. E. (1976). Stress and behavior in organizations. In M. D. Dunnette (Ed.), *Social and psychological factors in stress* (pp. 1351–1395). New York: Holt, Rinehart & Winston.

Mitchell, E. (1989). *Stress, health and examination performance in students.* Honours psychology thesis, University of Glasgow, Glasgow, Scotland.

Morris, L. W., & Liebert, R. M. (1970). Relationship of cognitive and emotional components of test anxiety to physiological arousal and academic performance. *Journal of Consulting and Clinical Psychology, 35,* 332–337.

Rotheiler, E., Hinton, J. W., & Mitchell, E. (1989, June). *The development and validation of a self-rating measure of general perceived coping incapacity.* Paper presented at the meeting of the International Society for the Study of Individual Differences, Heidelberg.

Rotheiler, E., Hinton, J. W., & Stewart, R. (1988). *The psychophysiological testing of a proprietary anti-perspirant.* Unpublished report, Psychophysiology Laboratory, University of Glasgow, Glasgow, Scotland.

Scheuch, K., & Schreinicke, G. (1983). *Stress: Gedanken, Theorien, Probleme: 1. Aufl.* [Stress: Thoughts, theories, problems: 1st edition]. Berlin, Verlag Volk und Gesundheit.

Schulz, P., & Schönpflug, W. (1982). Regulatory activity during states of stress. In W. Krohne & L. Laux (Eds.), *Achievement, stress and anxiety* (pp. 51–73). Washington, DC: Hemisphere.

Seligman, M. F. P. (1975). *Helplessness: On depression development and death.* San Francisco: Freeman.

Spielberger, C. D. (1983). *Manual for the State–Trait Anxiety Inventory.* Palo Alto, CA: Consulting Psychologists Press.

Vogel, H., Leuschner, G., Scheuch, K., Buhr, J., Koch, R., & Kulisch, E. (1987). Geschlechts-, Alters-und territoriale Besonderheiten der Beschwerdenkonstellation und Neurosentendenz bei Padagogen [Gender, age, and regional differences of ailment constellations and neurotic tendencies in teachers]. *Zeitschrift für die gesamate hygiene 33,* 588–591.

Vogel, H., Scheuch, K., Naumann, W., & Koch, R. (1988). Relationship of essential needs realization and social competence to functional health disorders and absenteeism. *Activitas Nervosa Superior, 30,* 174–182.

Weiss, J. M. (1970). Somatic effects of predictable and unpredictable shock. *Psychosomatic Medicine, 32,* 397–408.

Weiss, J. M. (1972). Influence of psychological variables on stress-induced pathology. In R. Porter & J. Knight (Eds.), *Physiology, emotion and psychosomatic illness* (Ciba Foundation Symposium 8, pp. 165–183). Amsterdam: Elsevier.

II

STRESS, CONFLICT, AND PERSONALITY

5

The Nature and Logic of Intrapsychic Conflicts

Paul McReynolds
University of Nevada–Reno, USA

The focus of this chapter is on intrapersonal conflicts—or, as they are usually termed, *intrapsychic conflicts*. Intrapsychic conflicts are one of the major contributors to anxiety and stress.

The word *conflict* calls up associations of disharmony, of turmoil, of forces or entities positioned against one another. The concept of mental conflict is of course a metaphor, derived from images such as two armies in battle, two antagonists in a court of law, and the like.

As a metaphor for certain dynamics, the term *conflict* is highly dramatic, because it tends to reify and anthropomorphize the opposing elements, as when we speak, for example, of conflicts between the ego and the id. My point is not that we should give up the term *conflict* in this context, but rather that we need to go beyond metaphor to develop a precise and detailed understanding of the nature of what we call mental conflicts.

I begin with several introductory observations.

First, actual conflicts in actual human beings are always very specific. They are never conflicts between something called the ego and something called the id, or between an approach tendency and an avoidance tendency, but instead are specific idiosyncratic oppositional experiences in the unique lives of particular individuals at particular times. For example, a man may be conflicted about whether to confront his supervisor about what he considers unfair treatment, a woman may be conflicted about whether to reveal an early experience of sexual abuse, or a child may be torn between feelings of love and hate for a parent. Even when an individual is confused and uncertain about the specific pushes and pulls of an inner conflict—and this frequently happens—the conflictual experience still is a very unique personal experience.

Second, though all conflictual experiences are unique, they do have certain characteristics by which they can be grouped into meaningful categories, and it is on this basis that we can search for an underlying semantic structure. This observation brings up the question of how fine-grained a taxonomy we should strive for. The current standard classificatory systems, which, as I have already noted, use

This chapter is based on a paper presented at a conference on stress and emotion preceding the 24th International Congress of Psychology, Sydney, Australia, August 1988. I am grateful to William Crabbe, Robert Jenkins, Ingrid Moore, Alexander Peer, Bruce Pither, and Patricia White for their assistance and collaboration in the development of the conceptualization presented in this chapter.

such broad divisions as conflicts between the ego and the superego or between approach and avoidance tendencies, are too all-embracing to be very useful, except as first approximations. On the other hand, it would obviously be a mistake to attempt a taxonomy so complex that it could not be reliably applied.

Third, inner conflicts vary in terms of magnitude or severity. It is a mistake to assume that conflicts are always of serious import. To be sure, conflicts may involve matters as distressing as whether to seek a divorce or as grim as whether to commit suicide, but they also encompass concerns such as which hairstyle to adopt or which entree to order for dinner. Indeed, the ongoing course of mental life is largely a succession of conflictual situations, varying in magnitude from the trivial to the heartbreaking. Unless evidence to the contrary arises we may assume that the same underlying grammar applies to all conflicts, of whatever degree of magnitude.

Finally, inner conflicts vary in terms of durability. Some intrapsychic conflicts appear to go on for years, even a lifetime, such that attempts to resolve them become part of one's personality structure, whereas others (probably most) have a very short life, being essentially ended and forgotten once resolved or bypassed.

HISTORICAL BACKGROUND

The general theme of intrapsychic conflicts has a long and fascinating history. The earliest written narrative that has survived—*Gilgamesh* (Mason, 1970), the Sumerian epic dating from about 2000 B.C.—contains elements of inner conflicts, as do the works of Homer and the earliest books of the Bible. The early Greek philosopher Empedocles, who lived in Sicily in the fifth century B.C., posited two fundamental forces, love and hate, engaged in eternal conflict (Leonard, 1908). This primitive pairing is suggestive of such later dichotomies as Freud's life and death instincts and the approach and avoidance tendencies in motivation theory.

Powerful depictions of inner conflicts are prominent in the dramas of Sophocles and Euripides, and by the time of Plato the notion of mental conflicts had been advanced considerably. From the psychological perspective, Plato divided the human being into three parts: reason, passions, and appetites. To illustrate the conflictual interactions among these parts, Plato employed his well-known analogy of a charioteer and two steeds (Hamilton & Cairns, 1961). The charioteer, who represents reason, has the task of controlling and managing the two horses. One of these, representing the appetites, is unruly and difficult to control, while the other, reflective of the passions, is somewhat helpful to the driver, who eventually gains control. Plato's theorizing elsewhere can be interpreted to also indicate the existence of unconscious conflicts.

The next figure in this brief historical account of conceptions of psychological conflicts is Saint Augustine. His autobiographical work, *The Confessions of Saint Augustine* (Augustine, c. 397/1932), includes numerous references to inner conflicts. The following brief quotation, which concerns the conflict between Augustine's desire to serve God and his personal appetites, is illustrative:

> But that new will which had begun to be in me, freely to serve Thee, and to wish to enjoy Thee,
> O God, the only assured pleasantness, was not yet able to overcome my former wilfulness,
> strengthened by age. Thus did my two wills, one new, and the other old, one carnal, the other
> spiritual, struggle within me; and by their discord, undid my soul. . . . Thus I understood, by my

own experience, what I had read, how the flesh lusteth against the spirit and the spirit against the flesh. (Augustine, c. 397/1932, p. 157; used by permission of Everyman's Library)

The theme of intrapsychic conflicts is central in—indeed is the very core of—much of the world's greatest literature. I have already noted in this connection the early Greek playwrights, but one could refer also to numerous other literary masterpieces, ranging from the ancient Hindu epic poem *Mahabharata* to Dostoyevsky's *Crime and Punishment*. I need quote only a single line—this from Shakespeare's *Hamlet* and familiar to everyone—to vividly illustrate the role of conflict in literature:

> *To be, or not to be, that is the question.*

Perhaps the most commonly recognized class of mental conflicts is that arising from disparate and contradictory motives. The first systematic delineation of intrapersonal conflicts in this context appears to have been made by Jeremy Bentham in 1789. In his book *An Introduction to the Principles of Morals and Legislation,* he included a subsection titled "Conflicts Among Motives," from which I quote the first two sentences:

> *When a man has it in contemplation to engage in any action, he is frequently acted upon at the same time by the force of divers motives: one motive, or set of motives, acting in one direction; another motive, or set of motives, acting as it were in an opposite direction. The motives on one side disposing him to engage in the action: those on the other, disposing him not to engage in it. (Bentham, 1789/1948, pp. 127–128; used by permission of Hafner Publishing Company, Inc.)*

With Bentham the idea of motives in conflict entered the mainstream of psychology, and in Alexander Bain's (1859) volume, *The Emotions and the Will,* we find a complete chapter devoted to the subject. The first American book to include a discussion of motive conflicts, to the best of my knowledge, was *Psychology: The Motive Powers,* by James McCosh (1890). McCosh, who was a disciple of the Scottish tradition in psychology, had come to this country in 1868 to accept the presidency of Princeton University. McCosh's discussion of appetences—his term for motive—was for its time quite insightful. He identified two different kinds of conflicts: first, the simultaneous operation of two inconsistent propensities, e.g., one's ambition prompting him to action at the same time a love of ease is inclining him to repose; and second, successive opposite motives toward the same object, as in the case of a man who alternately feels love and jealous anger toward a woman.

It is probable that most people, when they think of internal personal conflicts, think of Sigmund Freud, and of course it is true that the concept of conflict is an important hallmark of psychoanalytic theory. Freud began his psychodynamic theorizing in the 1890s—almost 100 years ago—and published his seminal work *Die Traumdeutung (The Interpretation of Dreams)* in 1900. Though various psychodynamic processes were involved in Freud's theory from the start, it was not until 1923, in his work titled *Das Ich und das Es (The Ego and the Id),* that the notion of internal conflicts became central in his system. The fundamental conflict in psychoanalytic theory is that between the ego and the id, with the possibility of the superego lining up on either side (Fenichel, 1945).

Conceptualizations of inner conflicts by mainstream experimental psychologists in this century have focused primarily on approach and avoidance tendencies, and the different permutations in which these may appear: approach–approach, approach–avoidance, avoidance–avoidance, and double approach–avoidance conflicts (Lewin, 1931; Miller, 1944) and, more recently, avoidance–approach conflicts (Epstein, 1978).

Contemporary theoretical attacks on the problem of intrapersonal conflicts include a revision of Freud's psychodynamic perspective (Brenner, 1982) and several approaches using a cognitive model (Honess, 1982; Lauterbach, 1975; Slade & Sheehan, 1979). Of these, the work of Lauterbach is most similar to my own.

Despite the long theoretical interest in mental conflicts, and the prominent role of conflictual dynamics in most conceptions of personality and psychopathology, little attention has been given to developing a comprehensive taxonomy of the elements involved in such conflicts. Rather, a common implicit assumption seems to be that intrapsychic conflicts, beyond such broad groupings as approach–avoidance tendencies and ego–id conflicts, are not in need of, or are even beyond, further analysis. My own view, in contrast, is that intrapsychic conflicts have a finer logic, a semantics, a grammar of their own, and that this structure can be identified and specified.

THE STRUCTURE OF INTRAPSYCHIC CONFLICTS

Intrapsychic conflicts always have two sides, and these two sides are in some sort of opposition—this, after all, is what makes a situation conflictual. To be sure, one can imagine an inner conflict with more than two sides, such as an individual's trying to decide which of three job offers to accept. Such multifaceted instances, however, can be reduced conceptually to a two-sided conflict, and this remains the paradigm case.

An intrapsychic conflict can be defined as a problem situation in mental life that involves two competing and mutually exclusive alternative resolutions. The general nature of a conflict can be succinctly stated in a "but statement," for example,

1. I want to go *but* I also want to stay.
2. I love her b I also hate her.

We may term the two alternatives in a conflict "sides," because that is the way they appear when written. Typically in a conflict one side is slightly stronger than the other side; by convention in our research, we place the weaker side on the left, and the stronger side on the right. If the right side is a great deal stronger than the left side, then that side prevails, at least temporarily, but when it is only slightly greater we have a continuing deadlock situation. In some instances there may be a reversal, and even an alternation, over time as to which alternative is dominant. Equality of strength can be represented in this way

3. I like candidate A $\bar{b}$ I also like candidate B.

If we employ the word *but* (b) to represent a disjunctive relationship between two possibilities, then the positive conjunctive *and* (a) can be used to indicate the relation between two units that are not in conflict. For example, consider

4. I want to do it *b* I am not able to do it.
versus
5. I want to do it *a* I am able to do it.

There are two different approaches that a theorist can employ in attempting to discern the structure of inner conflicts. The traditional approach is for the theorist to draw upon his or her own personal and/or clinical experiences in order to come up with an idealized picture of the typology of conflicts. The other, and I think preferable, approach, which my colleagues and I have followed, is to extensively sample real-life conflicts and then analyze these conflicts to discover their underlying order.

We have collected more than 500 instances of inner conflicts, from more than 200 individuals. The recorded conflicts all reflect disturbing personal concerns, though some of course were more serious than others. An immense diversity of problem topics is represented in our sample. These include intrapersonal problems of all kinds: feelings of depression, low self-esteem, and hostility; achievement concerns; sexual abuse; suicidal attempts; and a veritable roster of human distresses. Some of the instances of conflicts were lifted verbatim from therapy transcriptions, others were provided by therapists to represent their judgments of conflicts in certain patients, but most were provided by college students or other normal individuals who responded to our invitation to describe one or more serious personal problems.

The general formulation of intrapsychic conflicts that my associates and I have developed (McReynolds, 1987) is presented below. I should emphasize that the details of our system are somewhat tentative, and subject to revision as our research proceeds.

First, we substitute the term *mental discrepancy* for *inner conflicts*. This is a less dramatic, but preferable term because it directly expresses the essential fact that there are two mental contents that are strongly bound together in that both are constituents of an overall meaningful whole but differ (i.e., are discrepant) on an attribute common to both sides. Consider, for instance, the mental discrepancy noted earlier:

2. I love her *b* I also hate her.

Both sides are part of the same whole in that both include the constituents "I" and "her." Further, both include the same attribute, that is, "my feelings toward her." In one case, however, the sign on the attribute is positive (love), whereas in the other case it is negative (hate). There is, then, a *discrepancy* between the two values on the same attribute on the two sides of the statement.

Table 1 summarizes the major aspects of our system. The far left column lists the mental constituents, or elements, that may, according to our present conceptualization, be involved in intrapsychic conflicts. This list is a conservative one, and may well be too short.

Turning next to the syntax of mental discrepancies as summarized in the middle column of Table 1, I have already covered the signs for *disjunction* and *conjunction*. Specific categories can be described as being either *present* or *absent*, and as having either *positive* or *negative* valence. The rest of the data in the table can best be conveyed by specific illustrations. Consider this conflictual statement:

Table 1 Basic structure of taxonomic system for coding mental discrepancies (abridged)

Elements	Syntax	Category descriptors
A = action	Disjunctive symbol = b	Superscripts (subjects):
Af = affect	Conjunctive symbol = a	s = oneself
At = attitude	Status of categories:	o = other person
B = belief	$\wedge$ = presence	
C = capacity	$\vee$ = absence	
D = desire		
I = intention	Valence of categories:	Subscripts (objects):
M = moral	+ = positive	s = oneself
N = necessity	− = negative	o = other person
O = outcome		
P = possibility	Relationships among categories:	
Q = quality	$\overline{x,y}$ = to be treated as unit	
R = reality	m → n = m implies or leads to n	
U = unsterstanding	m ⇸ n = m does not imply or lead to n	
V = value	m $\xrightarrow{\text{sh}}$ n = m should imply or lead to n	

6. I want to leave him, but I also desire not to leave him.

$$\overline{_1D^s \wedge A_o^s}\ \bar{b}\ \overline{_2D^s \vee A_o^s}$$

where $_1D^s$ refers to one desire, $_2D^s$ refers to a second desire, the superscript "s" stands for "self," the subscript "o" represents the object, and A_o^s designates an action. The bars over the tops of the two sides indicate that the subtended elements are to be considered as a unit; $\bar{b}$ indicates *but*. The entire code can be read as follows:

There is a desire in the self to carry out a certain action but there is an equal desire in the self not to carry out the action.

Here is a second and somewhat more complex example:

7. I want to be independent and popular, but I feel that if I am independent I will not be popular.

$$\overline{D^s \wedge Q^s \wedge At_s^o+}\ b\ \overline{B^s \wedge Q^s \rightarrow \vee At_s^o+}$$

This code can be read as follows:

There is a desire in the self for a certain quality in the self and for a certain attitude by other persons toward the self, but there is a stronger belief in the self that the desired quality in the self will lead to the absence of the desired attitude of other persons toward the self.

Let us examine these two examples in order to gain an insight into the logical structure of inner conflicts. There are two immediate points to be noted. First, there are always *two elements in conflict*—one on each side of the code—in the sense that they have mutually exclusive behavioral (overt or covert) consequences.

In the first coded example (No. 6) above the conflicting elements are $_1$D and $_2$D—two different desires. In the second example (No. 7) the conflicting elements are D and B—a desire and a belief.

The second key point is that there is always one element that is found on both sides of the code but that has different values on the two sides. This can be referred to as the *discrepant element*. In example No. 6 the discrepant element is A, which is present ∧ on one side and absent ∨ on the other side. In example No. 7 the discrepant element is At +, which is present ∧ on one side and absent ∨ on the other side.

Although our research project is still underway, and thus these comments are in the nature of a progress report, some data are available. Table 2 presents a summary of the conflicting elements reported by 107 college students (White, 1982). The main point to be noted is that a variety of different element pairs are involved in inner conflicts. Table 3 shows the various discrepant elements that were involved in these same conflicts. Again the important thing to observe is the range and diversity of the elements involved.

THEORETICAL IMPLICATIONS

The intrapsychic conflicts that we have been studying are, for the most part, those directly reported by the subjects; that is, they are inner conflicts of which the subject is aware. Before turning to the issue of unconscious conflicts, I want to comment briefly on the nature of conscious conflicts. It would be a gross error to assume that conscious conflicts are rarely serious and that only unconscious conflicts are of monumental import in shaping human lives. On the contrary, the intensity, poignancy, and pervasiveness of many of the inner conflicts that are routinely reported in our research, among both patients and students, testify abundantly to their profound significance. Though many conscious conflicts are mundane and even trivial, others are life bending in their impact.

I shall now briefly describe the technique that I currently use to elicit reports of inner conflicts from normal adults. First, volunteer subjects are solicited who indicate that they are willing to describe, on an anonymous basis, a serious per-

Table 2 Conflicting elements reported by 107 college students for 114 mental discrepancies

Conflicting elements	Number of times coded
A/Af	3
B/AF	2
B/P	3
D/Af	22
D/At	2
D/B	12
D/D	11
D/N	4
D/P	11
D/R	17
N/Af	2
V/N	2
23 element pairs coded 1 time	23

Table 3 Discrepant elements reported by 107 college students for 114 mental discrepancies

Discrepant element	Number of times coded
A	61
Af	15
At	7
C	4
D	3
O	17
Q	4
U	3

sonal problem that they have or have had. The subjects, seen either individually or in groups, are asked to write a page or more describing this problem in detail. So far our subjects have had no difficulty in doing this. The printed instructions then inform the subject that personal problems typically involve matters about which a person has strong contradictory feelings. The instructions describe how such contradictory feelings can be written as two-part "but statements," and give three examples. The subject is then requested to indicate any contradictory feelings involved in the personal problem that he or she has just described, and to indicate the particular contradiction that was most difficult to deal with. Here, for example, are the internal contradictions identified by a young unmarried pregnant woman who was struggling with the question of whether to have an abortion:

1. The best thing to do is to have an abortion *but* it's wrong to have an abortion.
2. It's selfish to have an abortion *but* I'll destroy my life if I have this baby.
3. If John and I get married I may not feel so bad and could keep the baby, *but* I don't know if I love him enough and I'm not ready to have a baby.
4. I love children *but* I can't have this baby.

The several different mental discrepancies identified by this woman illustrate the fact that inner conflicts tend to come in closely interrelated clusters. The contradictions are listed above in the order of difficulty that the woman reported having in trying to cope with them. The most difficult contradiction, No. 1, can be restated and coded as follows:

1. It's wrong to have an abortion *b* I feel I must have an abortion.

$$\overline{M^s-} \vee A^s \, b \, \overline{D^s \wedge A^s}$$

In working with conflicts at the conscious level, I have naturally given considerable thought to the question of unconscious conflicts. The general wisdom among psychodynamic theorists is, I take it, that not only do unconscious conflicts exist, but they provide the really important dynamic influences in personality and psychopathology, and can be traced in many instances back to origins in infancy and childhood.

I have counted myself among the psychodynamic theorists, and yet I have come to feel that this particular conception is inadequate, and in some respects simply wrong. I propose an alternative formulation, with the caveat, however, that this alternative proposal is still in development and hence admittedly somewhat speculative.

Completely unconscious conflicts (i.e., conflicts in which both sides are unconscious) are, I believe, fairly rare and tend to be of low voltage and typically very transient. In contrast, conflicts in which one side is unconscious and the other side conscious are, I suggest, fairly common and often of great intensity and persistence. An example of such a split-level conflict, as we might call it, would be when an individual is strongly moved toward a certain act, attitude, or affect, but which is opposed by a powerful unconscious proposition the individual is unaware of, and in place of which he or she may devise elaborate but unconvincing explanations. Consider, for instance, a man who unconsciously wishes to molest children sexually but who at the conscious level finds such behavior completely abhorrent; that is, in code terms,

$$\overline{D^s} \wedge A_o^s + \ b \ \overline{M^s -} \wedge A_o^s + \ \rightarrow \ \vee A_o^s +$$

In this illustration the conscious side is dominant, but in the following example the unconscious side is dominant. Thus, consider a man who consciously desires marriage but who unconsciously is threatened by the mutual affectional intimacy that would be involved; that is,

$$\overline{D^s} \wedge A_o^s \ b \ \overline{Af -_{os}^{so}} \wedge A_o^s \ \rightarrow \ \vee A_o^s$$

In most intrapersonal conflicts, both sides, in my judgment, are conscious. These conflicts appear to be of two types. First, there are conflicts in which the two sides reflect understandable, actual alternatives without a major hidden agenda, such as whether to accept an offer of marriage, whether to change jobs, whether to confront an adversary, and so on. In the second, more complex and theoretically more interesting type, the conscious conflict is itself a *solution* to a potentially powerful unconscious conflict. This concept takes us to the heart of my present formulation. Intense emotionally unacceptable conflicts, I suggest, are not so much repressed as solved, with the solution being a new conflict that can be observed at the conscious level. This hypothesis can best be illustrated by an example. Imagine a young boy whose ability and competence are depreciated and belittled by his father. The boy's desire to be loved by his father, and his belief that he is not, leads to a conflict of the following form:

$$D_s^o \wedge Af_s^o + \ b \ \overline{B^s} \vee Af_s^o +$$

Years later the boy, now grown into a man, has no awareness of this conflict, and one might hypothesize that this is because the conflict has gone underground, that is, is active at an unconscious level. I think not. Rather, I suggest that in this example the boy, for one reason or another, came to the conclusion that if he excelled, if he accomplished great things, these would prove to his father that he was lovable and he would be loved. In other words, the original conflict does not reside in the unconscious—it simply does not exist at all, because it was solved by the commitment to excel. However, this conscious tendency, in the natural course of the realities of life, cannot, let us say, be adequately satisfied; hence we have a purely conscious conflict between the man's felt necessity to excel, on the one hand, and a belief that he lacks the capacity to excel, on the other hand; that is,

$$\overline{N^s \wedge A^s+}\ b\ \overline{B^s \vee C^s \wedge A^s+} \rightarrow \vee A^s+$$

The point is not to deny the reality of repression and the role of unconscious processes in the development of certain intrapsychic conflicts, but to reject the notion that the unconscious—in the strict Freudian sense—is in some manner a boiling cauldron of unresolved conflicts, and to give new credibility and clinical respectability to the powerful inner conflicts of which people are at least vaguely aware.

CONCLUSIONS

Intrapsychic conflicts should not be thought of as rare and isolated occurrences in the lives of individuals. Rather, such conflicts, including those that are minor and those that are intense, as well as those that are conscious and those that are unconscious, are part and parcel of the ongoing nature of human experience. Frequently, inner conflicts are construed, in the everyday vernacular, under such terms as decisions, choices, options, and dilemmas. The full nature of mental conflicts, especially if we include the interactions among the different conflicts within a person, is undoubtedly exceedingly complex. Among the important questions that conflict theory raises are these: Is there a relation between type of conflict and type of psychopathology? Are there gender differences in predominant types of conflict? Age differences? Cultural differences? And so on. All of these and similar questions depend for their examination and elucidation on the development of an adequate taxonomy of inner conflicts, a goal to which the present research I hope contributes.

In closing, I would like to reemphasize the relation of intrapersonal conflicts to anxiety and stress. Though there is not space to develop the theme, there are good reasons to believe—and indeed, it is a general clinical assumption—that intense unresolved inner conflicts contribute greatly to feelings of anxiety. Similarly, life situations presenting problems of the sort that an individual can in principle deal with very effectively may themselves become significant stressors if the person is at the same time struggling with difficult inner conflicts.

SUMMARY

The experiencing of inner conflicts is part of the human condition, and is a major contributor to feelings of stress and anxiety. Though many intrapsychic conflicts are minor and transient, others are of monumental import, and efforts of an individual to resolve them may permanently influence personality structure.

Interest in intrapersonal conflicts has a long history, and can be traced back to the savants of antiquity. Modern conceptions have been primarily psychoanalytic, which focus on conflicts between the ego and the id, or experimental, which focus on approach and avoidance tendencies. Both of these orientations, however, are overly simplistic.

The major theme underlying this chapter is that inner conflicts have a meaningingful and discernible logic—a grammar—in terms of which they can be described and compared. A preliminary taxonomic system for coding specific inner conflicts was presented. A conflict can be conceptualized as a "but statement" (e.g., "I want to go *but* I want to stay") in which the two sides of the conflict are part of the same whole, but include oppositional elements. Data gathered so far make it clear that conflicts may involve a variety of mental elements, including desires, affects, attitudes, actions, beliefs, and moral values. Though both sides of a conflict may be unconscious, a more frequent occurrence is for both sides to be conscious, or for one side to be conscious and the other unconscious.

REFERENCES

Augustine. (1932). *The confessions of Saint Augustine* (E. B. Pusey, Trans.). London: J. M. Dent & Sons. (Original work written c. 397)

Bain, A. (1859). *The emotions and the will.* London: Parker.

Bentham, J. (1948). *An introduction to the principles of morals and legislation.* New York: Hafner. (Original work published 1789)

Brenner, C. (1982). *The mind in conflict.* New York: International Universities Press.

Epstein, S. (1978). Avoidance–approach: The fifth basic conflict. *Journal of Consulting and Clinical Psychology, 46,* 1016–1022.

Fenichel, O. (1945). *The psychoanalytic theory of neurosis.* New York: W. W. Norton.

Freud, S. (1900). *Die Traumdeutung* [The interpretation of dreams]. Vienna: Franz Deuticke.

Freud, S. (1923). *Das Ich und das Es* [The ego and the id]. Vienna: In Internationaler Psychoanalytischer Verlag.

Hamilton, E., & Cairns, H. (Eds.). (1961). *The collected dialogues of Plato.* Princeton, NJ: Princeton University Press.

Honess, T. (1982). Accounting for oneself: Meanings of self-descriptions, and inconsistencies in self-descriptions. *British Journal of Medical Psychology, 44,* 41–52.

Lauterbach, W. (1975). Assessing psychological conflict. *British Journal of Social and Clinical Psychology, 14,* 43–47.

Leonard, W. E. (1908). *The fragments of Empedocles.* Chicago: Open Court. (Original work written c. 400 B.C.)

Lewin, K. (1931). Environmental forces in child behavior and development. In C. Murchison (Ed.), *A handbook of child psychology* (pp. 94–127). Worcester, MA: Clark University Press.

Mason, H. (1970). *Gilgamesh: A verse narrative.* New York: New American Library.

McCosh, J. (1890). *Psychology: The motive powers: emotions, conscience, will.* New York: Scribner's.

McReynolds, P. (1987). Self-theory, anxiety and intrapsychic conflicts. In N. Cheshire & H. Thomae (Eds.), *Self, symptoms and psychotherapy* (pp. 197–223). New York: Wiley.

Miller, N. E. (1944). Experimental studies of conflict. In J. McV. Hunt (Ed.), *Personality and the behavior disorders* (Vol. 1, pp. 431–465). New York: Ronald.

Slade, P. D., & Sheehan, M. J. (1979). The measurement of conflict in repertory grids. *British Journal of Psychology, 70,* 519–524.

White, P. (1982). *A study of cognitive anxiety and mental conflicts.* Unpublished doctoral dissertation, University of Nevada-Reno.

6

Intrapersonal Conflict, Life Stress, and Emotion

Wolf Lauterbach
J. W. Goethe Universität, Frankfurt, Germany

Intrapersonal conflicts are important and lasting stressors that operate independently of other stressful circumstances, such as life events, fight–flight responses, and the Type A behavior pattern. But what is intrapersonal conflict? Colloquially, it may be described by the contemporary saying "Everything that's fun is either unhealthy, immoral, or fattening." A person likes something that is incompatible with other valued aspects of life such as health.

In essence, an *intra*personal conflict implies the contradiction or incompatibility of attitudes, values, and opinions pertaining to personally relevant concepts in the significant areas of a person's life. It is neither *inter*personal conflict such as hostility, nor the unambiguous rejection of an idea, person, or life circumstances, but is more nearly equivalent to an approach–avoidance conflict.

Approach–avoidance conflicts have been used by Pavlov (1941) and others as a powerful stressor to produce states of great confusion and anxiety in animals, which generally result in the symptoms of experimental neurosis. Most theories of human neurosis and its psychological treatment, from Freud (1949) to Wolpe (1958), have considered intrapsychic conflicts to be a fundamental cause of emotional and behavioral disorders. Consequently, an important goal of psychotherapy is to identify those intrapersonal conflicts that are major sources of stress, and to find ways of resolving them.

Experiments with human subjects have demonstrated that inconsistent or dissonant cognitions cause tensions that may result in intense conflict (for reviews, see Cooper & Fazio, 1984; Insko, 1984), and cognitive dissonance reduces the emotional well-being of a person during an experiment. If this is true for the psychological laboratory and artificially manipulated stimuli and cognitions, is it also true for cognitions that reflect and interrelate relevant areas of a person's life? Can the intrapersonal conflict of a person be objectively measured? The complexity and ambiguity of this concept are a hindrance to its measurement that can, however, be overcome by a delimitation and definition of its meaning.

METHOD

The incompatibilities and contradictoriness of a person's life circumstances may be reflected by his or her cognitions. Intrapersonal conflict is therefore defined as the degree of inconsistency and contradiction in a cognitive field that consists of attitudes, values, and beliefs pertaining to a personally relevant range of topics.

This definition excludes, for example, interpersonal conflict, and it limits conflict measurement to a well-defined cognitive field, that is, to a section of the person's system of attitudes and beliefs.

The method of measuring intrapersonal conflict is indirect and based on the assumption that the incompatibilities of a person's real life circumstances are reflected by his or her conflicting cognitions. An interrelated, limited set of personally relevant cognitions and attitudes is elicited in a questionnaire and the degree of contradictoriness and inconsistency is calculated. Calculations are based on a model originating in Heider's (1946, 1958) social psychological model of cognitive balance and imbalance (Cartwright & Harary, 1956; Lauterbach 1975a, 1987, 1989).

An example of balanced versus imbalanced triads, taken from a questionnaire measuring pregnancy conflicts, may consist of the concepts "myself" (the person herself), "pregnancy," and "self-actualization" and their interrelations. The relations (arrows) in Figure 1 are transformed into questionnaire items:

1. Is pregnancy generally a positive or a negative experience for a woman?
2. How does pregnancy affect my quest for self-actualization?
3. Is self-actualization a positive or a negative goal?

A young woman may feel that pregnancy would be a positive value or an important experience for a woman (first relation is positive). She also thinks that self-actualization is a positive and important goal in life (third relation is positive). If she thinks that pregnancy would hinder her self-actualization (second relation is negative), this would be an element of conflict: two positive values that contradict each other. If she thinks that pregnancy may facilitate or be part of self-actualization (second relation is positive), then this triad of cognitions, this triad of two values and one belief, is balanced. Generally, a triad is imbalanced if the number of negative relations is odd (1 or 3, which implies that their product is negative) and balanced if this number is even (0 or 2, which implies a positive product). A computer can determine whether a triad of any content is balanced or imbalanced. Abelson and Rosenberg (1958) have coined the term "psycho-logic" for the description of cognitive consistency. Each of the three relations in Figure 1

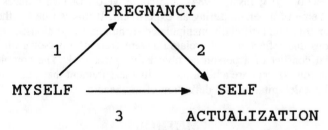

Figure 1   A triad of three interrelated cognitive elements including a
person's attitudes and beliefs. The triad is an element of
harmony or of conflict, depending on whether, for example,
two positive values (pregnancy and self-actualization) are
believed to be compatible or incompatible.

can be complemented by another relation in opposite direction (e.g., reflecting the attributed effect of self-actualization on the experience of pregnancy).

An imbalanced triad of three concepts and their interrelations constitutes an element of conflict; it does not yet describe a relevant section of an individual's intrapersonal conflicts. The model on which conflict measurement is based allows, however, for any number of concepts and their interrelations. This number is limited only by subjects' willingness to answer a lengthy questionnaire. A cognitive field that consists, for example, of 10 concepts can be descriptive of a relevant section of a person's problems, in which case the number of directed interrelations (and thus the number of items in a questionnaire) is 90. The number of possible triad combinations of these interrelations is 720, which can be either balanced and harmonious or imbalanced and contradictory. According to the definition of intrapersonal conflict (cf. Lauterbach, 1989), the degree of conflict (C) is the relative (or percentage of) imbalance in such a cognitive field. C ranges between 0.0 (implying no conflict and absolute harmony) and 1.0 (implying maximum contradictoriness and incompatibility).

RESULTS

In a series of group comparisons, subjects exposed to high degrees of life stress were shown to have higher degrees of intrapersonal conflict. For each group comparison, 8 to 10 concepts were identified that describe topics relevant for the groups that are to be compared.

Pregnancy Conflicts

The degree of conflict of pregnant women who wanted to have their child was compared with those who wanted an abortion in two independent studies (Lauterbach & Frübis, 1990). The topics used for testing the women's intrapersonal conflicts were: "myself," "pregnancy," "being a mother," "developmental resources for a child," "my partner," "self-actualization," "my job or education," and "my financial situation."

Conflict values were low for *birth* groups (Study 1 [n = 50]: C = .14; SD = .11; Study 2 [n = 52]: C = .13, SD = .16) and high for *abortion* groups (Study 1 [n = 50]: C = .36; SD = .09; Study 2 [n = 15]: C = .45; SD = .20), confirming the women's stressful life situation (in Study 1, t (98) = 10.95, p < .001; in Study 2, t (65) = 3.17, p < .05). Conflict in birth groups centered on the effects that "developmental resources for a child" and "being a mother" may have on the other concepts, particularly on the consequences for "financial situation."

In abortion groups, conflict centered on the effects of and the consequences for "developmental resources for a child," "pregnancy," "being a mother," and "my financial situation." The conflict generated by "my partner" and "my job or education" was relatively low; the reason may be that these concepts were unequivocally opposed to the birth of a child. It should be pointed out that if a woman were unequivocally opposed to giving birth to a child, her intrapersonal conflict would be low, because there would be few contradictions between her cognitions (attitudes, values, and beliefs) that reflect the various aspects of her life.

"Moonies" Versus Drug Addicts

A group of 17 members of the Unification Church (Moonies) was compared with 40 heroin addicts and 36 normal control subjects (Völp, 1984). Moonies seem to have found an aim in life, they are enthusiastic believers in the cause of their community, and they feel that they know what is right and what is wrong in this world. Their intrapersonal conflict was expected to be low. Heroin addicts, on the other hand, have many problems with their health, their addiction, the police, their lack of money, lack of friends, and so on. Their intrapersonal conflict was expected to be high. The cognitive field in which conflict was measured consisted of the following concepts: "myself," "my mother," "my friends," "finding answers to central existential questions," "the use of drugs," "believing in God," "my wishes and needs," "my life experiences," "the chance to have new, interesting experiences," and "my insecurity."

The various interrelations between these topics were transformed into questions for a cognitive questionnaire in the way described above for pregnancy and self-actualization. The percentage of imbalance in the answers of a Moonie or an addict was then calculated by computer. The differences in intrapersonal conflict were large: For Moonies, $C = .04$, $SD = .04$ (compared with controls, $t (51) = 3.39$, $p < .05$); for controls, $C = .12$, $SD = .10$; and for addicts, $C = .27$, $SD = .17$ (compared with controls, $t (74) = 4.62$, $p < .001$).

Competitive Swimmers

Similar contradictions between cognitions reflecting life circumstances were found in a study by the sports psychologists Völp and Keil (1987) for competitive swimmers. They tested 31 top-level swimmers (50% of them being members of the German national teams), 96 medium-level swimmers who used to participate in national and international competitions, and 34 hobby swimmers who practiced regularly but did not participate in competitions. The theory was that less success-ful swimmers, investing as much effort and sacrifice into their career, would have more conflict than more successful top stars that are in the lime light (which may be a stress factor other than conflict). The topics of the cognitive field were "my-self," "my competitive sport," "my proportion of success and failure," "my other hobbies," "my coach," "my training," "my partner," "my potential for athletic improvement," "my job," and "my teammates."

The answers of the highly successful top-level swimmers were less contradic-tory ($C = .11$, $SD = .09$) than were the answers of their less successful medium level comrades ($C = .18$, $SD = .12$) or those of hobby swimmers ($C = .17$, $SD = .11$), $t (63) = 2.39$, $p < .05$). The differences in conflict centered on the sports-related concepts: "my competitive sports," "my proportion of success and failure," "my training," and "athletic potential." When asked what their plans were, those members in the top and medium groups who wanted to continue their athletic career showed less conflict ($C = .16$, $SD = .11$, $n = 113$) than those who considered giving it up ($C = .21$, $SD = .14$, $n = 14$), $t (125) = 1.56$, NS).

CONFLICT AND MOOD

The preceding results of the studies on life stress show that intrapersonal conflict is higher in high-stress groups. However, conflict is not limited to cognitive stress. Early social psychological research (Cooper & Fazio, 1984; Insko, 1984) have shown that conflict has its emotional side, too.

Single-Case Studies

The correlations between the degree of conflict and the emotional state of a person were first investigated in clinical single-case studies (Lauterbach, 1975b). The main problem areas of depressed patients were individually described in terms of 10 or 12 concepts such as "being alone in a crowd," "performing socially," "inhibition to say what I feel," "emotional relaxation," "lack of self-confidence," "fear of being rejected," "taking pills," and "worrying about everything."

Patients were tested once a week over a period of 9 or 10 weeks for emotional state and intrapersonal conflict. One of the results was that negative emotions and conflict correlated highly in all patients ($r > 0.7$).

Alcoholics

Similar results were obtained in a group study (Klant, 1983) on intrapersonal conflict with hospitalized alcoholic patients. Concepts included "my partner," "my employment," "my spare time," "my friends," "independence," "sexual life," "my children," "my parents," "alcohol," and "relapse." The correlation between the consistency of patients' answers and their mood was .3, which was statistically significant ($p < .05$) but obviously smaller than correlations of .7 in single-case studies. Why was the correlation in the group study so much smaller than that in single-case studies? Could it be that people differ in their emotional response to cognitive inconsistency and conflict?

Conflict, Ambiguity, Intolerance and Mood

In search for appropriate personality variables, an old personality trait was selected: ambiguity intolerance (AIT; Frenkel-Brunswick, 1949), which describes a person's inability to deal with ambiguity, discrepancy, and uncertainty. This variable might well moderate the effects that contradictions and cognitive inconsistencies have on a person's emotional state. In order to make sure that subjects varied widely in respect to this variable, we included 65 art students near the end of their studies and 82 professional soldiers near the end of their careers.

The test of AIT included 16 items such as "There is a right or a wrong for nearly everything"; "When people cooperate, everyone should know exactly who is responsible for what"; and "If I were a research worker, I would hate the idea that my work is never really finished" (Zinke & Lauterbach, 1988; cf. Norton, 1975). Emotional state was tested by means of the Adjective Checklist (Janke & Debus, 1978), which includes 123 items that are grouped into 14 positive and negative subscales, such as Tiredness, Anger or Elation, Self-Certainty, which can be combined into a single score that indicates a negative affective state. The concepts or topics used to test intrapersonal conflict in both groups were "my partner," "my ambitions to perform well," "my financial security," "my professional prospects," "self-actualization," "being with people," "risk taking," and "the conditions of my work or study."

Results not only were obtained from the total sample but were cross-validated between the two subgroups (students and soldiers). AIT (range = 0 to 41) of soldiers (M = 23.7, SD = 5.13, n = 82) was somewhat higher than that of the students (M = 19.8, SD = 5.28, n = 65), t (145) 4.51; p < .001. Although soldiers were cognitively more consistent (C = .13, SD = .13) than were art students (C = .18, SD = .15), t (145) = 2.25, p < .05, these differences were smaller than would be expected on grounds of prejudices concerning the "squareness" and "orderliness" of professional soldiers and the "chaotic life-style" of art students.

The combined score of (negative) mood and the degree of conflict did, in fact, correlate (r = .44). Subjects with higher degrees of conflict were in a more negative (or less positive) emotional state. However, the correlations between mood and conflict were modified by AIT (Table 1); a multiple regression analysis with AIT as a moderator resulted in a multiple correlation coefficient of .52. When subjects were ordered into five subgroups according to their AIT, the correlation between conflict and mood increased with the degree of AIT from an insignificant correlation of .22 in the least intolerant group to correlation of .67 in the most intolerant group. In other words, the more a person is able to tolerate ambiguity, the less is mood affected by intrapersonal conflicts.

The most important section of a cognitive field appears to be the relations that are associated with the first element of a cognitive field, "myself" (e_1). These relations represent (a) a person's attitudes (e_{1-}) and (b) a person's "passive ego relations" (e_{1-}) (Lauterbach, 1989), reflecting the influence that the other elements are believed to have on "myself," or the degree to which a person identifies with the concepts of the cognitive field by saying, for example, that he feels financially secure or insecure, that he has or has not a chance for self-actualization and to what degree, and how good or bad the conditions of his work are. The conflict associated with answers to these questions (see ego conflict column in

Table 1 Correlation between intrapersonal conflict and (negative) mood

	r	
Group	Conflict	Ego conflict
AIT[a] <17	.22	.35
(n = 19)		
AIT = 17–19	.41*	.35
(n = 29)		
AIT = 20–23	.45**	.40*
(n = 38)		
AIT = 24–26	.49**	.55**
(n = 30)		
AIT >26	.67**	.83**
(n = 31)		

[a]Ambiguity intolerance.
*p < .05.
**p < .01.

Table 1) correlated highly with subjects' mood, and in the most ambiguity-intolerant subgroup the correlation was as high as .83 (Table 1).

Because these results were found in two diverse groups (soldiers and art students; Table 1 gives combined results), it seems justified to claim that the study succeeded in identifying (a) a personality variable (AIT) that moderates the effect of conflict on the emotional state of a person and (b) a section of a person's cognitions for which the association with emotional state is exceptionally strong.

CONCLUSIONS

Intrapersonal conflict can be an important cognitive and emotional stressor, and such conflict seems to be a reflection of a person's life stress. The contradiction between personally relevant cognitions related to life circumstances, aims, and values was higher in those groups whose life circumstances were difficult (e.g., drug addicts) or who felt threatened by major life changes (e.g., women who had applied for an abortion, unsuccessful athletes, or athletes considering giving up their athletic career). In each cognitive field, the topics and sources of intrapersonal conflict—that is, the patterns or structures of conflict and sources of cognitive stress—were identified.

The inconsistency and contradiction of attitudes and beliefs pertaining to topics that are important for a person's life are highly correlated with a person's general emotional state, particularly if subjects are intolerant of ambiguity, that is, if they are unwilling or unable to deal with uncertainty and ambiguity.

Measuring intrapersonal conflict allows testing for the ecological validity of hypotheses originating from laboratory research and helps to address questions concerning the correlates and possibly the origins and consequences of this cognitive stress factor. Until now these questions have been addressed only by clinicians and psychotherapists because objective assessment methods were not available.

SUMMARY

Cognitive approach–avoidance conflict (i.e., the incompatibility and inconsistency of attitudes, beliefs, and values pertaining to personally relevant topics) may contribute to and reflect a person's life stress. Comparisons of high versus low life stress groups confirm that intrapersonal conflict is higher in high-stress groups and that conflict is centered around those topics that characterize the problems of the groups concerned. As would be expected from social psychological theory (and from common sense), high degrees of conflict are correlated with negative affective states, and this is true particularly for those subjects who are unable or unwilling to deal with contradictions and inconsistency, that is, with ambiguity-intolerant subjects.

REFERENCES

Abelson, R. P., & Rosenberg, M. J. (1958). Symbolic psycho-logic: A model of attitudinal cognition. *Behavioral Science, 3,* 1–13.

Cartwright, D., & Harary, F. (1956). Structural balance: A generalization of Heider's theory. *Psychological Review, 63,* 277–293.

Cooper, J., & Fazio, R. H. (1984). A new look at dissonance theory. *Advances in Experimental Social Psychology, 17,* 229–265.

Frenkel-Brunswick, E. (1949). Intolerance of ambiguity as an emotional and perceptual personality variable. *Journal of Personality, 18*, 108-143.

Freud, S. (1949). *A general introduction to psychoanalysis.* New York: Garden City.

Heider, F. (1946). Attitude and cognitive organization. *Journal of Psychology, 1*, 107-112.

Heider, F. (1958). *The psychology of intrapersonal relations.* New York: Wiley.

Insko, C. A. (1984). Balance theory, the Jordan paradigm, and the Wiest tetrahedron. *Advances in Experimental Social Psychology, 18*, 89-140.

Janke, W., & Debus, G. (1978). *Die Eigenschaftswörterliste* [Adjective checklist]. Göttingen: Hogrefe.

Klant, M. (1983). Entwicklung und Anwendung eines einstellungs-fragebogens zur konfliktmessung bei alkoholikern [Development and application of an attitude questionnaire for measuring conflict in alcoholics]. Unpublished diploma thesis, Frankfurt.

Lauterbach, W. (1975a). Assessing psychological conflict. *British Journal of Social and Clinical Psychology, 14*, 43-47.

Lauterbach, W. (1975b). Covariation of conflict and mood in depression. *British Journal of Social and Clinical Psychology, 14*, 49-53.

Lauterbach, W. (1987). Intra-individuelle Konfliktmessung [Intraindividual conflict]. *Diagnostica, 33*, 319-338.

Lauterbach, W. (1989). *Intra-personal conflict measurement: Social psychological bases, methodology, and results.* Arbiten aus dem Institut für Psychologie der J. W. Goethe Universität.

Lauterbach, W. & Frübis, U. (1991). *Pregnancy conflicts.* Manuscript in preparation.

Norton, R. W. (1975). Measurement of ambiguity tolerance. *Journal of Personality Assessment, 39*, 607-619.

Pavlov, I. P. (1941). *Lectures on conditioned reflexes.* New York: International Universities Press.

Völp, A. (1984). Entwicklung und anwendung eines konflikt-fragebogens zum vergleich von drogenabhängigen und religiös gebundenen [Development and application of a conflict questionnaire for comparing drug addicts and religiously committed youths.] Unpublished diploma thesis, Frankfurt.

Völp, A., & Keil, U. (1987). The relationship between performance, intention to drop out, and intrapersonal conflict in swimmers. *Journal of Sports Psychology, 9*, 358-375.

Wolpe, J. (1958). *Psychotherapy by reciprocal inhibition.* Stanford, CA: Stanford University Press.

Zinke, B., & Lauterbach, W. (1988). *16-Fragen zur Ambiguitäts-Intoleranz* [16 ambiguity intolerance questions]. Unpublished manuscript.

7

Personality and Generalization as a Source of Stress

John Brebner
University of Adelaide, Australia

Among the questions used to differentiate individuals in terms of their introversion—extraversion (I–E) in the Eysenck Personality Questionnaire (EPQ; Eysenck & Eysenck, 1975) are some that relate to recreational or leisure pursuits, for example, "Do you have many hobbies?"; "I prefer reading to meeting people"; and "Do you tend to keep in the background on social occasions?" To some degree it might be suggested that responses to such questions reflect the sociability of extroverts. However, because recreation and leisure are such a large proportion of human behavior and involve such a variety of possibilities, many different factors are likely to be relevant, for example, the bias toward stimulus analysis in introverts and response organization in extraverts, as suggested by Brebner and Cooper (1974) or Brebner (1983). Differences between the personality groups in their sporting activities have been reviewed by Eysenck, Nias, and Cox (1982), and differences in movement have been considered by Brebner (1985). But, also, previous attempts to assess the characteristic mood and its variability (Hepburn & Eysenck, 1989) or the relative degree of general enjoyment experienced by the two groups from their leisure behavior (Brebner, 1990), suggest there is a possible difference between them.

Administration of the Personal State Questionnaire (PSQ), which is a 27-item questionnaire about enjoyment and leisure activities (Brebner, 1983b), gave the results shown in Table 1. Responses to the questions are made on a 11-point scale from 0% to 100% in 10% steps and the questions are deliberately very general. The test–retest reliability coefficient of the PSQ is .65 over short periods of around 5 weeks, and its internal consistency lies between alpha values of .83 and .85.

These results show that low scorers on extraversion stated they derived less enjoyment than high scorers claimed on almost anything. This seems to be due to extraversion rather than neuroticism since the high-neuroticism extraverts are much more like the low-neuroticism extraverts, than the high-neuroticism introverts. More recent results from a sample of second-year psychology students using the latest version of the PSQ show the same picture again with introverts lower on enjoyment (see Table 2).

These results could, of course, simply show that introverts do not use high numbers in answering questions. This might be tested by reversing the direction of the items to ask "how difficult or unpleasant" events had been to see if introverts still used lower numbers. However, the manual of the EPQ, which was used to select the groups, describes introverts as "pessimistic" and extraverts as "optimis-

Table 1 Items from the Personal State Questionnaire with mean scores for different personality
groups

	Introverts		Extraverts	
Item	High N[a] (n = 32)	Medium N (n = 31)	High N (n = 27)	Low N (n = 46)
What % of your time in the last few days has been spent in places that could be called beautiful or attractive?	42.2	39.7	49.6	56.5
What % of your time during the last few days have you actually spent enjoying yourself?	44.4	49.4	63.3	65.0
What % of the last few days was spent in leisure or recreational activities which you liked doing?	35.6	39.0	53.3	52.2
How much of tomorrow do you expect to be enjoyable?	53.8	65.5	71.5	78.3
How much have you enjoyed the scenery you have seen today?	44.4	52.3	57.8	64.6
What % of the food you have eaten in the last few days would you rate as delicious?	41.3	52.3	57.8	64.6
How enjoyable have you found any tourist visits or trips you have taken in the last few days?	37.8	49.0	55.9	66.1
To what degree have your hopes and expectations of what things would be like been satisfied over the last few days?	50.6	54.2	57.0	61.1
Grand mean	43.8	50.2	57.6	63.1

[a]Neuroticism.

tic," and there are earlier suggestions that extraverts tend to be happier than introverts (e.g., Wilson, 1967). Also, Gray (1981) has argued that introverts high on anxiety are more sensitive to negative events like punishment or nonreward, and also to novelty, and it could be argued that extraverts (described by Gray as high on impulsivity) are more sensitive to positive events such as reward or nonpunishment. Being "more sensitive" may mean having a stronger emotional impact, but it can also mean that the effect generalizes to affect more of the person's behavior. Very serious stress generalizes to have a unitary effect on all aspects of the stressed person's life. Less serious stresses can be compartmentalized more easily and possibly alleviated by the generalization of positive cognitive and emotional effects from other areas of the person's life. But a bias in a negative direction, a tendency to generalize negatively, that is, from negative events rather than from positive events, such as is indicated for introverts, would have wide-ranging effects, possibly even predisposing introverted individuals to chronic stress. In brief, negative generalization may be a source of stress. If this were the case, it would be expected that the behavior of introverts and extraverts would differ after experiencing a negative or a positive event.

To test this an experiment was performed on "stimulus generalization" in introverts and extraverts after exposure to a negative and a positive event. It is worth noting that, apart from ethical considerations, because it was the direction of generalization bias in introverts and extraverts that was being studied, it was not appropriate to use events that produce strong emotional effects. The emotional lability of individuals is measured by their neuroticism score rather than their extraversion score. If there is a strong emotional effect, that will generalize and will represent the emotionality of the person, but if there is a general direction of bias related to introversion–extraversion, this should be evident even in relatively unemotional conditions.

Moreover, although the literature has also related extraverts' greater happiness to their sociability and enjoyment of interpersonal interactions (Emmons & Diener, 1985; Wilson, 1967), and Argyle, Martin, and Crossland (1988) have broken this down further into the specific behaviors that characterize extraverts' social interactions with strangers, what was proposed in the present study is different and thus interpersonal factors were avoided as far as possible in this study.

Table 2 Items from the Personal State Questionnaire with mean scores and standard deviations for low, medium, and high scorers on extraversion (E) on the 5-point Eysenck Personality Questionnaire

Item	Low (E < 68; n = 19)	Medium ($-$) (E = 68–77; n = 23)	Medium ($+$) (E = 78–87; n = 23)	High (E > 87; n = 26)
How much of your recent time has been spent in places that could be called attractive?				
M	52.8	51.3	56.5	63.5
SD	26.5	25.1	22.5	21.5
How much of the time have you actually spent enjoying yourself recently?				
M	38.9	42.2	50.4	66.5
SD	26.0	22.2	23.1	22.6
How much of your recent time was spent in leisure or recreational activities?				
M	46.3	34.8	45.2	49.6
SD	26.1	20.9	28.1	22.2
How much have you enjoyed the scenery you have seen recently?				
M	56.3	60.4	64.4	73.9
SD	29.9	30.8	23.7	18.9
What proportion of the food you have eaten recently would you rate as delicious?				
M	54.7	58.3	57.8	68.1
SD	25.3	22.1	22.2	25.5
How enjoyable have you found any recent tourist activities?				
M	48.9	70.0	66.9	77.3
SD	29.8	18.6	29.5	22.4
To what degree have your recent hopes and expectations been satisfied?				
M	41.1	54.8	52.2	62.7
SD	27.5	16.8	25.6	22.4
Grand mean	48.4	53.1	56.2	65.9

METHOD

The method used involved a computer-controlled simulated betting game and had three phases. First, there was a discrimination phase in which subjects listened to seven tones of different frequencies and played them to themselves until they could pass a discrimination test that had a criterion of five successive correct discriminations. The tones varied between 150 and 1050 Hz in equal steps.

The second phase was a training session in which subjects began the simulated betting. They were presented with one of two tones, the lowest frequency (150 Hz) or the highest (1,050 Hz) in random order and had to "bet" either 20¢ or $1.00 on whether the tone predicted a win or a loss on a sort of computerized "fruit machine" (by entering their "bet"). They were instructed to maximize their winnings and, because the low tone had only a .15 probability of preceding a win, whereas the high tone's probability of winning was .85, after 50 trials all subjects had learned that the high tone was likely to win and the low tone was likely to lose.

The final, test, phase used only the five tones that were not used in the training phase. It was a similar betting game except that the probability of a "win" was .50 for all five tones, and subjects could choose between five different amounts to bet: 20¢, 40¢, 60¢, 80¢, or $1.00. Otherwise the procedure was the same—subjects listened to the tone, decided whether they thought it would "win" or "lose," placed their bet with the computer, and observed the result. There were 100 trials in the test phase, and the computer displayed running totals of the wins and losses and the amount won or lost.

HYPOTHESIS

If generalization occurred, subjects should bet low on the low-frequency tones and high on the high-frequency tones. Ideally, the lowest possible bet of 20¢ would always be placed on the lowest frequency tone in the test phase, then the next highest bet on the next highest frequency, and so on. However, because subjects are more likely to vary the amounts bet on any tone, the hypothesis was that generalization would be evidenced by an approximation to this ideal pattern. Also, if introverts' betting was more affected by the negative event of losing 85% of the time on the low tone and extraverts' betting affected by winning 85% of the time on the high tone, then, relative to extraverts, introverts should bet less on the higher tones and show a flatter "gradient of generalization" across the five tones.

SUBJECTS

For the reasons explained below, two experiments were conducted. Subjects in the first experiment were 23 students studying psychology at the University of Adelaide, of whom 11 were female. Fourteen of the students were extraverts and 9 were introverts according to their scores on the EPQ5pt. The EPQ5pt is the same as the EPQ except that, with the kind permission of the test's authors, a 5-point scoring scale is used instead of the standard 2-point scale. For extraverts scores ranged from 83 to 98, with a mean of 90.57, (SD = 5.00). For introverts the range was 54 to 65, with a mean of 59.67, (SD = 3.77). The mean age of extraverts was 20.36 years $(SD = 1.91)$ and that of introverts 22.89 years $(SD = 5.69)$.

RESULTS AND DISCUSSION

Two experiments were carried out; Figure 1 shows the results in the first of them. First, there was a gradient of generalization with a significant effect of tone, $F(4, 84) = 5.25, p < .01$. Analyzing the trends, the linear component was highly significant, $F(1, 84) = 15.63, p < .01$, and there was a smaller but also significant quadratic effect, $F(1, 84) = 4.72, p < .01$. Briefly, generalization occurred but, as expected, departed from the ideal linear progression and is instead curvilinear. In terms of the hypothesized differences between introverts and extraverts, the slope prediction was borne out and there was a significant Tone × Introvert–Extravert interaction, $F(1, 84) = 4.26, p < .01$. The prediction that introverts would bet less than extraverts, however, although true overall, did not hold for the two lowest tones, but in terms of a "gradient of generalization," the results support the notion that introverts have stronger negative generalization than do extraverts. If this is the case, then this tendency may attenuate positive effects derived from leisure and recreational pursuits as shown by the questionnaire results. Also, however, outside the laboratory where negative events may have much stronger effects, a tendency to generalize negatively would seem to be a recipe for chronic stress.

Table 3 shows the results of the other experiment. This experiment was intended to be the same as the first, and was in fact carried out first with different subjects. With the proviso below the method was the same. The 26 subjects were also psychology students, 9 of whom were male. Extraversion scores of the extraverted subjects $(n = 13)$, ranged from 83 to 104, with a mean of 90.85 $(SD = 5.87)$. For introverted subjects $(n = 13)$, the range was 36 to 64, with a mean of 54.77 $(SD = 9.24)$. Extraverts' mean age was 19.15 years $(SD = 1.57)$, and introverts' mean age was 20.54 years $(SD = 5.04)$.

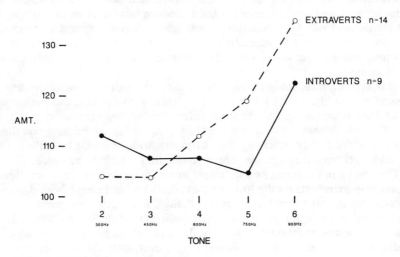

Figure 1 Results of the first experiment.

Table 3   Mean amounts (and standard deviations) bet on the five tones in the second experiment by both groups

	Tones				
Group	2	3	4	5	6
Introverts					
M	121.2	102.3	103.1	101.1	105.2
SD	31.5	20.6	18.4	26.1	28.9
Extraverts					
M	92.9	98.8	100.7	110.9	132.9
SD	30.7	27.9	22.8	33.7	30.1

In this experiment, extraverts behaved as predicted but the introverts did not. Introverts bet higher on the lowest tone than was expected. An analysis of variance performed on the data from the two lowest tones showed a significant Introversion–Extraversion $\times$ Tone interaction, $F(1, 24) = 6.03$, $p = .009$, with introverts betting higher on the lowest tone and extraverts on the higher tone. Moreover, analyzing the data from the three remaining tones gave a significant effect of tone, $F(1, 24) = 7.28$, $p = .002$, and a significant Introversion–Extraversion $\times$ Tone interaction, $F(1, 24) = 5.163$, $p = .009$. Extraverts' bets increased with tone frequency across the three highest tones, but introverts' bets did not.

These unexpected findings turned out to have been most likely due to a computer programming oversight that raised the probability of Tone 2 preceding a win from the intended .50 to .64. However, this makes the results very interesting because the extraverts did not respond to this unintended difference between Tone 2 and the others in the final test phase, although the introverts did. This suggests that introverts either work on shorter samples of events or base their behavior on estimates that they update more frequently than extraverts do, at least in this experimental context. That is, introverts update their population parameter estimates more often (possibly resetting them between tasks such as the training and test phases) and vary their behavior accordingly. In this experiment extraverts, on the other hand, were still generalizing from the training phase, and this implies they used either longer samples or longer intervals between updating their parameter estimates.

This serendipitous finding suggests various interesting possibilities: that extraverts are less affected by relatively infrequent negative events; that performance under partial reinforcement schedules differs for the two personality groups; or that if two-dimensional stimuli are used, after separately establishing one dimension as positive and the other negative, extraverts will generalize from the positive but introverts from the negative. These possibilities remain to be tested.

The results in the former experiment, in which introverts bet insignificantly higher than extraverts on the lowest tones, do not seem to have been due to the effect noted in this second experiment, that is, introverts recognizing that the probability of a win for particular tones had changed in the test phase. If this had been the case we would expect similar amounts to be bet across all of the tones, but this is not what was obtained. However, only the introverts' betting highest on the tone of highest frequency prevented this simple explanation from being acceptable. Perhaps introverts did generalize positively from past experience (though less than extraverts) if they could not discriminate between stimuli in terms of their probability of success in the test phase. Future research may show that both tendencies—to generalize negatively and to update their population parameters more frequently—operate for introverts. If so, the effects of positive events will be weaker and shorter lived for introverts than for extraverts.

The present results are unlikely to have been due to emotional differences or differences in skill in interpersonal interactions between introverts and extraverts though both of these may have general effects on the individual's sense of well-being (Hotard, McFatter, McWhirter, & Stegall, 1989). The tendency for introverts to generalize more strongly from negative events than from positive ones, and for extraverts to do the opposite, is a cognitive rather than emotional or social effect. This effect may be related to the "sadder but wiser" mode of behavior of depressives, which has been comprehensively reviewed by Alloy and Abramson (1979), or to the illusions that support well-being described by Taylor and Brown (1988). If further research establishes that the tendency to generalize negatively is characteristic of introverts in many situations, some interesting questions are raised. Is this tendency learned? Or is it the cognitive product of an inherent emotional tendency to fear and anxiety rather than anger and aggressivity that then selectively reinforces the perception of the world as lower on reward than punishment?

This study indicates that introverts update more frequently or operate on the basis of smaller samples. Given, however, that Broadbent (1958) has theorized that introverts operate on longer samples of information than extraverts do, it may be rather that introverts tend to input more information than extraverts do that results in introverts' updating more frequently. Findings like that of Ellgring (1970) that female introverts were better than female extraverts at discriminating which of seven points on their face another person was looking at may reflect this greater uptake of information. Together with a tendency to generalize more negatively, this would result in an approach to and assessment of events that is chronically more realistic but less positive than that of extraverts. If so, the PSQ results mentioned earlier may be an accurate reflection of the subjective status of introverts and extraverts.

Although the present experiments were not undertaken as a test of the Brebner-Cooper (Brebner & Cooper, 1974) model of extraversion, the results are in line with the view that introverts are more prone to stimulus analysis than extraverts. The relevant part of the model states that introverts generate central excitation from stimulus analysis whereas extraverts generate inhibition. Excitation is shown by the tendency to continue in or augment an activity; inhibition, by the cessation or attenuation of it. An interpretation of the results above in terms of introverts' making more use of available stimulus information than extraverts do, and updating their parameter estimates more frequently, is consonant with the greater stimulus analysis by introverts that the model attributes to them. However, because this is an interpretation of a serendipitous finding it is necessarily retrodictive and not a test of the model's predictive power.

SUMMARY

Two experiments were carried out to test the hypothesis that introverts would generalize negatively from a low-frequency tone previously associated with a probability of success as low as 0.15, rather than from a high-frequency tone with a success probability of 0.85, whereas extraverts would generalize positively from the successful, higher tone. The results from the first experiment provide support for the hypothesis. A computer programming error in the second experiment led to the serendipitous finding that introverts varied their behavior to match differences in the success probability of tones rather than generalizing from previous training. Extraverts generalized rather than matching their behavior to the unintended differences in success probability. On the basis of this result, it is suggested that introverts update their estimates of population parameters more frequently than extraverts do and make more use of available information to do so.

REFERENCES

Alloy, L. B., & Abramson, L. Y. (1979). Judgment of contingency in depressed and nondepressed students: Sadder but wiser? *Journal of Experimental Psychology: General, 108,* 441–485.

Argyle, M., Martin, M., & Crossland, J. (1988, August–September). *Happiness as a function of personality and social encounters.* Paper presented at the 24th International Congress of Psychology, Sydney, Australia.

Brebner, J. (1983a). A model of extraversion. *Australian Journal of Psychology, 35,* 349–359.

Brebner, J. (1983, September). *Personality factors in stress and anxiety.* Paper presented at the International Conference on Stress and Anxiety, Warsaw, Poland.

Brebner, J. (1985). Personality theory and movement. In B. Kirkcaldy (Ed.), *Individual differences in movement* (pp. 27–43). Lancaster: Medical and Technical Press.

Brebner, J. (1990). Personality factors in stress and anxiety. In C. D. Spielberger & R. Diaz-Guerrero (Eds.), *Cross-cultural anxiety, Volume 4,* (pp. 11–19). Washington, DC: Hemisphere.

Brebner, J., & Cooper, C. J. (1974). The effect of a low rate of regular signals upon the reaction times of introverts and extraverts. *Journal of Research in Personality, 8,* 263–276.

Broadbent, D. E. (1958). *Perception and communication.* London: Pergamon Press.

Ellgring, J. H. (1970). Judgment of glances directed at different points in the face. *Zeitschrift fur Experimentelle Angewandte Psychologie, 17,* 600–607.

Emmons, R. A., & Diener, E. (1985). Personality correlates of subjective well-being. *Personality and Social Psychology Bulletin, 11,* 88–97.

Eysenck, H. J., & Eysenck, S. B. G. (1975). *Manual of the Eysenck Personality Questionnaire.* London: Hodder & Stoughton.

Eysenck, H. J., Nias, D. K. B., & Cox, D. N. (1982). Sport and personality. *Advances in Behavior Research and Therapy, 4,* 1–56.

Gray, J. (1981). A critique of Eysenck's personality theory. In H. J. Eysenck (Ed.), *A model for personality* (pp. 246–273). New York: Springer-Verlag.

Hepburn, L., & Eysenck, M. W. (1989). Personality, average mood and mood variability. *Personality and Individual Differences, 10,* 975–983.

Hotard, S. R., McFatter, R. M., McWhirter, R. M., & Stegall, M. E. (1989). Interactive effects of extraversion, neuroticism, and social relationships on subjective well-being. *Journal of Personality and Social Psychology, 57,* 321–331.

Taylor, S. E., & Brown, J. D. (1988). Illusion and well-being: A social psychological perspective on mental health. *Psychological Bulletin, 103,* 193–210.

Wilson, W. (1967). Correlates of avowed happiness. *Psychological Bulletin, 67,* 294–306.

III

EMOTIONAL REACTIONS TO STRESS

8

Emotional Reactions of Pregnant Women to Ultrasound Scanning and Postpartum

Yona Teichman
Tel Aviv University, Israel

Dorit Rabinovitz and Yaron Rabinovitz
Shiba Hospital, Ramat Gan, Israel

Pregnancy and childbirth are considered stressful life events (Dohrenwend & Dohrenwend, 1974; Holmes & Rahe, 1967) or at least as experiences with crisis potential (Teichman, 1988). The stress is caused by physiological, psychological, and interpersonal experiences as well as by the close association with the medical profession and medical settings. As in many other stresses, investigators have attempted to determine factors that influence the way pregnant women deal with the stress. The most investigated factors have been social support and information. The study of individual differences has received less attention. Research on social support has focused mainly on support from the husband during pregnancy, childbirth, and early parenthood. As can be expected, women whose husbands are supportive manifest less anxiety, tension, and pain and report less complaints and more enjoyment (Huttel, Mitchell, Fischer, & Meyer, 1972; Norr, Block, & Charles, 1977). The topic of social support is not addressed in this chapter. As far as information was investigated, it applied to information obtained in childbirth preparation courses. Generally, findings indicate that such information is associated with less anxiety, less medication, and greater satisfaction (Davenport-Slack & Boylan, 1974; Klusman, 1975; Zax, Sameroff, & Farnum, 1975). We suggest that the ultrasound scanning during the first trimester of pregnancy can be considered as an additional source of information to the pregnant woman. This procedure provides information about the course of pregnancy and fetal sex. The purpose of the present study was to evaluate the influence of a general state of information versus no information. The impact of particular information, especially regarding the sex of the fetus, was presented elsewhere (Teichman, Rabinowitz, & Rabinowitz, 1988).

Since Janis's (1958) study, investigators have attempted to determine the role of information in coping with medical stress (surgery). Janis proposed that preoperative information would at first elevate patients' anxiety and initiate "work of worrying," which later in the postoperative stage would help in reducing anxiety. Janis's proposition was extensively investigated and failed to gain empirical support. Most of the findings indicated that in the preoperative stage, information about medical procedures and expected sensations does not elevate anxiety

(Vernon & Bigelow, 1974) and occasionally even reduces it (Wallace, 1984). In the postoperative stage, most findings support the idea that informed patients experience less distress (Hayward, 1975; Johnson & Leventhal, 1974; Johnson, Rice, Fuller, & Endress, 1978; Wallace, 1984). Findings about the effect of information given to pregnant women following ultrasound scanning indicate that such information, if properly delivered, is accepted enthusiastically, reduces postpartum anxiety, and enhances bonding between mother and child (Hyde, 1986; Kohn, Nelson, & Weiner, 1980; Milne & Rich, 1981; Reading & Cox, 1982).

On the basis of the conceptualization that pregnancy and childbirth resemble medical stress and previous findings with surgical patients and pregnant women, we suggest that Janis's (1958) theory can be investigated in this context as well. From this theoretical point of view we expected that information following an ultrasonic examination would first elevate emotional arousal but after the main stressful event, in the postpartum period, would reduce emotional arousal. Emotional arousal was evaluated by the level of reported state anxiety and depressed mood.

We also investigated the influence of individual differences (trait anxiety) on short- and long-term emotional reactions of pregnant women to the ultrasound procedure. The interaction between trait anxiety and information was examined as well. Trait anxiety is a very relevant variable to consider in this context. In Spielberger's (1966, 1972) trait–state theory of anxiety, the critical personality variable involved in determining an individual's experience of anxiety is anxiety proneness, that is individual predisposition to experience anxiety. Spielberger (1966, 1972) differentiated between two anxiety constructs: transitory or state anxiety (A—state) and anxiety proneness as a personality trait (A—trait). Trait-state anxiety theory predicts that persons high in trait anxiety are more prone to experience elevations in state anxiety in stressful situations. In order to measure these two aspects of anxiety, Spielberger, Gorsuch, and Lushene (1970) developed the State–Trait Anxiety Inventory (STAI). The STAI was translated and adapted to Hebrew by Teichman and Melnick (1985) and was used in the present study to evaluate both the independent variable (A—trait) and the dependent variable (A—state).

The influence of A—trait on reactions of surgical patients has been evaluated quite extensively. Most studies indicate that high A—trait patients manifest higher pre- and postoperative state anxiety (e.g., Auerbach, 1973; Chapman & Cox, 1977; Hodges, 1968; Hodges & Spielberger, 1966; Lamb, 1973; Spielberger, Auerbach, Wadsworth, Dunn, & Taulbee, 1973). In an attempt to explain these findings, Johnston (1988) and Eysenck (1988) suggested that high A—trait individuals engage a coping style that directs high attention to the dangers in the situation; that is, they are sensitizers. As a result, high A—trait individuals experience a higher A—state. This in turn makes them more vulnerable to physical and psychological problems, and a vicious circle that perpetuates anxiety starts to operate. If indeed this kind of sequence is set in motion, it has important implications for the psychological and physical well-being of the expectant mother, the new mother, and the baby.

Spielberger (1966, 1972) concentrated only on the relationship between the two types of anxiety; however, if Izard's (1972) theory that people typically experience more than one emotion and that emotions are related and organized in clusters is considered, it may be suggested that A—trait influences not only the level of experienced anxiety, but also the level of other emotions that are related to anxiety. One such emotion according to Izard (1972) is depression or, as he referred to it, distress. On the basis of this idea we have defined emotional arousal as elevation in anxiety and depressed mood and suggest that A—trait influences both emotions in a similar way.

Integrating the theoretical propositions and empirical findings regarding the effect of information and A—trait on emotional reactions of patients before and after a stressful event in a medical context, we tested the following hypotheses: (a) High A—trait women would report higher levels of A—state and depressed mood than low A—trait women, in the beginning of pregnancy, after the ultrasound scanning, and postpartum. (b) Uninformed women would report higher A—state and depressed mood than informed women after the examination and postpartum, and their level of anxiety was expected to stay stable. On the other hand, A—state level of informed women would be higher after the examination and drop postpartum. (c) Overall highest level of A—state and depressed mood will be reported by high A—trait, uninformed women.

METHOD

Subjects

Subjects were recruited from pregnant women who came for routine visits to prenatal clinics at a major medical center in Israel. The study was presented as research on the emotional reactions of pregnant women. The following inclusion criteria were requested: uncomplicated singleton pregnancy of married women, first time pregnant, no previous ultrasonic genetic evaluation, no history of involuntary infertility in the past, and no recorded history of psychopathology. The estimated gestational age was 25 to 27 weeks.

One hundred ninety-seven women were investigated. The age range was 17 to 43, with a mean age of 25.87. Subjects were middle-class women, and all of them had at least a partial high school education.

Women were randomly assigned to experimental and control groups. Following the ultrasound examination women in the experimental group ($n = 100$) received information about the course of pregnancy and about fetal sex. This information was disclosed only to women who declared a wish to receive it. No woman was convinced to obtain information or informed against her wish. Indeed, shortly after the study began, a group of women who chose to avoid information following the examination emerged. They formed a group of 56 subjects. The main reason mentioned by women for refusing to obtain information was unwillingness to know the fetal sex. Because this group did not differ on any demographic variable or any of the dependent variables from the original control group who received no information following the ultrasound examination ($n = 41$), the two groups were combined. Thus the control group included 97 women. Subjects in the control group had only minimal contact with the staff following the ultrasound scanning and received practically no information.

Using A—trait median score subjects in both groups were divided into low and high A—trait subgroups. In the experimental group 47 women were in the high

Table 1 Mean scores and standard deviations of state anxiety (A—state) and depressed mood
in the three evaluation periods (*n* = 197)

	Emotion			
	A—state		Depressed mood	
Situation	*M*	*SD*	*M*	*SD*
Preexamination	28.73	12.02	5.41	4.89
Postexamination	30.45	8.76	4.57	2.99
Postpartum	32.66	10.31	6.23	4.65

A—trait subgroup and 53 in the low A—trait subgroup. In the control group 50
women were in the high A—trait subgroup and 47 in the low A—trait subgroup.

Instruments

Anxiety was assessed by the Hebrew version (Teichman & Melnick, 1985) of
the STAI (Spielberger et al., 1970). Depressed mood was assessed by the Hebrew
version (Eyal, 1981) of Lubin's (1967) Depression Adjective Check List. In addition, subjects completed a short questionnaire in which they were asked to report
personal and socioeconomic information.

Procedure

In both groups, state anxiety and depression were evaluated three times: 10 to 14
days before the ultrasonic examination, immediately after the examination, and 38 to
48 hr postpartum. Trait anxiety was evaluated only once in the first evaluation.

RESULTS

Before reporting results about the specific hypotheses, it is important to determine whether in this study transition to motherhood was experienced as a stressful
life event and whether A—state and depressed mood are related emotions. In order
to answer the first question, A—state and depressed mood scores in the three
different evaluations were compared. The mean scores and standard deviations of
the two emotions in the different situations are presented in Table 1. The findings
regarding anxiety were very conclusive, they indicated a significant increase in
anxiety in all possible comparisons (preexamination–postexamination
$t(196) = 2.07, p < .05$; postexamination–postpartum $t(196) = 3.30, p = .001$;
preexamination–postpartum $t(196) = 4.29, p < .001$). Depressed mood scores
decreased significantly after the examination, $t(196) = 2.31, p = .02$, but then
elevated, and the postexamination–postpartum comparison indicates that this elevation was significant, $t(196) = 6.13, p < .001$, as was the overall elevation in
depression during the pregnancy (preexamination–postpartum $t(196) = 2.06$,
$p < .05$). As far as the relationship between A—state and depression is considered, our findings support Izard's (1972) idea that these two emotions are related.
The correlations between them in the three evaluations were as follows: Preexami-

nation $r = .32$, $p = .001$; postexamination $r = .43$, $p = .001$; and postpartum $r = .68$, $p = .001$.

After establishing that first-time transition to motherhood was accompanied by significant elevation in emotional arousal and that A—state and depression are related emotions especially when stress increases, we attempted to assess what factors contributed to the arousal.

In a $2 \times 2 \times 3$ analysis of variance, we examined the effect of A—trait (high or low), information (informed or uninformed) and situation (preexamination, postexamination, or postpartum) on A—state and depression. Results regarding A—state indicate a significant main effect of A—trait and situation— $F(1,195) = 54.98$, $p < .001$, and $F(2,195) = 12.24$, $p < .001$, respectively—and significant interactions of A—trait $\times$ Situation and Information $\times$ Situation—($F(2,195) = 12.89$, $p < .001$, and $F(2,195) = 4.43$, $p = .01$, respectively. The A—trait $\times$ Information interaction approached significance, $F(1,195) = 3.32$, $p = .07$. Main effect of information and the three-way interaction did not reach significance level. The three significant interactions are presented in Figures 1 through 3.

Results regarding depression indicate that all main effects and all two-way interactions reached significance or approached it: For A—trait, $F(1,195) = 18.93$, $p < .001$; for information, $F(1,195) = 3.85$ $p = .05$; for situation, $F(2,195) = 11.73$, $p < .001$; for A—trait $\times$ Situation, $F(2,195) = 1.69$, $p = .07$; for Information $\times$ Situation, $F(2,195) = 4.05$, $p = .02$; for A—trait $\times$ Information, $F(2,195) = 3.85$ $p = .05$. Again the three-way interaction did not reach significance. The three significant interactions are presented in Figures 4 through 6.

Post hoc analyses of the A—trait $\times$ Situation (Figure 1) interaction indicate that high A—trait women reported significantly higher levels of anxiety in all evaluations: Preexamination $F(1,195) = 66.10$, $p < .001$; postexamination $F(1,195) = 24.36$, $p < .001$; postpartum $F(1,195) = 11.36$, $p < .01$. However, none of the within-group comparisons reached significance level, indicating that their anxiety level remained almost the same. In contrast, the within-group comparisons in the low A—trait group yielded significant changes between all

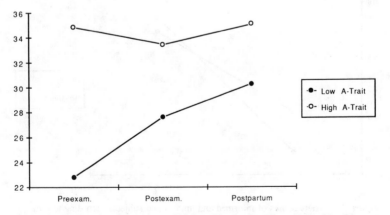

Figure 1 Changes in state anxiety of high and low trait anxiety (A—trait) subjects.

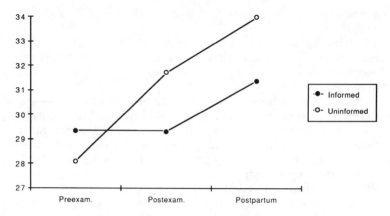

Figure 2 Changes in state anxiety of informed and uninformed subjects.

possible comparisons: Preexamination–postexamination $t(99)$ = 4.00, $p < .001$; postexamination–postpartum $t(99)$ = 3.04, $p < .001$; and preexamination–postpartum $t(99)$ = 5.58, $p < .001$.

High A—trait women also reported significantly higher depression in all evaluations (Figure 4): Preexamination $F(1,195)$ = 15.72, $p = .000$; postexamination $F(1,195)$ = 7.04, $p = .008$; postpartum $F(1,195)$ = 9.09, $p = .003$. Two of their within-group comparisons were also significant: Preexamination–postexamination $t(99)$ = 3.22, $p = .002$; postexamination–postpartum $t(99)$ = 5.24, $p = .001$. The preexamination–postpartum comparison did not reach significance. Among the low A—trait women only one comparison reached significance: preexamination–postpartum $t(99)$ = 2.00, $p = .05$.

Post hoc analyses of the information situation interaction (Figure 2) indicate that in the preexamination evaluation the difference in anxiety between the informed and uninformed groups was statistically unsignificant. After the examination and postpartum, uninformed women reported higher anxiety than informed

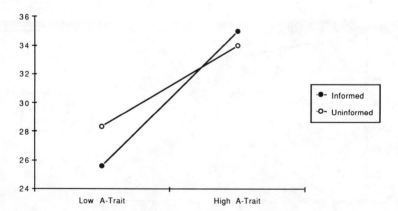

Figure 3 Anxiety scores of informed and uninformed subjects according to trait anxiety (A—trait) level (high/low).

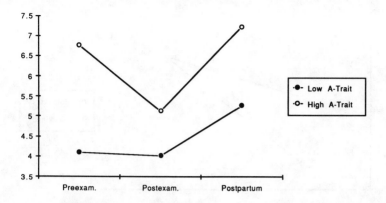

Figure 4 Changes in depressed mood of high and low trait anxiety (A—trait) subjects.

women: $F(1,195) = 3.79$, $p = .05$, and $F(1,195) = 3.24$, $p = .07$, respectively. The stability in the anxiety level of the informed women is also worth mentioning. Whereas the uninformed group experienced significant elevations in anxiety after the examination and postpartum—$t(96) = 2.92$, $p = .004$, and $t(96) = 2.14$, $p < .05$, respectively—and the overall elevation in anxiety was significant as well—$t(96) = 4.31$, $p < .001$—the informed group reported a significant elevation in anxiety only postpartum: Postexamination–postpartum $t(99) = 2.62$, $p = .01$; preexamination–postexamination $t(99) = 1.67$, $p = .10$.

The patterns of depression of informed and uninformed women resemble the patterns of their anxiety (Figure 5). Again both groups reported similar levels of depression in the preexamination stage and uninformed women reported significantly higher levels of depression after the examination, $F(1,195) = 9.34$, $p = .003$, and postpartum, $F(1,195) = 6.56$, $p = .01$. However, when stability was considered, within-group comparisons indicate that the uninformed group re-

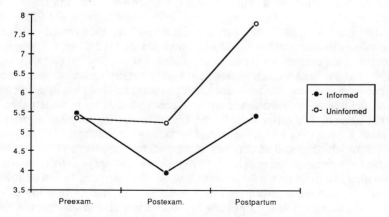

Figure 5 Changes in depressed mood of informed and uninformed subjects.

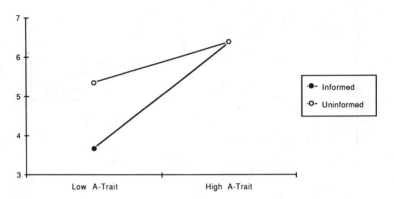

Figure 6   Depressed mood scores of informed and uninformed subjects according to
trait anxiety (A—trait) level (high/low).

ported a significant elevation in depression only postpartum—postexamination-
postpartum $t(96) = 4.71$, $p < .001$—and an overall elevation in anxiety—
preexamination-postpartum $t(96) = 3.12$, $p = .002$—whereas the informed
group reported a decline in depression in the postexamination evaluation,
$t(99) = 2.74$, $p = .007$, and a significant elevation postpartum, $t(99) = 3.94$,
$p < .001$. Despite this elevation, the informed subjects did not exceed their preexamination level of depression.

Post hoc analyses of the A—trait × Information interaction (Figure 3) indicate
that both informed and uninformed low A—trait women reported lower levels of
anxiety than high A—trait women—for informed women, $F(1,98) = 38.88$,
$p = .000$; for uninformed women, $F(1,95) = 17.5, p < .001$—but the information affected mainly low A—trait women. Whereas the difference between the two
groups of low A—trait women is significant, $F(1,98) = 5.33$, $p = .02$, the difference in the high A—trait group is negligible. The same pattern repeats itself
regarding depression (Figure 6). Low A—trait women reported significantly lower
levels of depression than high A—trait women—for the informed group,
$F(1,98) = 18.68$, $p < .001$, and for the uninformed group, $F(1,95) = 3.11$,
$p = .08$—and the differences between informed and uninformed groups approached significance only in the low A—trait group, $F(1,98) = 9.5, p = .003$.

Summarizing the results, it can be concluded that the first hypothesis was confirmed. High A—trait women experienced higher anxiety and depression than low
A—trait women during the pregnancy and postpartum. However, it is interesting
to note that low A—trait women manifested greater instability in anxiety than high
A—trait women. The differences in stability in depression in the two groups are
less clear. Findings regarding the second hypothesis indicate that in all the evaluations information reduced anxiety and depression but, contrary to the expectation,
increased emotional stability. The third hypothesis was only partially confirmed.
Information differentiated only between low A—trait women. Informed low A—
trait women reported significantly lower levels of state anxiety than low A—trait
uninformed women. The level of their depression was also lower than that of low
A—trait uninformed women, but this difference only approached significance.

DISCUSSION

Our findings support the notion that first-time childbirth is a stressful life event. A look at Table 1 reveals that following the ultrasound examination anxiety increased significantly and depressed mood decreased significantly but during the postpartum period both measures elevated significantly compared with preexamination and postexamination scores.

After concluding that first-time childbirth is a stressful situation that causes elevation in emotional arousal, it was interesting to examine what contributed to the arousal. The variables that were proposed in this study are A—trait, information, and the interaction between them.

Figures 1 and 4 show that high A—trait subjects reported significantly higher levels of anxiety and depression in all possible comparisons. When changes within the groups were considered, it must be pointed out that whereas A—state level of high A—trait women was stable and did not reveal any significant change between evaluations, A—state level of low A—trait women elevated significantly from one evaluation to the other and showed a significant overall increase in the preexamination–postpartum comparison.

The within-group comparisons regarding depressed mood are similar. Although high A—trait women reported a significant reduction in depression after the examination, and a significant increase postpartum, their overall level of depression remained almost the same. On the other hand, low A—trait women manifested a significant increase in depression only in the postexamination–postpartum comparison, but this elevation produced a significant change in the preexamination–postpartum comparison. Despite some differences between A—state and depressed mood responses of high and low A—trait subjects, it may be concluded that, as hypothesized in all the comparisons, high A—trait women experienced higher levels of anxiety and depression than low A—trait women. The differences between high A—trait and low A—trait subjects confirm Spielberger's (1966, 1972) theory regarding the relationship between trait and state anxiety, and can be added to previous findings that support the trait–state theory of anxiety (e.g., Auerbach, 1973; Glanzmann & Laux, 1978; Hodges, 1968; Hodges & Spielberger, 1966; Lamb, 1973; Spielberger et al., 1973; Spielberger, O'Neil, & Hansen, 1972).

It is important to note that on the basis of our findings, it is difficult to determine whether high or low A—trait subjects have a more difficult time during transition to motherhood. High A—trait subjects reported higher level of anxiety and depression, but because they have a high predisposition to experience arousal, this apparently is their usual way of experiencing life events. On the other hand, low A—trait subjects reported more emotional instability. The fact that low A—trait women experience emotional instability in stressful situations was also reported by Margalit, Teichman, and Levitt (1980). Emotional instability for women who are usually calm may be a very unpleasant experience.

The fact that in stressful situations low A—trait subjects are less stable than high A—trait subjects may be explained by Eysenck's (1988) proposition that there are two types of low A—trait subjects: subjects who indeed have very low predisposition to experience arousal and repressors. Repressors defend themselves against stress by avoiding it and when exposed to a stressful event may be even more threatened than high A—trait individuals (Schwartz, 1983; Weinberger, Schwartz, & Davidson, 1979). Our results indicate that such a differentiation within the low A—trait subjects may be worthwhile. As suggested by Eysenck (1988), the differentiation is possible using the Repression–Sensitization and Social Desirability scales.

Another explanation regarding the emotional instability of low A—trait subjects may be sex-related. It can be suggested that low A—trait women, who generally manifest low levels of anxiety, when confronted with an objectively defined stress situation, allow themselves freedom of emotional expression. On the other hand, high A—trait women, who tend to manifest high emotional arousal, and most probably often receive negative feedback to their behavior, when confronted with a stressful situation, may try to control their emotional reactions. Apparently they cannot change the level of their arousal, but its stability can be controlled. The different reaction patterns of low and high A—trait women to the developmental stress of becoming a mother suggests that when prevention is considered both groups have different needs. Whereas high A—trait women need help in reducing their arousal, low A—trait women would benefit from help in stabilizing their arousal.

Before concluding the discussion about the relationship between A—trait and emotional arousal during pregnancy and new motherhood, it should be mentioned that A—state and depressed mood correlated significantly in all three situations and that the level of both emotions could be predicted on the basis of A—trait level. These findings confirm Izard's (1972) theory that anxiety and depression are related emotions and not, as suggested by Cattell (1972), two distinct emotions. The fact that A—trait level predicted the level of depressed mood suggests that it can predict the level of additional emotions that were identified by Izard (1972) as belonging to the same cluster, that is, fear, guilt, anger, shame, and interest–excitement.

The results regarding the second hypothesis point out that information had a calming and stabilizing effect, but did not confirm Janis's two-stage theory. In the preexamination evaluation, A—state level of informed women was similar to that of the uninformed group, but after the examination and during the postpartum period, they manifested significantly, or almost significantly lower levels of anxiety. The stability in their anxiety is also worth mentioning. Whereas the uninformed group experienced significant elevations in anxiety after the examination and postpartum, the informed group experienced a significant elevation only postpartum.

In the preexamination evaluation depression level of the two groups was also similar, but whereas here information reduced depression, lack of information did not affect it. In the long range, however (i.e., postpartum), both groups manifested a significant elevation in depression. This elevation caused a significant overall elevation in depression only in the uninformed group.

The conclusion that may be suggested on the basis of these comparisons is that information reduced and stabilized anxiety and depression, whereas withholding of information elevated and fluctuated them. Contrary to Janis's (1958) thinking, receiving information did not cause an immediate elevation in emotional arousal. After receiving information, in the postexamination stage, subjects remained emotionally stable (Figure 2) or even, as in Wallace's (1984) study, reported a decrease in emotional arousal (Figure 5). In the second stage, however, our results confirm Janis's (1958) proposition and indicate that in the postpartum period the informed group manifested significantly lower emotional arousal on both measures. Thus the fact that information is effective in reducing emotional arousal was demonstrated again, except that it cannot be attributed, as Janis suggested, to the "work of worrying." An alternative explanation may be that of cognitive clarity and a sense of control that are enhanced through information (Johnston, 1988) or perhaps feelings of trust and security that develop as a result of the attention expressed by the medical staff. The practical conclusion that may be drawn from these findings is that ultrasound examinations that are followed by information have short- and long-range positive effect on the emotional well-being of pregnant women. Because there are findings that the emotional well-being of expectant mothers influences the well-being of the fetus, physiological and psychological reactions during childbirth, and the relationship between the mother and the neonate, such information has very important implications (Brown, 1964; Crandon, 1979; Davids & DeVault, 1962; Davids, Holden, & Gray, 1963; Gorsuch & Key, 1974; Sontag, 1958).

Results regarding the last hypothesis again draw attention to the low A—trait group. Significant interactions between A—trait and information were obtained regarding A—state and depression, but, contrary to the hypothesis, there was no difference in A—state or depression level between high A—trait informed and uninformed subjects (Figures 3 and 6). Regardless of information, both groups manifested significantly higher A—state and depression than low A—trait subjects. On the other hand, information made a difference in the low A—trait group. Informed low A—trait subjects reported significantly lower levels of state anxiety and depressed mood than uninformed low A—trait subjects. This finding points to the conclusion that mainly low A—trait subjects benefit from information. High A—trait subjects, because of their emotional arousal, may be in a state that interferes with information processing and with using constructively cognitive defenses.

Medical settings that develop prevention programs for pregnant women and possibly medical patients in general could apply the findings of this study according to the following guidelines: Recognize the short- and long-range value of information in coping with stressful events. Differentiate between high and low A—trait subjects and develop for each group programs according to their specific needs. High A—trait patients would benefit from interventions that focus on reducing anxiety level and only later can be expected to react positively to information. Low A—trait subjects benefit from information, but need interventions that focus on stabilizing emotional experiences.

SUMMARY

The effects of trait anxiety and giving information following ultrasound scanning on the emotional reactions of expectant and new mothers were investigated in this study. Changes in state anxiety and depression were evaluated for 197 first-time expectant mothers who were subdivided according to trait anxiety (A—trait) level (high or low) and exposure to information following an ultrasound examination (informed or uninformed). Anxiety and depression were measured preexamination, postexamination, and postpartum.

Based on Spielberger's trait–state theory of anxiety and Janis's propositions about the effects of information on coping with stress, the following hypotheses were evaluated: (a) High A—trait women would report higher levels of state anxiety (A—state) and depressed mood than low A—trait women in all assessments, (b) Anxiety and depressed mood of the informed women would be lower, but less stable, than the emotional reactions of uninformed women, (c) The highest level of A—state and depressed mood would be reported by the uninformed, high A—trait women.

As predicted, the high A—trait expectant mothers experienced higher levels of A—state and depressed mood, but the low A—trait women showed greater changes in these emotions. Information reduced A—state and depression, but, contrary to the second hypothesis, giving information increased emotional stability. However, information affected the emotions of only the low A—trait subjects. Informed low A—trait women reported significantly lower A—state than the uninformed low A—trait subjects. The informed women also reported less depression, but this difference only approached statistical significance. Theoretical and practical implications of the findings were discussed.

REFERENCES

Auerbach, S. M. (1973). Trait–state anxiety and adjustment to surgery. *Journal of Consulting and Clinical Psychology, 34,* 264–271.

Brown, J. (1964). Anxiety in pregnancy. *British Journal of Medical Psychology, 37,* 27–57.

Catell, R. B. (1972). The nature and genesis of mood states: A theoretical model with experimental measurements concerning anxiety, depression, arousal and other mood states. In C. D. Spielberger (Ed.), *Anxiety: Current trends in theory and research* (pp. 115–183). New York: Academic Press.

Chapman; C. R., & Cox, G. B. (1977). Determinants of anxiety in elective surgery patients. In C. D. Spielberger & I. G. Sarason (Eds.), *Stress and anxiety, volume 4,* (pp. 269–290). New York: Wiley.

Crandon, A. J. (1979). Maternal anxiety and obstetric complications. *Journal of Psychosomatic Research, 23,* 109–111.

Davenport-Slack, B., & Boylan, C. (1974). Psychological correlates of childbirth pain. *Psychosomatic Medicine, 24,* 215–233.

Davids, A., & DeVault, S. (1962). Maternal anxiety during pregnancy and childbirth abnormalities. *Psychosomatic Medicine, 5,* 464–470.

Davids, A., Holden, R. H., & Gray, G. B. (1963). Maternal anxiety during pregnancy and adequacy of mother and child adjustment eight months following childbirth. *Child Development, 34,* 993–1002.

Dohrenwend, B. S., & Dohrenwend, B. P. (1974). Overview and prospects for research on stressful life events. In B. S. Dohrenwend & B. P. Dohrenwend (Eds.), *Stressful life events: Their nature and effects.* New York: Wiley.

Eyal, N. (1981). *The Hebrew version of the Depression Adjective Check List: Reliability, validity and norms.* Master's thesis, Tel-Aviv University, Tel-Aviv, Israel.

Eysenck, M. W. (1988). Trait anxiety and stress. In S. Fisher & J. Reason (Eds.), *Handbook of life stress cognition and health* (pp. 476–482). Chichester, England: John Wiley & Sons.

Glanzmann, P., & Laux, L. (1978). The effect of trait anxiety and to kinds of stressors on state anxiety and performance. In C. D. Spielberger & I. G. Sarason (Eds.), *Stress and anxiety, volume 5* (pp. 145–164). Washington, DC: Hemisphere.

Gorsuch, R., & Key, M. (1974). Abnormalities of pregnancy as a function of anxiety and life stress. *Psychosomatic Medicine, 36,* 352–362.

Hayward, J. (1975). *Information: A prescription against pain.* London: RCN.

Hodges, W. F. (1968). Effects of ego threat and threat of pain on state anxiety. *Journal of Personality and Social Psychology, 8,* 364–372.

Hodges, W. F., & Spielberger, C. D. (1966). The effect of threat of shock on heart rate for subjects who differ in manifest anxiety and fear of shock. *Psychophysiology, 2,* 287–294.

Holmes, T. H., & Rahe, R. H. (1967). The Social Re-Adjustment Rating Scale. *Journal of Psychosomatic Research, 11,* 213–218.

Huttel, F., Mitchell, I., Fischer, W., & Meyer, A. (1972). A quantitative evaluation of psychoprophylaxis in childbirth. *Journal of Psychosomatic Research, 16,* 81–92.

Hyde, B. (1986). An interview study of pregnant women's attitudes to ultrasound scanning. *Social Science and Medicine, 22,* 587–592.

Izard, C. E. (1972). Anxiety; A variable combination of interacting fundamental emotions. In C. D. Spielberger (Ed.), *Anxiety: Current trends in theory and research* (pp. 55–106). New York: Academic Press.

Janis, I. L. (1958). *Psychological stress.* New York: John Wiley & Sons.

Johnson, J. E., & Leventhal, H. (1974). Effects of accurate expectations and behavioral instructions on reactions during a noxious medical examination. *Journal of Personality and Social Psychology, 29,* 710–718.

Johnson, J. E., Rice, V. H., Fuller, S. S., & Endress, M. F. (1978). Sensory information instruction in a coping strategy, and recovery from surgery. *Research in Nursing Health, 1,* 4–17.

Johnston, M. (1988). Impending surgery. In S. Fisher & J. Reason (Eds.), *Handbook of life stress, cognition and health* (pp. 79–100). Chichester, England: John Wiley & Sons.

Klusman, L. E. (1975). Reduction of pain in childbirth by alleviation of anxiety during pregnancy. *Journal of Consulting Clinical Psychology, 43,* 162–165.

Kohn, C. L., Nelson, A., & Weiner, S. (1980, March/April). Gravidas' responses to real-time ultrasound fetal image. *Journal of Obstetrics Gynecology and Nursing,* p. 88–100.

Lamb, D. H. (1973). The effect of two stressors on state anxiety for students who differ in trait anxiety. *Journal of Research in Personality, 7,* 116–126.

Lubin, B. (1967). *Depression Adjective Check List: Manual.* San Diego, CA: Educational and Industrial Services.

Margalit, C., Teichman, Y., & Levitt, R. (1980). Emotional reaction to physical threat: Reevaluation with female subjects. *Journal of Consulting and Clinical Psychology, 48,* 403–404.

Milne, L. S., & Rich, O. J. (1981). Cognitive and affective aspects of the responses of pregnant women to sonography. *Maternal–Child Nursing Journal, 10,* 15–39.

Norr, K. L., Block, C. R., & Charles, A. (1977). Explaining pain and enjoyment in childbirth. *Journal of Health and Social Behavior, 18,* 260–275.

Reading, A. F., & Cox, D. N. (1982). The effects of ultrasound examination on maternal anxiety levels. *Journal of Behavioral Medicine, 5,* 237–247.

Schwartz, G. E. (1983). Disregulation theory and disease: Applications to the repression/cerebral disconnection/cardiovascular disorder hypothesis. *International Review of Applied Psychology, 32,* 95–118.

Sontag, L. W. (1958). Maternal anxiety during pregnancy and fetal behavior. Physical and behavioral growth. Presented at Cross Laboratories Conference No. 26. Columbus, OH.

Spielberger, C. D. (1966). Theory and research on anxiety. In C. D. Spielberger (Ed.), *Anxiety and behavior* (pp. 3–20). New York: Academic Press.

Spielberger, C. D. (1972). Anxiety as an emotional state. In C. D. Spielberger (Ed.), *Anxiety: Current trends in theory and research* (Vol. 1, pp. 24–49). New York: Academic Press.

Spielberger, C. D., Auerbach, S. M., Wadsworth, A. P., Dunn, R. M., & Taulbee, E. S. (1973). Emotional reactions to surgery. *Journal of Consulting and Clinical Psychology, 40,* 33–38.

Spielberger, C. D., Gorsuch, R. L., & Lushene, R. L. (1970). *State–Trait Anxiety Inventory manual.* Palo Alto, CA: Consulting Psychologists Press.

Spielberger, C. D., O'Neil, H. F., & Hansen, D. N. (1972). Anxiety, drive theory, and computer-assisted learning. In B. A. Maher (Ed.), *Progress in experimental personality research* (Vol. 6) New York: Academic Press.

Teichman, Y. (1988). Expectant parenthood. In S. Fisher & J. Reason (Eds.), *Handbook of life stress, cognition and health* (pp. 3–22). Chichester, England: John Wiley.

Teichman, Y., & Melnick, H. (1985). *The Hebrew manual for the State–Trait Anxiety Inventory.* Tel-Aviv: Ramot.

Teichman, Y., Rabinowitz, D., & Rabinowitz, Y. (1988, September). *Gender preferences of pregnant women and emotional reactions to information regarding fetal gender.* Paper presented at the International Council of Psychologists, Singapore.

Weinberger, D. A., Schwartz, G. E., & Davidson, R. J. (1979). Low-anxious, high-anxious, and repressive coping styles. Psychometric patterns and behavioral and physiological responses to stress. *Journal of Abnormal Psychology, 88,* 369–380.

Vernon, D. T., & Bigelow, D. A. (1974). Effects of information about potentially stressful situation on responses to stress impact. *Journal of Personality and Social Psychology, 29,* 50–59.

Wallace, L. M. (1984). Psychological preparation as a method of reducing the stress of surgery. *Journal of Human Stress, 10,* 62–77.

Zax, M., Sameroff, A., & Farnum, J. (1975). Childbirth education, maternal attitudes and delivery. *American Journal of Obstetrics and Gynecology, 123,* 185–190.

9

Determinants of Changes in Trait Anxiety

Peter B. Defares
University of Amsterdam, the Netherlands

A legitimate question to be addressed in anxiety research pertains to the assessment of basic underlying variables that contribute to the maintenance of trait anxiety levels. Many authors have pinpointed neuroticism as a major concomitant of trait anxiety. In this chapter, it is contended that a multimodel approach that references specific intrapsychic preconditions related to previous experiences will facilitate an understanding of the causation of trait anxiety. The rationale for this view stems partly from the outcome of several intervention studies that involved deliberate efforts to reduce trait anxiety levels over time in which very different approaches were found to be effective in producing substantial reductions in trait anxiety.

Four intervention studies carried out in cooperation with the present author are briefly summarized: (a) a study in which psychophysiological functioning was altered by a biofeedback procedure, (b) a study involving psychotherapeutic interventions with victims suffering from the stress response syndrome, (c) a study in which the anxiety of subjects suffering from a speech disorder (stuttering) was altered by applying a behaviorally oriented intervention strategy, and (d) a study using cognitive recoding of threatening situations that aimed at enhancing the coping capability of Type A individuals.

In order to account for the outcomes of these studies, an integrative theoretical model is presented that highlights the differential causation of trait anxiety (Frijda, 1986). An important feature of the proposed integrative model is the search for common elements that may be operative in a variety of areas of psychological functioning.

THE EMOTION PROCESS

Theoretical issues with regard to the causal determinants of changes in trait anxiety have emerged because highly divergent interventions have been equally successful in reducing this trait. Interpretations of the causes of trait anxiety lean heavily on emotion theory, such as the versatile and comprehensive theoretical framework recently proposed by Frijda (1986). A core assumption in Frijda's cognitively oriented emotion theory is that "concerns" underlie emotions. To quote Frijda,

> *Concern is defined as a disposition to desire occurrence or non-occurrence of a given kind of situation. The dispositions can be conceived as internal representations serving as standards against which actual situations are tested. . . . Concerns bear relevance for elicition of emo-*

tional responses, when actual conditions deviate from their satisfaction conditions. (Frijda, 1986, pp. 335-336).

According to Frijda, the situation corresponding to the standard is called the concern's "satisfaction condition." In Frijda's model of emotion, which is presented in Figure 1, the initial stage comprises a stimulus event that engenders information coding. The stimulus event is subsequently appraised as to its relevance for one or more of the person's concerns. If a discrepancy is perceived between the potential repercussions of the event and the "satisfaction condition" of a particular concern, the emotion induction process will proceed. In contrast, if the comparison indicates a concurrence of event potentialities and the satisfaction conditions of the concern, no emotional response is evoked.

The second stage of the model implies a context of evaluation. The stimulus

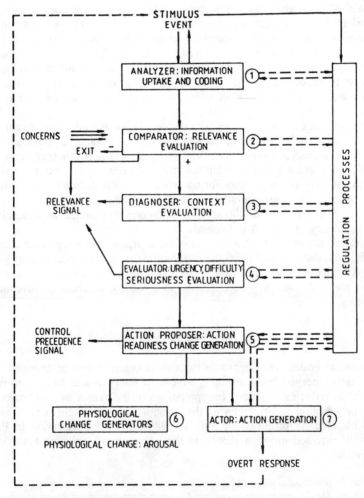

Figure 1 Frijda's (1986) emotional process model.

situation as a whole is appraised in terms of what the subject can or cannot do about it. The outcome is a precursor for entrance in the next stage: evaluation of urgency, seriousness, or difficulty. Depending on signals that indicate the degree of perceived control, action readiness change is generated. And eventually physiological change is effected in accordance with the action readiness mode generated before, ultimately mediating how the overt emotional response will become manifest.

Relevance evaluation of concern and subsequent evaluation of urgency and seriousness, with due reference to perceived control–lability, are thus the most decisive factors in eventuating the emotional response. An additional important derivation of the theory asserts that intensity of emotion is related to the strength of the underlying concern.

THE STATE–TRAIT ANXIETY DISTINCTION IN RELATION TO ASSESSMENT OF INTERVENTIONS

The applicability of Frijda's (1986) model to the problem of trait anxiety changes shall be addressed next. A preliminary methodological matter concerns the status of state and trait anxiety in systematic intervention studies (Spielberger, Gorsuch, & Lushene, 1970). In any intervention study in which a control group acts as a comparable reference group, in order to ascertain between-group differences of trait anxiety decrements due to the net effect of an experimental manipulation, a methodological problem pertains to the assessment of the reported alterations in trait anxiety levels. Given a stable level of trait anxiety as the baseline score, marking a divergent score after the experimental manipulation presupposes a learning process in the subject, mediated by repetitious reappraisals of potentially threatening stimuli in real-life situations (Spielberger, 1972).

Whatever the efficacy of the intervention strategy may have been, a retrospective evaluation necessarily implicates that the subject engages in a sort of reappraisal of his own functioning in diverse threat-provoking situations. The extent to which state anxiety was actually experienced in these situations ultimately leads the subject to conclude whether he or she has indeed attained trait anxiety changes.

To put it another way: An overall evaluation of experienced state anxiety levels during the manipulation, or the follow-up period that is after the commencement of the intervention and prior to the assessment date, to a large extent determines the newly reported trait anxiety outcomes. This reasoning implies that as long as a newly acquired stable trait anxiety level has not yet been firmly established, the causal chain of events is partially the reverse of what is generally depicted in overall anxiety models (Spielberger, 1972). The labile intermediary state during the intervention period in which gradual changes in the direction of a newly acquired trait anxiety level are engendered point to cognitive reappraisals of one's own functioning that are based on the actual experience of state anxiety in diverse situations. The foregoing signifies that in applying the emotion process model to clarify alterations in trait anxiety, it suffices in the first instance to restrict the analysis to state anxiety changes.

TRAIT ANXIETY CHANGES OF DISPOSITIONAL
HYPERVENTILATORS

A flowchart is presented in Figure 2 to illustrate the disrupting influence of excessive hyperventilatory breathing on psychological functioning. According to this schematic representation, dispositional hyperventilation is a concomitant of trait anxiety that strongly hampers an individual's coping capability in stressful situations.

Figure 3 shows the extremely high levels of trait anxiety and neurosomatic instability of hyperventilators that were found in our study (Grossman, de Swart, & Defares, 1985). From an emotion theory perspective, other factors should also be taken into account, such as the significance of concerns. As previously indicated, the concept of concern is a core construct within emotion theory for explaining observed alterations in emotional states. In describing the conditions that influence the anxiety status of an individual, an ethological frame of reference should be adopted.

A causal analysis in which the antecedents of concerns are elucidated serves to reveal the crucial steps of the emotional change process. What are the concerns of severe hyperventilators who suffer from excessive trait anxiety? The dynamics of the hyperventilation syndrome depicted in Figure 4 offer a possible explanation. This model suggests that severe symptoms may materialize, mediated by a substantial drop in carbon dioxide in the blood and a shift in acidity level in the direction of alkalosis. Physical complaints like dizziness, palpitations, feeling a lump in the throat, and insecurity of movement and posture may also lead to a sense of alienation, disorientation, and contact loss (Defares & Grossman, 1988).

A tendency to resort to rigid preoccupation with one's own physical deficiencies may also complicate the picture (Lum, 1981). An implicit primary concern is the strong desire to regain contact with one's environment in order to attain a state

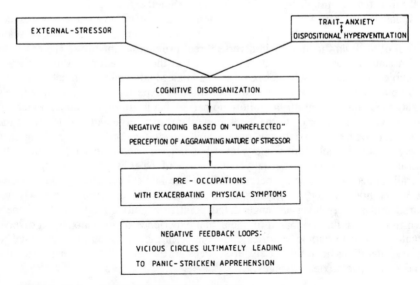

Figure 2 Trait anxiety of dispositional hyperventilators.

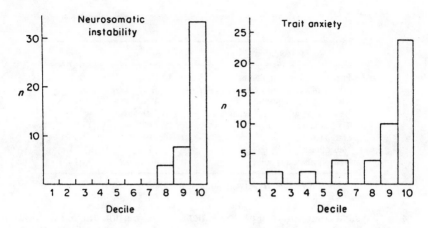

Figure 3 Neurosomatic instability and trait anxiety of hyperventilators

of physical well-being. Because the experience of a debilitating state is in sharp contrast with the intensity of the relevant concerns, extremely negative appraisals ensue, resulting in high levels of anxiety. Biofeedback therapy can be directed toward restoring the subject's physical well-being. In guiding a return to normal respiration, biofeedback therapy ameliorates the physical complaints, which are the crucial antecedents of psychological dysfunctioning.

The results of an intervention study are presented in Table 1. As carbon dioxide levels are normalized, psychosomatic complaints largely disappear (Defares & Grossman, 1988). Normalization of physical complaints not only induces a sense of physical well-being, but also permits an individual to regain contact with the environment and engage in interactive communications. Because of the influence

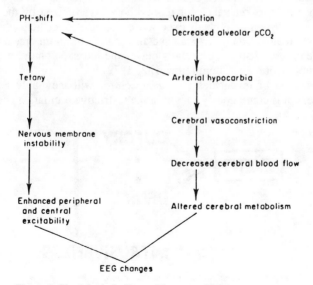

Figure 4 Physiological effects of hyperventilation.

Table 1 Physiological and psychological effects of biofeedback
intervention

Effects	F	p
Psychosomatic complaints	13.288	.001
HVPT pCO$_2$ (5 min)	8.133	.007
Recovery capnogram	6.408	.015
Baseline breathing frequency	8.749	.005
Trait anxiety	3.914	.05
State anxiety	4.519	.039
Neuroticism	3.758	.021
Neurosomatic instability	4.480	.04

Note. HVPT = Hyperventilation provocation test.

of the physical condition on a person's mental state, carbon dioxide restoration in a very direct fashion induces a weakening of the intensity of the relevant concerns and an attenuation of the emotional process that results in ·a reduction in state anxiety.

EFFECTS OF TREATMENT OF THE STRESS RESPONSE SYNDROME ON CHANGES IN TRAIT ANXIETY

A schematic representation of Horowitz's (1976) stress response syndrome is presented in Figure 5. The victim of this syndrome oscillates between intrusions (i.e. vivid reexperiencing of the hazardous event) and a state of debilitating numbness, due to denial and passive avoidance. This deplorable state of affairs induces extreme vulnerability and helplessness as important antecedents of the emotion process (Lazarus, 1981; Peterson & Seligman, 1984; Seligman, 1975).

Which concern bears relevance for those who are victimized by the stress response syndrome? When individuals experience a state of utter helplessness, they find themselves in an existential crisis. The anticipation of an imminent danger or the experience of utter distress, especially during the intrusion phase, might evoke fantasies of annihilation and doom (Horowitz, 1979).

The mobilization of tendencies to regain control will inevitably be in vain, because the person is continuously caught in the restrictive oscillation of intrusions

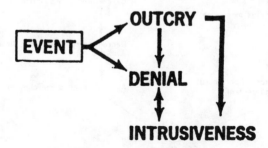

Figure 5 Stress response syndrome according to
Horowitz (1976).

and lethargic numbness. The implications are obvious: A strong impetus for regaining existential control will sensitize an individual to stimulus events that might affect his or her vulnerability.

A sharp discrepancy between an emotional state and the condition for satisfying the concern actualizes negative evaluations and aggravates the subjective appraisal of uncontrollability. These factors set the stage for the completion of the emotion process, ultimately resulting in heightened state anxiety levels.

Now, coming to our own research, an overview of the stressors is presented in Table 2.

In fact our study comprised a systematic comparison of three different therapies: trauma desensitization, hypnotherapy, and a psychodynamic approach along the lines developed by Horowitz.

In assessing therapy effects of the treatment procedure, a waiting-list group acted as a control or reference group. A systematic comparison is based on the differences between pre- and posttreatment measurements. Discrepancy scores of the treatment group are compared with discrepancy scores of the control group for both before–after and before–follow-up comparisons.

For the present discussion it suffices to present the outcomes of trauma desensitization (Brom, Kleber, & Defares, 1989). Because of the gradual diminution of the impact of the original stressor and the subject's simultaneous recoding that the harmfulness of the event was definitely passed, a direct effect was exerted on the alternation of intrusions and denial. Dramatic improvements on the Dutch version of the Impact of Event scale, devised by Horowitz, were ascertained by means of T statistics for before and after comparisons of treatment and waiting-list groups ($p < .01$).

This result is all the more significant because the statistical analysis was subjected to a rigorous procedure using residual gain scores.

This outcome evidently signifies that trauma desensitization very effectively alleviated the main antecedents of helplessness and concomitant uncontrollability: intrusion and numbness. By the same token, reduction of helplessness augments the satisfaction condition of the concern, or, to state it differently, amelioration of the precariousness of the concern for regaining existential equilibrium is conducive for positive evaluation of seriousness and difficulty, thus tempering the strength of the emotional response, which factually amounts to lowering of state anxiety and, over time, trait anxiety. This was indeed found in our study, because the outcomes of T tests for before–after and before–follow-up comparisons of treatment and waiting-list groups proved to be significant on the .05 level.

Table 2 Severe stressors of subjects in the intervention study

Loss of beloved person or victimization due to:

- Murder or suicide, $n = 17$ (15%)
- Traffic accidents, $n = 17$ (15%)
- Acute illness, $n = 16$ (14%)
- Brief illness, $n = 15$ (13%)
- Chronic illness, $n = 18$ (16%)
- Violent offenses, $n = 19$ (17%)
- Miscellaneous, $n = 10$ (9%)

Total $n = 112$

THE TREATMENT OF STUTTERING AND ANXIETY CHANGES

The third approach to be dealt with relates to the impact of a major speech deficiency: stuttering. Stuttering is a handicap that strongly hinders interpersonal communication. Subjects who suffer from speech disturbances of this kind are extremely sensitive about becoming the victim of negative judgments of other people (Bloodstein, 1969; Webster, 1980).

What are the salient concerns of the stutterer? The desire to communicate smoothly, exempt of judgmental stress, seems the most dominant concern. The conspicuous failure to express oneself properly is an antecedent of event evaluations, which deviate from the satisfaction condition of the concern.

To tackle the problem, in this case, the treatment was based on principles derived from behavior therapy. For reasons of brevity, specifics are left out; let it suffice to say that the treatment was mainly focused on the speech deficiencies themselves. Sessions were devoted to regular exercises, to promote fluency of speech. Reinforcement procedures were applied in such a manner that self-regulatory behavior with reference to erroneous speech and reading difficulties would be enhanced. Subjects were instructed to ward off negative self-appraisals, if these might arise, subsequent to stuttering or faulty utterances.

Basically, then, the therapy aimed at improvement of the subject's condition, focusing on the speech disturbances in a direct and straightforward manner.

What did the intervention accomplish? Aside from considerable improvements with reference to speech fluency, therapeutic gain also comprised other aspects of stuttering such as reading aloud and the assignment to give oral comments on presented cartoons.

This outcome not only mitigates the intensity of the relevant concern, but also moderates urgency of appraisals regarding judgmental stress. Both aspects are of decisive significance as to how the emotion process further unfolds. According to the emotion process model, the overt emotional response, presently state and trait anxiety, will eventually be less vehement.

Empirical outcomes seemed to corroborate the aforementioned reasoning. For all three variables—speech fluency, reading, and oral comments—discrepancy scores of baseline–posttreatment comparisons of treatment and waiting-list groups amounted to significant differences on the .05 level, two-tailed. Further analysis based on comparisons of follow-up data of the treatment group and postmeasurement data of the waiting-list group yields a significant difference on the .01 level, indicating that elapse of time even enhances therapeutic gain.

As for the effects on trait anxiety, discrepancy scores of the treatment group exceeded those of the waiting-list group significantly on the .05 level, thus establishing a clear-cut effect of the treatment.

TYPE A BEHAVIOR, SOMATIC COMPLAINTS, AND ANXIETY CHANGES

Classically, Type A individuals are depicted as though outside pressures are continually bearing down on them, are engaged in ambitious striving, and suffer from impatience and perpetual restlessness. Furthermore, they feel uneasy about relaxing, engage themselves in obstinate behaviors to ward off what they perceive to be blocking agents that stand in the way, and devote all their energy to gain control over their environment (Friedman & Rosenman, 1974).

Whenever an external stressor remains beyond the subject's control, especially subsequent to fierce attempts to master the situation, exhaustive helplessness may temporarily ensue, as Glass (1977) demonstrated in his work on the impact of unpredictable stressors. To what extent do the original suppositions still hold?

The concept is still under skeptical scrutiny and theories vary from sheer denial of the legitimacy of the Type A classification to the introduction of various subdistinctions, with strong emphasis on situational determinants (Burke & Weir, 1980; Cooper, Detre, & Weiss, 1981; Dembroski, MacDougall, Elliot, & Buell, 1983; Mathews, 1982).

Another hot issue pertains to subtypifications: delicate versus more robust Type A individuals, or those susceptible to angina versus subjects who run the risk of full-fledged infarction (Mathews, 1982).

Interestingly, Friedman and Rosenman in the pioneer phase traced the historical roots of the Type A distinction to Sir William Osler, a famous cardiologist. Osler argued on the basis of commonsense psychology that "It is not the delicate neurotic person, who is prone to angina, but the robust, the vigorous in mind and body, the keen and ambitious man, whose engine indicator is always "at full speed ahead" (1910, p. 696).

Today judgments are more subtle, and ironically there seems to be abundant evidence that, more and more, anxious, less stable and vigorous, yet ambitious and hostile Type A individuals are entering the scene of competitive struggle. In other words, psychosomatic instability, anxiety, and neuroticism are, at least in a substantial proportion of Type A persons, intricately intermingled with the strong urge to become the A-1 person (Appelbaum, 1981).

In line with an assessment put forward by Karen Mathews, it is our contention that the condition of Type A persons, typified by excessive striving, time urgency, inability to relax, anger, and inclination to lose control, is strongly worsened if they also suffer from high anxiety levels and psychosomatic instability (Mathews, 1982).

The Intervention Study

Type A individuals who attained high scores on the Dutch version of the Jenkins Activity Scale (JAS), introduced in the Netherlands by Appels, were admitted for participation in our intervention study, provided they also suffered from psychosomatic instability (Appels, De Haes, & Schuurman, 1979; Ros, Winnubst, Defares, Joppen, & van Leeuwen, 1985). The subjects were employees in industrial settings in the eastern part of Holland, mostly male blue-collar workers, with an average age of 42 years. Prior to assignment to the experimental and control groups, precautions were taken not to include subjects with psychosomatic complaints that might be caused by physical ailments. Of 107 potential subjects, 74 met these criteria; 28 were randomly assigned to the treatment group, and 16 to a waiting-list control group. Although the size of the control group was relatively small, it was within the range of statistical requirements.

The relaxation training intervention consisted mainly of exercises based on

Jacobson's (1988) muscle relaxation technique. The subjects were instructed to practice the relaxation exercises daily at regular time intervals. The core of the intervention included procedures aimed at changing the habitual cognitive appraisal of stressors, particularly with respect to the threat of loss of control. Cognitive restructuring was further supplemented with elements derived from Meichenbaum's (1977) inoculation technique, and included use of behavioral rehearsal and rational emotive treatment procedures (Ellis, 1970).

Correlations for the total sample of the JAS with the pretreatment trait anxiety and anger measures, psychosomatic complaints, and other relevant variables are reported in Table 3. It is worth noting that average baseline anxiety scores approximated the scores of population samples suffering from neuroticism.

The treatment outcomes corroborated the vulnerability of this specific sample. In the present context, only the effects of the intervention on trait anxiety and psychosomatic complaints shall be considered. Comparison of treatment and control groups on pretreatment and posttreatment tests of trait anxiety and psychosomatic complaints are reported in Table 4, which shows that the scores for the treatment group decreased on both measures, whereas the control group was unchanged.

Discussion

It seems plausible that Type A persons who suffer from psychosomatic complaints are led by a concern for physical well-being. If a person is confronted with symptoms, signaling that ill health might insidiously materialize, and is simultaneously alert not to lose control, then a strong desire to restore physical well-being is generated. In considering what aspects of the therapeutic intervention may have contributed to lower the concern about physical well-being, it seems that relaxation training may have attained a dual effect. On the one hand, arousal levels are reduced, directly soothing the subject's heightened activation. In addition, the subject cognitively reinterprets his or her health state, not only because disagreeable symptoms gradually vanish, but also because it is noticed that restoration of defective functioning augments vigor and competence. Thus, the improved state of the organism indirectly facilitates the subjective perception of controllability.

Controllability is of extreme importance for the Type A person. In contrast to

Table 3 Correlations of Jenkins Activity Scale with other measures for the total sample: Pretreatment mesurements before assignments to either treatment or control group

Measure	r	F	n^a
Trait anxiety (Spielberger)	.39	.001	63
Anger scale (Spielberger)			
Total	.48	.000	64
Temperament	.42	.000	64
Reaction	.38	.001	64
Somatic complaints	.43	.002	73
Neuroticism	.37	.001	73
Grievance	.30	.005	73

$^a n$ varies because of missing values in some cases.

Table 4 Comparison of pre- and posttreatment measurements for treatment and control groups (Type As)

Time of measurement	Trait anxiety[a]				Psychosomatic complaints[b]			
	Treatment (n = 24)		Control (n = 16)		Treatment (n = 24)		Control (n = 9)	
	M	SD	M	SD	M	SD	M	SD
Pretreatment	40.21	8.81	42.07	7.57	1.52	.34	1.63	.36
Posttreatment	36.46	6.83	43.40	7.79	1.29	.25	1.67	.59

[a]$F = 5.32, p = .03$
[b]$F = 4.65, p = .04.$

victims of the stress response syndrome, this need for controllability does not pertain to preservation of existential equilibrium, but to maintenance of competence in demanding situations. In terms of the emotion process model, the salient concern of the Type A person is to maintain competence at all costs. When overt anxiety responses are elicited, this results from the appraisal of seriousness and urgency of actual demands that may thwart controllability.

In accordance with the foregoing analysis, attempts to alter the coping strategies of vulnerable Type A persons should focus primarily on their attitudes toward threat to control in demanding situations. Recoding the harmfulness of the potential loss of control as more benign than previously suspected would mitigate evaluations of seriousness of the threat and shift the threshold of perception of defective controllability in a positive direction. Consequently, subsequent stages of the emotion process further reduce overt state anxiety responses. The preceding analysis is summarized schematically in Figure 6.

SPECIFIC CONCERNS AS GUIDANCE FOR ADEQUATE INTERVENTIONS

Figure 7 schematically depicts the general conclusion that lessening of concerns is a crucial intermediary step to engender furthering of the emotion process. The nature of the specific concern that relates to a particular stressor may guide the implementations of adequate interventions. It should be emphasized that the analysis presented in Figure 7 does not pretend to be exhaustive. It is hoped that insights derived from general emotion theory can be fruitfully applied in unraveling the determinants of changes in trait anxiety. The search for concerns that underlie anxiety responses that occur in diverse settings may prove to be a promising strategy for devising the most adequate interventions.

SUMMARY

A legitimate question to be addressed in trait anxiety research is the assessment of basic underlying variables that contribute to the maintenance of given trait anxiety levels. It is contended in this chapter that one should adopt a multimodel approach with reference to specific intrapsychic preconditions related to specific previous experiences in order to unravel the cause of trait anxiety. The rational for this stand stems partly from the outcome of several intervention studies, involving deliberate attempts to reduce trait anxiety levels over time. It was found that very different approaches proved to be effective in attaining substantial reductions of trait anxiety levels. The intervention studies were carried out in cooperation with the present author. Four different studies are briefly summarized:

- An intervention study in which psychophysiological functioning was steered via a biofeedback procedure;
- A study involving psychotherapeutic interventions (trauma desensitization, and a psychoanalytic approach along the lines proposed by Horowitz, 1979) with victims suffering from the stress response syndrome;
- An intervention study in which anxiety levels of subjects suffering from a

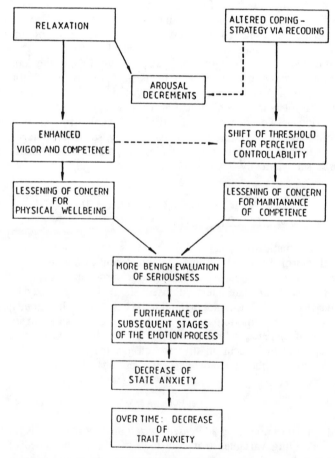

Figure 6 Causal chain of state/trait anxiety decrements in vulnerable Type A persons.

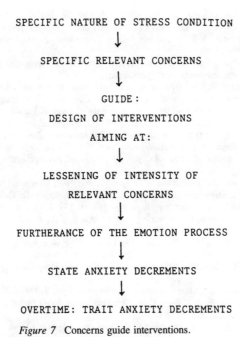

SPECIFIC NATURE OF STRESS CONDITION
↓
SPECIFIC RELEVANT CONCERNS
↓
GUIDE:
DESIGN OF INTERVENTIONS
AIMING AT:
↓
LESSENING OF INTENSITY OF
RELEVANT CONCERNS
↓
FURTHERANCE OF THE EMOTION PROCESS
↓
STATE ANXIETY DECREMENTS
↓
OVERTIME: TRAIT ANXIETY DECREMENTS

Figure 7 Concerns guide interventions.

speech disorder (stuttering) was altered in a positive direction by applying a behaviorally oriented intervention strategy;

• A fourth study, mainly using cognitive recoding of threatening situations, aimed at enhancing the coping capability of the individual (this led to a substantial reduction of trait anxiety with Type A individuals).

In order to account for the outcomes of these studies, an integrative theoretical model derived from Frijda (1986) is presented that may highlight the differential causation of trait anxiety. An important aspect of the model involves the differential significance of concerns. The nature of the specific concern that related to a specific stressor may guide the implementation of adequate interventions.

REFERENCES

Appelbaum, S. H. (1981). *Stress management.* London: Aspen.
Appels, A., De Haes, W. S., & Schuurman, J. (1979). Een test ter meting van "coronary behavior pattern" Type A. *Nederlands Tijdschrift voor de Psychologie, 34,* 181–188.
Bloodstein, O. (1969). *A handbook on stuttering.* Chicago: Easter Seal Society.
Brom, D., Kleber, R. J., & Defares, P. B. (1989). Brief psychotherapy for posttraumatic stress disorders. *Journal of Consulting and Clinical Psychology, 5,* 607–612.
Burke, R., & Weir, T. (1980). The Type A experience: Occupational and life demands, satisfaction and well being. *Journal of Human Stress, 6,* 28–38.
Cooper, T., Detre, T., & Weiss, S. M. (1981). Coronary-prone behavior and coronary heart disease: A critical review. *Circulation, 63,* 1199–1215.
Defares, P. B., & Grossman, P. (1988). Hyperventilation, anxiety and coping with stress. In C. D. Spielberger, I. G. Sarason, & P. B. Defares (Eds.), *Stress and anxiety, volume 11* (pp. 127–140). Washington, DC: Hemisphere.

Dembroski, Th. M., Mac Dougall, J. M., Elliot, R. S., & Buell, J. C. (1983). A social-psychophysiological model of biobehavioral factors and coronary heart disease. In C. D. Spielberger, I. G. Sarason, & P. B. Defares (Eds.), *Stress and anxiety, volume 9* (pp. 177–190). Washington, DC: Hemisphere.

Ellis, A. (1970). *The essence of rational psychotherapy: A comprehensive approach to treatment.* New York: Institute for Advanced Study in Psychotherapy.

Friedman, M., & Rosenman, R. M. (1974). *Type A behavior and your heart.* Greenwich, CT: Fawcet.

Frijda, N. H. (1986). *The emotions.* Cambridge, England: Cambridge University Press.

Glass, D. C. (1977). *Behavior patterns, stress and coronary disease.* Hillsdale, NJ: Erlbaum.

Grossman, P., de Swart, J. C. G., & Defares, P. B. (1985). A controlled study of breathing therapy for treatment of hyperventilation syndrome. *Journal of Psychosomatic Research, 29,* 49–58.

Horowitz, M. J. (1976). *Stress response syndromes.* New York: Jason Aronson.

Horowitz, M. J. (1979). *States of mind: Analysis of change in psychotherapy.* New York: Plenum Press.

Jacobson, E. (1988). *Progressive relaxation.* Chicago: University of Chicago Press.

Lazarus, R. S. (1981). The stress and coping paradigm. In C. Eisdorfer, D. Cohen, A. Kleinman, & P. Maxim (Eds.), *Models for clinical psychopathology* (pp. 177–214). New York: Spectrum.

Lum, L. C. (1981). Hyperventilation and anxiety state. *Journal of the Royal Society of Medicine, 74,* 1–4.

Mathews, K. A. (1982). Psychological perspectives on the Type A behavior pattern. *Psychological Bulletin, 2,* 293–323.

Meichenbaum, D. (1977). *Cognitive behavior modification: An integrative approach.* New York: Plenum.

Osler, W. (1910). The Lumleian lectures on angina pectoris. *Lancet, 1,* 696–700, 839–844, 974–977.

Peterson, C., & Seligman, M. E. P. (1984). Causal explanation as a risk factor for depression: Theory and evidence. *Psychological Review, 91,* 347–374.

Ros, W. J. G., Winnubst, J. A. M., Defares, P. B., Joppen, J. G. G. M., & van Leeuwen, G. M. (1985). *Omgaan met stress* [Coping with stress: An intervention study with Type A subjects] (pp. 1–69). Nijmegen: Stress Groep Nijmegen.

Seligman, M. E. P. (1975). *Helplessness.* San Francisco: Freeman.

Spielberger, C. D. (1972). Current trends in theory and research on anxiety. In C. D. Spielberger (Ed.), *Anxiety: Current trends in theory and research* (Vol. 1, pp. 3–19). New York: Academic Press.

Spielberger, C. D., Gorsuch, R. L., & Lushene, R. E. (1970). *Manual for the State-Trait Anxiety Inventory.* Palo Alto, CA: Consulting Psychologists Press.

Webster, R. L. (1980). Establishment of fluent speech in stutterers. In F. J. McGuigan, W. E. Sime, & J. Macdonald Wallace (Eds.), *Stress and tension control* (pp. 197–206). New York: Plenum Press.

10

Influence of Coping Dispositions and Danger-Related Information on Emotional and Coping Reactions of Individuals Anticipating an Aversive Event

Heinz Walter Krohne and Joachim Fuchs
Johannes Gutenberg University
Mainz, Germany

THEORETICAL FOUNDATIONS

Numerous studies in the field of coping research have examined how people deal with threat-relevant information in aversive situations and which cognitive and emotional processes can be observed under those circumstances.

These studies differ according to the type of information that is presented to the individuals while they await the aversive event. Some experiments use cues that allow a temporal prediction or an instrumental control of the aversive event (cf., e.g., Averill, O'Brien, & DeWitt, 1977; Averill & Rosenn, 1972; Kohlmann, 1990; Miller, 1979). Other studies offer the subjects more complex informative items, in which case numerous aspects of information are of interest and are varied. Thus Miller and Mangan (1983), for instance, investigated the effects of extensive, detailed information versus brief information given to patients prior to surgery on stress indices manifested by these same patients. Johnson (1975) as well as Calvert-Boyanowsky and Leventhal (1975) focused on the diverse effects of information that related either to emotions and sensations or to objective features of an aversive event. Finally, Cornelius and Averill (1980) used cue-relevant versus cue-irrelevant information during the anticipation phase preceding an aversive stimulus.

In addition to the type of information that is presented, personality dispositions (such as coping styles, anxiety, and locus of control) should exert a significant amount of influence on the way a person deals with information and on the cognitions and emotions resulting thereof (cf. Krohne, 1986, 1989; Miller, 1980). In this context it is of special interest to examine the interactive effects of information presented and personality dispositions on cognitive and emotional variables. The analysis of these relationships was the focus of our investigation.

We would like to thank Carl-Walter Kohlmann for his valuable comments on an earlier draft of this chapter.

The theoretical basis of the present study is the model of dispositionally determined coping modes, as outlined in more detail by Krohne (1986, 1989). This model focuses on those (cognitive or intrapsychic, respectively) coping strategies that aim at *changing the perception of a threatening event,* that is, the subjective representation of objective elements inherent in an aversive situation. Such strategies include, among others, attentional diversion, reinterpretation, or selective information search.

These cognitive coping strategies may be combined into two classes of higher order strategies: (a) attempts to obtain information relating to a threatening event and (b) avoidance of threat-related cues. The former class is defined as *vigilance* and the latter as *cognitive avoidance,* based on the two central concepts used to analyze cognitive aspects of the coping process that have been described by many researchers (Horowitz, 1979; Krohne, 1978; Krohne & Rogner,1982; Lazarus, 1966; Lazarus & Launier, 1978; Miller, 1980; Roth & Cohen, 1986; Suls & Fletcher, 1985).

These two classes of strategies describe actual stress-related operations as well as interindividual differences with respect to the habitualized preference (i.e., the frequency) of specific coping strategies. Regarding the habitual aspect, it is postulated that the dimensions cognitive avoidance and vigilance vary independently of one another (see Figure 1).

The model further postulates that subjective uncertainty is the central anxiety elicitor for persons displaying a high degree of vigilance. This uncertainty is due to specific aspects of ambiguity inherent in danger situations, such as the possibility of being surprised by an unpleasant event. These persons attempt to reduce the anxiety by employing vigilant behavior (e.g., intensified information searching or construing a scheme related to the anticipated confrontation). Accordingly, for persons high in cognitive avoidance the essential threat is the emotional arousal that is triggered by cues prior to the confrontation with an aversive event. These persons try to deal with this threat by diverting attention from these cues. Because the dimension vigilance describes persons who are stressed in varying degrees by subjective uncertainty in an aversive situation, this variable can also be defined as "intolerance of uncertainty or negative surprise." Correspondingly, the dimension cognitive avoidance differentiates persons who are stressed by the experience of emotional arousal. Therefore, we can also call this dimension "intolerance of emotional arousal" (Krohne, 1989).

Assuming the independence of both the dimensions of habitualized coping, four configurations can be distinguished. These groups are called *coping modes* and constitute the central unit of analysis in many of our studies. First, persons with high vigilance and low avoidance are called "sensitizers." They are primarily stressed by experienced uncertainty in a situation of threat and hence show an increased tendency over diverse situations of threat to seek out information about the stressor in order to construe a scheme of the anticipated confrontation.

Second, persons with high cognitive avoidance and low vigilance are named "repressers." They feel stressed mainly by the possibility of strong emotional arousal in situations of threat and therefore relatively consistently display the tendency to pay little attention to threat-relevant characteristics of situations.

Third, persons with high vigilance and high avoidance are called "anxious persons." They are stressed by uncertainty in aversive situations as well as by the emotional arousal triggered by cues. This is supposed to elicit *instable* coping

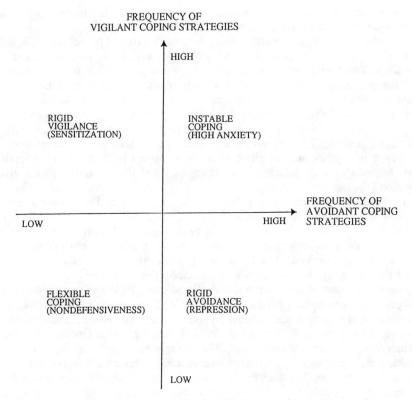

Figure 1 A two-dimensional conceptualization of habitual cognitive avoidance and
vigilance.

behavior. When trying to reduce the uncertainty that they experience as stressful
by increased preoccupation with the stressor, they simultaneously increase their
emotional arousal to a level exceeding their tolerance. If they turn away from the
stressor in order to reduce anxiety, then their uncertainty increases together with
the strain resulting from it.

Fourth, persons with low vigilance and low avoidance are called "nondefensives." In a situation of threat, they are oriented neither toward dealing with the
anticipated aversive confrontation in an essentially cognitive manner, nor toward
avoiding the possibility of emotional arousal at any cost. Instead, they preferably
try to affect the situation instrumentally. This can also include increased information search, if this enhances the subject's control over the situation.

Thus, within the two-dimensional system these four coping modes can be defined by the following scores on the dimensions vigilance and cognitive avoidance:
sensitization—high vigilance, low avoidance scores; *repression*—high avoidance,
low vigilance scores; *nondefensiveness*—low scores on both scales; and *high
anxiety*—high scores on both scales. Whereas the definitions of the modes sensitization and repression are unequivocal, another dimension should actually be introduced in order to measure nondefensiveness and high anxiety. This dimension
should represent the systematic relationship between the person's behavior and the

coping requirements in a stress situation. This relationship is expected to be high in the case of nondefensive persons, and low for anxious persons.

The recently developed Mainz Coping Inventory (MCI; Krohne, Rösch & Kürsten, 1989; Krohne, Wigand, & Kiehl, 1985) permits the separate assessment of the dimensions vigilance (VIG) and cognitive avoidance (CAV). In the manner of stimulus-response inventories used in anxiety research (cf. Endler, Hunt, & Rosenstein, 1962), it contains descriptions of potentially anxiety-evoking situations (see also Miller, 1987). Depending on the topic to be investigated (such as coping during surgery or in the course of examinations), only situations that involve physical threat (MCI-P) or ego threat (MCI-E) are taken into consideration. A repertoire of vigilant and cognitive avoidant strategies is assigned to each situation. Subjects indicate which of the strategies listed they would use in a given situation (Figure 2).

The present study analyzed the instrumental, cognitive, and emotional reactions of persons of the aforementioned four coping modes while awaiting an aversive event. When persons of different coping modes anticipate such an event, differences between them with respect to the use of threat-relevant information and to their emotional reactions should emerge. Thus in the present study we hypothesized the following: Repressers would constantly manifest little cognitive and instrumental orientation toward the threat-related cues. In keeping with central assumptions relating to the operation of this mode (Lazarus, 1966), we furthermore postulated that despite this attentional diversion the autonomic reactions of repressers should be comparably high (Asendorpf & Scherer, 1983; Gudjonsson, 1981; Weinberger, Schwartz, & Davidson, 1979; Weinstein, Averill, Opton, & Lazarus, 1968). Sensitizers were hypothesized to constantly focus their attention on threat-relevant information. The question as to whether this information contributes to an increase in controllability of the situation was presumed to be of secondary importance. Rather, it is of central significance to sensitizers to be able to construe a "scheme" of the aversive confrontation in such situations. Nondefensives would be oriented toward the information that was presented only if they were under the impression that the controllability over the situation could be increased by doing so. Anxious persons would oscillate in an unsystematic manner between diversion and information search.

METHOD

Subjects

A total of 62 female students enrolled at Mainz University in the Federal Republic of Germany, whose ages ranged from 18 to 39 years, participated in the experiment. Participation was on a voluntary basis; there was no pay. Depending on the scores that subjects obtained on the dimensions CAV and VIG of the MCI, 10 persons each were assigned to the groups of sensitizers, repressers, nondefensives, or anxious subjects. Subjects whose score was located in the median range of either dimension were not taken into consideration for the rest of the experiment. Subjects in each group were then randomly divided into two groups of equal size and assigned to the experimental conditions of "valid" or "redundant" information. Next, the t test was used to check every coping mode to find out whether

Imagine that you haven't been to the dentist for quite a long time. You are now sitting in his waiting room because you are having problems with your teeth.

In this situation ...

I remember previous unpleasant dental treatments.   VIG

I tell myself: "It won't be all that bad."   CAV

I try to look at the patients who were treated
ahead of me to see whether it was an unpleasant
procedure.   VIG

I try not to think about the treatment and, instead,
I read the magazines that are on display.   CAV

I read the leaflets informing about diseases of the
teeth and treatment procedures that are on display
in the waiting room. I try to imagine what exactly
the dentist will do to my teeth.   VIG

I tell myself: " I can trust my dentist. He'll find
out what's causing the problem and he'll give me the
best treatment possible for my teeth."   CAV

Figure 2 Sample items of the Mainz Coping Inventory (MCI): VIG = vigilance,
CAV = cognitive avoidance.

the subjects of either experimental condition differed from each other in terms of their CAV or VIG scores. This was not the case.

Experimental Conditions

Subjects anticipated a very unpleasant loud noise exactly 3 min after the beginning of the experiment. While awaiting this aversive event they had the choice of either listening to information about the impending stimulus or listening to music. Depending on the experimental condition, the information was either useful ("valid") or of no value ("redundant") in terms of increasing controllability over the impending event. Although no informative item permitted an instrumental (primary) control over the aversive stimulus, valid information did show the subjects ways of reducing the aversive character of the situation in another manner (secondary control). (Example of a valid informative item: "It's best if you open your mouth slightly already a couple of seconds before the stimulus is presented.") Redundant items contained references of a general nature referring to the noise event without suggestions regarding secondary control (e.g., "As a relatively artificial noise is involved, there is hardly any way of comparing it with unpleasant noises encountered in everyday life").

In a pretest, the question of whether either group of informative items differed from the other in degree of rated usefulness or other coping-related aspects had been clarified. In this context, 25 subjects different from the experimental subjects rated all items on a 4-point scale as to whether they were "useful and helpful," "distracting," or "soothing." By means of the sign test, significant differences between valid and redundant items concerning rated usefulness, but not regarding their distracting or soothing effect, could be ascertained. Thus, the items differed from each other only in terms of appraised secondary control of the stressor, and not where the support of other coping reactions was concerned.

Dependent Variables

Listening to information versus music. For every minute of the 3-minute anticipation interval, the amount of time subjects spent listening to either information or music was measured in seconds. Subjects could oscillate at wish between the two channels. Because these choices were complementary events, it sufficed to register the choice of information (INFSEC).

Cognitive coping reactions. In order to assess the cognitive coping reactions during the anticipation interval, immediately after the experiment subjects were confronted with a modified form (Monat, 1976) of the Attention Deployment Scale (ADS; Monat, Averill, & Lazarus, 1972). The scale contains four items each measuring either a vigilant or a cognitive avoidant orientation toward the stressor. Subjects were instructed to answer each item separately for the first, second, and last third of the anticipation time on a 4-point scale. The sum of the four vigilance items minus the sum of the four avoidance items (ADS) served as the score. Negative values thus indicated a preponderance of avoidant thoughts; positive values, a preponderance of vigilant ones.

Psychophysiological parameters. As indicators of psychophysiological arousal, heart rate (HR) and number of spontaneous electrodermal fluctuations (NSR) were registered. As tonic measures, difference values between the values of experimental phases and those of the resting phases were calculated. The resting value was based on the average of one baseline measurement each prior to and following the actual experiment.

To register HR a photoplethysmographic measuring procedure was used (Jennings et al., 1981; Schandry, 1981). The mean resulting from the measurements of the last 15 s of each minute in the pre- and postexperimental assessment of the resting condition (HRB) served as the baseline value. Four separate experimental

1. Preparation of the physiological measurements

2. Responding to the Mainz Coping Inventory (MCI)

3. Baseline measurement 1 (3 minutes)

4. Instruction

5. Anticipation of the aversive stimulus (3 minutes)

  Heart rate: Seconds 1-15 = HR 1, 45-60 = HR 2,
  105-120 = HR 3, 165-180 = HR 4.

  Spontaneous electrodermal fluctuations: Seconds
  1-30 = NSR 1, 30-60 = NSR2, 90-120 NSR 3,
  150-180 = NSR 4.

6. Presentation of the aversive stimulus (5 seconds)

7. Responding to the Attention-Deployment Scale (ADS)

8. Postexperimental assessments (PE 1 to 5)

9. Baseline measurement 2 (3 minutes)

Figure 3 Design and variables of the study.

values were obtained (see Figure 3): within the first 15 s after the beginning of the measurement (HR 1) as well as during the last 15 s of every minute of the 3-min anticipation phase (HR 2 through HR 4). The change value that was of actual interest (DHR) was calculated for every subject as the difference between the readings HR 1 through HR 4 and HRB.

In order to measure NSR (i.e., the short-term changes of skin conductance not related to a discernible stimulus), the frequency method was used. This means that the NSR occurring during a specific time span was counted. A minimal amplitude of 0.02 μS was chosen as the criterion for one spontaneous fluctuation (Vossel, 1990).

In all other respects, the procedure that was used to obtain the respective NSR values (NSR 1 to NSR 4, NSRB, and DNSR) was analogous to that used for HR. Because our electrodermal measure, in contrast to the registration of HR, was based on discrete and rare single events (the resting level is six to eight reactions per minute), a registration interval of 30 s instead of 15 s was chosen.

Postexperimental assessments. In a postexperimental interview subjects indicated on a 5-point scale how unpleasant the noise stimulus was (PE 1), whether the information was useful (PE 2), or distracted them from the aversive situation (PE 3), and whether the content of the information (PE 4) or the voice of the speaker (PE 5) had a calming effect.

Statistical Analysis

To test the influence of coping variables (vigilance and avoidance) and experimental conditions on the dependent variables, three-way analyses of variance (ANOVAs) were calculated. Vigilance and avoidance (high vs. low) served as the first and second independent variables, and experimental condition (valid vs. redundant information) constituted the third independent variable. In the case of those variables recorded several times, repeated measurement was added as the fourth independent variable. This latter had three levels in the case of the variables INFSEC and ADS, and four levels for the two psychophysiological measures DHR and DNSR. In the designs of repeated measurement, a correction of the degrees of freedom according to Greenhouse and Geisser (1959) was carried out.

In the case of significant effects, multiple comparisons of means between the various groups and time points were conducted by means of analysis of the single main effects and Scheffé tests.

Material and Experimental Procedure

The experiment was conducted in the soundproof cubicle of an experimental room at the Psychological Institute of Mainz University. Next to a comfortable armchair with a monitoring switch attached to its armrest there were a table, a monitor, and a set of headphones in the cubicle. Immediately after the subject's arrival, preparations were begun to record the physiological measures. Following the procedure described by Walschburger (1975), the skin areas were prepared for the conduction of electrodermal activity. For conduction, nonpolarizable Ag/AgCl-electrodes with a surface of $0.79\ cm^2$ were used. The readings were carried out with the help of the constant-voltage procedure (0.5 V) with a time constant of 5 s. The acuity of the instrument was $0.005\ \mu S$. In order to register HR, a photoplethysmograph was attached to the finger pad of the middle finger of the nondominant hand.

After this preparation, the subject filled out the MCI-P. Next, the subject was told that prior to the experiment the physiological resting values had to be registered. Without any further instructions regarding the actual experiment, baseline measurement 1 was carried out.

Subsequently, instructions regarding the way the experiment was to proceed (actual instructions about the monitor, headphones, and monitoring switch, and definition of the noise stimulus as unpleasant yet not painful) were given to the subjects by the experimenter. The instructions regarding the experiment were transmitted to the subjects via headphones. Parallel to the auditive instructions, a condensed form of the latter was presented on the monitor in print (audiovisual instruction). The trial started immediately after the instructions had been presented. During the total time of anticipating the aversive stimulus, the instructions remained on the screen. In addition, a digital clock kept time, indicating how much time was left until the stimulus would be displayed. Immediately after the 3-min anticipation phase, the stimulus was presented. This was a pure tone of 1000 Hz lasting 5 s with an amplitude of 0.9 V. When a measuring sensor was held between the earpieces, 100 dB (A) were measured. This means that the value was clearly below the pain threshold of 120 dB (A); on the other hand, such a tone is perceived as markedly unpleasant (cf. Terasaki, 1981).

After the experiment the subject responded to the ADS and the questionnaire regarding the postexperimental assessments. Next, baseline measurement 2 was carried out. Stimulus presentation and data registration were computerized and proceeded under automatic control.

RESULTS

First, a number of basic requirements had to be tested. In order to find out whether the experimental manipulation really induced stress, the mean values of the psychophysiological (pre- and postexperimental) baseline measurements (HRB and NSRB) were compared with the average values derived from the four experimental readings (HRE and NSRE). In each case, highly significant higher values were found in the experimental measurement (for both comparisons, $p < .001$). Furthermore, a nonsignificant correlation ($r = -.12$) between VIC and CAV demonstrated that the hypothesis of an independent variation of the dispositional coping dimensions vigilance and cognitive avoidance was true.

Table 1 shows the correlations among the psychophysiological, cognitive, and behavioral reactions (averaged across the separate measurements). The two psychophysiological parameters were highly correlated ($r = .47, p < .01$); the same applied to the cognitive (ADS) and behavioral (INFSEC) measures ($r = .42, p < .01$). Furthermore, HR was positively associated with vigilant cognitive coping ($r = .36, p < .05$) and information intake ($r = .28, p < .10$). Finally, NSR and vigilant orientation show a positive covariation ($r = .28, p < .10$).

Table 2 contains the results of the ANOVAs (F values and significance levels). A marginally significant main effect ($p < .08$) of the variable avoidance on the variable INFSEC could be observed. Persons high in avoidance spent less time

Table 1 Correlations among the aggregated state variables

	ADS[a]	DHR[b]	DNSR[c]
INFSEC[d]	.42***	.28*	.13
ADS		.36**	.28**
DHR			.47***

[a]Attention Deployment Scale (Monat, Averill, & Lazarus, 1972).
[b]Difference in heart rate.
[c]Difference in number of spontaneous electrodermal fluctuations.
[d]Choice of information.
*$p < .10$. **$p < .05$. ***$p < .01$.

Table 2 Results of the analyses of variance

Source of variation	F	p
Choice of information		
Vigilance (A)	<1	NS
Avoidance (B)	3.32	.08
Condition (C)	<1	NS
A × B	7.90	.01
A × C	<1	NS
B × C	1.84	NS
A × B × C	<1	NS
Time (D)	11.19	.00***
A × D	<1	NS
B × D	<1	NS
C × D	<1	NS
A × B × D	2.33	NS
A × C × D	<1	NS
B × C × D	3.04	.06*
A × B × C × D	<1	NS
Attention Deployment Scale		
Vigilance (A)	1.59	NS
Avoidance (B)	1.66	NS
Condition (C)	<1	NS
A × B	<1	NS
A × C	1.20	NS
B × C	<1	NS
A × B × C	<1	NS
Time (D)	3.19	.05**
A × D	1.19	NS
B × D	<1	NS
C × D	3.67	.04**
A × B × D	3.24	.05**
A × C × D	3.29	.05**
B × C × D	3.04	NS
A × B × C × D	<1	NS
Difference in heart rate		
Vigilance (A)	1.14	NS
Avoidance (B)	<1	NS
Condition (C)	4.03	.06
A × B	2.11	NS
A × C	<1	NS
B × C	<1	NS
A × B × C	8.17	.01
Time (D)	4.52	.01***
A × D	<1	NS
B × D	<1	NS
C × D	<1	NS
A × B × D	2.72	.05**
A × C × D	1.34	NS
B × C × D	<1	NS
A × B × C × D	1.30	NS

Table 2   Results of the analyses of variance (*continued*)

Source of variation	F	p
Difference in number of spontaneous electrodermal fluctuations		
Vigilance (A)	< 1	NS
Avoidance (B)	< 1	NS
Condition (C)	4.58	.04
A × B	3.69	.06
A × C	2.90	.10
B × C	3.69	.06
A × B × C	10.49	.00
Time (D)	3.78	.02**
A × D	< 1	NS
B × D	< 1	NS
C × D	2.27	.09*
A × B × D	1.66	NS
A × C × D	< 1	NS
B × C × D	< 1	NS
A × B × C × D	2.72	.05**
Noise unpleasant[a]		
Vigilance (A)	< 1	NS
Avoidance (B)	< 1	NS
Condition (C)	3.84	.06
A × B	1.84	NS
A × C	< 1	NS
B × C	< 1	NS
A × B × C	< 1	NS
Information useful[a]		
Vigilance (A)	3.70	.06
Avoidance (B)	< 1	NS
Condition (C)	< 1	NS
A × B	1.20	NS
A × C	1.20	NS
B × C	< 1	NS
A × B × C	< 1	NS
Information distracting[a]		
Vigilance (A)	3.04	.09
Avoidance (B)	< 1	NS
Condition (C)	13.65	.00
A × B	< 1	NS
A × C	< 1	NS
B × C	1.32	NS
A × B × C	2.56	NS
Information calming[a]		
Vigilance (A)	7.76	.01
Avoidance (B)	< 1	NS
Condition (C)	< 1	NS

(*Table continued on following page*)

Table 2 Results of the analyses of variance (continued)

Source of variation	F	p
Information calming[a]		
A × B	1.06	NS
A × C	2.81	NS
B × C	1.69	NS
A × B × C	4.13	NS
Voice soothing[a]		
Vigilance (A)	4.72	.04
Avoidance (B)	<1	NS
Condition (C)	<1	NS
A × B	<1	NS
A × C	<1	NS
B × C	1.23	NS
A × B × C	<1	NS

[a]Postexperimental assessment.
$*p < .10$, $**p < .05$, $***p < .01$ (Greenhouse-Geisser correction).

listening to stressor-related information than did low avoiders. However, a more differentiated picture emerged when we looked at the highly significant ($p < .01$) Vigilance × Avoidance interaction. It was, in fact, the high avoidance/high vigilance group (the so-called high-anxiety coping mode) who preferred to listen to music, that is, renounced information (INFSEC = 63.2 s; i.e., 116.8 s listening to music). The other three groups exhibited a preponderance of information intake to attentional diversion. In the Scheffé test, however, significant differences emerged among all four groups, with sensitizers (160.1 s) taking in more information than repressers (140.8 s), and the latter, in turn, being higher than so-called nondefensives (120.1 s).

In addition, a highly significant time effect was obtained ($p < .001$). Listening to information was less pronounced in the last minute of the anticipation period (32.3 s) than in the two preceding minutes (45.7 and 43.1 s, respectively). Again, this main effect was part of a more complicated pattern. As the Avoidance × Condition × Time interaction ($p < .06$) exhibits (Figure 4), subjects high in avoidance who received redundant information as well as persons low in avoidance who were exposed to valid information manifested a sharp decline of information intake as the aversive confrontation approached. On the other hand, high avoiders with valid and low avoiders with redundant information showed only a modest decline of attentional orientation when the aversive event was imminent, with the former group remaining at a medium (40.2, 40.6, and 34.0 s) and the latter at a high (54.0, 53.7, and 48.0 s) level of information intake.

For the cognitive coping reactions (ADS) during the anticipatory phase a time effect was registered ($p < .05$). Immediately prior to the aversive confrontation, the focus of the subjects' cognitions on this event (vigilance) was greater than at the beginning of anticipation. This effect, however, implies an interaction between experimental condition and time ($p < .04$). Vigilance increased only under valid information conditions, so that immediately prior to the aversive event a significant difference regarding the degree of concentration on the stressor existed between valid and redundant information conditions.

These effects of time and condition, however, were modified by dispositional influences. The significant Vigilance × Avoidance × Time interaction ($p < .05$; see Figure 5) demonstrates that sensitizers remained at a high level of threat-related cognitions throughout the entire anticipation period. Compared with those subjects, repressers manifested a constantly low level of attentional orientation. The two other groups heightened their vigilance with the approaching noxious event, with nondefensives exhibiting the most dramatic increase (0.7, 2.2, and 5.0 units). The significant Vigilance × Condition × Time interaction ($p < .05$; see Figure 6) shows that subjects who were exposed to valid information manifested an increase in vigilant cognitions, regardless of their degree of dispositional vigilance. With redundant information, however, a marked difference between high and low vigilance subjects was observed. Whereas persons low in dispositional vigilance remained at a low level of attentional orientation, subjects who were high in vigilance manifested a significant decrease in threat-related cognitions.

Significant effects for condition ($p < .06$) and time ($p < .01$) were observed for the baseline corrected HR (DHR). Valid information about the stressor was associated with a higher HR than redundant information. Furthermore, as Figure 7 illustrates, HR immediately prior to the aversive event was clearly higher than HR at points 2 and 3. Again, these situational effects were shaped by dispositional coping orientations. As the highly significant Vigilance × Avoidance × Condition interaction exhibits ($p < .01$; see Figure 8), repressers and sensitizers manifested, in contrast to the two other coping modes, significantly greater HR levels under the condition of valid information than under redundant information. Conse-

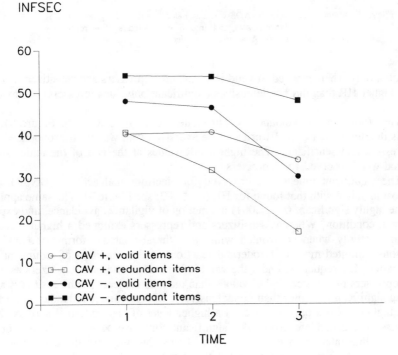

Figure 4 Listening to information (INFSEC) as a function of cognitive avoidance (CAV), experimental condition, and time.

ADS

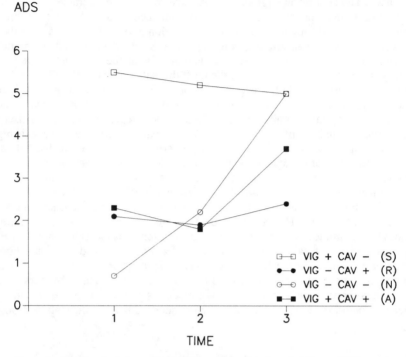

Figure 5 Attention deployment (ADS-vigilance) as a function of vigilance (VIG),
cognitive avoidance (CAV), and time; S = sensitizers, R = repressers,
N = nondefensives, A = anxious subjects.

quently, only when exposed to valid information, repressers and sensitizers exhibited higher HR than did nondefensives (significant only for repressers) or anxious
persons.

The Vigilance × Avoidance × Time interaction ($p < .05$; see Figure 9) reveals that the increase in HR prior to the aversive event was most pronounced for
repressers and sensitizers. The highest HR values at the end of the anticipation
period were observed for repressers.

The significant time effect observed for electrodermal activity (DNSR) was
almost identical with that found for HR ($p < .02$; see Figure 7). The same applied
to the highly significant ($p < .001$) interaction of vigilance, avoidance, and experimental condition. Whereas sensitizers and repressers exhibited a higher electrodermal activity when confronted with valid threat-related information, anxious
persons exhibited more electrodermal reactions in the condition of redundant information. Consequently, under the valid information condition sensitizers as well
as repressers manifested higher values than anxious subjects (with sensitizers also
being significantly higher than nondefensives), whereas under redundant information highly anxious persons reached a higher level of electrodermal activity than
repressers and nondefensives. The significant Vigilance × Avoidance × Condition × Time interaction basically repeated this finding, with the exception that
repressers and sensitizers manifested the described difference between the two
conditions of valid and redundant information in particular immediately prior to

confrontation, whereas the difference for anxious persons remained constant across the four time points.

The postexperimental assessments yielded a number of significant findings as well. Persons high in dispositional vigilance experienced the information as more useful (PE 2, $p < .06$), but also as more distracting (PE 3, $p < .09$) and calming (PE 4, $p < .01$), and rated the speaker's voice as more soothing (PE 5, $p < .04$). Furthermore, the noxious stimulus was rated as more unpleasant if previously little useful (redundant) information was offered (PE 1, $p < .06$). Redundant items were also perceived as distracting more from the impending aversive confrontation than the valid information (PE 3, $p < .001$). Finally, repressers rated valid information as more calming than redundant information (PE 4, $p < .05$).

One problem with the analysis so far reported results from the fact that 27 out of 40 subjects turned to one channel at the very beginning and stayed with it for the entire anticipation period. Of these "nonchangers" 19 consistently listened to information (9 in the valid and 10 in the redundant conditions), while 8 subjects (5 in the valid and 3 in the redundant condition) consistently tuned to the music channel. Of the 13 "changers" 6 were in the valid and 7 in the redundant condition. There was no significant relationship between this "channel preference" and coping dispositions. We therefore decided to run a second series of ANOVAs, replacing the two variables vigilance and avoidance by the three-level variable channel preference (change, information, and music). Table 3 shows the results for the dependent variables ADS, DHR, and DNSR.

ADS

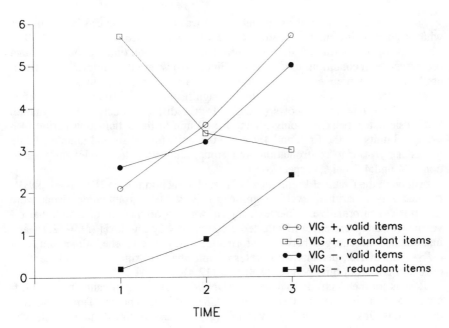

Figure 6 Attention deployment (ADS vigilance) as a function of vigilance, experimental condition, and time.

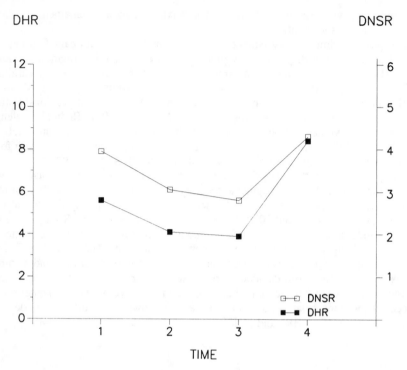

Figure 7 Heart rate (DHR) and electrodermal activity (DNSR) as a function of time.

Self-reported actual vigilant coping (ADS) was more pronounced in individuals who listened to information than in those who were tuned to music ($p < .02$). This was especially true for the valid information condition (interaction of channel preference with condition: $p < .04$; see Figure 10) where the "information listeners" exhibited a preponderance of vigilance (6.9 units) and the "music listeners" of avoidance (-0.7 units). As the highly significant ($p < .001$) Channel Preference × Time interaction shows (Figure 11), the difference between information and music listeners existed only for the first 2 min of the anticipation period (4.3 vs. -2.8 units for the first, and 4.7 vs. -0.1 units for the second minute), while immediately prior to confrontation both groups showed a clearly vigilant orientation (5.4 and 4.3 units, respectively).

Although the Channel Preference × Time interaction for the HR values (DHR) reached only a marginal level of significance ($p < .10$), group comparisons were nevertheless informative. Whereas subjects with an orientation of attentional diversion (music preference) manifested a comparatively low level ($M = 2.4$), and individuals who changed between information and music reached a medium level ($M = 5.2$) of HR, persons who preferred information exhibited a significant increase in HR from time point 3 (4.8) to 4 (12.4).

Results for the electrodermal activity (DNSR) indicate significant Channel Preference × Condition ($p < .02$) as well as Channel Preference × Time ($p < .07$) interactions. Taking the condition variable (Figure 12), we found that subjects who attended to the information channel exhibited more electrodermal activity in the valid than in the redundant condition. In addition, under valid information persons tuned to the information channel showed higher DNSR values than did information avoiders (i.e., subjects who preferred music). As the interaction between channel preference and time indicates (Figure 13), the characteristic, U-shaped curve observed for electrodermal activity (Figure 7) only existed for those subjects who consistently avoided information intake (time 1 < time 2). Compared with this group, information seekers and changers exhibited no significant changes in this autonomic parameter over time (with changers manifesting significantly higher values than music listeners at time 2 and 3).

DISCUSSION

The dispositional coping dimensions vigilance and cognitive avoidance varied independently of each other, confirming previous results (Krohne, 1989). As far as the state variables were concerned, significant positive associations could be observed (with the exception of the correlation between informational orientation and electrodermal activity). The more people attended to the information channel, the higher their HR and cognitive orientation toward the stressor (vigilance). Correspondingly, the more vigilant cognitions they reported, the higher their autonomic reactions.

All state variables also exhibited a significant change during the anticipation period. The instrumental behavior of information intake decreased with the approaching aversive event, thus indicating that searching for additional information

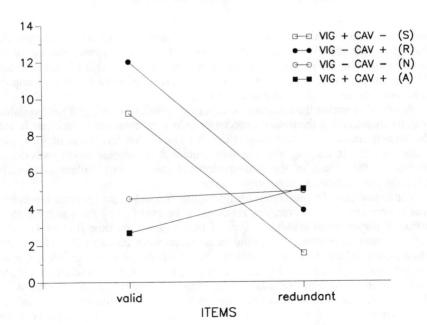

Figure 8 Heart rate as a function of vigilance (VIG), cognitive avoidance (CAV), and experimental condition (For definition of symbols, see Figure 6).

DHR

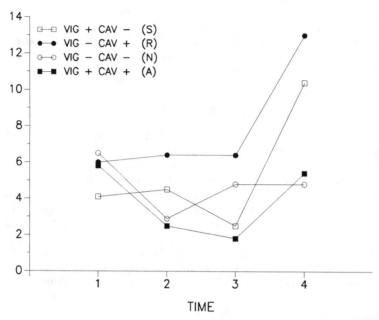

Figure 9   Heart rate as a function of vigilance (VIG), cognitive avoidance (CAV), and time (For definition of symbols, see Figure 6).

lost its adaptational value when the danger was imminent. Conversely, intrapsychic vigilant coping as well as the autonomic reactions increased immediately prior to the stressor, with the physiological indicators exhibiting a U-shaped curve. These findings are typical of the anticipation of a noxious event when the time of impact is known (Monat, 1976; Monat et al., 1972).

Results concerning the influence of coping dispositions on the INFSEC variable only partly supported theoretical expectations. As predicted, sensitizers manifested the highest amount of information-search behavior. That this behavior served to reduce anxiety, in keeping with the assumptions of our coping model, was documented by the results of the postexperimental assessment: Vigilant individuals rated the information as especially calming.

The hypothesis of a preference for distraction (music) in the group of repressers was not confirmed. However, this result has to be qualified by the observed interaction of dispositional avoidance, type of information, and time (Figure 4). Low avoiders who were exposed to valid information were tuned to the information channel most of the time (approximately 50 out of 60 s) during the first 2 min of the anticipation period. During the last minute, however, they manifested a sharp decline in informational orientation, indicating that they no longer considered information search as adaptational. On the other hand, low avoiders with redundant information remained at a very high level of information intake throughout the entire anticipation period. Because this type of information did not increase control of the stressor, its adaptational value did not change with the approaching aversive event. High avoiders with redundant information showed a steady decline in informational orientation as they approached the noxious stimulus, whereas high avoiders with valid information exhibited (on average) a medium level of information intake.

Unexpectedly, subjects high in both vigilance and avoidance showed the strongest inclination toward attentional diversion (music). In the model of coping modes these persons were defined as highly anxious. It was expected that they would change in a nonsystematic way between information intake and attentional diversion. However, as the results with the channel preference variable indicate, the mode of high anxiety was not significantly associated with the group of subjects who frequently changed between the two channels. One could assume that so-called high-anxiety persons manifest an adaptational style of coping: In a situation where the stressor is predictable but not (really) controllable they avoid threat-related instrumental and cognitive coping reactions. Consequently, their level of physiological arousal remains comparatively low. However, as HR data of high- and low-anxiety subjects obtained by Lykken, Macindoe, and Tellegen (1972) indicate, this might only be true for the anticipation period, not for the impact and postimpact phases.

Contrary to expectations, nondefensive persons were not affected by the degree of usefulness inherent in the information offered. Generally, they took in less information than repressers or sensitizers. This finding might indicate that they

Table 3 Influence of channel preference on cognitive and psychophysiological variables

Source of variation	F	p
Attention deployment scale		
Channel preference (A)	4.99	.02
Condition (B)	<1	NS
A × B	3.61	.04
Time (C)	7.45	.00***
A × C	6.98	.00***
B × C	1.93	NS
A × B × C	<1	NS
Difference in heart rate		
Channel preference (A)	2.28	NS
Condition (B)	2.43	NS
A × B	1.12	NS
Time (C)	2.62	.06
A × C	1.81	.10
B × C	<1	NS
A × B × C	<1	NS
Difference in number of spontaneous electrodermal fluctuations		
Channel preference (A)	<1	NS
Condition (B)	<1	NS
A × B	4.42	.02
Time (C)	5.38	.01***
A × B	2.01	.07*
B × C	2.21	.09
A × B × C	<1	NS

$*p < .10, **p < .05, ***p < .01$ (Greenhouse-Geisser correction).

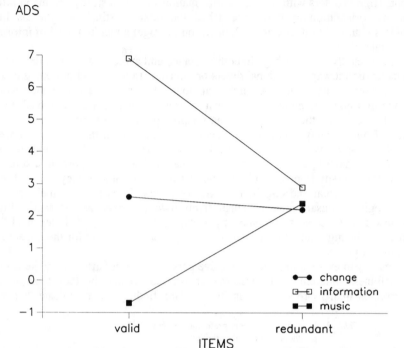

Figure 10 Attention deployment (ADS vigilance) as a function of channel preference
and experimental condition.

prefer other forms of instrumental reactions, options not offered in this experiment.

A possible explanation of the unexpected results could be found in the fact that, depending on the individual's orientation, the offered information could have different functions. It might help one type of person (e.g., sensitizers) to construe a "scheme" of the impending aversive confrontation. This hypothesis is supported by the finding that the stimulus was experienced as less aversive whenever valid information (i.e., information facilitating secondary control over the stressor) was presented prior to its occurrence (see also Lykken et al., 1972; Perkins, 1968). For other persons (such as repressers) information might serve as a distractor while waiting for the confrontation. This means further research is required to investigate the *intention* people have in selecting a certain coping strategy.

Results with the cognitive reactions (attention deployment) clearly confirmed our hypotheses. Sensitizers manifested a high level of vigilant cognitions throughout the entire anticipation period, whereas repressers exhibited a constantly low level of attentional orientation. Nondefensive as well as anxious persons increased their vigilance as they approached the aversive event. Obviously, sensitizers and repressers reacted according to their *dispositional* preference. Sensitizers intended to construe a scheme of the forthcoming confrontation and, hence, realized vigilant coping behavior. Repressers generally preferred attentional diversion and, consequently, minimized their orientation toward the stressor. On the other hand, nondefensives (so-called flexible copers) as well as anxious persons (instable copers) exhibited a stronger *situational* dependency in their behavior. As they approached the confrontation they increased their preoccupation with the stressor.

Persons who were exposed to valid information manifested an increase in vigilant cognitions as they approached confrontation. Obviously, valid information is less serviceable as a distractor than redundant information, an interpretation supported by the postexperimental assessment that indicated that redundant items were perceived as distracting more from the impending confrontation than valid information.

The latter results find their correspondence in the effects for the physiological variables (HR and electrodermal activity). Valid information about the stressor was associated with higher changes in both parameters than redundant information. However, this was true only for repressers and sensitizers, that is, for those individuals who clearly preferred information to music. Because valid information allows the exercise of preparatory reactions (Perkins, 1968), this elevated physiological arousal could reflect the higher level of activation in persons exposed to valid information.

Both physiological variables, taken together with the cognitive coping variable, also yielded information concerning a possible discrepancy between cognitive and physiological stress reactions in the case of repressers (Kohlmann, Singer, & Krohne, 1989; Weinstein et al., 1968). Although repressers reported a low degree of cognitive orientation toward the stressor, their autonomic reactions (HR) were markedly elevated, especially immediately prior to the aversive confrontation

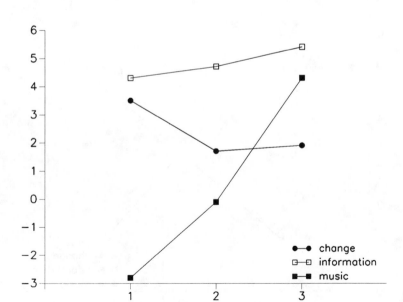

Figure 11 Attention deployment (ADS vigilance) as a function of channel preference and time.

(Figure 9). Interestingly, sensitizers did not exhibit the reversed pattern (low physiological and high cognitive reactions), but reached high levels in both response
modalities.

Results with the channel preference variable basically repeated correlational
findings, qualified, however, by interactions with the variables time and type of
information. The association between instrumental coping behavior (information
vs. music orientation) and cognitive coping reactions (vigilance) was confined to
valid information as well as to the first part of the anticipation period. Most
noticeable was the marked increase in preoccupation with the stressor in persons
who avoided listening to threat-related information (Figure 11). We assume that
these subjects, instead, monitored the clock that indicated how much time was left
until the noxious stimulus was to be delivered.

Whereas the insignificant correlation between informational orientation and
electrodermal activity ($r = .13$) might indicate that both parameters varied independently of each other, the significant interaction of channel preference and type
of information demonstrates that this was not the case: Under valid information,
persons who listened to information showed higher levels of spontaneous fluctuations than individuals who avoided information. This reflects the well-known fact
that spontaneous fluctuations are an indicator of focused attention (Vossel, 1990).
Redundant information exhibited the reverse pattern (with group differences, however, being insignificant). Persons who did not listen to information showed a
marked U-shaped curve for this parameter (Figure 13). Because this curve is

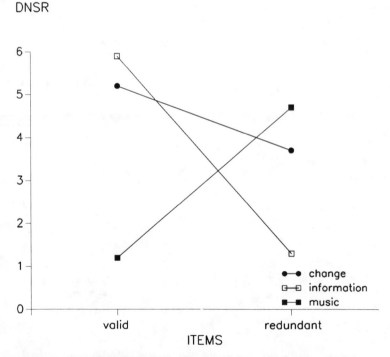

Figure 12 Electrodermal activity as a function of channel preference and
experimental condition.

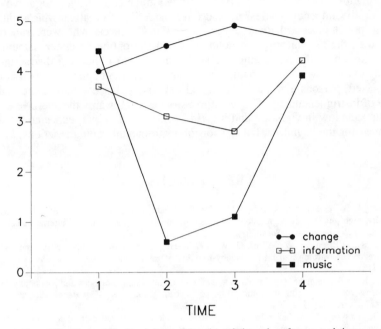

Figure 13 Electrodermal activity as a function of channel preference and time.

typical of relatively short anticipation periods where the time of impact is known (Monat, 1976; Monat et al., 1972), we conclude that these persons coped with the situation by closely monitoring the time display. This hypothesis has to be tested, of course, in a following investigation.

Thus, the findings of our experiment can be summarized as follows: Hypotheses for sensitizers were clearly confirmed. They exhibited the highest degree of instrumental as well as cognitive orientation toward the aversive event. With repressers, however, expectations were confirmed only for the cognitive, not for the instrumental coping reactions. Instead, repressers showed a comparatively high amount of orientation toward information related to the aversive event. In their case, however, the possibility exists that they tuned to the available information mainly in order to bridge the unpleasant waiting period. This has to be tested in future experiments by systematically assessing the intentions underlying the selection of specific options. Despite their low level of cognitive orientation toward the threat, repressers exhibited a high degree of emotional arousal, thus confirming the discrepancy hypothesis for repressers. For sensitizers, however, instrumental, cognitive, and autonomic reactions were in accordance with each other.

SUMMARY

This study investigated the interaction between dispositional coping modes and types of preimpact information on emotional, cognitive, and instrumental reactions of Ss awaiting an aversive event. Regarding the personality dispositions, two dimensions, vigilance and cognitive avoidance, were distinguished while two forms of information were realized: "valid" information which improved cognitive control over the impending stressor, and "redundant" information which did not increase potential control over the stressor. Forty subjects who were randomly assigned to the two information conditions had the option of either listening to information about the impending aversive stimulus or of choosing distraction by listening to music while anticipating an aversive event (an unpleasant, loud noise). As expected, persons high in vigilance and low in avoidance exhibited the highest degree of instrumental as well as cognitive orientation towards the aversive event. With subjects low in vigilance and high in avoidance, however, expectations were confirmed for the cognitive, but not for the instrumental coping reactions.

REFERENCES

Asendorpf, J. B., & Scherer, K. R. (1983). The discrepant repressor: Differentiation between low anxiety, high anxiety, and repression of anxiety by autonomic facial-verbal patterns of behavior. *Journal of Personality and Social Psychology, 45*, 1334–1346.

Averill, J. R., O'Brien, L., & DeWitt, G. W. (1977). The influence of response effectiveness on the preference for warning and on psychophysiological stress reactions. *Journal of Personality, 45*, 395–418.

Averill, J. R., & Rosenn, M. (1972). Vigilant and nonvigilant coping strategies and psychophysiological stress reactions during the anticipation of electric shock. *Journal of Personality and Social Psychology, 23*, 128–141.

Calvert-Boyanowsky, J., & Leventhal, H. (1975). The role of information in attenuating behavioral responses to stress: A reinterpretation of the misattribution phenomenon. *Journal of Personality and Social Psychology, 32*, 274–277.

Cornelius, R. R., & Averill, J. R. (1980). The influence of various types of control on psychophysiological stress reactions. *Journal of Research in Personality, 14*, 503–517.

Endler, N. S., Hunt, J. M., & Rosenstein, A. J. (1962). An S–R inventory of anxiousness. *Psychological Monographs, 76*(17, Whole No. 536).

Greenhouse, S. W., & Geisser, S. (1959). On methods in the analysis of profile data. *Psychometrika, 24*, 95–112.

Gudjonsson, G. H. (1981). Self-reported emotional disturbance and its relation to electrodermal reactivity, defensiveness, and trait anxiety. *Personality and Individual Differences, 2*, 47–52.

Horowitz, M. (1979). Psychological response to serious life events. In V. Hamilton & D. M. Warburton (Eds.), *Human stress and cognition: An information processing approach* (pp. 237–265). Chichester, England: Wiley.

Jennings, J. R., Berg, W. K., Hutcheson, J. S., Obrist, P., Porges, S., & Turpin, G. (1981). Committee report. Publication guidelines for heart rate studies in man. *Psychophysiology, 18*, 226–231.

Johnson, J. E. (1975). Stress reduction through sensation information. In I. G. Sarason & C. D. Spielberger (Eds.), *Stress and anxiety, volume 2* (pp. 361–378). Washington, DC: Hemisphere.

Kohlmann, C.-W. (1990). *Rigid and flexible modes of coping: The role of coping preferences* (Mainzer Berichte zur Persönlichkeitsforschung No. 30). Mainz: Johannes Gutenberg-Universität, Psychologisches Institut.

Kohlmann, C.-W., Singer, P., & Krohne, H. W. (1989). Coping disposition, actual coping, and the discrepancy between subjective and physiological stress reactions. In P. Lovibond & P. Wilson (Eds.), *Proceedings of the XXIV International Congress of Psychology: Volume 9. Clinical and abnormal psychology* (pp. 67–78). Amsterdam, the Netherlands: Elsevier.

Krohne, H. W. (1978). Individual differences in coping with stress and anxiety. In C. D. Spielberger & I. G. Sarason (Eds.), *Stress and anxiety, volume 5* (pp. 233–260). Washington, DC: Hemisphere.

Krohne, H. W. (1986). Coping with stress: Dispositions, strategies, and the problem of measurement. In M. H. Appley & R. Trumbull (Eds.), *Dynamics of stress* (pp. 209–234). New York: Plenum.

Krohne, H. W. (1989). The concept of coping modes: Relating cognitive person variables to actual coping behavior. *Advances in Behaviour Research Therapy, 11*, 235–248.

Krohne, H. W., & Rogner, J. (1982). Repression-sensitization as a central construct in coping research.

In H. W. Krohne & L. Laux (Eds.), *Achievement, stress and anxiety* (pp. 167-193). New York: McGraw-Hill.

Krohne, H. W., Rösch, W., & Kürsten, F. (1989). Die Erfassung von Angstbewältigung in physisch bedrohlichen Situationen [The assessment of coping in physical threat situations]. *Zeitschrift für Klinische Psychologie, 18,* 230-242.

Krohne, H. W., Wigand, A., & Kiehl, G. E. (1985). Konstruktion eines multidimensionalen Instruments zur Erfassung von Angstbewältigungstendenzen [Construction of a multidimensional instrument for the assessment of coping tendencies]. In H. W. Krohne (Ed.), *Angstbewältigung in Leistungssituationen* (pp. 63-77). Weinheim: Edition Psychologie.

Lazarus, R. S. (1966). *Psychological stress and the coping process.* New York: McGraw-Hill.

Lazarus, R. S., & Launier, R. (1978). Stress-related transactions between person and environment. In L. A. Pervin & M. Lewis (Eds.), *Perspectives in interactional psychology* (pp. 287-327). New York: Plenum.

Lykken, D. T., Macindoe, I., & Tellegen, A. (1972). Perception: Autonomic response to shock as a function of predictability in time and locus. *Psychophysiology,* 318-333.

Miller, S. M. (1979). Controllability and human stress: Method, evidence and theory. *Behavior Research and Therapy, 17,* 287-304.

Miller, S. M. (1980). When is a little information a dangerous thing? Coping with stressful life events by monitoring vs. blunting. In S. & U. Levine H. (Ed.), *Coping and health* (pp. 145-169). New York: Plenum Press.

Miller, S. M. (1987). Monitoring and blunting: Validation of a questionnaire to assess styles of information seeking under threat. *Journal of Personality and Social Psychology, 52,* 345-353.

Miller, S. M., & Mangan, C. E. (1983). Interacting effects of information and coping style in adapting to gynecologic stress: Should the doctor tell all? *Journal of Personality and Social Psychology, 45,* 223-236.

Monat, A. (1976). Temporal uncertainty, anticipation time, and cognitive coping under stress. *Journal of Human Stress, 2*(2), 32-43.

Monat, A., Averill, J. R., & Lazarus, R. S. (1972). Anticipatory stress and coping reactions under various conditions of uncertainty. *Journal of Personality and Social Psychology, 24,* 237-253.

Perkins, C. C. (1968). An analysis of the concept of reinforcement. *Psychological Review, 75,* 155-172.

Roth, S., & Cohen, L. J. (1986). Approach, avoidance, and coping with stress. *American Psychologist, 41,* 813-819.

Schandry, R. (1981). *Psychophysiologie. Körperliche Indikatoren menschlichen Verhaltens* [Psychophysiology. Bodily indicators of human behavior.]. München: Urban & Schwarzenberg.

Suls, J., & Fletcher, B. (1985). The relative efficacy of avoidant and non-avoidant coping strategies: A meta-analysis. *Health Psychology, 4,* 249-288.

Terasaki, M. (1981). Manifest anxiety, noise, and serial reaction performance. *Japanese Journal of Psychology, 52,* 53-56.

Vossel, G. (1990). *Elektrodermale Labilität: Ein Beitrag zur Differentiellen Psychophysiologie* [Electrodermal lability. A contribution to differential psychophysiology.]. Göttingen: Hogrefe.

Walschburger, P. (1975). Zur Standardisierung und Interpretation elektrodermaler Meßwerte in psychologischen Experimenten [On the standardization and interpretation of electrodermal readings in psychological experiments.]. *Zeitschrift für experimentelle und angewandte Psychologie, 22,* 514-533.

Weinberger, D. A., Schwartz, G. E., & Davidson, R. J. (1979). Low-anxious, high-anxious, and repressive coping-styles: Psychometric patterns and behavioral and physiological responses to stress. *Journal of Abnormal Psychology, 88,* 369-380.

Weinstein, J., Averill, J. R., Opton, E. M., & Lazarus, R. S. (1968). Defensive style and discrepancy between self-report and physiological indexes of stress. *Journal of Personality and Social Psychology, 10,* 406-413.

11

Panic Disorder and Responses to Naturally Occurring and Experimentally Induced Stressors

Nola Biddle
Department of Psychiatry,
University of Melbourne, Australia

Michael C. F. Pain
Thoracic Medicine,
Royal Melbourne Hospital, Australia

John W. G. Tiller
Department of Psychiatry,
University of Melbourne, Australia

A panic attack, although circumscribed in duration, is one of the more over-whelming stressors likely to be experienced by individuals with panic disorder. The fear of dying or of losing control in some unacceptable way during an attack is generally strong, as is the belief that there must be some undiagnosed disease process causing the symptoms, so that the growth of a generalized anxiety between attacks is not uncommon. With avoidance of situations in which an attack may occur, agoraphobia, social phobia, and interpersonal problems can all develop, compounding the difficulties faced by individuals with the disorder and further limiting their adaptability.

In attempting to determine etiological and maintaining factors in panic disorder, two complementary models have become foci of recent research interest. One, a cognitive–behavioral model, postulates that the inappropriate and fearful interpretation of interoceptive change is crucial to the development of a panic attack (Clark, 1986; Ley, 1987; Salkovskis & Clark, 1986). The other, a biological model, postulates that the interoceptive changes are the attack, a dysfunction or abnormality of the central carbon dioxide chemoreceptors conferring a vulnerability to such change (Carr & Sheehan, 1985; Fyer et al., 1987). Biological vulnerability is assumed if a panic attack is induced during a provocation test such as lactate infusion or inhalation of a carbon dioxide mixture (Dillon, Gorman, Liebowitz, Fyer, & Klein, 1987; Fyer et al., 1987).

Recent reviews of the above biological model have highlighted methodological flaws in the control of psychological factors in provocation studies (Margraf, Ehlers, & Roth, 1986a, 1986b) and have presented a case for interpreting results in favor of a cognitive–behavioral model. Induced panic attacks have rarely been operationally defined, and in some studies subjects were asked whether the changes experienced with testing were similar to a panic attack, raising the possibility of response bias, experimental set, and expectancy effects (Orne, 1962). An equally important and related problem is the use of subjective reports as if the data are as reliable as physiological measures.

The ventilatory response to carbon dioxide (VRC), where a carbon dioxide mixture is rebreathed for up to 4 min, has been reported as inducing a greater than normal frequency of panic attacks in panic disorder (Woods et al., 1986). In its original role of estimating sensitivity of the central carbon dioxide chemoreceptors to increasing carbon dioxide (Read, 1967), the VRC is a direct test for the dysfunction held to be fundamental to this biological model. As a provocation test, effects of experimental manipulation of psychological factors on the induction of panic attacks can be observed without affecting the biological measure, which is stable (Sullivan & Yu, 1984) and not susceptible to psychological manipulation. Our study replicated the Woods et al. study (1986) except that, to minimize apprehension and expectancy effects, a neutral explanation for sensations induced by the VRC was given to subjects. The possibility of panic attacks was not broached until after the test.

To reduce bias, subjects were not told that VRC responses and panic attacks were to be compared. Records of panic attacks and other acute episodes in response to naturally occurring stressors were kept by patients with panic disorder for the week before testing. A control group was included to determine normal responses during acute episodes and to the VRC.

Our hypotheses, in contrast to the biological and cognitive–behavioral models of panic disorder, were that when a neutral explanation for the interpretation of symptoms induced by the VRC is tendered (a) responses of patients to the VRC are not distinguishable from normal responses and (b) panic attacks are qualitatively and quantitatively different from responses to the VRC. The study also enabled us to determine whether the patients were more generally anxious than the normal controls and whether their responses to daily stressors were more severe.

METHOD

Subjects

Twenty patients diagnosed by psychiatrists as having panic disorder ($n = 16$) or agoraphobia with panic disorder ($n = 4$) according to criteria in the *Diagnostic and Statistical Manual of Mental Disorders* (*DSM-III*; American Psychiatric Association [APA], 1980) were referred to the study. Panic attacks had preceded agoraphobia in patients with agoraphobia. Median duration of the disorder was 1 year, with a range of 4 months to 13 years. Mean age was 33.9 ($SD = 10.4$) years; 6 subjects were male. Patients were matched for age (Kronenberg & Drage, 1973) and gender with 20 normal controls; mean age was 33.8 ($SD = 10.8$) years. Subjects' urine samples were negative for benzodiazepines (Emit, Sylva, Palo Alto, CA).

Psychological Assessment

The major instrument to record subjective assessment of change in sensations with panic attacks, other acute episodes, and the experimental stressor was the Anxiety-related Symptoms Checklist (ASC), prepared by the authors and consisting of 57 state-dependent anxiety-related symptoms, including the 12 *DSM-III* (APA, 1980) panic disorder symptoms (PDS) for diagnosis of panic disorder and "fear." Each item can be rated from 0 to 5, where 0 = *none,* 1 = *slight,* 2 = *mild,* 3 = *moderate,* 4 = *severe,* and 5 = *very severe.* The PDS items only were the focus of the study.

The observer-rated Diagnostic Interview Schedule (Robins, Helzer, Croughan, & Ratcliff, 1981) and Hamilton Anxiety Rating Scale (HARS; Hamilton, 1967) were administered. Self-assessment measures included the State–Trait Anxiety Inventory (STAI; Spielberger, Gorsuch, & Lushene, 1970).

The Provocation Test

The subject, wearing a nose-clip, rebreathed a carbon dioxide/oxygen mixture through a mouthpiece and tube connected to the VRC circuit (Read, 1967). Over the test period of 4 min the proportion of carbon dioxide increased from 7% to about 10%. The ASC was used to record subjective responses. The regression of increase in ventilation with increasing carbon dioxide provided the measure of sensitivity. The method and sensitivity of the carbon dioxide chemoreceptors are described elsewhere (Pain, Biddle, & Tiller, 1988).

Preparation of Subjects

The subjects were familiarized with the testing procedure on three occasions: (a) a week before testing, when an explanation sheet was given to each subject; (b) on the morning of the test, when the subject was given a verbal explanation before signing the consent form; and (c) just prior to testing, with the equipment in full view. A neutral context was provided by describing the original use of the VRC, to determine biological sensitivity to carbon dioxide in respiratory disease (Singh, 1984) and athletics (Saunders, Leeder, & Rebuck, 1976). The generation of symptoms by carbon dioxide was described as similar to that of strenuous exercise. Control over the test procedure was arranged by demonstrating to the subject how to stop the test and remove him- or herself from the system. The possibility of a panic attack being provoked by the VRC was not discussed until after the completion of testing.

Design

Week before testing.   Each subject kept the ASC as a daily diary. An ASC was also completed whenever a subject had a panic attack or other acute episode. The subject summarized perceived causes of the episodes.

Test morning.—Each subject had been asked not to drink alcohol or caffeine-containing products (Charney, Heniger, & Jatlow, 1985) for at least 12 hr before testing and to eat a light breakfast. Following psychological assessment, refreshment, collection of a urine specimen, the recording of baseline respiratory measures (Pain et al., 1988) and a 10-min rest period, the subject completed the ASC. Then the subject, after exhaling, was switched into the VRC circuit. Immediately after the test, the subject completed the ASC. Discussion of the morning's experiences included being asked about panic attacks.

Definitions of Responses

A *panic attack* was defined by (a) the subject's reporting a panic attack or (b) the satisfaction of modified *DSM-III* criteria (APA, 1980)—a discrete period of fear or apprehension accompanied by the appearance of at least 4 of the 12 diagnostic symptoms, and (c) no apparent environment precipitant. The "appearance" of a symptom was defined as a change in severity of at least 2. For the VRC, criterion c did not apply. An *acute episode* was defined by reported changes in any of the 12 PDS symptoms, with or without "fear" but not fulfilling panic attack criteria.

Analyses

Analyses were performed using SPSS^x programs (SPSS, Inc., 1983). Parametric or non-parametric tests were used for comparisons according to whether variables met the appropriate conditions. Frequency distributions were compared using the chi-square statistic.

RESULTS

The panic disorder patients were significantly more anxious than the normal controls, according to the HARS, PDS, and State and Trait scales of the STAI (Table 1). At baseline, all but two subjects scored PDS items at 2 or less, indicating little potential for ceiling effects with the VRC.

Week Before Test Day

Twenty-seven acute episodes were recorded by the panic disorder patients; 12 satisfied the study criteria for a panic attack. Panic attacks were significantly more severe than other acute episodes (Table 1). The 12 acute episodes recorded by normal subjects were significantly less severe than those recorded by patients. Acute episodes were related to interpersonal factors in many cases.

For panic attacks, the percent frequencies of reported PDS symptoms are displayed, in order, in Figure 1. Of the five symptoms reported by more than 80% of patients, "fear of dying or losing control" and "trembling or shaking" were reported less frequently during acute episodes: $\chi^2 (1, N = 27) = 7.13, p < .01$; $\chi^2 (1, N = 27) = 4.22, p < .05$, respectively. Ninety-seven of a possible 144 responses were recorded during panic attacks and 70 of a possible 180 were recorded during acute episodes, $\chi^2 (1, N = 324) = 26.84, p < .001$. For acute

Table 1 Anxiety measures at baseline, in response to the ventilatory response to carbon dioxide (VRC) test, and during the week pre-VRC

	Normal control (n = 20)		Panic disorder (n = 20)		
	Median	Range	Median	Range	Mann-Whitney z
Hamilton Anxiety Rating Scale	0.0	0–6	21.5	12–33	5.47**
State–Trait Anxiety Inventory[a]					
State anxiety (STAI-X1)	26.9	4.6	45.1	12.4	6.02**
Trait anxiety (STAI-X2)	32.0	7.4	51.5	7.6	8.14**
PDS[b] in response to VRC					
Baseline	0	0–6	4	0–53	4.26**
VRC change	8	1–33	8	−26–27	0.04
PDS week pre-VRC					
General level	0	0–2	11	1–50	5.18**
Panic attacks	—	—	24[c]	17–36	
Acute episodes	3[c]	1–6	11[d]	4–25	3.15*

[a]Values for this measure are means and standard deviations.
[b]The 12 Diagnostic and Statistical Manual of Mental Disorders symptoms for diagnosis of panic disorder.
[c]n = 12.
[d]n = 15.
*p < .002. **p = .0000.

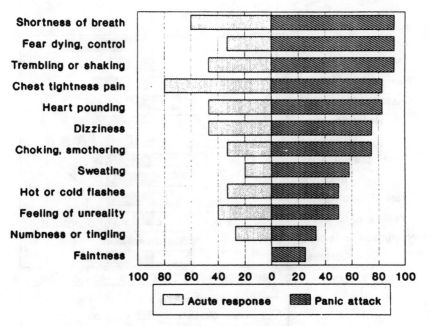

Figure 1 Percent frequencies of the 12 *Diagnostic and Statistical Manual of Mental Disorders* symptoms for panic disorder during panic attacks and other acute episodes in 20 panic disorder patients.

episodes and normal subjects, the 21 of a possible 144 responses were less than for patients, χ^2 (1, N = 324) = 20.45, p < .001.

The Provocation Test

None of the 40 subjects reported having a panic attack in response to the VRC. Three normal subjects and 4 panic disorder patients fulfilled the operational criteria for a panic attack, giving a sensitivity of 20%, specificity of 75%, and diagnostic confidence of 57%. All were female.

Responses to the VRC were similar in severity for patients and normal controls (Table 1). Controls and patients reported 91 and 96 increases in PDS symptoms, respectively, and distributions across symptoms were similar (Figure 2). Thirty-one decreases in symptom severity were reported by patients and one by a control, the greatest decrease (5) being for "tightness or pain in the chest."

Ventilatory Response to Carbon Dioxide, Panic Attacks, and Acute Episodes

For the patients, fewer VRC responses than panic attack responses were recorded (96 of 240 and 97 of 144, respectively, χ^2 (1, N = 384) = 25.87, p < .001. Panic attacks and VRC responses differed significantly in severity (Table 1) and in symptom distribution (Figure 2). Of the five panic attack symptoms re-

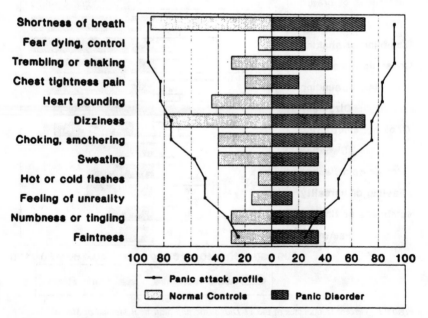

Figure 2 Percent frequencies of the 12 *Diagnostic and Statistical Manual of Mental Disorders* symptoms for panic disorder for panic attacks and for the ventilatory response to carbon dioxide for 20 panic disorder patients and 20 normal controls.

ported by more than 80% of the patients, three were reported less frequently in response to the VRC; they were "fear of dying or losing control," "tightness or pain in the chest," and "trembling or shaking": χ^2 (1, N = 32) = 10.80, $p <$ .005; χ^2 (1, N = 32) = 9.79, $p <$ .005; and χ^2 (1, N = 32) = 5.12, $p <$ .05, respectively. Acute episodes and VRC responses were similar in severity (Table 2) and symptom distribution (Figures 1 and 2), apart from "tightness or pain in the chest," χ^2 (1, N = 35) = 10.13, $p <$ .01, and "faintness," χ^2 (1, N = 35) = 4.55, $p <$ .05.

DISCUSSION

The biological model for panic disorder that has as a central tenet a greater than normal vulnerability to induction of panic attacks with inhalation of carbon dioxide mixtures (Carr & Sheehan, 1985; Fyer et al., 1987) was not supported in this study. When psychological factors considered by proponents of a cognitive–behavioral model of panic disorder to influence the induction of panic attacks by provocation tests (Clark, 1986; Margraf et al., 1986a, 1986b) were controlled, there were no differences between panic disorder patients and normal controls in satisfying modified *DSM-III* (APA, 1980) criteria for a panic attack during the VRC.

At least two outcomes in response to the VRC should have been observed if the biological model of panic disorder was to have been supported. More panic disorder patients than normal controls should have fulfilled *DSM-III* criteria for a panic attack, and, in the patient group, the profile of symptoms for panic attacks should have been similar to that for the VRC. Neither of these occurred. In addition, not only was the patient profile of symptoms in response to the VRC different from the panic attack profile, it was similar to the normal profile, strengthening the validity of the results. There were even reports of reductions in symptom intensity. The lack of subjective reports of panic attacks with rebreathing, although perhaps not conclusively weakening the biological model, supports a cognitive–behavioral model of panic disorder by demonstrating control over the responses upon which the biological model has been based.

A major feature of the study was to try to ensure that the subjects did not feel unduly apprehensive or expect to experience a panic attack during testing. The literature abounds with reports of studies in which panic attacks have been induced by the inhalation of carbon dioxide mixtures when similar psychological preparation was not part of the design (e.g., Fyer et al., 1987; van den Hout, van der Molen, Griez, Lousberg, & Nansen, 1987; Woods et al., 1986). As a consequence, we did not consider it ethically justifiable to have a control group of panic disorder patients who were not prepared in this way.

This study confirms that individuals with panic disorder experience life in a state of arousal considerably higher than normal. Generalized anxiety in the patients was severe, their trait anxiety scores placing them as a group at about the 95th percentile of a normal population (Spielberger et al., 1970). Acute responses, mostly to psychosocial stressors in the study, were less severe than panic attacks but more severe than similar responses for the normal controls. Most responses for the normal subjects were trivial compared with those for the panic disorder patients, indicating a tendency of the latter to "overreact" to stressors and a lowered ability to cope with them.

The results do not exclude the possibility of biological differences between normal individuals and those with panic disorder, but even if there is a difference (Pain et al., 1988), the study indicates that cognitive factors can limit its expression. This has important consequences for treatment of panic disorder and the control of panic attacks and of reactions to events. It also emphasizes that caution must be exercised in the preparation and interpretation of results from provocation tests in panic disorder.

SUMMARY

Induction of panic attacks with challenge tests, such as lactate infusion and inhalation of carbon dioxide mixtures, has been used as evidence of a biological dysfunction in individuals with panic disorder. However, these responses are open to psychological manipulation. To help minimize the experimental induction of anxiety during the rebreathing of 7% carbon dioxide by 20 panic disorder patients and 20 normal controls matched for age and gender, the possible range of responses was likened to response to a normally occurring stressor, strenuous exercise. Although baseline symptoms were more severe than normal for the panic disorder patients, induced responses were similar in severity and distribution for both groups. Responses were different from panic attacks and the event-related attacks recorded over the week prior to testing. It was concluded that, to determine biological dysfunction, the use of psychologically sensitive responses to an experimentally induced stressor is not appropriate.

REFERENCES

American Psychiatric Association. (1980). *Diagnostic and statistical manual of mental disorders* (3rd ed.). Washington, DC: Author.

Carr, D. B., & Sheehan, D. V. (1985). Panic anxiety: A new biological model. *Journal of Clinical Psychiatry, 45,* 323-330.

Charney, D. S., Heniger, G. R., & Jatlow, P. I. (1985). Increased anxiogenic effects of caffeine in panic disorders. *Archives of General Psychiatry, 42,* 233-243.

Clark, D. M. (1986). A cognitive approach to panic. *Behaviour Research and Therapy, 24,* 461-470.

Dillon, D. D., Gorman, J. M., Liebowitz, M. R., Fyer, A. J., & Klein, D. F. (1987). Measurement of lactate-induced panic and anxiety. *Psychiatry Research, 20,* 97-105.

Fyer, M. R., Uy, J., Martinez, J., Goetz, R., Klein, D. F., Fyer, A., Liebowitz, M. R., & Gorman, J. (1987). CO_2 challenge of patients with panic disorder. *American Journal of Psychiatry, 144,* 1080-1082.

Hamilton, M. (1967). Diagnosis and rating of anxiety. In M. Lader (Ed.), *Studies of anxiety* (pp. 76-79). Ashford, Kent: Headly.

Hout, M. A. van den, Molen, G. M. van der, Griez, E., Lousberg, H., & Nansen, A. (1987). Reduction of CO_2-induced anxiety in patients with panic attacks after repeated CO_2 exposure. *American Journal of Psychiatry, 144,* 788-791.

Kronenberg, R. S., & Drage, C. W. (1973). Attenuation of the ventilatory and heart rate responses to hypoxia and hypercapnia to aging in normal men. *Journal of Clinical Investigations, 52,* 1812-1819.

Ley, R. (1987). Panic disorder and agoraphobia: Fear of fear or fear of the symptoms produced by hyperventilation? *Journal of Behavioral Therapy and Experimental Psychiatry, 18,* 305-316.

Margraf, J., Ehlers, A., & Roth, W. T. (1986a). Biological models of panic disorder and agoraphobia—a review and critique. *Behaviour Research and Therapy, 24,* 553-567.

Margraf, J., Ehlers, A., & Roth, W. T. (1986b). Sodium lactate infusions and panic attacks: A review and critique. *Psychosomatic Medicine, 48,* 23–51.

Orne, M. T. (1962). On the social psychology of the psychological experiment: With particular reference to demand characteristics and their implications. *American Psychologist, 17,* 776–783.

Pain, M. C. F., Biddle, N., & Tiller, J. W. G. (1988). Panic disorder, the ventilatory response to carbon dioxide, and respiratory variables. *Psychosomatic Medicine, 50,* 541–548.

Read, D. J. C. (1967). A clinical method for assessing the ventilatory response to carbon dioxide. *Australian Annals of Medicine, 16,* 20–32.

Robins, L. N., Helzer, J. E., Croughan, J., & Ratcliff, K. S. (1981). The NIMH Diagnostic Interview Schedule: Its history, characteristics, and validity. *Archives of General Psychiatry, 38,* 381–389.

Salkovskis, P., & Clark, D. M. (1986). Cognitive and physiological processes in the maintenance and treatment of panic attacks. In I. Hand & H. U. Wittchen (Eds.), *Panic and phobias* (pp. 90–102). Berlin: Springer.

Saunders, N. A., Leeder, S. R., & Rebuck, A. S. (1976). Ventilatory response to carbon dioxide in young athletes: A family study. *American Review of Respiratory Disease, 113,* 497–502.

Singh, B. S. (1984). Ventilatory response to CO_2. I. A psychobiological marker of the respiratory system. *Psychosomatic Medicine, 46,* 333–344.

Spielberger, C. D., Gorsuch, R. L., & Lushene, R. E. (1970). *Manual for the State–Trait Anxiety Inventory.* Palo Alto, CA: Consulting Psychologists Press.

SPSS, Inc. (1983). *SPSS^x User's Guide.* New York: McGraw-Hill.

Sullivan, T. Y., & Yu, P.-L. (1984). Reproducibility of CO_2 response curves with ten minutes separating each rebreathing test. *American Review of Respiratory Disease, 129,* 23–26.

Woods, S. W., Charney, D. S., Loke, J., Goodman, W. K., Redmond, D. E., & Heninger, G. R. (1986). Carbon dioxide sensitivity in panic anxiety. *Archives of General Psychiatry, 43,* 900–909.

12

The Spielberger Anger Expression Scale: Factor Structure and Correlations with Blood Pressure

Robert G. Knight and Barbara J. Chisholm
University of Otago, New Zealand

Judith M. Paulin and Hendrika J. Waal-Manning
Otago Medical School, New Zealand

Mode of anger expression has been frequently linked with the development of coronary heart disease (CHD) and essential hypertension (e.g., Diamond, 1982; Gentry, Chesney, Gary, Hall, & Harburg, 1982; Jenkins, Zyzanski, & Rosenman, 1978; Williams et al., 1980). The impressive evidence from the Western Collaboration Group Study (Rosenman et al., 1964) of an association between the Type A behavior pattern and subsequent development of CHD provided a major impetus for further research in this area. Friedman and Rosenman (1974) listed hostility and aggressiveness among the most important components of the Type A behavior pattern.

Alexander (1939) was among the first to describe the hypertensive individual as a person whose chronic suppression of anger eventually resulted in the persistent elevation of blood pressure (BP). The experimental study of the effects of anger expression on the cardiovascular system dates back to the work of Funkenstein, King, and Drolette (1954), who were among the first to distinguish between anger-in and anger-out. Persons classified as anger-in tended to suppress anger and to withdraw from conflict without overtly dissipating their feelings of irritation and frustration. Persons classified as anger-out overtly displayed their anger and vented their feelings when frustrated.

Evidence that suppressed anger was associated with elevated BP was reported by Harburg, Gentry, and colleagues (e.g., Gentry, Chesney, Hall, & Harburg, 1981; Harburg, Blakelock, & Roeper, 1979). These investigators found that city dwellers living in high-stress areas who tended to suppress anger had higher diastolic blood pressure than those with high anger-out scores and that this relation between suppressed anger and elevated BP was particularly true for black males.

The research described in this chapter was supported in part by a grant from the Otago University Research Committee. We gratefully acknowledge the continued support of this research of the people of Milton, the Medical Research Council of New Zealand, and the National Health Foundation. We are also grateful to Professor C. D. Spielberger for making available the experimental form of his Anger Expression Scale.

A major obstacle to establishing a coherent pattern of research results in this field has been the lack of valid psychometric procedures for assessing anger. In response to this need, Spielberger and his associates developed the State–Trait Anger Scale (STAS; Spielberger, Jacobs, Russell, & Crane, 1983) to assess the experience of anger, and the Anger EXpression Scale (AX; Spielberger et al., 1985) to measure "individual differences in anger expression as a personality trait" (p. 14).

The construction of the AX Scale began with the administration of a preliminary version to a large sample of high school students. In subsequent factor analyses of responses to individual items, two factors were identified, which were labeled Anger/In and Anger/Out on the basis of item content. These findings led to the construction of a 20-item version of the AX Scale, with 8-item AX/In and AX/Out subscales. Three of the four remaining items (e.g., "I keep my cool" and "I control my angry feelings") were tentatively identified as measuring a third construct, anger control (AX/Con). The total Anger Expression (AX/EX) score provides a measure of the overall tendency to overtly or covertly express angry feelings. For a detailed review of the development of the AX Scale, see Spielberger, Krasner, and Solomon (1988).

The AX Scale has been found to have satisfactory levels of reliability in several studies (e.g., Johnson, 1984; Spielberger et al., 1985, 1988) and good convergent and discriminant validity. Moreover, the AX/In and AX/Out subscales have been consistently found to be uncorrelated with each other; the items from the AX/In, AX/Out, and AX/Con subscales have substantial loadings on independent factors (Johnson, 1984; Pollans, 1983).

The primary aim of the present study was to present further factor analytic evidence of the independence and validity of the AX/In, AX/Out, and AX/Con subscales based on a large sample of the general adult population of New Zealand. We were interested in whether the factor structure of the AX Scale could be replicated in an adult sample recruited outside of the United States. Another aim of this study was to determine if the AX subscales could predict casually recorded BP levels.

METHOD

Subjects

All households within the boundaries of the borough of Milton, New Zealand, a rural community 54 km south of Dunedin, were visited by a Rotary Club member. The residents were asked for volunteers over the age of 15 to attend a testing center as part of a regular health survey conducted every 3 years. During a 5-day period in May 1985, 1,120 persons attended, which was approximately 78% of the total adult population of Milton. Of the total sample, 96% identified themselves as European in ethnic origin, 2% as Maori, and 2% as Chinese.

Of the males ($n = 551$) in the sample, 13% were students, retired, or not looking for employment. The occupations reported by the remaining male subjects in the sample as compared with figures based on the 1981 New Zealand census statistics for males (in parentheses) were as follows: professional and technical, 7% (11%); administrative and managerial, 10% (12%); salespersons, 7% (9%); farmers and agricultural workers, 17% (13%); workers in transport occupations,

6% (5%); craftsmen, process workers, and laborers, 48% (42%); service workers, 1% (4%); and unemployed, 3% (4%).

Procedure

The total time required to participate in the health survey was about 1½ hr for each person. During this time, subjects moved systematically through a series of procedures that included medical history questionnaires; recording of height, weight, and BP; and administration of the 20-item AX Scale. BP was measured with an electric sphygmomanometer for epidemiologists developed at the Otago Medical School.[1] Each subject was seated and the last of three readings of BP was used in the data analyses.

The AX Scale was scored in accordance with the professional manual prepared by Spielberger (1988), which is similar to the method described by Spielberger et al. (1985). The AX/In score comprised the sum of the scores on Items 3, 5, 6, 10, 12, 14, 15, and 18; the AX/Out score was the sum of scores on Items 2, 7, 9, 11, 13, 19, and 20; and the AX/Con score was the sum of Items 1, 8, and 16. AX/EX scores were computed by summing the scores on the AX/In and AX/Out subscales, plus the score for Item 4 and a constant of 15, minus the AX/Con score.

RESULTS

Those volunteers who failed to answer any of the AX Scale items were excluded from the study; a total of 1,023 subjects (506 male and 517 female) responded to all 20 items. None of the subjects reported any difficulty in interpreting the items, suggesting that the AX Scale was suitable for a general adult sample outside the United States. The means and standard deviations of the scores on the AX/In and AX/Out subscales, and the reliability statistics for these scales, have been reported in detail elsewhere (Knight, Chisholm, Paulin, & Waal-Manning, 1988). No significant differences between males and females were found at any age range. The correlations between the AX/In and AX/Out subscales were negligible for both males ($r = .13$) and females ($r = .17$) but nevertheless statistically significant ($p < .001$) because of the large number of subjects in the sample.

The factor analysis procedures used in this study were similar to those employed by Spielberger et al. (1985). Separate analyses for males and females were carried out using the principal axis method, with squared multiple correlations as the initial estimates of communalities. The factors extracted by this method were subsequently rotated, employing the Kaiser varimax procedure. Four factors were found to have latent roots greater than 1.00 for both sexes; therefore, the four-, three-, and two-factor solutions were examined further. Overall, the three-factor solution provided the best approximation to simple structure and could be most meaningfully interpreted. The factor loadings for this solution are presented in Table 1.

The most striking feature of the results of the factor analysis is the clear emergence of the same three factors that were found for high school and undergraduate university students by Johnson (1984) and Spielberger et al. (1988). The three

---

[1] This instrument was based on the random zero sphygmomanometer developed for epidemiologists by the London School of Hygiene and Tropical Medicine.

Table 1 Factor loadings of the Anger EXpression Scale Items for males and females

Factor	Factor 1		Factor 2		Factor 3	
	M	F	M	F	M	F
Anger/Out						
2. Express my anger	.42	.45	.06	.00	.21	.19
7. Sarcastic comments	.58	.52	.20	.15	.08	.07
9. Slam doors	.36	.43	.07	.19	.08	.15
11. Argue with others	.41	.46	.12	.04	.16	.17
13. Strike at what infuriates me	.40	.45	.15	.16	.10	.03
17. Say nasty things	.67	.62	.20	.07	−.02	.07
19. Lose my temper	.57	.59	.06	.03	.31	.32
20. If someone annys me, tell them how I feel	.42	.40	.00	.06	.09	.00
Anger/In						
3. Keep things in	−.37	−.35	.35	.48	−.04	−.13
5. Put or sulk	.26	.26	.29	.25	.14	.28
6. Withdraw from people	.09	.05	.47	.56	.14	.08
10. Boil inside	−.11	−.26	.57	.63	−.02	.02
12. Harbor grudges	.14	.12	.48	.53	.00	.05
14. Secretly critical	.20 ·	.15	.52	.34	.00	.03
15. Angrier than willing to admit	.10	.15	.62	.57	−.06	−.05
18. Irritated more than others are aware	.15	.20	.55	.56	.05	−.05
Other Items						
1. Control my temper	.26	.25	−.06	−.07	.55	.62
8. Keep my cool	.26	.16	.05	.00	.61	.60
16. Calm down faster	.07	.02	.17	.01	.55	.44
4. Make threats	.24	.37	.21	.26	.13	.27

Note. M = Male; F = Female.

factor solutions were also remarkably consistent for both males and females. The consistency of these results with previous findings provides strong evidence for the validity of the distinction between anger-in and anger-out as independent variables. In addition, the three types of the preliminary AX/Con scale (1, 8, and 16) clearly defined a third factor.

Some minor deviations from simple structure should be noted, however. Surprisingly, Item 3 ("I keep things in") had loadings of comparable magnitude on Factor 1 (Anger/Out) and Factor 2 (Anger/In), though the loadings on the first factor were negative. No other item behaved in this way, and this anomaly has not been observed in other factor studies of the AX Scale. The finding that "I pout or sulk" loaded positively on both Factors 1 and 2 can possibly be explained by noting that this item describes two behaviors: pouting, which is an overt expression of displeasure, and sulking, which is not necessarily observable and may be similar to "withdrawal," as in Item 6. Our subjects appeared to be divided as to whether the regarded this item as indicating overt or covert expression of anger.

Item 4 ("make threats") also loaded positively on both Factors 1 and 2, though more strongly on the former. A similar finding for this item was reported by Spielberger and his colleagues and it has been deleted from the revised 24-item version of the scale. It is somewhat surprising that this item has been singularly unsuccessful, given the close approximation in content to Items 7 and 17, which also describe the verbal expression of anger.

Correlations of the AX Scale with age and BP are reported in Table 2. Age was significantly correlated with both systolic and diastolic BP, which is consistent with the well-documented finding that BP increases with age. Only AX/Out correlated significantly with BP; higher AX/Out scores were found to be associated with lower BP for both women ($p < .001$) and men ($p < .05$). Because of the significant intercorrelations of AX scores with age and BP, partial correlations between the AX subscales and BP were computed with age held constant. Controlling for age had the effect of marginally reducing the size of AX–BP correlations. The amount of variance in BP explained by the AX/Out scores was small, however, being less than 3%.

DISCUSSION

The present study confirmed, in part, previous findings of an association between anger expression and BP. With age held constant, there was a small but significant inverse relation between AX/Out scores and BP for female subjects. Women who reported being less prone to express anger overtly were more likely to have elevations in both systolic and diastolic BP. The magnitude of these correlations for the AX/Out scale were almost identical to those found by Spielberger et al. (1985). However, the significant positive correlations between AX/In and BP reported by Spielberger et al. were not found in this study.

The magnitude and pattern of results in the present study were similar to those reported by Harburg, Gentry, and colleagues, who also found that subjects with high anger-out scores had lower levels of casual BP. The reason for the failure to find a concurrent association between AX/In scores and BP, as was reported by Spielberger et al. (1985), is not obvious.

A major difference between the present study and that of Spielberger et al. (1985) was in the demographic characteristics of the samples. In the Spielberger et al. study, the subjects were high school students and approximately 40% were black. Their subjects also had higher AX Scale scores and lower average BP

Table 2 Correlations between the Anger EXpression (AX) scales and systolic and diastolic blood pressure (BP) for males and females

	Age	Systolic BP		Diastolic BP	
Age					
M		.50***		.36***	
F		.63***		.43***	
AX/In					
M	−.01	.01	(.02)[a]	.01	(.02)
F	.02	.02	(.01)	.00	(.00)
AX/Out					
M	−.14**	−.08*	(−.05)	−.09*	(−.04)
F	−.18**	−.16***	(−.14)***	−.08*	(−.07)*
AX/EX					
M	−.07	−.03	(−.00)	−.04	(−.02)
F	−.09	−.07	(−.01)	−.04	(−.01)

[a]Age-controlled partial correlations are reported in parentheses.
*$p < .05$. **$p < .01$. ***$p < .001$.

readings than the present adult sample. The heterogeneous age range of the adult sample of the present study also presents problems. There are many physical or medical reasons why BP may be elevated in subjects over the age of 30, which may override any trend for the personality factors to predict BP levels.

The factor analytic results of the present study provide strong evidence for the construct validity of the AX/In and AX/Out scales. Overall, the factor pattern was essentially equivalent to the findings that have been reported for student samples by Spielberger and his colleagues. As in previous studies, the correlation between AX/In and AX/Out subscales proved to be negligible, confirming the independence of these two scales.

Overall, the factor analytic results described in the present report and the psychometric data that are reported elsewhere (Knight et al., 1988) provide strong and independent support for the reliability and validity of the AX Scale. This new scale has an important potential as a measure of mode and style of anger expression in psychosomatic medicine. The revised AX Scale that now comprises 24 items (Spielberger, 1988; Spielberger et al., 1988) includes eight anger-control items that will serve to enhance the usefulness of this subscale.

SUMMARY

The Spielberger Anger EXpression (AX) Scale was administered to a large adult sample as a part of a general health survey of a small New Zealand community. Blood pressure (BP) readings were concurrently measured. Factor analysis of the AX items confirmed previous findings that the AX Scale is comprised of Anger/In, Anger/Out, and Anger/Control factors. The validity and independence of the AX/In and AX/Out subscales were also supported. With age held constant, women who reported expressing anger overtly were found to be have lower BP levels than those who did not. A similar trend was also noted for males.

REFERENCES

Alexander, F. G. (1939). Emotional factors in essential hypertension: Presentation of a tentative hypothesis. *Psychosomatic Medicine, 1*, 175–179.

Diamond, E. L. (1982). The role of anger and hostility in essential hypertension and coronary heart disease. *Psychological Bulletin, 92*, 410–433.

Friedman, M., & Rosenman, R. M. (1974). *Type A behavior and your heart.* Greenwich, CT: Fawcett.

Funkenstein, D. M., King, S. H., & Drolette, M. E. (1954). The direction of anger during a laboratory stress-inducing situation. *Psychosomatic Medicine, 16*, 404–413.

Gentry, W. D., Chesney, A. P., Gary, H. G., Hall, R. P., & Harburg, E. (1982). Habitual anger-coping styles: I. Effect on mean blood pressure and risk for essential hypertension. *Psychosomatic Medicine, 44*, 195–202.

Gentry, W. D., Chesney, A. P., Hall, R. P., & Harburg, E. (1981). Effect of habitual anger-coping pattern on blood pressure in black/white, high/low stress area respondents. *Psychosomatic Medicine, 43*, 88–90.

Harburg, E., Blakelock, E. H., & Roeper, P. J. (1979). Resentful and reflective coping with arbitrary authority and blood pressure: Detroit. *Psychosomatic Medicine, 3*, 189–202.

Jenkins, C. D., Zyzanski, S. J., & Rosenman, R. H. (1978). Coronary-prone behavior: One pattern or several? *Psychosomatic Medicine, 40*, 25–34.

Johnson, E. H. (1984). *Anger and anxiety as determinants of elevated blood pressure in adolescents.* Unpublished doctoral dissertation, University of South Florida, Tampa, FL.

Knight, R. G., Chisholm, B. J., Paulin, J. M., & Waal-Manning, H. J. (1988). The Spielberger Anger Expression Scale: Some psychometric data. *British Journal of Clinical Psychology, 27*, 279–281.

Knight, R. G., Paulin, J. M., & Waal-Manning, H. J. (1987). Self-reported anger intensity and blood pressure. *British Journal of Clinical Psychology, 26,* 65–66.

Pollans, C. H. (1983). *The psychometric properties and factor structure of the Anger EXpression Scale.* Unpublished master's thesis, University of South Florida, Tampa, FL.

Rosenman, R. H., Friedman, M., Strauss, R., Wurm, M., Kosicheck, R., Hahn, W., & Werthessen, N. T. (1964). A predictive study of coronary heart disease: The Western Collaborative Group study. *Journal of the American Medical Association, 189,* 15–22.

Spielberger, C. D. (1988). *Professional manual for the State–Trait Anger Expression Inventory (STAXI)* (research ed.). Tampa, FL: Psychological Assessment Resources, Inc.

Spielberger, C. D., Jacobs, G. A., Russell, S. F., & Crane, R. J. (1983). Assessment of anger: The State–Trait Anger Scale. In J. N. Butcher & C. D. Spielberger (Eds.), *Advances in personality assessment* (Vol. 2, pp. 159–187). Hillsdale, NJ: Erlbaum.

Spielberger, C. D., Johnson, E. H., Russell, S. F., Crane, R. F., Jacobs, G. A., & Worden, T. J. (1985). The experience and expression of anger: Construction and validation of an Anger Expression Scale. In M. A. Chesney & R. H. Rosenman (Eds.), *Anger and hostility in cardiovascular and behavioral disorders* (pp. 5–30). New York: Hemisphere/McGraw-Hill.

Spielberger, C. D., Krasner, S. S., & Solomon, E. P. (1988). The experience, expression and control of anger. In M. P. Janisse (Ed.), *Health psychology: Individual differences and stress* (pp. 89–108). New York: Springer/Verlag.

Williams, R. B., Haney, T. L., Lee, K. L., Kong, Y., Blumenthal, J., & Whalen, R. E. (1980). Type A behavior, hostility and coronary atherosclerosis. *Psychosomatic Medicine, 42,* 539–549.

IV

PHYSIOLOGICAL REACTIONS TO STRESS

13

Neurophysiological Studies of Stress, Arousal, and Anxiety

Rick Howard
University of Otago, New Zealand

Conceptualizations of stress and anxiety as a complex psychobiological process (e.g., Spielberger, Pollans, & Worden, 1984) recognize the centrality of cognitive appraisal processes in the evocation of an anxiety state and the importance of state and trait anxiety as psychological constructs. Lazarus and colleagues (e.g., Folkman, Schaeffer, & Lazarus, 1979) have highlighted the role of "primary" and "secondary" appraisal processes in mediating the cognitive, affective/ physiological, and motoric responses to stressors (see Figure 1).

The stressor is first appraised for its potential *threat* with reference to the individual's "personal agenda" (his or her beliefs, values, goals, and so forth). If it is perceived as threatening, then the secondary appraisal process is engaged, and the stressor is appraised for its potential *controllability*. As a result of this, coping activity is mobilized: cognitive, affective/physiological, and motoric. This coping activity and its results are then *reappraised* (indicated by feedback arrow in Figure 1), and this process continues until the person–environment equilibrium is restored. As indicated in Figure 1, the cognitive appraisal processes are subject to predisposing influences. In particular, personality traits bias the individual's appraisal of the environment, so that, for example, anxious, socially withdrawn individuals show a heightened appraisal of threat.

The studies reviewed herein all tapped, as dependent measures, the outputs shown in Figure 1. The cognitive output was tapped using a measure of perceived control called Judgment of Control (JOC). The JOC uses an analogue scale to measure the degree of control the person perceives he or she has over onset of the aversive stimulus, and is based on a measure used in previous studies of learned helplessness by Alloy and Abramson (1979).

The affective/physiological output was tapped in two ways. First, subjective mood was measured using a mood-adjective checklist called the Stress Arousal Checklist (SACL; Mackay, Cox, Burrows, & Lazzerini, 1978). This is a 30-item self-rated inventory that taps into two independent dimensions of mood, namely, stress and arousal. Stress items (e.g., "jittery," "calm," and "distressed") reflect the individual's hedonic tone, whereas arousal items (e.g., "sleepy," "alert," and "sluggish") reflect the individual's level of activation or alertness.

The second way in which this affective/physiological output was tapped was by measuring the contingent negative variation (CNV), an electrocortical measure first described by Walter, Cooper, Aldridge, McCallum, and Winter (1964), in

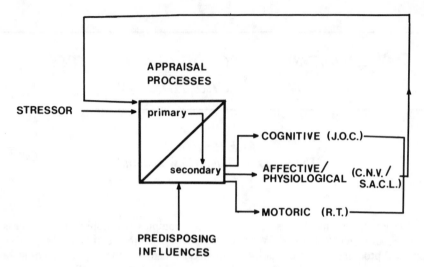

Figure 1 A psychobiological model of interacting factors influencing coping, including cognitive mediating mechanisms, stressful environmental events, and predisposing influences.

tasks involving effortful active coping. The most commonly used task was a go/no go avoidance task that combines active and passive avoidance in two interleaved conditions, go and no go (see Figure 2). In one condition (go) the subject is warned by a tone of a particular pitch that a button-press response is required to a second tone of like pitch, with response omission or too slow a response (outside a given time window) being punished by a burst of aversive white noise. Interleaved with go trials are other trials (no go condition) in which the subject is warned by a

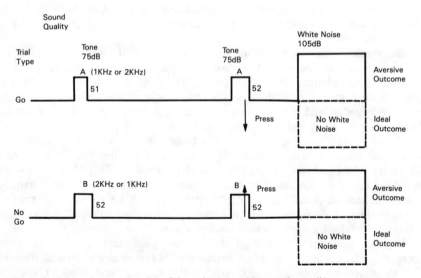

Figure 2 Schematic representation of the go/no go avoidance task paradigm.

different tone that he or she must refrain from responding to the second tone, on pain of being punished by a burst of white noise. Sample CNVs generated in this task are shown in Figure 3, where it may be seen that the go condition (upper trace) generates a large negative shift, whereas the no go condition (lower trace) generates a lack of negativity. Sometimes a positive shift (contingent positive variation) develops during the foreperiod in the no go condition.

RESEARCH STRATEGIES

The studies reviewed herein made use of three main strategies for looking at stress and coping. The first strategy involved manipulating stress experimentally, using a "helplessness" paradigm, illustrated in Figure 4. In this paradigm, subjects are tested on 2 days, a control day and an experimental day, each comprising three go/no go sessions. The only difference between days is that, notwithstanding the

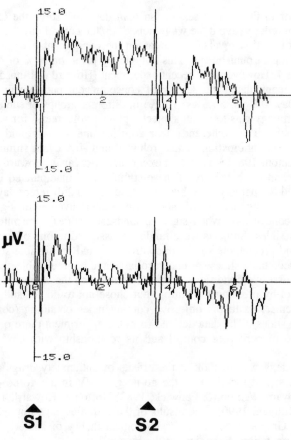

Figure 3 Go (upper trace) and no go (lower trace) contingent negative variations recorded from the vertex in a single subject. Averages are of 16 trials in each case. The interstimulus interval is 3.5 s.

Experimental Method

Helplessness

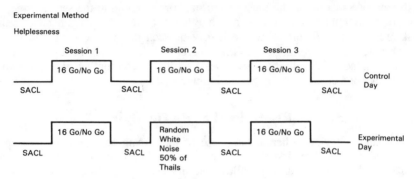

Figure 4 Schematic representation of the "helplessness" paradigm.

instruction prior to the middle session on *both* days to "solve the change in task requirements in order to avoid the white noise," on the control day the subject has to solve the discrimination reversal, whereas on the experimental day the subject receives noncontingent punishment. This is typically given on 50% of trials, as indicated in Figure 4. However, in a recent experiment (Howard & Lumsden, 1990) we systematically manipulated the density of noncontingent punishment given on the experimental day (0% vs. 50% vs. 100%) in different groups of subjects.

A second strategy was to select subjects (phobic volunteers) for whom particular classes of stimuli are inherently fear arousing and stressful and to record the CNV generated in anticipation of fear-relevant and -irrelevant stimuli (Lumsden, Howard, & Fenton, 1986). In a recent experiment (Regan & Howard, in press) the controllability and predictability of these stimuli were manipulated in the context of a forewarned RT paradigm. Subjects were tested on 2 different days: an experimental day, when signaled blank slides were interleaved with signaled phobic slides, and a control day, when signaled landscape slides were interleaved with signaled blank slides. Subjects were randomly assigned to one of four conditions: controllable and predictable slides, uncontrollable and predictable slides, controllable and unpredictable slides, or uncontrollable and unpredictable slides. Figure 5 illustrates the first two conditions. Subjects were given the option of attempting to exercise control by pressing the button, but chose not to do so, and therefore did not expose themselves to the objective contingencies obtaining (controllable vs. uncontrollable slides). The data derived from the experiment therefore highlighted the importance of perceived control and its relationship with CNV, stress, and arousal.

A third strategy was to look at the effects of antianxiety drugs (barbiturates, benzodiazepines, and nicotine) on the go/no go CNV in the go/no go avoidance paradigm (Howard, Fenton, & Fenwick, 1982; Norton & Howard, 1988; Norton, Howard, & Milligan, 1990). The results of these studies have implications for the application of Gray's (1982) neuropsychological theory of anxiety, derived from animal experimentation, to anxiety at the human level.

Results from studies using the first two aforementioned strategies shall be reviewed first (see summary in Table 1). These have resulted in a working schema of the relationships between mood, perceived threat, and perceived control. Results

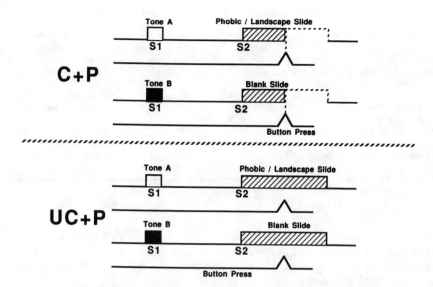

Figure 5 Task paradigm for experiment in which controllability and predictability of slide stimuli were independently manipulated in different groups of subjects. The figure shows the conditions where slides were controllable and predictable (C + P) and uncontrollable and predictable (UC + P).

pertaining to the third strategy are then outlined, and then their implications for Gray's neuropsychological theory of anxiety are discussed.

RELATIONSHIPS BETWEEN MOOD
AND CONTINGENT NEGATIVE VARIATION

Subjective Stress and Go Contingent
Negative Variation

Our studies have found a consistent association between the amplitude of the go (but not the no go) CNV, measured at both temporal and central sites, and subjective stress (Brown, Fenwick, & Howard, 1989; Norton & Howard, 1988; Howard & Lumsden, 1990; Regan & Howard, in press). However, the sign of this association varied with resting level of stress, indicating a nonlinear (inverted U) relationship. At low initial levels of stress, stress was found to be positively correlated with CNV amplitude, particularly at temporal recording sites (Brown et al., 1989). However, if high levels of stress were induced, either by helplessness (Howard & Lumsden, 1990) or by phobic slide stimulation (Regan & Howard, in press), the CNV amplitude decreased with increasing stress. This was shown particularly clearly in the Howard and Lumsden (1990) helplessness study. Across all subjects, there was a modest but significant negative correlation between change in go CNV amplitude and change in subjective stress consequent upon the helplessness procedure, $r = -0.38, p < .05$. However, in this paradigm some subjects (responders) reacted to the helplessness procedure with an increase in subjective stress, whereas others (nonresponders) did not. For responders, the correlation between change in

Table 1 Summary of studies of interrelationships among mood, contingent negative variation
(CNV), and perceived control

Study	Subjects	Paradigm	Measures
Brown, Fenwick, & Howard (1989)	12 males	Go/no go	CNV, SACL[a]
Norton & Howard (1988)	12 male smokers	Go/no go	CNV, SACL, JoC[b]
Petticrew, Howard, & McCullagh (1990)	Male and female, high and low hostility	Go/no go with "helplessness"	Heart rate, pulse transit time, SACL, JoC
Regan & Howard (in press)	16 female phobics	"Phobia CNV"	CNV, subjective fear, SACL, JoC
Howard & Lumsden (1990)	36 females	Go/no go with "helplessness"	CNV, SACL, JoC

[a]Stress Arousal Checklist.
[b]Judgment of Control scale.

go CNV and change in subjective stress was strong, $r = -0.68$, $p < .01$. It is interesting to note that this nonmonotonic relationship between go CNV and subjective stress is identical to that originally proposed by Tecce (1972) to obtain between CNV and what he termed "arousal."

Subjective Arousal and the No Go Contingent Negative Variation

In contrast to the go CNV, the no go CNV amplitude has been found to relate to changes in subjective arousal (Brown et al., 1989a; Norton & Howard, 1988). However, again the relationship appeared to be nonlinear. Brown et al. found an inverse relationship between no go CNV and SACL arousal, $r = -0.68$, $p < .01$. Norton and Howard found a positive relationship between changes in arousal consequent upon cigarette smoking and change in the no go CNV, $r = 0.67$, $p < .05$. In this case, therefore, there appears to have been a U shaped relationship between arousal and no go CNV amplitude. At low levels of arousal, a negative relationship obtains between arousal and no go CNV. At higher levels of arousal (such as are induced by cigarette smoking), no go CNV increases as arousal increases. This is in contrast to the inverted-U relationship originally suggested by Tecce (1972) to obtain between CNV and what he referred to as "arousal."

RELATIONSHIP BETWEEN CONTINGENT NEGATIVE VARIATION AND PERCEIVED CONTROL

No relationship has been found between the go/no go CNV and perceived control (Howard & Lumsden, 1990; Norton & Howard, 1988). Howard and Lumsden in their helplessness study were able to successfully manipulate perceived control by varying density of noncontingent punishment in a between-groups design (see Figure 6). The go/no go CNV, however, did not change systematically between groups. In contrast to the go/no go CNV, amplitude of the CNV in anticipation of phobic slides ("phobic slide CNV"), but not that of the

CNV in anticipation of blank slides ("blank slide CNV"), was found by Regan and Howard to be positively correlated ($r = 0.89$, $p < .01$) with perceived control.

RELATIONSHIPS BETWEEN MOOD AND PERCEIVED CONTROL

A consistent inverse relationship has been found between stress and perceived control (Norton & Howard, 1988; Petticrew, Howard, & McCullagh, 1990; Regan & Howard, in press). Thus, with increasing stress, perceived control was reduced. A fairly consistent *positive* relationship was found between arousal and perceived control by Norton and Howard (1988) and Petticrew et al., (1990). However, in the latter study, in which high-hostility subjects were compared with low-hostility subjects, the significant relationships between mood and perceived control were restricted to the high hostiles on the control (low stress) day.

A WORKING SCHEMA

The results described above led to the development of a working schema that is outlined in Figure 7. Two orthogonal dimensions are shown, a perceived control (secondary appraisal) dimension and a perceived threat dimension, the latter corresponding to the balance between lateralized activation and arousal processes as proposed by Tucker and Williamson (1984). Activation is a left-hemisphere process related to motor readiness and (at a trait level) to anxiety/social withdrawal. Arousal is a right-hemisphere process related to response to novel perceptual input and habituation and (at a trait level) to low anxiety/social withdrawal (Brown et al., 1989; Carter, Johnson, & Borkovec, 1986).

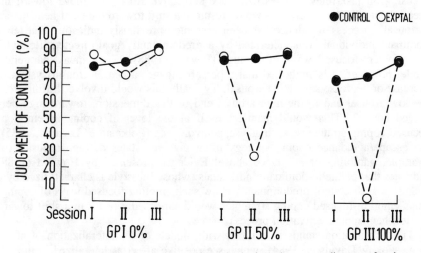

Figure 6 Perceived control over the aversive noise in the go/no go paradigm as a function of density of noncontingent noise (0% vs. 50% vs. 100%) delivered in the middle session of the experimental day using the "helplessness" paradigm. Noise was response contingent throughout on the control day.

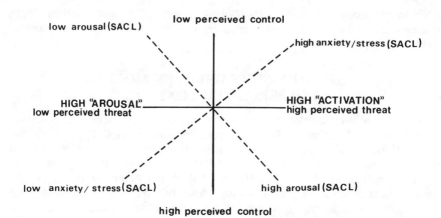

Figure 7 Primary (perceived threat) and secondary (perceived control) appraisal processes
represented as orthogonal dimensions. "ACTIVATION" and "AROUSAL" refer
to processes said by Tucker and Williamson (1984) to reflect left- and
right-hemisphere activation, respectively. Arousal (SACL) and anxiety/stress
(SACL) refer to subjective arousal and stress as measured by the Stress Arousal
Checklist (SACL; Mackay, Cox, Burrows, & Lazzerini, 1978).

We can consider that the balance between activation and arousal might be manipulated in either of two ways: (a) by engaging or disengaging a neural *stress*
system to increase or decrease subjective stress or (b) by engaging or disengaging
a neural *arousal* system to increase or decrease subjective arousal. It is suggested
that when a person is in a goal-directed or, to use the language of reversal theory
(Apter, 1982), "telic" mode, he or she engages in problem-focused coping by
focusing on task-relevant cues to reduce subjective stress and move toward increased perceived control. This would result in a shift toward the right-hemisphere
"arousal" process. Evidence has been presented previously indicating that telic-
dominant individuals (characterized by a predominantly goal-directed life-style)
use problem-focused ways of coping (Howard, 1988). When in a "paratelic"
mode, however, it is suggested that a person engages a neural arousal system to
increase or decrease subjective arousal. Typically this would involve shifting from
the low arousal end to the high arousal end of this dimension, toward high perceived control. This would manifest itself at the level of coping as emotion-
focused coping strategies, such as escape/avoidance (Folkman & Lazarus, 1985).
An escape/avoidance coping strategy often involves states of high arousal, for
example, gambling or substance abuse. Evidence presented by Howard (1988)
indicates that paratelic-dominant individuals (whose life-style is characterized by a
lack of goal direction) predominantly show such emotion-focused ways of coping.
Thus emotion-focused coping strategies would supposedly result in a shift toward
the left-hemisphere activation process.

  This formulation stands in contrast with models of the lateralization of affect
(e.g., Fox & Davidson, 1984), which see positive affect as lateralized in the left
hemisphere and negative affect as lateralized in the right hemisphere. The present
view sees positive affect as associated with *either* hemisphere, depending on the
individual's metamotivational state (telic vs. paratelic).

NEUROPSYCHOLOGICAL THEORIES OF ANXIETY

Gray's Theory

In *The Neuropsychology of Anxiety*, Gray (1982) amasses a considerable body of evidence based on animal research that attributes anxiety to a brain system (the behavioral inhibition system; BIS) sensitive to signals of response-contingent punishment or frustrative nonreward, as well as to novel stimuli and "innate fear" stimuli. In general, the effects of such stimuli are inhibitory and are counteracted by a variety of antianxiety drugs such as benzodiazepines (BZDs), barbiturates, and alcohol. In particular, these drugs counteract the inhibition of responding caused by punishment of normally reinforced responses (passive avoidance) as well as by novel or innately fear-arousing stimuli. On the basis of this research, Gray equates anxiety with level of activity in the BIS.

Gray (1982) suggests that the septal–hippocampal system (SHS), the supposed neuroanatomical substrate of the BIS, acts as a "mismatch detector." When an unexpected (nonpredicted) outcome is encountered and involves nonreward, punishment, or novelty, the SHS switches from a "just checking" mode to a "control" mode. This has three important consequences: First, there is inhibition of ongoing motor programs. Second, the current motor program is labeled as faulty and in need of checking. Third, exploratory behavior is initiated aimed at the source of the mismatch. The SHS receives ascending excitatory inputs through noradrenergic, serotonergic, and cholinergic pathways, resulting in enhanced activity in the SHS/BIS and hence in anxiety. Anxiolytic drugs are said to work by inhibiting these ascending excitatory inputs to the SHS. There is also a descending excitatory input to the SHS from the orbitofrontal cortex. As well as transmitting to the SHS information about ongoing motor programs, the orbitofrontal cortex permits (in humans) neocortical control of the SHS/BIS, through verbally coded information. Thus the orbitofrontal cortex may be said to be a cortical extension of the SHS/BIS at the human level. Finally, an excitatory noradrenergic output from the SHS to hypothalamic mechanisms primes the organism for vigorous activity ("fight/flight").

Gray's (1982) theory can be construed as an attentional model of anxiety, insofar as high activation of the SHS/BIS in its just-checking mode results in *overattention* to potentially anxiety-provoking stimuli (cues signaling punishment, nonreward, and so forth). This state of "hypervigilance" would be analogous to a state of generalized anxiety in humans. A high state of activation of the SHS/BIS in its control mode, by contrast, would be analogous to an obsessional–compulsive state.

A number of unresolved problems remain in Gray's theory. One concerns the problem of assessing and defining "anxiety" in animals. Gray's theory rests on the assumption that a description of the psychological processes that are altered by antianxiety drugs is equivalent to a description of the psychology of anxiety (Gray, 1982). By psychological processes Gray refers to behaviors such as passive avoidance. There is a degree of circularity in Gray's argument that we can use the level of "behavioral inhibition" as a measure of the anxiolytic effects of drugs, because the prime reason for equating behavioral inhibition with anxiety is that anxiolytic drugs affect it. A disinhibiting effect of anxiolytic drugs on animal behavior as passive avoidance can as well be interpreted as reflecting an increase in siveness as a decrease in anxiety. Therefore the BIS/SHS could as well be seen, at the human level, as the substrate of impulsiveness as of anxiety (Fenwick, Howard, & Fenton, 1983). It becomes imperative, therefore, that theories derived from animal studies be directly tested on human subjects, in whom subjective state can be independently assessed.

Another problem with Gray's (1982) model of anxiety is that it associates anxiety primarily with behavioral inhibition, rather than with the activation of behavior. The commonsense everyday experience of anxiety, however, frequently relates it to situations such as hurrying for a train, taking an examination, or attending an interview. In all of these situations active responding rather than passive avoidance is required. Although Gray explicitly acknowledges the role of the BIS/SHS in priming hypothalamic motor systems involved in fight/flight, still this does not seem to do justice to the fact that anxiety in people is often experienced when they are in a state of behavioral activation.

Perhaps the most important problem with Gray's theory, however, is that it focuses on subcortical, noncognitive aspects of anxiety rather than on the cortical, cognitive aspect. At the level of experience this manifests itself as "worry," which has been described as consisting of "uncontrollable verbally mediated cognitive activity, or thoughts, about self-relevant issues such as interpersonal relations, finances and work, and is concerned primarily with future events" (Carter et al., 1986, p. 193). At the level of cognitive mechanisms, anxiety involves the appraisal processes alluded to earlier (see Figure 1). Translating from cognitive to neural mechanisms, we might relate the "primary appraisal" process to Gray's SHS in its just-checking mode, whereas the "secondary appraisal" process may be related to Gray's SHS in its control mode.

The Tucker and Williamson (1984) Model

Tucker and Williamson (1984) suggested that anxiety at the human level reflects a predominance of a left-hemisphere "activation" process involved in mediating motor readiness. This process, contrasted with a right-hemisphere, noradrenergically mediated "arousal" process, is said to be dependent on dopaminergic neurotransmission. As Tucker and Williamson stated,

> The primary subjective experience of activation may be anxiety. As it operates to prime the motor system, activation engages an active attentional mode with experiential as well as cybernetic features. In anxiety, a tonic alertness is maintained in anticipation of negative events. (1984, p. 209)

Like Gray's (1982) model, Tucker and Williamson's conceptualization is an attentional model of anxiety; that is, anxiety entails hypervigilance to environmental signals of potential threat. However, Tucker and Williamson are suggesting the existence of neural mechanisms of anxiety at the cortical level in humans, whereas Gray's animal model merely postulates an input from the orbitofrontal cortex to the subcortical system (SHS), which itself mediates anxiety.

Tucker and Williamson (1984) adduced behavioral evidence of their own to support their hypothesis. More recently, Carter et al. (1986) have provided electroencephalogram (EEG) evidence to support Tucker and Williamson's hypothesis.

Worry was found to be associated with high overall cortical (EEG) activation and with relatively greater left-hemisphere activation. Progressive relaxation was associated with attenuation of this EEG asymmetry. Further support for Tucker and Williamson's hypothesis has been provided by results of a study using event-related brain potential measures (Howard, Fenwick, & Brown, 1990). In this study, a CNV paradigm was developed that produced hemispherically lateralized CNVs related to verbal and visuospatial cognitive functions. It was found that lateralization of the CNV reflected trait anxiety/social withdrawal, such that high-anxiety subjects showed relatively greater CNVs in the left hemisphere, regardless of task (verbal vs. visuospatial), whereas low-anxiety subjects showed greater CNVs in the right hemisphere.

An Integration of the Two Models

It has been suggested by Brown et al. (1989) that the dynamic balance between Tucker and Williamson's (1984) "activation" and "arousal" processes may represent the cortical extension of Gray's (1982) BIS at the human level. However, the question arises whether, at the human level, Gray's SHS is the substrate of subjective stress or of subjective arousal. This question can be addressed by looking at the effects of anxiolytic drugs on the go/no go CNV, given (as indicated above) that the go CNV relates to stress, while the no go CNV relates to arousal. According to Figure 7, a reduction in anxiety/activation could be achieved either by a reduction in stress or by a reduction in arousal, or, indeed, through a reduction in both stress and arousal. Intuitively, one might expect an effect of anxiolytics on the stress dimension. On the other hand, some authors have suggested an effect on arousal (e.g., Blaha & Brückman, 1983). The demonstrated relationship between the SHS and behavioral inhibition in the rat might lead one to expect that anxiolytics would operate on the arousal dimension, because this is related to the CNV recorded in the passive avoidance (no go) situation.

Effects of Anxiolytics on the Go/No Go Contingent Negative Variation

Studies on the effects of three different classes of anxiolytic drug—barbiturates, BZDs, and nicotine—are summarized in Table 2. It may be seen from Table 2 that the only common effect of all drugs is a reduction in the go CNV; effects of the drugs on the no go CNV are variable and inconsistent.

Table 2　Summary of studies of the effects of anxiolytic drugs on the go/no go contingent negative variation (CNV)

Study	Drug (dose)	Subjects	Effect on go CNV	Effect on no go CNV
Howard, Fenton, & Fenwick (1982)	Secobarbital (200 mg)	Male mentally abnormal offenders	Reduced	Increased
Norton & Howard 1988)	Nicotine (self-titrated)	Male smokers	Reduced/increased	Reduced/increased
Norton, Howard, & Milligan (1990)	Midazolam (15 mg)	Male medical students	Reduced	Unchanged

From this we may conclude, first, that the common anxiolytic action of these drugs is via an effect on the "stress" dimension shown in Figure 7; that is to say, the drugs result in movement toward the "low stress" pole of this dimension. This is hardly a dramatic or surprising conclusion, being what one might intuitively expect.

The go CNV is thought to be mediated by a cortically represented "action acceptor" or expectancy for reward/nonpunishment that modulates activity in a subcortical reward motivational (go) system (Howard et al., 1982). We can therefore conclude that the common anxiolytic effect of these drugs in people is mediated by an inhibitory effect either directly on the cortical action acceptor or on its excitatory input to the subcortical go system. This leads to the conclusion that Gray's (1982) SHS at the human level mediates behavioral activation rather than inhibition. Although this may appear paradoxical, given the association between Gray's SHS and behavioral inhibition in rats, we need to bear in mind, as was pointed out in the beginning of this chapter, that anxiety at the human level is associated with behavioral activation and motor readiness. This conclusion implies that behavioral inhibition in the rat (as indexed, for example, by passive avoidance) is not a valid behavioral model of human anxiety.

Finally, our interpretation of the effects of anxiolytic drugs clarifies two paradoxes contained within Gray's (1982) theory of anxiety. The first paradox relates to Gray's proposition that the BIS functions to detect mismatch, particularly between expected reward/nonpunishment and obtained nonreward/punishment. When such a mismatch is detected, the BIS enters control mode, with inhibition of ongoing motor programs, labeling of ongoing motor programs as faulty, and instigation of exploratory behavior. This being the case, it would be reasonable to expect that the strength of the mismatch would be determined by the strength of the expectancy for reward/nonpunishment. However, the strength of this expectancy is, by Gray's own argument, related to impulsivity, not to anxiety. This paradox is resolved if one views anxiety (rather than impulsivity) as related to the level of activity in the cortical action acceptor for reward/nonpunishment.

The second paradox concerns the supposed poor ability of anxious individuals to suppress incorrect responses. As Gray (1982, p. 457) stated, "If anxious individuals are genuinely worse at reversal learning, it is strange that, in animals, antianxiety drugs impair the ability to suppress dominant incorrect responses and thus hinder reversal learning." In the present formulation, the mismatch pathway from the reward/nonpunishment action acceptor is also instrumental in the extinction of previously reinforced responses, so that if activity in this pathway is reduced by BZDs, then failure of response suppression (e.g., in extinction) will occur.

DISCUSSION AND CONCLUSIONS

It is suggested that the two independent mood dimensions stress and arousal as defined by Mackay et al. (1978) reflect activity in go and no go brain systems, respectively. Each system has associated with it its own action acceptor or expectancy—in the case of the go system, an action acceptor for reward/nonpunishment; in the case of the no go system, an action acceptor for punishment/nonreward. Thus subjective stress and arousal are said to reflect activation of reward/nonpunishment and punishment/nonreward action acceptors, respectively. The hemispheric balance between Tucker and Williamson's (1984) activation and arousal processes is said to be the cortical correlate of trait anxiety. This hemispheric balance is manipulable in either of two ways: by reducing subjective stress via a change in the brain go system, or by reducing subjective arousal via a change in the brain no go system. It is suggested that the option selected will depend on the individual's "metamotivational state" (Apter, 1982). When in a goal-directed (telic) state, activity in the go system and its associated action acceptor may be modified to bring about changes in subjective stress. This will typically result (in the overstressed individual) in a hemispheric shift in favor of the right-hemisphere arousal process of Tucker and Williamson. When in a non-goal-directed (paratelic) state, activity in the no go system and its associated action acceptor may be modified to bring about changes in subjective arousal. This will typically result (in the individual suffering from acute boredom) in a hemisphere shift in favor of the left-hemisphere activation process of Tucker and Williamson. Thus brain go and no go systems are said to be under the higher level control of metamotivational state.

Some support for the idea that modulation of the no go system is operating when in a paratelic state is provided by analysis of the P300 component of the auditory evoked potential in people who are either telic or paratelic dominant as indexed by the Telic Dominance Scale of Murgatroyd, Rushton, Apter, and Ray (1978). Changes in the P300 amplitude reflect changes in level of alertness/arousal as indexed by performance measures, for example, errors in the go/no go task (Svebak, Howard, & Rimehaug, 1987) and choice reaction time and critical flicker fusion frequency (Milligan, Lumsden, Howard, Howe, & Dundee, 1989). The P300 amplitude is enhanced or diminished by doses of nicotine, which produce opposite effects on subjective arousal (Norton & Howard, 1990). Thus there are good grounds for suggesting the P300 reflects the relative state of activation of the no go system, assuming that this system mediates changes in subjective arousal. Paratelic-dominant individuals have been found to show more variability in their P300, depending on task conditions. Stimuli that do not require an immediate response (warning stimuli in the go/no go paradigm) have been found to elicit small P300s in paratelic-dominant individuals (Svebak et al., 1987). On the other hand, in an unpublished study using the auditory "oddball" paradigm, in which some (rare) stimuli require an immediate response whereas other (frequent) stimuli do not, paratelic-dominant individuals showed, in comparison with telic-dominant individuals, shorter latency P300s to frequent (nontarget) stimuli but longer latency P300s to rare (target) stimuli. P300 amplitude, on the other hand, did not vary in this task between telic- and paratelic-dominant individuals. It seems, therefore, that paratelic-dominant individuals show a more variable sensitivity or "gain" control of their no go system.

SUMMARY

Studies are reviewed in which cognitive (perceived control) and affective/ physiological (contingent negative variation [CNV] and subjective stress and arousal), as well as motoric responses were measured in tasks involving effortful active coping. Three main strategies were used for looking at stress and coping: experimental manipulation of stress via changes in controllability of aversive stimuli, use of subjects for whom particular classes of stimuli are inherently aversive, and use of antianxiety drugs. A working schema is outlined for describing the interrelationships found among mood, perceived control, and the CNV. Two recent neuropsychological models of anxiety are discussed. Results are summarized from studies examining the effects of antianxiety drugs on the CNV measured in a go/no go avoidance task incorporating both active and passive avoidance. Their implications for a neuropsychological theory of anxiety are discussed.

REFERENCES

Alloy, L. B., & Abramson, L. Y. (1979). Judgement of contingency in depressed and non-depressed students: Sadder but wiser? *Journal of Experimental Psychology: General, 108,* 441–485.

Apter, M. J. (1982). *The experience of motivation: The theory of psychological reversals.* London: Academic Press.

Blaha, L., & Brückman, J. -U. (1983). Benzodiazepines in the treatment of anxiety (Angst): European experiences. In E. Costa (Ed.), *The benzodiazepines: From molecular biology to clinical practice* (pp. 287–293). New York: Raven Press.

Brown, D., Fenwick, P. B. C., & Howard, R. C. (1989). The contingent negative variation in a go/no go avoidance task: Relationships with personality and subjective state. *International Journal of Psychophysiology, 7,* 35–45.

Carter, W. R., Johnson, M. C., & Borkovec, T. D. (1986). Worry: An electrocortical analysis. *Advances in Behavior Research and Therapy, 8,* 193–204.

Fenwick, P. B. C., Howard, R. C., & Fenton, G. W. (1983). Review of cortical excitability, neurohumoral transmission, and the dyscontrol syndrome. In M. Parsonage, (Ed.), *Advances in epileptology: XIVth Epilepsy International Symposium* (pp. 181–191). New York: Raven Press.

Folkman, S., & Lazarus, R. S. (1985). If it changes it must be a process. A study of emotion and coping during three stages of a college exam. *Journal of Personality and Social Psychology, 48,* 150–170.

Folkman, S., Schaeffer, C., & Lazarus, R. S. (1979). Cognitive processes as mediators of stress and coping. In V. Hamilton & D. M. Warburton (Eds.), *Human stress and cognition: An information processing approach* (pp. 265–298). New York: John Wiley & Sons.

Fox, N. A., & Davidson, R. J. (1984). Hemispheric substrates of affect: A developmental model. In N. A. Fox & R. J. Davidson (Eds.), *The psychobiology of affective development* (pp. 353–380). Hillsdale, NJ: Lawrence Erlbaum.

Gray, J. A. (1982). *The neuropsychology of anxiety: An enquiry into the function of the septo-hippocampal system.* Oxford, England: Oxford University Press.

Howard, R. C. (1988). Telic dominance, personality and coping. In M. J. Apter, J. H. Kerr, & M. P. Cowles (Eds.), *Progress in reversal theory* (pp. 129–141). Amsterdam: Elsevier (North Holland).

Howard, R. C., Fenton, G. W., & Fenwick, P. B. C. (1982). *Event related brain potentials in personality and psychopathology: A Pavlovian approach.* New York: John Wiley.

Howard, R. C., & Lumsden, J. (1990). *Uncontrollability and the contingent negative variation (CNV): Relationships with perceived control and subjective stress.* Manuscript in preparation.

Howard, R. C., Fenwick, P. B. C., & Brown, D. (1990). *Relationship of personality to laterality and performance in cognitive tasks.* Manuscript in preparation.

Lumsden, J., Howard, R. C., & Fenton, G. W. (1986). The contingent negative variation (CNV) to fear-related stimuli in acquisition and extinction. *International Journal of Psychophysiology, 3,* 253–261.

Mackay, C., Cox, T., Burrows, G., & Lazzerini, I. (1978). An inventory for the measurement of self-reported stress and arousal. *British Journal of Social and Clinical Psychology, 17,* 283–284.

Milligan, K. R., Lumsden, J., Howard, R. C., Howe, J. P., & Dundee, J. W. (1989). Use of auditory evoked responses as a measure of recovery from benzodiazepine sedation. *Journal of the Royal Society of Medicine, 82,* 595–597.

Murgatroyd, S., Rushton, C., Apter, M. J., & Ray, C. (1978). The development of the Telic Dominance Scale. *Journal of Personality Assessment, 42,* 519–528.

Norton, R., & Howard, R. C. (1988). Smoking, mood and the contingent negative variation (CNV) in a go–no go avoidance task. *Journal of Psychophysiology, 2,* 109–118.

Norton, R., & Howard, R. C. (1990). *Changes in the P300 induced by cigarette smoking.* Manuscript in preparation.

Norton, R., Howard, R. C., & Milligan, K. (1990). *Effects of a benzodiazepine (midazolam) on the contingent negative variation (CNV) in a go/no go avoidance task.* Manuscript submitted for publication.

Petticrew, M. P., Howard, R. C., & McCullagh, P. (1990). *Hostility, coping with stress and cardiovascular reactivity.* Manuscript in preparation.

Regan, M., & Howard, R. C. (in press). Controllability, predictability, and event related potentials to fear-relevant and fear-irrelevant stimuli. *Journal of Psychophysiology.*

Spielberger, C. D., Pollans, C. H., & Worden, T. J. (1984). Anxiety disorders. In S. M. Turner & M. Hersen (Eds.), *Adult psychopathology and diagnosis* (pp. 263–303). New York: John Wiley & Sons.

Svebak, S., Howard, R. C., & Rimehaug, T. (1987). P300 and quality of performance in a forewarned go/no go reaction time task: The significance of goal-directed lifestyle and impulsivity. *Personality and Individual differences, 8,* 313–319.

Tecce, J. (1972). Contingent negative variation (CNV) and psychological processes in man. *Psychological Bulletin, 77,* 73–108.

Tucker, D. M., & Williamson, P. A. (1984). Asymmetric neural control systems and human self-regulation. *Psychological Review, 91,* 185–215.

Walter, W. G., Cooper, R., Aldridge, V. J., McCallum, W. C., & Winter, A. L. (1964). Contingent negative variation: An electric sign of sensorimotor association and expectancy in man. *Nature, 203,* 380–384.

14

Emotional and Cortisol Response to Uncontrollable Stress

Petra Netter, Serge Croes, Peter Merz, and Matthias Müller
University of Giessen, Germany

This chapter reports research findings on emotions and physiological reactions to uncontrollable stress. This research was guided by three general theoretical concepts: First, Seligman's revised theory of learned helplessness (Abramson, Teasdale, & Seligman, 1978) defines an internal, stable, and global attribution style (AS) as one of the prerequisites for the development of depression. The other prerequisite for depression, derived from Seligman's (1975) earlier theory, states that an experienced noncontingency between behavior and an aversive uncontrollable stimulus elicits helplessness that is manifested in emotional, motivational, and cognitive deficits (Seligman, 1975).

If a person who has developed the expectancy of incompetence on the basis of a negative attribution style (i.e., interpreting negative events contingent on behavior as reliable, as due to personal shortcomings, and as referring to all similar events) is exposed to a *controllable* situation, helplessness will develop with motivational, emotional, and cognitive deficits (Petermann, 1987). However, the theory does not make clear predictions regarding how subjects with depressive AS react to *uncontrollable* situations, that is, whether such situations match the subjects' expectations and elicit less anxiety and associated deficits, or whether uncontrollability heightens these anxiety-related deficits.

The second concept was derived from endocrinological research on depression. Higher plasma levels of cortisol, as well as nonsuppression of adrenocorticotropic hormone (ACTH), and cortisol release upon challenge by the dexamethasone suppression test, have been reported for patients suffering from endogenous depression (Depue, 1979). However, little is known about the cortisol responses of such patients to stress. Furthermore, because many clinical studies have confirmed predictions from Seligman's theory of a higher incidence of depressive AS in depressed patients, a positive relationship would be expected between AS and plasma cortisol level.

The third basis for our experiments was the animal model proposed by Henry and Stephens (1977). This model predicts higher cortisol responses in individuals who employ subordinate, passive coping behaviors rather than dominant, fight-or-flight behaviors. The cortisol response results from activation of the hippocampus–septum–hypothalamus–pituitary–adrenal axis under conditions of unavoidable stress in contrast to activation of the amygdala–sympathomedullary system when the individual tries to control the situation. Several investigators have successfully related these biochemical findings to Seligman's model of learned helplessness in animals (Maier, 1984; Overmier & Wielkiewicz, 1983; Swenson & Vogel, 1983). Although reports on cortisol responses under conditions of uncontrollability in humans are scarce, they tend to confirm higher cortisol responses to uncontrollable stress (Breier et al., 1987).

The purpose of the present two experiments was to elucidate the relationship between experimental uncontrollability and AS as derived from the two parts of Seligman's theory and to combine the three concepts of AS, clinical depression, and cortisol response in uncontrollable conditions.

Experiment 1 was designed to answer the following questions confined to the emotional deficit:

1. Does uncontrollable stress elicit higher anxiety and unpleasant emotions than controllable stress and is this difference larger in subjects of depressive attribution style (ASQ+) than in those of nondepressive attribution style (ASQ−)?

2. Are there differences in these responses with respect to types of stressors (mental vs. physical)?

3. How do physiological responses reflect the emotional responses in groups ASQ+ and ASQ−?

Experiment 2 studied the following questions:

4. Is cortisol response to uncontrollable stress higher than to controllable stress?

5. Do depressives show higher cortisol responses to failure than nondepressed matched controls and are differences in cortisol responses to uncontrollable stress and to controllable stress more pronounced in depressed patients than in controls?

6. Does therapy for depression bring the depressed patients' cortisol responses closer to control values?

7. Does preceding failure affect cortisol responses to success and is this different for groups of different levels of depression?

8. How does the subject's state depression and attribution style when rating his or her (manipulated) test performance match respective cortisol responses?

METHOD

Experiment 1

Subjects were 20 healthy male students who were exposed to the following types of stressors in balanced order:

• two cognitive stressors (number completion and adding; Klutmann, 1980) and modified d_2 letter cancellation (Brickenkamp, 1972);
• one emotional stressor (two short videos of accidents);
• two physical stressors (electrical pain stimulus and its anticipation; threat of blood sampling that did not take place).

These conditions were either controllable or uncontrollable. In the case of the cognitive tasks the time for reaching a goal set by the subject was manipulated to induce failure; in the case of the videos, the instruction and button to switch off the video were not presented, as they were in the controllable condition; and in case of the electrical stimulus the intensity (ampères) was not to be operated by the subject, as it was in the controllable situation. The order of stressors was balanced so that a subject exposed to a given uncontrollable stress was yoked to a subject who had been exposed to the same set and order of stressors before and was now exposed to a controllable stress. This again was balanced for two groups of 10 subjects each divided according to a questionnaire on depressive attributional style (Brunstein, 1986) into above and below median scores.

Dependent variables included ratings on emotional state and subjective sensations of heart rate after each stressor and recordings of heart rate prior to and after each of the stressors.

Composite scores were computed for anxiety from ratings on helplessness, disappointment, depression, and anxiety and for negative emotional state composed of the adjectives nervous, excited, aroused, and calm (inverted).

Experiment 2

Two groups of 12 hospitalized endogenous depressive patients each, one group with acute depression (depressed less than 1 week) and one having had 3 weeks or more of antidepressant treatment, and a control group of 12 surgical patients all individually matched for age and sex were subjected to a control day on which one specimen of saliva for analysis of cortisol was taken and a modified German version (Brunstein, 1986) of the Attributional Style Questionnaire (ASQ; Peterson et al., 1982) was administered. On the two consecutive experimental days they were subjected to the number completion and addition test (Klutmann, 1980). Success and failure were induced in balanced order by either letting patients reach a previously set goal or stopping them prior to the target.

In order to disguise manipulation of success (S) and failure (F), the order of the five trials on the day of success was SFSSS and on the day of failure was FSFFF. Specimens of saliva for cortisol determination were taken three times at 5-min intervals prior to and after the stressor and 30 min after the test. Ratings on attribution of experimentally experienced success and failure were obtained after the test and ratings on state depression before and afterwards.

Saliva specimens were stored at $-20\,°C$ and free cortisol was analyzed in saliva by radioimmunoassay with a commercial kit (Mallinckrodt Diagnostica) according to the method described by Hiramatsu (1981). Experiment 2 was approved by the Ethics Committee of the Hessian Hospital Association.

Statistical evaluation in Experiment 1 was performed by analysis of variance with the independent variables ASQ+/ASQ- and uncontrollable/controllable stress and in Experiment 2 by analysis of covariance with pretest values as covariates and with groups and order of success and failure as independent variables and success/failure as a repeated measurement factor. In one analysis of cortisol the 3 points of measurement were included as a second repeated measurement factor. Furthermore, correlations between state depression and ASQ state ratings for experimental performance on the one hand and corresponding cortisol change scores and cortisol baseline values of respective days on the other were computed for the total sample.

RESULTS

Experiment 1

One of the stressors, the number test, yielded significantly higher anxiety values in uncontrollable than in controllable stress, whereas the video stress and threat of blood sampling merely revealed differences between groups, with ASQ+ subjects showing significantly higher levels of anxiety than ASQ− subjects in controllable as well as in uncontrollable video stress and under threat of blood sampling (Figure 1). An interaction between controllability and AS revealing higher increases of anxiety with uncontrollable stress in the number test in ASQ+ subjects was only significant on the 10% level (Figure 1, left).

This tendency did become significant for the composite score of unpleasant arousal (Figure 2, left), whereas electrical stimulation (Figure 2, right) elicited the opposite pattern. Subjects with depressive AS felt more unpleasant arousal when having to decide on the intensity of the electrical current themselves whereas ASQ− subjects felt more uneasy when they did not have stimulus control.

When analyzing physiological response of heart rate and concomitant ratings on palpitation for groups and stressors, the following picture emerged for mental and emotional stress (Figure 3): Subjective ratings on palpitation were higher in ASQ+ subjects in the uncontrollable than in the controllable situation, whereas the reverse was true for ASQ− subjects (interaction $p < .05$). Actual heart rate relationships for controllable versus uncontrollable stress corresponded to those obtained for palpitation in ASQ−, but not in ASQ+, subjects and although objective heart rate recordings for the mental stressor (letter cancellation d_2) did not

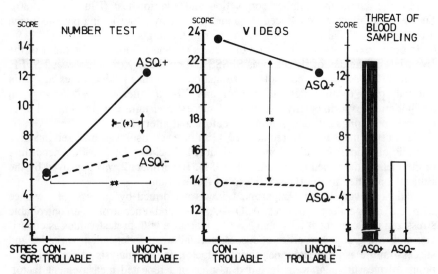

Figure 1   Anxiety ratings after controllable and uncontrollable mental stress (left) and emotional stress (center), and after uncontrollable physical threat (right) in subjects of depressive (ASQ+) and nondepressive attributional style (ASQ−). Number test: $^{**}p < .01$ for stressor; $^{(*)}p < .10$ for ASQ × Stressor interaction. Videos and blood sampling: $^{**}p < .01$ for ASQ. ASQ = Attributional Style Questionnaire.

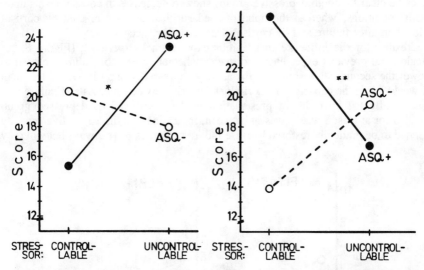

Figure 2 Ratings on unpleasant emotional state after controllable and uncontrollable stress. In number test (mental stress) (left),* $p < .05$ for ASQ × Stressor interaction. In electrical stimulation (physical stress) (right),** $p < .01$ for ASQ × Stressor interaction. ASQ = Attributional Style Questionnaire.

yield significant effects there was a tendency to generally higher values for ASQ− subjects.

For the emotional stressor of videos, the interaction for palpitation was the opposite of the one observed with the mental stressor: ASQ+ subjects felt less palpitation when they were not able to control the stressor and more when they had a chance to escape from the stressor ($p < .05$). Again, for objective recordings of heart rates the ASQ+ subjects showed a pattern opposite to their subjective ratings, that is, higher responses when exposed to uncontrollable stress than to controllable stress and clearly higher than the ASQ− group.

Palpitation ratings both for anticipation of electrical stimuli and for actual electrical stimulation showed a significant interaction of the type observed for palpitation with videos ($p < .05$ each), that is, lower levels for ASQ+ subjects in the uncontrollable than in the controllable situation and vice versa for ASQ− subjects. Actual changes of heart rate did not differ significantly for groups and stressors in either of the "electrical conditions."

Experiment 2

Figure 4 gives adjusted means for cortisol responses (averaged across three measurements) after success and failure for the three clinical groups. The significantly larger values after failure ($p = .01$) are mainly due to the control group. With this group the difference between success and failure was much greater than that of both the depressive groups, a finding that was responsible for the near-significance interaction between group and condition ($p = .06$).

When values were plotted as percent difference from baselines (Figure 5) it became clear that both depressive groups showed decreases in cortisol levels upon both conditions, whereas the nondepressed surgical patients reacted by cortisol elevation after failure and by cortisol decrease after success.

Testing for the influence of previous experimental experience (Figure 6) revealed that previous experience, no matter whether success or failure, seemed to lower the second-day response in the acutely depressed group (depressed less than 1 week) while the capacity to discriminate clearly between success and failure was hardly affected by order of presentation in the controls. The depressed group treated for at least 3 weeks was in between, indicating that discriminative capacity tended to be gradually restored because failure responses were always but still only

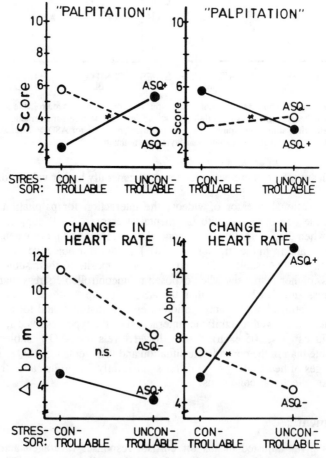

Figure 3 Scores on palpitation ratings (upper figures) and changes of heart rate (lower figures) for letter cancellation test d_2 (mental stress) (left) and videos (emotional stress) (right) in subjects of high and low depressive attribution style (ASQ+/ASQ−, respectively). ASQ = Attributional Style Questionnaire; n.s. = not significant. $^*p < .05$ for ASQ × Stress interaction.

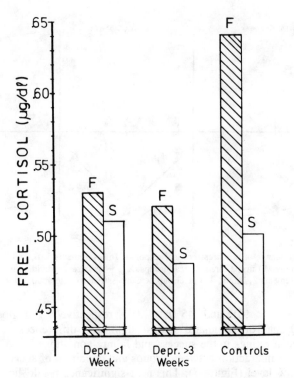

Figure 4 Means of cortisol (adjusted for respective baseline
values) under conditions of failure (F) and success
(S) in the three clinical groups. For condition
(failure/success), $p = .01$; for Failure/Success $\times$
Group interaction, $p = .06$.

slightly higher than respective success responses in the same subgroup of the
treated depressed patients.

Although prestress depressive state was significantly higher in the psychiatric
groups than in surgical controls ($p < .01$), there was no significant difference in
change scores due to condition of success/failure or order of presentation.

Depressive AS as measured by the ASQ on habitual behavior (ASQ trait) when
confronted with imagined negative situations differed in the predicted manner between depressed and control subjects for the dimensions internality ($p < .001$)
and globality ($p < .05$). For globality both depressed groups had equally higher
values than controls (32.1, 32.8, and 24.9 points, respectively, for the acutely
depressed, treated depressed, and control groups). In addition to showing a corresponding difference, the values for internality of the treated depressive group
exceeded those of the acutely depressed group ($p < .05$): 26.2, 30.1, and 18.0
points, respectively, for the acutely depressed, treated depressed, and control
groups.

Among corresponding dimensions of the ASQ state obtained for ratings on
experimental performance, only globality ratings for failure situations and stability
ratings for success situations were significantly correlated with those of the ASQ

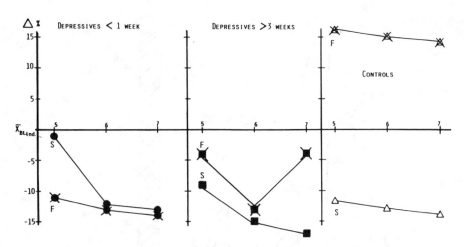

Figure 5 Percent change of poststress cortisol responses (measurements 5, 6, and 7) to success (S) and failure (F) in the three clinical groups. X_{ind} = prestress individual means across measurements 2, 3, and 4. For Group × Success/Failure interaction, $p < .05$.

trait: rs = .48 ($p < .01$) and .45 ($p < .01$), respectively. For globality ratings only for ASQ state questionnaire scores, significant differences of means were obtained between ratings in the success and failure conditions ($p < .05$), but significance for the interaction between groups and condition of success/failure only reached the 10% level (Figure 7). This near-significance result, however, reveals that acutely depressed subjects seemed to rate their failures as more global than their successes, whereas the other two groups exhibited the nondepressive AS, that

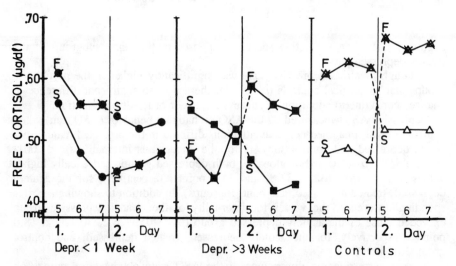

Figure 6 Means of cortisol adjusted for baseline values after failure (F, crossmarked symbols) and success (S, blank symbols) according to order of success/failure conditions and clinical groups. For Group × Order × Condition × Measurement interaction, $p = .06$.

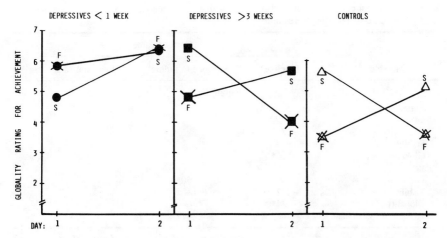

Figure 7 Globality ratings of subjects' achievement in arithmetic test according to experimental
condition of success (S) and failure (F) and order of presentation in the three
experimental groups. For group effect, $p < .10$; for effect of success/failure, $p < .05$;
for Group $\times$ Success/Failure interaction, $p < .10$.

is, higher globality for success than for failure (Figure 7). Furthermore, acutely
depressed patients seemed less capable of differentiating between success and failure than the treated depressed and the control groups, in particular when their first
experience was failure.

Sample sizes were too small to obtain separate correlations between cortisol
response and ASQ scores for each group, but correlations computed for the total
sample yielded the coefficients given in Table 1 in which trait and state dimensions
of AS for failure and success were correlated with cortisol baseline values (computed across pretest measurements from both days) and with cortisol response
values of corresponding days of success and failure, respectively.

Two dimensions each of the habitual and state AS upon failure were negatively
correlated with cortisol *baselines* (rs = $-.24$ and $-.26$ for habitual and $-.32$
and $-.24$ for state), and corresponding dimensions of the ASQ for ratings of
successful situations were positively associated with tonic cortisol levels
(rs = $.24, .24, .41, .25,$ and $.25$ for the three failure and two success AS dimensions, respectively). This was reflected by a negative relationship between change
of depression in the successful condition and pretest cortisol levels ($r = -.33$).
This implies that a depressive AS is related to lower and the nondepressive AS to
higher cortisol levels.

Cortisol *response* values in the failure condition were lower in those who attributed their negative experience to themselves (correlation with internality,
rs = $-.34$ for trait and $-.30$ for state) but higher in subjects who became more
depressed by their bad results in the test ($r = .31$). Under conditions of success
the coefficient for trait internality reflected the correlation for failure (higher cortisol response with higher tendencies to feel responsible for one's success;
$r = .29$), and the coefficient for state globality ($r = -.37$) reflected the one
obtained for change of depression upon failure (the less a subject dared to believe
in general success the higher his cortisol increase).

Table 1 Significant correlations of cortisol values with attribution style scores and with test-induced change of depression scores in the total group

Variable	Cortisol value		
	Baseline[a]	Respone to failure[b]	Response to success[b]
		Failure	
Attribution style			
Trait[c]			
Internality	− .24*	− .34**	
Stability	—	—	
Globality	− .26*	—	
State[d]			
Internality	—	− .30**	
Stability	− .32**	—	
Globality	− .24*	—	
Change of depressive state	—	.31**	
		Success	
Attribution style			
Trait			
Internality	.24**		.29*
Stability	.24**		—
Globality	.41***		—
State			
Internality	—		—
Stability	.25*		—
Globality	.25*		− .37**
Change of depressive state	− .33**		—

[a]Average across pretest measurements 2, 3, and 4 for the success and failure days together.
[b]Highest of the three consecutive values.
[c]For imagined situations.
[d]For test performance.
***$p < .01$. **$p \leq .05$. *$p \leq .10$. — = not significant.

DISCUSSION

Our first hypothesis—whether uncontrollable stress elicits higher anxiety and negative emotional response—in Experiment 1 was confirmed only in the number test, where for neither letter cancellation d_2 nor stressful videos or anticipation and experience of electrical stimuli did uncontrollability seem to increase negative arousal beyond the level elicited by respective controllable conditions. The reason for this may be that the number test was perceived as the mildest stressor and therefore the condition of uncontrollability had a chance of making a difference to the subjects. The other tasks were so aversive that awareness of personal influence could not reduce arousal felt without stimulus control. A separate analysis for scores on the visual analogue scale of the term "helpless" revealed, however, that subjects were well aware of uncontrollability in the shock condition ($p < .01$ for controllable vs. uncontrollable stress).

Differences between emotional arousal experienced under controllable versus uncontrollable stress were larger for ASQ+ than for ASQ− subjects, although only for mental stressors in the direction mentioned above for the total group. This may be taken as evidence that uncontrollability represented by failure in performance tended to be experienced as a clearly greater threat to the ASQ+ subjects than performance under controllable (i.e., success) conditions, whereas for nondepressive attributers there was equally low arousal in both conditions.

The difference between scores of unpleasant emotion with controllable versus uncontrollable stress was equally large but in the opposite direction in subjects with depressive AS under electrical stimulation. This observation, in combination with the previous one, refers to Question 2, regarding stressor specificity. ASQ+ subjects did not object to uncontrollability so much when subjected to physical pain; however, when the shock had to be operated by themselves they were more irritated and nervous than the ASQ− group (Figure 2, right). Two principles from anxiety research may have been operating to produce these results: Because there is a positive correlation between depressive AS and trait anxiety as measured by the State–Trait Anxiety Inventory by Spielberger ($r = .56$), ASQ+ subjects, like highly anxious ones, will experience ego threat as applied by failure in performance (uncontrollable stress) as much more aversive than physical pain applied by the experimenter (Schwenkmezger, 1985; Spielberger, 1972), whereas easy mental tasks in which they perform successfully may be experienced as fairly pleasant, as was the case for ASQ+ subjects in the controllable number test condition (Figure 2, left). The second principle is the one described by Gray (1982) that mismatch between expected and environmental stimuli recorded by the comparator system in the hippocampus–septum area of the brain will induce anxiety by activating the behavioral inhibition system. Because our subjects with depressive AS expected to be uncontrollably exposed to manipulations by the experimenter, the condition of being responsible for their own pain intensity was in contrast to their general experience of helplessness and would elicit more unpleasant arousal than electrical stimulation itself.

The emotional stressor (videos) did not show this interaction between group and controllability but just higher anxiety levels in the ASQ+ group, as was also observed for threat of blood sampling. This may be explained by positive state/trait correlations frequently observed in anxiety stress research.

Question 3, regarding correspondence between physiological and psychological response, may be answered by relating depressive AS to sensitization as defined by Byrne (1964) or by the combined scores from anxiety and social desirability scales (Krohne, 1975; Weinberger, Schwartz, & Davidson, 1979). In the uncontrollable mental stress, ASQ+ subjects, as would be predicted for sensitizers (Weinstein, Averill, Opton, & Lazarus, 1968), admitted higher palpitation, but exhibited lower actual heart rate increases than did ASQ− subjects (Figure 3, left), while ASQ− subjects, who might resemble repressors, exhibited the opposite pattern. Strikingly, conditions were reversed for the emotional stressor (Figure 3, right), where ASQ+ subjects displayed a marked rise in heart rate that corresponded to their general level of anxiety (Figure 1, center) and that, however, was evidently not perceived by them (Figure 3, right, upper part) and was not present in the controllable emotional stress condition although palpitation here was sensed more strongly. Whether it was greater involvement in the uncontrollable situation when subjects were not distracted by remembering their own responsibility and thus did not become aware of their physiological reactions and were carried away by the emotional impact of the accidents shown on the video remains an unresolved question.

Regarding Question 4, from Experiment 2 it may be concluded that, overall, uncontrollable stress did elicit higher cortisol levels than controllable stress. There is agreement in the literature with respect to this observation in animal experiments (Coover, Ursin, & Levine, 1973; Dess, Linwick, Patterson, Overmier, & Levine, 1983; Henry & Stephens, 1977; Swenson & Vogel, 1983) as well as in studies on humans (Breier et al., 1987; Lundberg & Forsman, 1979; Lundberg & Frankenhäuser, 1978; Nesse, Curtis, & Thyer, 1985). Only a few studies, however, have reported that controllable mental stress can induce a decrease in cortisol level, as was observed in our surgical control group. This was, for instance, reported by Lundberg and Frankenhäuser (1978) for working under noise conditions and by Hyyppä, Aunola, Lahtela, Lahti, and Marniemi (1983) for subjects exposed to a 1-hr mental stress. In an unpublished study on healthy males exposed to mental arithmetics, we observed a similar trend in plasma cortisol decrease from pre- to post-stress values, and the same was observed in certain subgroups of female subjects in a study performed on saliva cortisol (Hemmeter, Burkhardt, & Netter, in press). Direction of cortisol response may depend on stress intensity, with highly controllable stress eliciting stress-induced cortisol increases with increasing intensity, but if stress has the quality of monotony, decrease of cortisol may be observed (Lundberg & Forsman, 1979). Our healthy subjects probably perceived the very simple task of completing and adding numbers in which they achieved their self-selected goals without effort as relatively boring and may have responded by relaxation, that is, reduction of expectation induced cortisol levels.

Regarding Question 5, contrary to our prediction, the depressed subjects did not show higher increases upon failure than did healthy controls, but their cortisol was decreased when confronted with stress, no matter whether it was controllable or uncontrollable. This means they were less able to discriminate between the emotional and motivational impact of the situation.

It has been observed in the literature that subjects already in a very stressed emotional state when exposed to additional stressors may not respond by further increases of cortisol but may seem unresponsive or may even react by cortisol decrease. This has been reported for some phobic subjects when exposed to their phobic stimuli in a session of flooding therapy (Curtis, Nesse, Buxton, & Lippman, 1978) and was interpreted by the authors as indicating "desynchrony of fear." It was also reported to occur in healthy but highly stressed NASA scientists and administrative staff members who showed a decrease of cortisol upon additional stress (Caplan, Cobb, & French, 1979), which may be interpreted as an uneconomic style of physiological coping (Wittersheim, Brandenberger, & Follenius, 1985) or as an indicator of adrenal exhaustion as described in Selye's (1950) model of the general adaptation syndrome. Thus, although tonic levels may be elevated as has been described for depressed patients (Depue, 1979; Sachar, Halbreich, Asnis, Nathan, & Halpern, 1980) and for healthy subjects exposed to a continuous threat, as observed in the population of Three Mile Island (Schaeffer & Baum, 1984), the acute responsivity may be reduced. This is probably due not only to higher initial values, which tend to be negatively correlated to changes, but also, as in our depressive groups who did not show overall elevated baseline levels (possibly because of antidepressant therapy, which indirectly may affect ACTH and cortisol release), to their incapacity to discriminate between controllable and uncontrollable stress.

This addresses Question 6 regarding whether therapy can effect change in cortisol level. The reorganization of discriminative power as reflected by cortisol responses in Figure 6 would match reports in the literature on the endocrinology of depression that positive relationships between severity of desease and tonic levels of cortisol are frequently observed (Depue, 1979; Zerssen & Doerr, 1980).

The performance scores obtained by the three groups (computed as completed items per minute) nicely reflect this progress of therapy since performance has seemed to correspond to cortisol response in some studies (Vaernes & Darragh, 1982). This would corroborate our finding that with reobtaining the feeling of control over everyday life requirements, the subjects learned to increase their cortisol on demand when active coping was felt to be feasible. This would confirm the hypothesis that mild cortisol increases may reflect successful coping and response to challenge (Brandenberger, Follenius, Wittersheim, & Salamé, 1980; Vaernes & Darragh, 1982).

Question 7 referred to the influence of preceding stress on subsequent responses. It is a well-established observation that repeated exposure to the same stressor leads to reduced cortisol responses with subsequent exposure (Rose, 1984). This has been shown with different stressors such as catheterization (Rose & Hurst, 1975), exposure to physical exercise (Davis, Gass, & Bassett, 1981), and parachute jumping (Ursin, Baade, & Levine, 1978). The finding by Wittersheim et al. (1985) that one mental stressor (a multiple-choice task) preceded by another one (a short-term memory task) did not elicit lower cortisol responses than obtained in unpreceded presentation, would still be compatible with the hypothesis of cortisol increase as an indicator of novelty claimed by Rose (1984), Levine, Weinberg, and Brett (1979), or Davis et al. (1981).

In our experiment, however, there was no overall effect of this kind of adaptation from Days 1 to 2; that is, cortisol levels of the total group on Days 1 and 2 were not significantly different. However, in the acutely depressed group this type of carryover effect was observed, no matter whether the first experience was failure or success (Figure 6). Furthermore, one purpose of investigating the effect of consecutive stressors was to answer the question whether learned helplessness expected to be induced by primary failure would be reflected in subsequent cortisol responses upon success, which, however, was not the case, since there was no overall significant Order × Condition interaction in the analysis of covariance; nor was there a threefold interaction, which would have established this relationship for one of the depressive groups.

Question 8, which related to correspondence between cortisol and emotional responses, is answered by Table 1, which shows only a few and fairly low correlations. Correlations between behavioral and biochemical measures tend to be low anyhow (Ursin et al., 1978), but in the case of cortisol the bidirectional nature of the hormone (Wittersheim et al., 1985) may also be responsible for this finding. On the one hand, increase in cortisol may indicate stress and fear and on the other hand may represent response to novelty, challenge, and adaptive coping. Conversely, nonresponsiveness may indicate emotional stability or adrenocortical exhaustion (Curtis et al., 1978).

Yet, if we tentatively try to draw conclusions from Table 1 (which is based on the heterogeneous sample of healthy and depressed subjects), we might speculate that higher baseline levels indicate nondepressive AS and cortisol increases indicate depressive reactions to failure for which, however, the subject does not feel responsible.

Controversy over psychological traits correlated to habitually high cortisol levels is also encountered in the literature. Positive correlations of cortisol levels as well as responses have been reported with cooperativeness in young hemophiliacs (Mattson, Gross, & Hall, 1971) and with low aggression and high social involvement in school children (Tennes & Kreye, 1985) but also with higher anxiety and concern with illness (Bunney, Mason, & Hamburg, 1965). Furthermore, increases of cortisol with age must be considered as a confounding relationship (Jacobs, Mason, Kosten, Brown, & Ostfeld, 1984). Since optimistic AS is not known to be positively related to age, this factor is unlikely to have been responsible for our findings relating baseline levels and ASQ trait.

But failure induction, if experienced as unavoidable and out of personal control, as indicated by ASQ state scores, seems to be accompanied by increases in cortisol in the manner predicted by learned helplessness theory. The increasing discriminative ability from acutely depressed patients to healthy controls is also reflected in the increase in discrimination between success and failure for state globality ratings (Figure 7), which—although only suggested by parallel development of means and not be correlations—would also support the interpretation of cortisol–AS relationships given above.

SUMMARY

Experimentally induced uncontrollable stress was investigated in healthy subjects of high and low depressive attribution style (ASQ + /ASQ −) for emotional effects and in depressive patients for effects on saliva cortisol response.

Higher arousal upon uncontrollable than upon controllable stress of performance was experienced in ASQ + but not in ASQ − subjects, while (un)controllability of physical pain yielded opposite effects. The relationship between perceived and measured increases in heart rate tended to show the pattern of sensitizers in ASQ + subjects and of repressors in ASQ − subjects under uncontrollable stress of performance and the reverse pattern under emotional uncontrollable stress. Cortisol was increased upon uncontrollable stress and decreased upon controllable stress (failure and success) in nondepressed controls, but reduced under both conditions in depressive patients. Treatment made the latter more capable of discriminating endocrinologically between controllable and uncontrollable stress.

Results are discussed with respect to stimulus specificity and to the Henry and Selye models relating stress to cortisol response.

REFERENCES

Abramson, L. Y., Teasdale, J. D., & Seligman, M. E. P. (1978). Learned helplessness in humans: Critique and reformulation. *Journal of Abnormal Psychology, 87*, 49–74.

Brandenberger, G., Follenius, M., Wittersheim, G., & Salamé, P. (1980). Plasma catecholamines and pituitary adrenal hormones related to mental task demand under quiet and noise conditions. *Biological Psychology, 10*, 239–252.

Breier, A., Albus, M., Pickar, D., Zahn, T. P., Wolkowitz, O. M., & Paul, S. M. (1987). Controllable and uncontrollable stress in humans: Alterations in mood and neuroendocrine and psychophysiological function. *American Journal of Psychiatry, 144*, 1419–1425.

Brickenkamp, R. (1972). *Test d₂—Aufmerksamkeitsbelastungstest* [Test d₂—A test for attention demands]. Göttingen: Hogrefe.

Brunstein, J. C. (1986). Attributionsstil und Depression: Erste Befunde zur Reliabilitat und Validität eines deutschsprachigen Attributionsstilfragebogens [Attribution style and depression: Preliminary results for reliability and validity of a German version of a questionnaire on attribution style]. *Zeitschrift für Differentielle Diagnostik und Psychologie, 7*(1), 45–53.

Bunney, W. E., Mason, J. W., & Hamburg, D. A. (1965). Correlations between behavioral variables and urinary 17-hydroxycorticosteriods in depressed patients. *Psychosomatic Medicine, 27,* 299–308.

Burkhardt, H., Hemmeter, U., & Netter P. (in press). The influence of fasting, body weight, and stress on cortisol in women with eating disorders. In C. Kirschbaum & D. Hellhammer (Eds.), Hormone and drug assessment in saliva. Bern: Huber.

Byrne, D. (1964). Repression-sensitization as a dimension of personality. In B. A. Maher (Ed.), *Progress in experimental personality research* (Vol. 1, pp. 169–220). New York: Academic Press.

Caplan, R. D., Cobb, S., & French, J. R. P. (1979). White collar work load and cortisol: Disruption of a circadian rhythm by job stress? *Journal of Psychosomatic Research, 23,* 181–192.

Coover, G., Ursin, H., & Levine, S. (1973). Corticosterone and avoidance in rats with basolateral amygdala lesions. *Journal of Comparative Physiological Psychology, 85,* 111–112.

Curtis, G. C., Nesse, R., Buxton, M., & Lippman, D. (1978). Anxiety and plasma cortisol at the crest of the circadian cycle: Reappraisal of a classical hypothesis. *Psychosomatic Medicine, 40,* 368–378.

Davis, H. A., Gass, G. C., & Basett, J. R. (1981). Serum cortisol response to incremental work in experienced and naive subjects. *Psychosomatic Medicine, 43,* 127–132.

Depue, R. A. (Ed.). (1979). *The psychobiology of depressive disorders.* New York: Academic Press.

Dess, N. K., Linwick, D., Patterson, J., Overmier, J. B., & Levine, S. (1983). Immediate and proactive effects of controllability and predictability on plasma cortisol responses to shocks in dogs. *Behavioral Neuroscience, 97,* 1005–1016.

Gray, J. A. (1982). *The neuropsychology of anxiety: An inquiry into the function of the septo-hippocampal system.* Oxford, England: Clarendon.

Henry, J. P., & Stephens, P. M. (1977). *Stress, health, and the social environment.* New York: Springer.

Hiramatsu, R. (1981). Direct assay of cortisol in human saliva by solid phase radioimmunoassay and its clinical applications. *Clinica Chemica, 117,* 239–249.

Hyyppä, M. T., Aunola, S., Lahtela, K., Lahti, R., & Marniemi, J. (1983). Psychoneuroendocrine responses to mental load in an achievement oriented task. *Ergonomics, 26,* 1155–1162.

Jacobs, S., Mason, J., Kosten, T., Brown, S., & Ostfeld, A. (1984). Urinary free cortisol excretion in relation to age in acutely stressed persons with depressive symptoms. *Psychosomatic Medicine, 46,* 213–222.

Klutmann, B. (1980). Vergleich zwischen Depressiven und Nichtdepressiven hinsichtlich ihrer Kausalattribution in einer Leistungssituation [A comparison of attribution style between depressed and nondepressed subjects in a performance task]. In M. Hautzinger & W. Schultz (Eds.), *Klinische Psychologie und Psychotherapie: 3. Depression/Psychosomatik* (pp. 33–45). Tubingen: DGVT.

Krohne, H. W. (1975). *Angst und Angstverarbeitung [Anxiety and Coping].* Stuttgart: Kohlhammer.

Levine, S., Weinberg, J., & Brett, L. P. (1970). Inhibition of pituitary adrenal activity as a consequence of consummatory behavior. *Psychoneuroendocrinology, 4,* 275–286.

Lundberg, U., & Forsman, L. (1979). Adrenal-medullary and adrenal-cortical responses to understimulation and overstimulation: Comparison between Type A and Type B persons. *Biological Psychology, 9,* 79–87.

Lundberg, U., & Frankenhäuser, M. (1978). Psychophysiological reactions to noise as modified by personal control over noise intensity. *Biological Psychology, 6,* 51–59.

Maier, S. F. (1984). Learned helplessness and animal models of depression. *Progress in Neuropsychopharmocology and Biological Psychiatry, 8,* 435–446.

Mattson, A., Gross, S., & Hall, T. W. (1971). Psychoendocrine study of adaptation in young hemophilics. *Psychosomatic Medicine, 33,* 215–225.

Nesse, R. M., Curtis, G. C., & Thyer, B. A. (Eds.). (1985). Endocrine and cardiovascular responses during phobic anxiety. *Psychosomatic Medicine, 47,* 320–332.

Overmier, J. B., & Wielkiewicz, R. M. (1983). On unpredictability as a causal factor in learned helplessness. *Learning and Motivation, 14,* 324–337.

Petermann, F. (1987). Nachwort: Zehn Jahre Erlernte Hilflosigkeit: In Theorie, Forschung und Anwendung [Ten years of theoretical and applied research on learned helplessness]. In M. E. P. Seligman (Ed.), *Erlernte Hilflosigkeit* (2nd ed., 251–263). München: Urban & Schwarzenberg.

Peterson, C., Semmel, A., Metalsky, G., Abramson, L. Y., Baeyer, C. V., & Seligman, M. E. P. (1982). The Attribution Style Questionnaire. *Cognitive Therapy and Research, 6,* 287–300.

Rose, R. M. (1984). Overview of endocrinology of stress. In G. M. Brown, S. H. Koslow, & S. Reichlin (Eds.), *Neuroendocrinology and psychiatry* (pp. 95–122). New York: Raven.

Rose, R. M., & Hurst, M. W. (1975). Plasma cortisol and growth hormone response to intravenous catheterization. *Human Stress, 1,* 22–36.

Sachar, E. J., Halbreich, U., Asnis, G., Nathan, R. S., & Halpern, F. S. (1980). Neuroendocrine disturbance in depression. In I. Brambilla, G. Racagni, & D. de Wied (Eds.), *Progress in psychoneuroendocrinology* (pp. 263–281). Amsterdam: Elsevier.

Schaeffer, M. A., & Baum, A. (1984). Adrenal cortical response to stress in Three Mile Island. *Psychosomatic Medicine, 46,* 227–238.

Schwenkmezger, P. (1985). *Modelle der Eigenschafts und Zustandsangst* [*Models of State and Trait Anxiety*]. Göttingen: Hogrefe.

Seligman, M. E. P. (1975). *Helplessness: On depression, development and death.* San Francisco: Freeman.

Selye, H. (1950). Stress and general adaptation syndrome. *British Medical Journal, 1,* 1383–1392.

Spielberger, C. D. (1972). Anxiety as an emotional state. In C. D. Spielberger (Ed.), *Anxiety: Current trends in theory and research* (Vol. 1, pp. 24–48). New York: Academic Press.

Steinmeyer, E. M. (1984). *Depression und Hilflosigkeit* [*Depression and Helplessness*]. Berlin: Springer.

Swenson, R. M., & Vogel, W. H. (1983). Plasma catecholamine and corticosterone as well as brain catecholamine changes during coping in rats exposed to stressful footshock. *Biochemistry, Pharmacology and Behavior, 18,* 689–693.

Tennes, K., & Kreye, M. (1985). Children's adrenocortical response to classroom activities and tests in elementary school. *Psychosomatic Medicine, 47,* 451–460.

Ursin, H., Baade, E., & Levine, S. (1978). *The psychobiology of stress.* New York: Academic Press.

Vaernes, R. J., & Darragh, A. (1982). Endocrine reactions and cognitive performance at 60 meters hyperbaric pressure. *Scandinavian Journal of Psychology, 23,* 193–199.

Weinberger, D. A., Schwartz, G. E., & Davidson, J. R. (1979). Low-anxious, high-anxious and repressive coping styles: Psychometric patterns and behavioral and physiological responses to stress. *Journal of Abnormal Psychology, 88,* 369–380.

Weinstein, J., Averill, J., Opton, E., & Lazarus, R. (1968). Defensive style and discrepancy between self report and physiological indices of stress. *Journal of Personality and Social Psychology, 10,* 406–415.

Wittersheim, G., Brandenberger, G., & Follenius, M. (1985). Mental task-induced strain and its aftereffect assessed through variations in plasma cortisol levels. *Biological Psychology, 21,* 123–132.

Zerssen, D. V., & Doerr, P. (1980). The role of the hypothalamopituitary adrenocortical system in psychiatric disorders. In J. Mendelwicz & H. M. van Praag (Eds.), *Psychoneuroendocrinology and abnormal behavior* (pp. 85–106). Basel: Karger.

15

Stress and Steroid Hormone Modulation of GABA-Mediated Responses

David I. B. Kerr, Jennifer Ong, and Graham A. R. Johnston
Department of Pharmacology, University of Sydney, Australia

Considerable changes in mood and behavior are induced by stress, but their underlying physiological basis is still obscure. This is partly due to the variety of substances released by stress in the brain itself, or into the circulation, many of which can alter neural function (De Wied & Jolles, 1982). In seeking the particular agent(s) most likely to be responsible, it is necessary to find those agents that can disturb the delicate balance of neural excitation and inhibition that characterizes normal brain function. At the therapeutic level this notion is familiar from the use of pharmacological agents that restore this balance and so relieve the symptoms of depression and anxiety. However, in the context of stress, one is seeking anxiogenic substances that can act in a manner opposite to that of the tranquilizing drugs.

In this chapter we point out that circulating steroid hormones, released from the adrenal gland in response to stress, may well represent one important class of anxiogenic substances, because they are capable of inducing profound alterations in brain excitability. In particular, it is emphasized that steroids are able to modify the actions of the amino acid gamma-aminobutyric acid (GABA), which is a major inhibitory transmitter in the central nervous system (CNS). Of course, such an action might not be the only mechanism whereby steroid hormones in general can influence the brain. Indeed, several different types of steroid are already known to modify the responses to diverse CNS neurotransmitters (Biegon, Reches, Snyder, & McEwen, 1983; Hruska, 1986; McEwen, 1981). But the GABA system is very likely to be of particular relevance in stress because it is also the target for many well-known tranquilizing drugs capable of opposing anxiety.

Steroid hormones are released from the cortex of the adrenal gland in response to stress and subsequently alter the metabolic activity in most tissues of the body. In particular, these circulating steroids lead to the synthesis of glucose from body protein and for this reason are referred to as "glucocorticoids"; the principal such hormones are cortisol and cortisone. The CNS has long been known as a target for these circulating adrenal steroid hormones. Indeed, excessive circulating glucocorticoid, as in Cushing's syndrome with overactivity of the adrenal cortex, is characteristically associated with increased CNS excitability. At the behavioral level, this

We thank the National Health and Medical Research Council of Australia for financial support, and the Australian National Research Fellowships Advisory Committee for the award of a Queen Elizabeth II Fellowship to Jennifer Ong.

leads to insomnia, euphoria, and irritability, and may advance to frank psychotic episodes in extreme cases.

A similar pattern of altered mood and behavior is seen when cortisone is used as an antiinflammatory agent. Conversely, in conditions where the circulating levels of these hormones are low, the patients show a marked depression of CNS activity ("mental fatigue") that is readily reversible with steroid therapy. Previously, the underlying mechanisms for these effects of steroids on mood have been little understood, but recently we have found that glucocorticoid hormones are potent modulators of inhibitory mechanisms mediated by GABA in the CNS. As will be seen, this action offers some explanation for the alterations in mood and behavior that result from excessive steroid release in stress.

GABA is well recognized as a major inhibitory transmitter in the CNS, where it regulates the overall CNS excitability. This inhibition depresses neural discharges as well as dampening transmission, and is mediated through GABA acting at specific receptor sites on the surface membrane of neurons. These receptors are special protein domains on the cell surface that have been rather precisely characterized (Barnard, Darlison, & Seeburg, 1987). Importantly, they contain regions at which benzodiazepine tranquilizers and barbiturate anesthetics act to enhance CNS inhibition.

It is now evident that there are additional regions at the GABA receptor complexes where steroids can also influence GABA-induced inhibitory transmission (Johnston, Kerr, & Ong, 1987). There are two possible effects of steroids on this inhibition—either enhancing it or depressing it. Some steroid sex hormones act like benzodiazepines to increase the inhibition. In doing so, they appear to have tranquilizing actions, or to be anesthetics, whereas other steroids such as cortisone and cortisol oppose this action. This is of particular relevance to our present concern because the latter are the major steroids released in stress.

Because GABA-induced inhibition is so profoundly modified by benzodiazepines and barbiturates, it has seemed likely that naturally occurring substances, elaborated in the brain, might act in the same ways as do these therapeutic agents. Curiously enough, apart from some steroids, the only substances so far found act as antagonists to oppose these therapeutic agents (Medina, Novas, De Robertis, Pena, & Paladini, 1986). Paradoxically, these compounds are pro-conflict in effect, and not tranquilizers as one might expect for a naturally occurring "benzodiazepine." This action is so powerful that their administration will elicit panic attacks in human subjects (Dorow, Horowski, Paschelke, Amin, & Braestrup, 1983). From this it can be seen that antagonism of GABA-induced inhibition can profoundly alter human emotions, and it is likely that the steroid hormones, cortisol and cortisone act in a similar manner. A useful test for examining the behavioral effects of these and similar agents is the drinking-shock paradigm (Beer, Chasin, Clody, Vogel, & Horovitz, 1972), in which both benzodiazepines and barbiturates alleviate the conflict behavior. However, there do not seem as yet to be any comparable behavioral studies using any of the steroids known to modulate GABA-mediated inhibition.

It was Hans Selye, almost 50 years ago, who popularized the idea of adrenal steroid involvement in the general "alarm reaction" to stress, the adrenal glands being activated by the brain through the release of adrenocorticotropic hormone from the pituitary gland under the influence of the hypothalamus. Selye originally emphasized the slower, nonneural aspects of the body responses to the adrenal steroids, but went on to show that there are also direct steroid actions on nervous function, including the anesthetic properties of some hormones (Selye, 1942). The compounds explored in the latter study were mainly sex steroids and their metabolites. As a result of this, very effective steroid anesthetics were eventually developed, but fell into disrepute because of their adverse side effects. Nevertheless, such steroids have been shown to act like barbiturates and stimulate GABA-induced inhibition, which leads to anesthesia (Harrison & Simmonds, 1984; Ong, Kerr, & Johnston, 1988). Interestingly, the sex steroids progesterone and estrogen have opposing actions in the brain: Progesterone increases GABA-mediated inhibition, whereas estrogen enhances the actions of excitatory amino-acid transmitters. Such actions of sex steroids may be involved in premenstrual tension (Smith, Waterhouse, & Woodward, 1987) and point to profound interactions between steroid hormones and brain function. The glucocorticoid steroids, released in stress, share this ability to modify CNS activity.

That stress rapidly modifies GABA inhibitory actions in the brain is well documented (Maddison, Dodd, Johnston, & Farrell, 1987; Schwartz, Wess, Labarca, Skolnick, & Paul, 1987; Skerritt, Triskidoon, & Johnston, 1981), the effects of swim stress being prevented by prior removal of the adrenal glands. These actions are of very rapid onset, as rapidly as the brain–pituitary–adrenal axis can respond. In the experimental animal, even seemingly minor stress such as unfamiliar surroundings and handling can elevate blood steroid levels with surprising speed, as can more direct insults such as swim stress and administration of injections. Similar rapid increases in steroid levels are also seen in humans subjected to various degrees of stress. Our own studies have emphasized that such steroids released in stress can have two actions, either potentiating or preventing GABA-induced responses. These are most easily studied in a convenient isolated model that allows quantitative studies of GABA actions and of modulators such as benzodiazepines, barbiturates, and steroids (Ong et al., 1988).

Cortisol, the major human glucocorticoid, as well as cortisone and corticosterone are all potent modulators of GABA. In general, they enhance GABA when present in very low concentrations, but oppose GABA when at higher concentrations such as occur during stress (Johnston et al., 1987; Ong, Kerr, & Johnston, 1987). These results are in good agreement with those found in other systems (Harrison, Majewska, Harrington, & Barker, 1987; Majewska, 1987). Most striking is the observation that cortisol is 1,000 times more potent than any other steroid in enhancing GABA-mediated actions. This makes cortisol the most potent enhancer of GABA actions so far found. However, higher cortisol concentrations, equivalent to those found in stress, have the opposite effect and block GABA. In this regard, the related hormone cortisone is the most potent GABA-blocking agent yet known. It is this blocking, or antagonist, action that would make a major contribution to the cortisone-induced alterations in mood that are characteristic of cortisone therapy. Moreover, because both cortisol and cortisone are released at high concentrations in stress, it is likely that they are candidates for naturally occurring anxiogenic compounds. Functionally, this action could be directed toward ensuring arousal, tension, and alertness to times of sudden acute stress. This is not to say that GABA is the only neural transmitter whose function may be altered by steroids in stress, or that steroids are the only mediators of altered brain function in stress. But certainly, the possibility of steroid involvement at the neural level in stress should not be overlooked.

SUMMARY

It is well known that steroid hormones are rapidly released from the adrenal cortex during stress, resulting after some delay in altered metabolism and other physiological functions. However, there is now increasing evidence that steroid hormones not only have such actions on peripheral tissues, but also rapidly and effectively alter neural function. Most important, they can interfere with neural transmission in the central nervous system. In particular, steroids released in stress have marked depressant actions on neural inhibitory processes mediated through the inhibitory transmitter gamma-aminobutyric acid (GABA). This action is opposite to that of benzodiazepine tranquilizers, all of which act by increasing GABA functions. In consequence, the adrenal steroid hormones, released in considerable amounts during stress, can increase arousal and anxiety. It is suggested that this interference with normal brain function may in part provide a physiological basis for the psychological manifestations of stress.

REFERENCES

Barnard, E. A., Darlison, M. G., & Seeburg, P. (1987). Molecular biology of the GABA$_A$ receptor: The receptor/channel superfamily. *Trends in Neuroscience, 10,* 502–509.

Beer, B., Chasin, M., Clody, D. E., Vogel, J. R., & Horovitz, Z. P. (1972). Cyclic adenosine monphosphate phosphodiesterase in brain: Effect on anxiety. *Science, 176,* 428–430.

Biegon, A., Reches, A., Snyder, L., & McEwen, B. S. (1983). Serotonergic and noradrenergic receptors in the rat brain: Modulation by chronic exposure to ovarian hormones. *Life Science, 42,* 1407–1417.

De Wied, D., & Jolles, J. (1982). Neuropeptides derived from pro-opiocortin: Behavioral, physiological and neurochemical effects. *Physiological Reviews, 62,* 976–1059.

Dorow, R., Horowski, R., Paschelke, G., Amin, M., & Braestrup, C. (1983). Severe anxiety induced by FG 1742, a beta-carboline ligand for benzodiazepine receptors. *Lancet, 2,* 98–99.

Harrison, N. L., Majewska, M. D., Harrington, J. W., & Barker, J. L. (1987). Structure–activity relationships for steroid interaction with the gamma-aminobutyric acid$_A$-receptor complex. *Journal of Pharmacology and Experimental Therapeutics, 241,* 346–353.

Harrison, N. L., & Simmonds, M. A. (1984). Modulation of the GABA receptor complex by a steroid anesthetic. *Brain Research, 323,* 287–292.

Hruska, R. W. (1986). Elevation of striatal dopamine receptors by estrogen: Dose and time studies. *Journal of Neurochemistry, 47,* 1908–1915.

Johnston, G. A. R., Kerr, D. I. B., & Ong, J. (1987). Stress, steroids and GABA receptors. In M. J. Rand & C. Raper (Eds.), *Pharmacology* (pp. 121–124) Amsterdam: Elsevier Science Publishers, Biomedical Division.

Maddison, J. E., Dodd, P. R., Johnston, G. A. R., & Farrell, G. C. (1987). Brain GABA receptor binding is normal in rats with thioacetamide-induced hepatic encephalopathy despite elevated plasma GABA-like activity. *Gastroenterology, 93,* 1062–1068.

Majewska, M. D. (1987). Antagonist-type interaction of glucocorticoids with the GABA-receptor-coupled chloride channel. *Brain Research, 418,* 377–382.

McEwen, B. S. (1981). Neural gonadal steroid actions. *Science, 211,* 1303–1311.

Medina, J. H., Novas, M. L., De Robertis, E., Pena, C., & Paladini, A. C. (1986). Identification of a potent endogenous benzodiazepine binding inhibitor from bovine cerebral cortex. In G. Racagni & A. Donoso (Eds.), *GABA and endocrine function* (pp. 47–56). New York: Raven Press.

Ong, J., Kerr, D. I. B., & Johnston, G. A. R. (1987). Cortisol: A potent biphasic modulator at GABA$_A$-receptor complexes in the guinea-pig isolated ileum. *Neuroscience Letters, 82,* 101–106.

Ong, J., Kerr, D. I. B., & Johnston, G. A. R. (1988). Alfaxalone potentiates and mimics GABA-induced contractile responses in the guinea-pig isolated ileum. *British Journal of Pharmacology, 95,* 33–38.

Schwartz, R. D., Wess, M. J., Labarca, R., Skolnick, P., & Paul, S. M. (1987). Acute stress enhances the activity of the GABA receptor-gated chloride ion channel in brain. *Brain Research, 411,* 151–155.

Selye, H. (1942). Correlations between the chemical structure and the pharmacological actions of the steroids. *Endocrinology, 30,* 437–453.

Skerritt, J. H., Triskidoon, P., & Johnston, G. A. R. (1981). Increased GABA binding in mouse brain following acute swim stress. *Brain Research, 215,* 398–403.

Smith, S. S., Waterhouse, B. D., & Woodward, D. J. (1987). Sex steroid effects on extrahypothalamic CNS. II. Progesterone, alone and in combination with estrogen, modulates cerebellar responses to amino acid neurotransmitters. *Brain Research, 422,* 52–62.

16

One State's Agony, the Other's Delight: Perspectives on Coping and Musculoskeletal Complaints

Sven Svebak
University of Bergen, Norway

Psychological factors in skeletal muscle tension and complaints are the focus of this chapter. Part of the research discussed is taken from a research program that has been going on for several years in my laboratory and that has involved a number of collaborators. We have made use of a wide range of paradigms, methods, and dependent variables. The electromyographical (EMG) findings from these experiments have been summarized elsewhere (e.g., Apter & Svebak, in press). Here the focus is not on physiological data, but rather on survey data derived from using a recently developed scale called the Tension and Effort Stress Inventory (TESI; see Appendix). Responses to this scale have been related to verbal reports on musculoskeletal complaints, and findings have presented new perspectives on psychogenic risk factors in back complaints.

CONSCIOUSNESS AND SKELETAL MUSCLES

The phenomenological orientation to motivation and emotion in reversal theory has been the converging theoretical basis in the present research. This theory has developed a systematic account of motivational states of consciousness and related emotional experiences (e.g., Apter, 1982, 1988; Lachenicht, 1988). In light of this phenomenological orientation, reversal theory presents a new challenge to research on psychological factors in musculoskeletal tension and complaints. Pioneering experimental studies of cognitive and other conscious processes that relate to striate muscle activity were reported by Jacobsen (1932) and Malmo (see Malmo, 1965). Reversal theory presents a more structured and systematic account of the conscious processes that may be involved than was available to the pioneering empirical studies.

The cortex of the brain is the biological substrate for consciousness, and the monosynaptic connection of the motor cortex to skeletal muscles, because of nerve fibers in the corticospinal tract, is the unique case where a part of the motor system

The Norwegian Research Council for Social Science and the Humanities (Sections for Social Science and Medical Science; the HEMIL program), as well as different sources at the University of Bergen, supported research described in this chapter. The research on back complaints was made possible by collaborative efforts from a number of colleagues including Holger Ursin, Inger Endresen, and Michael Apter.

mediates intended changes according to specific conscious commands. This corticospinal pathway is known as the pyramidal pathway to the skeletal muscles. A number of nerve connections are of subcortical origins and give rise to four other pathways of musculoskeletal control that are only indirectly moderated by conscious processes. These extrapyramidal pathways account for a range of postural changes, and one of them (the reticulospinal pathway) is responsible for the orchestration of a relatively general level of activation throughout the central nervous system as well as the motor systems of the body.

MUSCULOSKELETAL COMPLAINTS IN MODERN SOCIETIES

Musculoskeletal pain and discomfort are responsible for a substantial proportion of time lost through sick leave in industrialized societies (Sejersted & Westgaard, 1988). Some studies have estimated this proportion to be in the range of 30%, and thus it presents the major reason for absenteeism from work (e.g., Aaras & Westgaard, 1987; Lee, Helewa, Smythe, Bombardier, & Goldsmith, 1985; Westgaard & Aaras, 1985). From this perspective, it is thought compelling that underreporting is a significant problem for the assessment of the epidemiology of musculoskeletal complaints (Biering-Sørensen, 1985). Often the individual troubled with pain and discomfort from skeletal muscles regards him- or herself as not being ill in the "proper" sense and may therefore not see a general practitioner or a physiotherapist. Self-administered treatment regimens are invoked to compensate for "proper" treatment, and they include the use of analgesics and taking the occasional day off from work.

The subjective experience of pain, discomfort, and stiffness is the basis for a decision to see a general practitioner and to ask for professional treatment. This simple phenomenological fact is often taken as evidence for specific *physiological* changes of muscles in the actual body area. Typically, it is assumed that pain and discomfort reflect enduring states of increased muscle tension, and it is implied that pain is more intense the higher the level of tension. In light of the almost linear relation between EMG activity and intensity of static and dynamic power production in the muscle, it is assumed that tension can be indexed by level of EMG activity (e.g., Radcliffe, 1962; see Basmajian, 1967, for a review). Furthermore, the assumption that high EMG responses emerge in muscle areas with high levels of presenting complaints and pain has been empirically supported in several studies (e.g., Davis & Malmo, 1951).

These assumptions, taken together, present a risk for overestimating the role of muscle tension in musculoskeletal complaints. In part, neurological disorders may give rise to a range of symptoms in skeletal muscles. Some complaints are due to inflammatory states affecting the muscles, their sheaths, the facial layers, and neural pathways of the locomotor system (cf. rheumatism and myofibrositis). Moreover, the dose–effect relationship is not well known in the relation of muscle tension and muscle pain. One challenge to research in this latter domain is the implication of marked individual differences in proportions of different muscle fibers across individuals. The important distinction at this point is that of the aerobic (Type I) and the anaerobic (Type II) fibers: The former are designed to produce energy at a low to moderate level over enduring time periods, whereas the latter are specially designed to provide acute increases of high energy levels and have little tolerance for enduring states of elevated energy output.

The distinction between the Type I and Type II muscle fibers has not yet attracted much attention among psychophysiologists. Our ongoing research on psychogenic muscle tension is now also searching for the possible implications of individual differences in striate muscle fiber composition for psychogenic sources to musculoskeletal complaints. In this way our research has an orientation that differs from a significant proportion of the more recent orientation of EMG research that has been toward the psychophysiology of affective facial displays. Such displays are regulated by a separate neural control system, and their EMG activity may relate only indirectly to psychogenic factors in the regulation of symptom-related changes in the *load-bearing* muscles of the neck, shoulders, low back, and the extremities.

The unique corticospinal arrangement of the pyramidal pathway was pointed out above. This arrangement calls on an increased understanding among psychophysiologists of the potential of subjective experience as a data base in their EMG research. In this respect, reversal theory is an interesting challenge in the way it presents a systematic account of motivational states and their ways of organizing the experience of emotions. Such experience may present the epiphenomenon of mechanisms in the brain that mediate the biopsychosocial processes implicated in psychogenic muscle tension and discomfort. (See Pennebaker, 1982, for an extensive and more general presentation of relations between physiological processes and psychological symptoms.)

AEROBIC AND ANAEROBIC METABOLISM IN STRIATE MUSCLES

Most of the energy production in the human body takes place in the striate muscles. Approximately 80% of this output is in the form of heat production. This means only some 20% of the energy production is available for work in the everyday sense.

The muscle fibers produce energy by contraction in response to stimulation from nerve fibers. In the present context it is important to point out two different processes that are involved in this energy production: One takes place in the so-called Type I muscle fibers and is referred to as the *aerobic* type of metabolism. The Type I fibers get access to energy from carbohydrate molecules (the primary source of energy) by oxidation. This means breathing is implicated for the lungs to make oxygen available and transported to the aerobic muscle fibers by the cardiovascular system. This circulatory system is also implicated in the transport of carbon dioxide and water from the aerobic fibers and back to the lungs. Carbon dioxide and water are the waste products of aerobic metabolism.

Psychophysiologists have put much effort into unfolding the relationship between cardiovascular changes that are metabolically provoked, because of need for oxygen, and changes that are due to *psychological* factors (see, e.g., Obrist, 1981). In this research, practically no attention has been paid to the complicating fact that the *anaerobic muscle* fibers need no oxygen, and produce no carbon dioxide and water, in getting access to energy from carbohydrate molecules. Instead, these fibers metabolize the molecule in a way that has lactic acid as an end product. However, one should keep in mind that this anaerobic access to energy, which takes place in the Type II fibers (the so-called fast-twitch fibers), is far less efficient in exploiting the energy potential of the carbohydrate molecule. These different metabolic processes are illustrated in Figure 1.

We know from studies of elite performers of endurance and explosive sports (e.g., marathon and sprint runners, respectively) that the proportion of endurance and fast-twitch fibers are markedly different: Long distance runners may have four times the number of endurance fibers, relative to the number of explosive fibers, in their leg muscles, whereas elite sprint runners typically show the same proportion in favor of the fast-twitch fibers. These individual differences are genetically coded, and physical training has the primary effect of making the fiber more efficient in producing energy according to its aerobic or anaerobic disposition. Individual differences in the distribution of aerobic and anaerobic muscle fibers are probably less marked among a random sample of the population at large, compared with the elite level of sport performers. These genetically coded differences among individuals are, nonetheless, intriguing in light of the assumption that enduring muscle tension is a major risk factor in chronic pain and discomfort of skeletal muscles. There is still no biopsy data at hand on muscle fiber classification, from a sample of different muscles throughout the human body, that would permit normative estimates of distributions of Type I and Type II fibers of skeletal muscles in a large-scale population.

There are two obvious and contrasting hypotheses that come out of these perspectives on relations between muscle complaints and distribution of muscle fibers: One is the possibility that individuals with a high proportion of endurance fibers in their muscles are at higher risk of suffering from enduring muscle tension

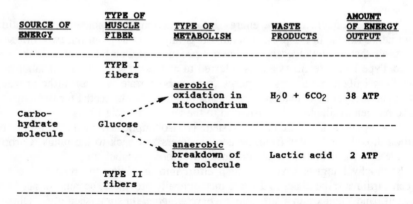

AEROBIC AND ANAEROBIC PRODUCTION OF ENERGY

IN STRIATE MUSCLE FIBERS

SOURCE OF ENERGY	TYPE OF MUSCLE FIBER	TYPE OF METABOLISM	WASTE PRODUCTS	AMOUNT OF ENERGY OUTPUT
	TYPE I fibers			
		aerobic oxidation in mitochondrium	$H_2O + 6CO_2$	38 ATP
Carbo-hydrate molecule	Glucose			
		anaerobic breakdown of the molecule	Lactic acid	2 ATP
	TYPE II fibers			

Figure 1 Schematic illustration of the differences between Type I (aerobic) and Type II (anaerobic) muscle fibers in their production of energy from a glucose molecule. Note that the term "waste product" is somewhat misleading for lactic acid because this molecule can be made available for subsequent aerobic metabolism in Type I fibers. ATP = adenosine triphosphate.

than are individuals with a relative bias toward explosive fibers. Another hypothesis is that muscles with a relatively large proportion of Type I fibers are biologically "talented" for enduring tension levels and thus are *less* at risk of suffering from complaints. A related hypothesis concerns the case in which the individual is "equipped" with a relative bias toward the fast-twitch fibers. In this case, enduring levels of tension, and the resulting output of lactic acid, may cause tissue damage that puts these individuals at high risk of suffering from musculoskeletal complaints. These genetically oriented hypotheses are neutral to the distinction between psychogenic and ergonomic risk factors, and some individuals may be suffering from genetic, ergonomic, as well as psychogenic risks.

ERGONOMIC AND PSYCHOGENIC RISKS: ACUTE AND ENDURING LOADS

The most common musculoskeletal disorders are those of neck and shoulder pain and stiffness, low back pain, and tension headache. There are a number of local origins to such symptoms. Some of them occur immediately after the muscle has been exposed to load, whereas others are delayed or prolonged reactions (e.g., Hagberg, 1982). Ruptures of muscle tendons and ischemia (i.e., deficiency of blood supply) of the muscles present acute complaints. A typical example of delayed complaints are those experienced in the legs of an individual who goes for a run after several months of inactivity. These symptoms of pain and stiffness are most marked 2 to 3 days after exposure to muscular strain, and they are caused by factors such as ischemic lesions and energy depletion. The chronic symptoms reflect degenerative tendinitis or chronic myalgia. This means that inflammatory states are often implicated as local tissue factors in prolonged musculoskeletal pain and discomfort.

Although ergonomic and psychogenic factors may play central causal roles in the development of symptoms from skeletal muscles, their roles may be less exclusive throughout the more enduring course of these complaints. This is due to the possibilities for different types of vicious circles that are often nested in the dynamics of such enduring symptoms. These dynamics are indicated in Figure 2 as follows: Muscle strain may be acute or enduring and caused by ergonomic and/or psychogenic factors. The effect on the strained muscle is (a) local muscle fatigue that (b) causes accumulation of metabolites and energy depletion that (c) induces tissue damage. A secondary consequence of this damage is (d) prolonged pain and inflammation which trigger (e) compensatory contractions of surrounding muscle fibers. These compensatory spasms complete the circle by inducing and maintaining the local muscle fatigue. These local effects may have side effects on psychogenic and ergonomic factors, for example, by inducing compensatory body postures and efforts to cope as well as worries about one's ability to cope. The experience of a threatening and overly demanding work environment is a likely catalyst of this psychogenic risk, and the final sections of this chapter point out some of the complexities involved in this kind of risk factor.

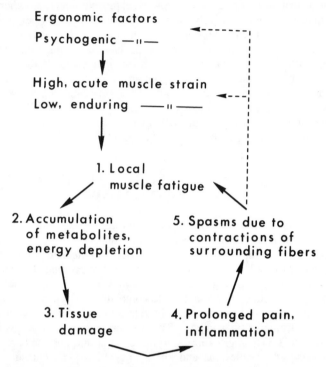

Figure 2 The vicious circle of events that may induce and maintain
tension and discomfort in striate muscles. From *Progress in
Psychology* (p. 148) by S. Svebak, 1988, Amsterdam:
North-Holland. Copyright 1988 by North-Holland.
Reproduced by permission.

EXPERIMENTAL STUDIES OF ENDURING
AND ACUTE ELECTROMYOGRAPHIC ACTIVATION

Experimental studies of facilitation and inhibition in the motor system have
pointed to a difference in preparatory myoelectric outflow to muscles of the trunk
and extremities and to the facial muscles. The former are referred to as the load-
bearing muscles, and they are mainly involved in performance of work and in
"fight or flight" behavior. For example, the increased tension in the preparatory
foreperiod of a reaction time task serves as a stabilizing platform for phasic (fast,
stimulus-elicited, forceful) motor responses. Facial muscles are of primary significance in the communication of affect (e.g., Brunia, 1984; Dimberg, 1988). In our
own laboratory, a number of studies have pointed to psychological factors in the
buildup of such stabilizing platforms in muscles of the extremities. Most of these
studies have made use of so-called continuous perceptual–motor tasks that induce
EMG activation gradients in muscles not strictly called on by the extrinsic nature
of the tasks. Some of these studies manipulated incentives and documented, for

example, that a threatening context to such tasks provokes steeper EMG gradients (e.g., Svebak, 1982). Similar effects were provoked by rewarding incentives (Rimehaug & Svebak, 1987).

Overall, the findings from our experiments, using the continuous perceptual–motor task paradigm and related paradigms, have identified a role for intrinsic motivation, such as goal-directed, serious-minded, planning-oriented involvement in effortful performance where EMG gradients are marked (e.g., Apter & Svebak, 1986; Rimehaug & Svebak, 1987; Svebak & Murgatroyd, 1985). It is important to note here that these gradients have occurred in seemingly passive parts of the skeletal muscle system, for example, in the left forearm flexor area when the right (dominant) forearm operated the joystick to perform a car-racing video task. In this way the laboratory tasks provoked EMG activation of the kind that parallels that provoked in studies of musculoskeletal load that may cause pain in the worksite (e.g., Westgaard & Aaras, 1985). In the laboratory, like in everyday life, these changes were not intended by the subjects, and they were not perceived by them as taking place. Also, the changes were not explicitly required by the structure of the task. This means the EMG gradients appeared to have been mediated by the extrapyramidal, multisynaptic pathways of subcortical origin that cause unintended changes of tension in skeletal muscles.

Subjects who performed these video tasks for fun, impulsively focusing on the momentary actions, rather than on their consequences, and expending effort when performing in this playful state, have presented only trivial, if any, tonic EMG changes. In contrast, subjects performing in this intrinsic state of playfulness have yielded high power amplitudes of acute phasic increases of the active forearm EMG due to joystick operation. These acute changes were consciously implemented to cope with sensory input. In this way, the phasic changes were mediated by the monosynaptic, pyramidal discharges of corticospinal fibers to the active forearm. It should be added that results from a recent study of elite performers of sports (Braathen & Svebak, 1990) showed high tonic, as well as phasic, EMG changes in the endurance sport performers. These subjects scored higher on "stress" and lower on "arousal" (see Mackay, 1980) despite having liked performing the task. Thus, elite performers of endurance sports may be efficient at organizing effortful discharges in both extrapyramidal and pyramidal pathways to the skeletal muscles.

These more recent studies from my laboratory add to previous reports, such as those by Malmo (1965, 1975), who identified a close relation between anxiety and tonic changes (slow, unrelated to any specific stimulus). Our studies also brought out evidence for effort and task involvement as factors that provoked such EMG gradients. More precisely, the psychogenic factors that contribute to the enduring electromyographic "load," can be described from these studies as a constellation of (a) serious-mindedness and planning orientation (referred to in reversal theory as the telic state), (b) the experience of unpleasant high arousal, and (c) the investment of efforts to cope (see Svebak, 1988).

The recent developments in this research program have included a systematic conceptualization of the relations among (a) experience of exposure to stressors, (b) the experience of a range of "basic" pleasant and unpleasant emotions, and (c) the experience of efforts invested to cope. This development provided the basis for constructing the TESI.

THE TENSION AND EFFORT STRESS INVENTORY

The TESI was designed according to assumptions about the structure and dynamics involved in the subjective experience of stress. These assumptions have been presented earlier by Apter and Svebak (1989). A *stressor* is defined in reversal theory as any source that gives rise to the recognition of a discrepancy from a preferred level of some variable. This is referred to in systems theory as the detection of an "error." In the present context, an "error" is the experience ("detection") of negative hedonic tone or unpleasant mode of some kind. This general state of anhedonia is referred to as *tension-stress*. Apter (1988) has developed a systematic account of unpleasant emotional experiences, each being dependent on the operation of a particular motivational state or constellation of such states (in reversal theory, such states are referred to as metamotivational; see, e.g., Apter, 1982). *Effort-stress* is a term used in reversal theory to account for the expenditure of negative feedback that is undertaken to overcome or reduce the discrepancy that gives rise to tension-stress. Therefore, effort-stress is the experience of exerting will power, concentrating harder, pushing oneself, or working harder to reduce tension-stress. Briefly stated, then, the theory argues that a stressor is any source that provokes tension-stress, and effort-stress is action taken to reduce or overcome the tension-stress.

Apter (1988) presented a systematic account of pleasant and unpleasant emotions, being dependent upon the operation of particular modes of consciousness. Four pairs of such opposite modes have been proposed in reversal theory (e.g., Apter & Smith, 1985). One of these pairs is arousal avoiding and arousal seeking. The three other pairs are conformity and negativism, mastery and sympathy, and allocentrism versus autocentrism.

Arousal avoidance is defined as a state in which the preferred level of felt arousal is low, the opposite end of the felt arousal continuum being the preferred one in the arousal-seeking state. In the conformist state, the individual wants, or feels compelled to comply with some requirement, whereas wanting to act against some requirement is the defining feature of the negativistic state. Mastery is a state in which the individual seeks to master (dominate, control, etc.) the other with whom he or she is interacting at the time. In this state transactions are seen as involving taking or yielding up, whereas in the opposite state, the sympathy state, transactions with others are seen as involving giving or being given. In the allocentric state, pleasure and displeasure derive from what happens to someone else, rather than what happens to oneself, whereas in the opposite state, referred to as autocentrism, pleasure and displeasure derive from what happens to oneself rather than from what happens to someone else (Apter, Fontana, & Murgatroyd, 1985).

The theory makes a distinction between somatic and transactional emotions. The former are related to the experience of arousal, whereas the nature of outcome in transactions with the other person is of a primary importance to the experience of the latter emotions. It is assumed that somatic tension-stress can be experienced in four different ways as anxiety, boredom, anger, and sullenness. The pleasant counterparts are experienced as relaxation, excitement, placidity, and provocativeness, respectively. It is also assumed that transactional tension-stress takes the basic forms of humiliation, shame, resentment, and guilt, whereas the pleasant counterparts are experienced as pride, modesty, gratitude, and virtue, respectively. The relation of each of these emotions or moods with specific motivational states is illustrated in Figure 3. In this figure, the term "winning" refers to an outcome that is experienced by the individual as fulfilling the intrinsic "goal" of the states that are in operation (e.g., the pleasant experience of excitement reflects the achievement of high arousal in the arousal-seeking mode in conjunction with the conformist mode, whereas provocativeness is the pleasant experience of high arousal in the constellation of the arousal-seeking and negativistic modes). The term "losing" on the other hand, is the experience of any outcome that is contrary to the intrinsic "goal" of the states in operation (e.g., the unpleasant experience of guilt comes out of seeing oneself as not being able to care successfully for the other person, which is, a negative outcome in the constellation of the sympathy and allocentric states).

The reasoning behind the relations between motivational states and emotional outcome shown in Figure 3 has been given elsewhere (Apter, 1988). However, the TESI presents an account of four different stressor domains in people's life, each of which can give rise to the experience of stressors (demands, pressure, and challenge) resulting in tension-stress of some kind. For most adult individuals it is assumed that these domains can be subsumed as work, family, economy, and one's own body. The latter domain has often been neglected in traditional stress research where situational (extrinsic) sources have been at focus. From a phenomenological

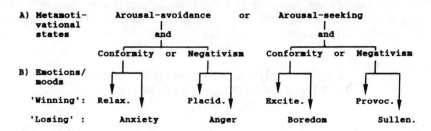

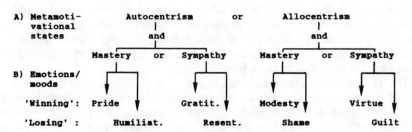

Figure 3 The relations between so-called metamotivational states and basic emotions or moods as seen in reversal theory (Apter, 1988). Felt level of arousal is assessed to be of particular significance to the somatic emotions, whereas outcomes in transaction with the other person is of particular significance to the transactional emotions. The terms "winning" (pleasant) and "losing" (unpleasant) refer to an outcome that is experienced by the individual as fulfilling, and as being contrary to, respectively, the intrinsic "goal" of the states that are in operation.

point of view, however, one's own body is likely, in some circumstances, to be a more powerful stressor than any of the other three domains. One example would be the case of enduring pain from one's neck and shoulder when performing work such as word processing. Although an ergonomic "stressor" may have provoked the pain in the first place, the experience of pain is likely to represent a major psychological stressor as a secondary consequence.

The TESI asks for separate estimates of the experience of stressors within each of the above-mentioned domains. This means responses to the TESI permit analyses of, for example, relations between particular body symptoms and the experience of stressors in these four domains. Also, the TESI permits the exploration of associations between exposure to different domains of stressors and musculoskeletal complaints, and how they relate to the experience of a systematic range of pleasant and unpleasant emotions (i.e., different forms of tension-stress).

Finally, it was pointed out above that effort-stress is the experience of action undertaken to reduce or overcome tension-stress. Theoretically, it is possible to invest effort that is dysfunctional for different reasons. One example is the case in which efforts to cope with tension-stress orient to the wrong domain (e.g., investing efforts in the domain of economy when one's body is the primary stressor). Another is the case of effort invested in the appropriate domain of stressors but reduction of tension-stress fails because of inappropriate skills or an overwhelming stressor. The assessment of effort-stress within each of the four domains provides a specific and empirical basis for assumptions on where to start a process of intervention: (a) in which domain, (b) working to identify and moderate the stressor or any particular emotion, and/or (c) the expenditure of more skillful, efficient, and appropriate efforts to cope.

BACK COMPLAINTS AND RESPONSES TO THE TENSION AND EFFORT STRESS INVENTORY

The TESI has been developed in versions that ask for estimates over different periods in time. One focuses on the last 12 months, and another on the last 7 days. The latter version is given in the Appendix. These time periods are also included in a Nordic Questionnaire (NQ) for the recording of musculoskeletal symptoms (Kourinka et al., 1987). The NQ permits detailed assessment of musculoskeletal discomfort and pain in the separate areas defined as neck, shoulders, and low back. (Complaints from other parts of the body are also recorded in the NQ, but those sections are not of concern here).

The TESI and NQ were distributed to more than 300 female office workers as part of a larger collaborative survey on psychosocial factors in musculoskeletal complaints. Most of these subjects reported the experience of only trivial complaints over the preceding 12 month period. Most of the subjects with mild, if any, complaints, were therefore excluded from the analyses, and the remaining 96 subjects presented back complaints distributed across a scale from "mild" to "very severe" pain in the neck, shoulders, and low back.

Stepwise multiple regression analyses documented a significant association between pain in the neck and overall expenditure of efforts to cope, $r^2 = .14$, $F(1,93) = 14.83$, $p < .0002$, and experience of negative transactional emotions (humiliation, shame, resentment, and guilt), $r^2 = .18$, $F(2,92) = 10.45$, $p < .0001$.

The overall experience of negative transactional emotions also was high with pain in shoulders, $r^2 = .07$, $F(1,93) = 7.24$, $p < .008$, and a similar association emerged for low back pain with negative transactional emotions, $r^2 = .08$, $F(1,93) = 7.80$, $p < .006$.

Scores reflecting sum of pain and discomfort in neck, shoulders, and low back also significantly related to total effort scores, $r^2 = .11$, $F(1,93) = 11.86$, $p < .009$, and negative transactional emotions $r^2 = .18$, $F(2,92) = 10.08$, $p < .0001$. These results from stepwise multiple regression analyses indicate that the experience of efforts to cope and negative transactional emotions explained their unique parts of the variance of back complaint scores.

In bivariate analyses of correlation, the TESI scores for one's body indicated a more significant stressor, and target of efforts to cope, than did the domains of work, family, and economy in relation to back pain. For emotions, relatively high positive correlations were found for the transactional emotions of guilt, $r = .42$, $p < .01$, and resentment, $r = .55$, $p < .001$ with pain in shoulders. For total back pain scores, these two variables accounted for 25% and 46% of the variance, respectively.

Thirty subjects participated in a 5-month follow-up, and change scores were calculated for TESI and back pain variables. In case of a causal relation between the psychological factors of perceived stress, efforts, and emotions with the experience of back pain, a reduction of, for example, transactional displeasure should be parallel with a reduction in back pain. Conversely, increase of such displeasure should occur with increased back pain.

Total stressor change scores were significantly associated with shoulder pain change scores (27% of pain variance explained), $F(1,23) = 8.05$, $p < .007$. The change in perceived exposure to stressors due to economy was a particularly significant contributor to this overall association of stressor change with change of shoulder pain over the 5-month period (17.1% of pain variance explained), $F(1,29) = 5.99$, $p < .021$. This finding was consistent with that of change in efforts to cope with stressors due to economy (37% of variance in shoulder pain change scores explained), $F(1,28) = 16.43$, $p < .0004$.

Forty-one percent of the variance in change scores for total back pain was explained by TESI change scores for efforts to cope with economy, $F(1,21) = 14.58$, $p < .001$, whereas change scores for efforts to cope with work explained an additional 20% of this variance, $F(2,20) = 15.64$, $p < .0001$. This indicates that 61% of the total back pain change variance was accounted for by change scores for efforts to cope with stress from economy and at work.

Bivariate analyses of change scores for emotions and back pain change scores confirmed a role for reduced guilt with reduced pain from shoulders and the low back area, $r = .31$ and .39, respectively, ($p < .05$). Resentment change scores, however, proved unrelated to change scores for back complaints. Interestingly, the increase of gratitude was significantly associated with a reduction in neck pain. According to reversal theory (Apter, 1988), gratitude is the pleasant emotional counterpart of resentment. This means reduction in unpleasant emotions may be of importance to reduction in back pain, but the increased experience of pleasant emotions and moods (i.e., a relative shift from "losing" to "winning") may be equally important for the induction of reduced back pain.

The preceding hypothesis implies that reduction in the experience of, for example, resentment may not automatically increase the experience of the opposite emotion of gratitude. A neutral mood may take over and only a less intense experience of resentment may prevail. In this way a mood change often reflects nothing more than a reduction in level of unsuccessful coping. A pleasant mood state, in contrast, is provoked by cognitive appraisal, or reappraisal, with a positive outcome or self-talk that causes the experience of successful coping (e.g., Averill, 1973; Ursin & Murison, 1983).

CONCLUSION

Results from our EMG studies of psychogenic muscle tension, and from survey data on the experience of stress and back pain, confirm the important role of cognition, motivation, and emotions in these biological changes and symptoms. It is a major challenge in our current research to uncover the psychobiological relation between EMG activation patterns and the experience of back pain. High phasic amplitudes of EMG discharges, expended on impulse and in play behavior (e.g, sports) just for fun, as well as enduring elevations of tonic EMG discharges, expended in serious-minded and goal-directed behavior, may both present elevated risks of musculoskeletal discomfort and pain (acute and enduring, respectively; see Figure 2). The significance of individual differences in muscle fiber composition (see Figure 1) is one of the issues to be sorted out next in this project.

However, despite the biological risk factors that are involved in back pain, our findings on psychogenic factors are in concert with recent findings from an independent and contemporary study: Flor and Turk (1988) studied the role of psychological factors in chronic back pain and rheumatoid arthritis. They concluded that the combination of situation-specific and general cognitive variables explained 32% and 60% of the variance in pain and disability, respectively. Caution is needed in the evaluation of their and our findings. Our laboratory data on EMG lend support to a causal role for some psychological variables in tonic and phasic response patterns. For the experience of back pain, the causal relations may be more complex because of the tendency for perceived pain to elicit increased and compensatory tension in the painful area (see Figure 2).

Despite the complexity of causal factors in back pain, our results lend support to the importance of cognitive change, away from catastrophizing and towards coping self-statements, as a point of intervention in the treatment and prevention of back pain.

SUMMARY

This chapter presents a biological and ergonomic context for the study of psychogenic factors that influence musculoskeletal pain and discomfort. Psychophysiological findings on the role of arousal avoidance (including serious-mindedness and planning orientation) and arousal seeking (including playfulness and impulsivity) for tonic (enduring) and phasic (acute) electromyographic changes are reported. A new survey measure designed to assess the experience of stress and efforts to cope, the Tension Effort Stress Inventory (TESI), is also described. Findings for the TESI related to survey measures of musculoskeletal back complaints indicate that unsuccessful efforts to cope with stressors expended in the "sympathy" mode (orientation toward caring, rather than controlling) give rise to guilt and resentment, as well as to back pain. Analyses of relations between change scores for TESI responses and back complaints over a 5-month period provide further evidence of this relation between coping behavior and musculoskeletal pain.

REFERENCES

Aaras, A., & Westgaard, R. H. (1987). Further studies of postural load and musculo-skeletal injuries of workers at an electro-mechanical assembly plant. *Applied Ergonomics, 18,* 211–29.

Apter, M. J. (1982). *The experience of motivation: The theory of psychological reversals.* London: Academic Press.

Apter, M. J. (1988). Reversal theory as a theory of the emotions. In M. J. Apter, J. H. Kerr, & M. P. Cowles (Eds.), *Progress in reversal theory* (pp. 43–62). Amsterdam: Elsevier/North-Holland.

Apter, M. J., Fontana, D., & Murgatroyd (Eds.). (1985). *Reversal theory: Applications and developments.* Cardiff, Wales: University College Cardiff Press/Elsevier.

Apter, M. J., & Smith, K. C. P. (1985). Experiencing personal relationships. In M. J. Apter, D. Fontana, & S. Murgatroyd (Eds.), *Reversal theory: Applications and developments* (pp. 161–178). Cardiff, Wales: University College Cardiff Press/Elsevier.

Apter, M. J., & Svebak, S. (1986). The EMG gradient as a reflection of metamotivational state. *Scandinavian Journal of Psychology, 27,* 209–219.

Apter, M. J., & Svebak, S. (in press). Reversal theory as a biological approach to individual differences. In A. Gale & M. W. Eysenck (Eds.), *Handbook of individual differences: Biological perspectives.* Chichester, England: John Wiley.

Apter, M. J., & Svebak, S. (1989). Stress from the reversal theory perspective. In C. D. Spielberger & J. Strelau (Eds.), *Stress and emotion, volume 12* (pp. 29–50). Washington, DC: Hemisphere.

Averill, R. J. (1973). Personal control over aversive stimuli and its relationship to stress. *Psychological Bulletin, 80,* 286–303.

Basmajian, J. V. (1967). *Muscles alive: Their functions revealed by electromyography* (2nd ed.). Baltimore: Williams & Wilkins.

Biering-Sórenson, F. (1985). National statistics in Denmark: Back trouble versus occupation. *Ergonomics, 28,* 25–29.

Braathen, E. T., & Svebak, S. (1990). Task-induced tonic and phasic EMG response patterns and psychological predictors in elite performers of endurance and explosive sports. *International Journal of Psychophysiology, 8,* 55–64.

Brunia, C. H. M. (1984). Facilitation and inhibition in the motor system: An interrelationship with cardiac deceleration. In M. G. H. Coles, J. R. Jennings, & J. A. Stern (Eds.), *Psychological perspectives: Festschrift for Beatrice and John Lacey* (pp. 199–215). New York: Van Nostrand Reinhold.

Davis, F. H., & Malmo, R. B. (1951). Electromyographic recording during interview. *American Journal of Psychiatry, 107,* 908–916.

Dimberg, U. (1988). Facial electromyography and the experience of emotions. *Journal of Psychophysiology, 2,* 277–282.

Flor, H., & Turk, D. C. (1988). Chronic back pain and rheumatoid arthritis: Predicting pain and disability from cognitive variables. *Journal of Behavioral Medicine, 11,* 251–265.

Hagberg, M. (1982). Local shoulder muscular strain—symptoms and disorder. *Journal of Human Ergology, 11,* 99–108.

Jacobsen, E. (1932). Electrophysiology of mental activities. *American Journal of Psychology, 44,* 677–694.

Kourinka, I., Jonsson, B., Kilbom, A., Vinterberg, H., Biering-Sórensen, F., Andersson, G., & Jórgensen, K. (1987). Standardized Nordic Questionnaires for the analysis of musculo-skeletal symptoms. *Applied Ergonomics, 18,* 233–237.

Lachenicht, L. (1988). A critical introduction to reversal theory. In M. J. Apter, J. H. Kerr, & M. P. Cowles (Eds.), *Progress in reversal theory* (pp. 1–42). Amsterdam: Elsevier/North-Holland.

Lee, P., Helewa, A., Smythe, H. A., Bombarider, C., & Goldsmith, C. H. (1985). Epidemiology of musculoskeletal disorders (complaints) and related disability in Canada. *Journal of Rheumatology, 12,* 1169–1173.

Mackay, C. J. (1980). The measurement of mood and psychophysiological activity using self-report techniques. In I. Martin & P. H. Venables (Eds.), *Techniques in psychophysiology* (pp. 501–562). Chichester, England: Wiley.

Malmo, R. B. (1965). Physiological gradients and behavior. *Psychological Bulletin, 64,* 225–234.

Malmo, R. B. (1975). *On emotions, needs, and our archaic brain.* New York: Holt, Rinehart & Winston.

Obrist, P. A. (1981). *Cardiovascular psychophysiology: A perspective.* New York: Plenum Press.

Pennebaker, J. W. (1982). *The psychology of physical symptoms.* New York: Springer-Verlag.

Radcliffe, C. W. (1962). The biomechanics of below-knee prostheses in normal, level, bipedal walking. *Artificial Limbs, 6,* 10–24.

Rimehaug, T., & Svebak, S. (1987). Psychogenic muscle tension: The significance of motivation and negative affect in perceptual–cognitive task performance. *International Journal of Psychophysiology, 5,* 97–106.

Sejersted, O. M., & Westgaard, R. H. (1988). Occupational pain and injury: Scientific challenge. *European Journal of Applied Physiology, 57,* 271–274.

Svebak, S. (1982). The effect of task difficulty and threat of aversive electric shock upon tonic physiological changes. *Biological Psychology, 14,* 113–128.

Svebak, S. (1988). Psychogenic muscle tension. In M. J. Apter, J. H. Kerr, & M. P. Cowles (Eds.), *Progress in reversal theory* (pp. 143–162). Amsterdam: Elsevier/North-Holland.

Svebak, S., & Murgatroyd, S. (1985). Metamotivational dominance: A multimethod validation of reversal theory constructs. *Journal of Personality and Social Psychology, 48,* 107–116.

Ursin, H., & Murison, R. C. (1983). The stress concept. In H. Ursin & R. C. Murison (Eds.), *Biological and psychological basis of psychosomatic disease* (pp. 7–13). Oxford: Pergamon Press.

Westgaard, R. H., & Aarås, A. (1985). The effect of improved workplace design on the development of work-related musculo-skeletal illnesses. *Applied Ergonomics, 16,* 91–97.

APPENDIX

The Tension and Effort Stress Inventory (TESI)

Subject code _____

Sex _____   Age _____

Please give your answers by *circling* the appropriate figures.

A. Estimate the degree of *pressure,* stress, challenge, or demand that you have been exposed to over the *last seven days* as due to:

	No pressure Very much
Work:	1–2–3–4–5–6–7
Family:	1–2–3–4–5–6–7
Finance:	1–2–3–4–5–6–7
Your own body:	1–2–3–4–5–6–7

B. Estimate the degree of *effort* that you have put up over the *last seven days* to cope with pressure etc. from:

	No effort Very much
Work:	1–2–3–4–5–6–7
Family:	1–2–3–4–5–6–7
Finance:	1–2–3–4–5–6–7
Your own body:	1–2–3–4–5–6–7

C. Estimate here the degree to which you have experienced the following *moods or emotions* in everyday life over the *last seven days:*

	Not at all	Very much
Relaxtion:	1–2–3–4–5–6–7	
Anxiety:	1–2–3–4–5–6–7	
Excitement:	1–2–3–4–5–6–7	
Boredom:	1–2–3–4–5–6–7	
Placidity:	1–2–3–4–5–6–7	
Anger:	1–2–3–4–5–6–7	
Provocativeness:	1–2–3–4–5–6–7	
Sullenness:	1–2–3–4–5–6–7	
Pride:	1–2–3–4–5–6–7	
Humiliation:	1–2–3–4–5–6–7	
Modesty:	1–2–3–4–5–6–7	
Shame:	1–2–3–4–5–6–7	
Gratitude:	1–2–3–4–5–6–7	
Resentment:	1–2–3–4–5–6–7	
Virtue:	1–2–3–4–5–6–7	
Guilt:	1–2–3–4–5–6–7	

Thank you!

Designed 1987 by Sven Svebak, Department of Somatic Psychology,
Årstadveien 21, N-5009 Bergen, Norway

V

STRESS, TYPE A BEHAVIOR, AND HEART DISEASE

17

Occupational Stress, Type A Behavior, and Risk of Coronary Disease

Don G. Byrne and Anne E. Byrne
Australian National University, Canberra, Australia

Despite long-standing recognition of the fact, coronary heart disease (CHD) continues to be the major cause of death and disability among middle-aged and older people in Western urbanized societies. Rates of incidence, reflecting both mortality and morbidity, vary somewhat between countries but Australian data give some indication of the magnitude of the problem. In 1986 some 48% of all deaths (males and females of all ages) was attributable to vascular disease in some form with 39% being directly related to CHD (National Heart Foundation of Australia, 1986). This compared with 24% for neoplastic disease of all forms. The data present an even more prominent picture when males and females are examined separately: In 1986, the mortality rate from CHD in males 30 to 64 years old (premature deaths) was around 150/100,000 whereas in females in the same age range, the mortality rate from CHD approximated 45/100,000. (Death from carcinoma of the breast, uterus, and lung account for greater female mortality in this age group.)

Australia is by no means unique in this regard. Mortality from CHD in Australian males 30 to 64 years old ranks 13th in a risk list of 18 countries prepared by the World Health Organization (National Heart Foundation of Australia, 1986). Mortality from CHD for the United States and England ranks slightly above that of Australia. Countries such as Finland show CHD mortality rates at twice the level to be found in Australia or the United States while Japan's mortality from CHD is exceptionally low. Not surprisingly, international variation of this magnitude has given rise to much speculation on the causes of CHD (Byrne, 1987). By and large, however, attention has been focused on physiological and metabolic regulation of cardiovascular functioning in an effort to understand the pathology underlying this recognized epidemic.

Epidemiological investigation over three decades has identified a multitude of risk factors supposedly related to the incidence of CHD (Willerson, Hillis, & Buja, 1982). Among these, high levels of serum cholesterol, hypertension and cigarette smoking have been most strongly implicated (Frick, Elo, Haapa, Heinonen, Heinsalmi et al., 1987). Only relatively recently has serious consideration been given to the possible roles that psychosocial factors, broadly defined, might play in the pathological process of atherogenesis and the precipitation of clinical CHD (Byrne & Rosenman, 1989).

Reviews of the contemporary literature on psychosocial risks for CHD (Booth-Kewley & Friedman, 1987; Byrne, 1987; Jenkins, 1976; Siegel, 1984) have generally concluded that stress from whatever source poses, at best, an ambiguous threat to the functional integrity of the cardiovascular system. Greater credence has been given to the more specific role of the Type A behavior pattern (TABP) as a risk factor for CHD (Rosenman & Chesney, 1981), and, although the epidemiological evidence is by no means unequivocal (Byrne, 1987), it is broadly accepted that the TABP endows an independent risk of CHD of a similar magnitude to that associated with elevated serum cholesterol (National Heart, Lung and Blood Institute, 1981).

Reference to common descriptions of the TABP (Byrne, 1981; Friedman, 1969; Herman, Blumenthal, Black, & Chesney, 1981) indicates a pattern of behaviors characterized by ambition, competitiveness, personal striving, achievement orientation, time urgency, and anger/hostility. Even a cursory overview of these attributes alerts one to the idea that they are likely to be associated with an individual's occupational milieu. There is clear support for the view that the TABP is positively related to occupational status (Byrne, Rosenman, Schiller, & Chesney, 1985; Chesney & Rosenman, 1980; Zyzanski, 1978) with the basis for this seemingly encapsulated in Jenkins's (1978) comment that

> "Type A behavior, its achievement orientation, in all likelihood leads to upward mobility, and similarly, the culture of professions and administrations values the same traits that are at the foundation of the Type A value system."

By way of extension, Byrne and Reinhart (1989a) were led to suggest that the TABP and the occupational environment, acting in concert, endow a unique risk for CHD. It is certainly the case that particular occupational environments precipitate observable episodes of the TABP more readily than others (Kittel, Kornitzer, & Dramaix, 1980).

The emergence of occupation as a variable of interest in the study of CHD risk resurrects an area that has for some time discarded by the psychosocial perspective on CHD. It is reasonably widely accepted that occupational status relates to risk of CHD; however, contrary to the popular view, current evidence favors the notion that CHD is more prevalent among blue collar than among executive or managerial occupational groups (Bolm-Audorff & Siegrist, 1983). However, the evidence suggesting that simple measures of occupational demand or work stress related causally to risk of CHD was sufficiently equivocal in outcome and questionable in methodology (Jenkins, 1971) that it has not been accorded serious consideration for some years.

Studies attempting to relate aspects of occupations to risk of CHD have accumulate into a large mass of material, but there is noticeable variability both in the methodological quality of the work and the degree of support it lends to causal links between occupation and CHD. Much of the work has invoked the concept of occupational stress as a mediating mechanism interposed between the nature of occupations or characteristics of occupational environments (however defined or measured) and risk of CHD. Thus, some occupations have come to be labeled as "stressful" relative to others (though there is often little consistency between studies as to what these occupations are) and, therefore, to endow a particular risk of CHD. Evidence of this kind has relied typically on studies involving simple conceptualizations both of stress and of the characteristics of occupations considered to produce this state. More recent research has placed greater emphasis on interactive conceptualizations in which aspects of occupations are seen to interact with individual characteristics to produce combinations that are either adaptive (and healthy) or maladaptive (and threatening future health breakdown). Before examining this view, however, we briefly survey the material attempting to relate simple conceptualizations of occupation and occupational stress to risk of CHD.

OCCUPATION AND CORONARY HEART DISEASE

Sources of Occupational Stress

A major source of occupational stress relates to the type of occupation engaged in. Both differences within (Russek, 1960) and differences between (French & Caplan, 1970) occupations are potentially important sources of stress. In addition, occupational stress may result from the manner of remuneration, that is, self-paid versus salaried employment (Magnus, Matroos, & Strackel, 1983). In addition, employment status for women per se may be a source of occupational stress (Haynes & Feinleib, 1980). The nature of work demands (Haynes, Feinleib, Levine, Scotch, & Kannel, 1978), the nature of workload (Magnus et al., 1983), and the degree of satisfaction workers feel in their employment and situation (Sales & House, 1971) may also contribute significantly to stress in the workplace. Further sources of occupational stress relate to the personality of workers and the amount of social support workers receive (Haynes & Feinleib, 1980) and the degree of personal control workers experience over the work demands that confront them (Karasek, Baker, Marxer, Ahlborn, & Theorell, 1981).

Exploring the Relationship Between Occupational Stress and Coronary Heart Disease

Differences within particular occupational groups have been shown to link with the incidence of CHD. The exemplary work of Russek (1960) demonstrated that a group of general practitioners ages 40 to 69 had a markedly higher prevalence of CHD than a group of same-age specialists working in the less stressful area of dermatology. In a further study (Russek, 1965) the CHD prevalences among specialities within the professions of medicine, law, and dentistry were investigated. As expected, there was a trend toward higher prevalence of CHD among the more stressful specialties within each of these occupational groups. Friedman and Hellersten (1968), however, failed to replicate this finding in a study investigating stress ratings and their relationship to CHD in a sample of individuals involved in a number of legal specialities.

Working within the public versus the private sector for any single occupational group may also affect the rates of CHD experienced. In a longitudinal study (Kornitzer, Kittel, Debacker, & Dramaix, 1981; Kornitzer, Tilly, Van Roux, & Balthazar, 1975) involving samples of bank employees working in either the public or private sector, it was found that the incidence of CHD was greater in the sample of private basic employees; the explanation given by the authors for this finding had to do with the much greater pressure experienced by employees in private as compared with public banking institutions.

Apart from differences in the incidence of CHD within occupations, there is evidence that consistent differences between occupational groups exist in terms of

CHD prevalence. The high rate of deaths from CHD in sea officers in Norway compared with the population average led Mundal, Erikssen, & Rodahl (1982) to conclude that occupational stress was the major cause of the inflated figure. Occupational stress was also given as a possible explanation for the high rates of death from CHD among sea officers in West Germany (Zorn, Harrington, & Goethe, 1977). In a study investigating occupational differences in cardiovascular disease prevalence, French and Caplan (1970) found that blue collar trade employees and managers had a much higher incidence of cardiovascular disease than engineers or scientists—this was found to be the case irrespective of the age comparisons employed. The researchers argued that these differences were due to the higher levels of occupational stress in blue collar workers and managerial staff compared with the engineers and scientists. Other studies have shown that professions of roughly equal social status experience widely disparate rates of CHD (Kasl, 1978). For instance, the teaching profession was shown to have lower CHD rates as a group when compared with the total population whereas other professional cohorts (e.g., lawyers, surgeons, and real estate agents) had a much higher incidence of CHD than the population as a whole. Again, different levels of occupational stress would seem a likely explanation for these differences across occupational groups.

In a major study of the occupational characteristics of patients who had experienced their first episode of acute myocardial infarction (Bolm-Audorff & Siegrist, 1983), it was found that blue collar occupations were significantly overrepresented when compared with the incidence of myocardial infarction in the total population. Stress in the workplace was posited as the likely reason for this finding. Within the white collar group, differences between the incidence of acute myocardial infarction were also evident. For example, pilots, air traffic controllers, and managers had a higher prevalence of infarcts than other occupational groupings; again, work stress was offered as a likely explanation.

Individuals who are self-employed have been found to have a much higher incidence of CHD than those with employee status. More specifically, Magnus et al. (1983) concluded that self-employed persons are at twice the risk of CHD than those persons not self-employed. It is worth noting that very little work has been done with female samples, though the little that is available seems to corroborate the evidence for male samples. Certain groups of working women have been found to be at higher risk for CHD than other groups: In particular, clerical workers have been found to have a higher risk of CHD than for women generally (Haw, 1982; Haynes & Feinleib, 1980). The picture is more complicated for women than for men, however, because a large percentage of women do not work and the dual roles of working and caring for a family may add additional stress that may not be evident in male samples. The relationship between work demands and CHD is far from clear. Whereas early research (Liljefors & Rahe, 1970) supports a positive association between work demands (in this case, number of hours worked) and the incidence of myocardial infarction, later research has not, for the most part, confirmed this association. Although the Framington study (Haynes, Feinleib, & Kannel, 1980; Haynes, Feinleib, Levine, Scotch, & Kennel, 1978) examined a relationship between work demands (measured by an index and a work load) and CHD among a sample of older workers, it failed to establish such an association for younger age groups. Moreover, the work demand measure did not make a significant independent contribution to the prediction of the prevalence of CHD. Magnus et al. (1983) failed to find a relationship between excessive working hours and time pressure and the incidence of CHD. In addition, Maschewsky (1982) found only equivocal support for the association between work demands (measured by items covering length of working hours, pressure on time, and responsibilities at work) and acute coronary events. Although workers experiencing myocardial infarction rated significantly higher on some measures of work demands, a control group (comprising healthy workers) were shown to rate significantly higher on other work demand indices. Theorell and Rahe (1971) reported similar equivocal patterns in their comparison of the work demands experienced by a group of workers who had experienced an episode of myocardial infarction and a group of healthy workers: The former rated significantly higher on some measures of work demands but the latter rated higher on other dimensions of this variable.

Results from cross-cultural research have further confused the picture. In one study (Orth-Gomer, 1979), groups of Swedish and American persons who had suffered from coronary heart disease were compared with healthy samples in each country. Whereas the Swedish sample of CHD victims reported higher rates of job demand than the comparison sample, the opposite pattern emerged for the American sample. Overall the links between work demands and the prevalence of acute coronary disorders seem tenuous at best and perhaps nonexistent.

One reason for the failure to find more consistent results in the study investigating the link between work demands and CHD may be the simplicity of the measures of work demand that have been employed. It has been suggested that composite measures of work load (including psychosocial as well as physical work stressors) are necessary to adequately assess the relationship between work stressors and CHD. Composite measures of work stress have been found to be positively associated with CHD in samples of individuals recovering from CHD (Magnus et al., 1983). In a further study employing a composite measure of workload Theorell and Floderus-Myrhed (1977) found that frequency of work load was significantly higher for samples of myocardial infarcts than for the population as a whole.

It has been suggested that job satisfaction is positively associated with the occurrence of CHD (Sales & House, 1971), but this interpretation is under review (cf. Frank & Weintraub, 1973). For the most part, no association has been found between job satisfaction and the incidence of CHD (Theorell & Rahe, 1971).

The lack of control that an individual feels at work and the excessive demands that individuals feel control them in the workplace have both been found to be positively related to CHD. Alfredson, Karasek, and Theorell (1982) assessed whether high work demands and low opportunities for control at work were risk factors for CHD. Employing a large and representative sample of individuals engaged in a wide range of occupations in Sweden, they found that the hectic nature of work coupled with a lack of control over work practices was significantly associated with the risk of myocardial infarction. Also they found that shift work (high demand characteristic) and monotony (low control characteristic) were significantly though independently related to the risk of myocardial infarction. It needs to be pointed out, however, that where physical job requirements and traditional risk factors (e.g., cigarette smoking and low education level) were taken into consideration, the relationship between shift work and CHD disappeared (Alfredson & Theorell, 1983). All other relationships were maintained.

In a further study, Karasek et al. (1981) investigated the relationship between job characteristics and the risk of CHD. The latter was found to be predicted by high job demands and low intellectual discretion. By matching the characteristics of control subjects who had died from coronary heart or vascular disease, the same authors report that the risk of coronary heart or vascular disease was significantly increased for individuals experiencing both high work demands and high work demands coupled with low personal freedom.

In a longitudinal study, Langosch, Brodner, and Borcherding (1983) investigated the association between job demand and control characteristics, on the one hand, and the severity and progression of coronary disease on the other. It was reported that high work demands (including doing too many tasks at the same time) and lack of job control (uncontrollable job stress) were positively and significantly related to the severity of CHD as well as to the progression of that disease.

Siegrist (1984) assessed the relationship between low levels of control and high levels of demand at work and CHD. He found that time urgency (high demand characteristic) and feelings of hopelessness and anger and severe sleep disturbances (low control characteristics) were significantly related to the incidence of CHD. These findings also support the notion that high work demands and low control at work at important contributors to CHD.

Although personality and social support variables are believed to be useful predictors of the incidence of CHD, there is, with one exception, little empirical support for this contention. In an attempt to explain the finding (reported earlier) that women holding clerical jobs were at greater risk of coronary heart disease than other groups, Haynes and Feinleib (1980) provided evidence that personality factors and social support mechanisms were both significant contributors to CHD among clerical workers.

Methodological Limitations

Although the evidence on occupational stress and CHD presents a persuasive picture, at least at face value, a number of methodological problems, particularly in design and measurement, somewhat limit the conclusions that may be drawn from the data. The term "occupational stress" has suffered from inadequate definition (just as the general notion of "stress" has posed conceptual problems in the past). Measurement of occupational stress has, therefore, been neither precise nor consistent. Moreover, sampling has frequently been unrepresentative of either the general population or more specific occupational groups of interest. Research designs have typically been retrospective in nature, giving rise to potential contamination from unmeasured and unanticipated variables and obscuring interpretations of the data. Finally, studies have frequently relied on simplistic conceptualizations of occupational stress or similar factors, thus reducing the sophistication of the work. As a result, the import of this entire area of research is restricted to rather vague pronouncements regarding broad and nonspecific effects.

OCCUPATION AND THE TYPE A BEHAVIOR PATTERN

Clearly, the evidence cited above does not allow a complete dismissal of the view that at least some attributes of individual occupations, or the environments within which they are practiced, relate statistically to risk of CHD. Nonetheless, the evidence is neither unequivocal nor consistent in its support for such a link. This raises the possibility that it is not occupation or the occupational environment per se that endows a risk for CHD but some interaction between the occupational situation and other characteristics of the individual. The idea of interactive risk is presently capturing some attention in epidemiology (Byrne & Reinhart, 1989a). A major contender for consideration within this context involves the interaction between aspects of the occupation and the TABP.

As noted earlier, occupation and the TABP present two not dissimilar realms of discourse. The relationship between crudely measured occupational status and at least some measures of the TABP is well documented, with high-status occupations being associated with high scores on scales of the TABP (though as Chesney et al. [1981] point out, this may not be so for all measures of TABP). The detailed relationship which the occupational situation bears to the TABP may therefore shed some light on the mediation of coronary risk by way of these variables.

Regrettably, little work has been done to document the potentially informative details of this relationship. A study reported by Byrne and Reinhart (1989b) did examine relationships between a self-reported measure of the TABP (the Jenkins Activity Survey [JAS]; Jenkins, Zyzanski, & Rosenman, 1979) and a range of occupational measures of reflecting both organizational and individual imposed work demands. Subjects in this study were 432 persons employed in professional and managerial positions within government departments; that is, subjects were selected on the grounds that their generally senior levels of occupation should ensure generally high levels of the TABP within the sample. Occupational measures examined together with associations emerging with subscales of the JAS (Global Type A behavior, Speed and Impatience [S], Job Involvement [J], and Hard Driving [H]) are shown in Table 1.

The Global scale of the JAS was significantly related to occupational level but the relationship was more strongly evident where the TABP was reflected by the J scale. As expected, the presence of the TABP coincided with higher occupational

Table 1 Correlations between Jenkins Activity Survey scale scores, occupational level, and job characteristics

Occupational measures	Type A behavior pattern				
	Global Type A	Speed	Job Involvement	Hard Driving	Occupational Level
Occupational level	.15**	.07	.21***	.01	—
No. of people supervised	.12**	.06	.03	.06	.31***
No. of years in present position	−.09	−.08	−.17***	.01	.06
Time of arrival at work	−.08	−.07	.07	.03	−.11**
Time of leaving work	.23***	.13**	.34***	.21***	.28***
Length of training period required for present position	−.12**	−.02	−.06	−.09	.05
Perceived likelihood of promotion	.18***	.06	.20***	.16**	.02
Standard working hours per week	.32***	.19***	.26***	.24***	.33***
Excess working hours per week	.27***	.08	.32***	.29***	.17***
Feelings about overtime	.16***	.02	.30***	.17***	.14***
Frequency of weekend work	.31***	.15**	.44***	.24***	.32***

$**p < .01.$ $***p < .001.$

levels. These scales, together with the H scale, also correlated consistently and significantly with, response to most items reflecting job characteristics. Inspection of the correlation coefficients suggests, however, that it is aspects of the job under individual control rather than those imposed by the nature of the occupational organization that relate most strongly with measures of the TABP. By contrast, that aspect of the TABP measured by the S scale of the JAS failed to correlate appreciably with the great majority of job characteristics, and it would seem that measures reflecting personal effort rather than those indicating time pressure and impatience distinguish high occupational achievers from persons remaining lower in occupational status.

Although associations among the TABP, occupational level, and job characteristics are interesting as independent data, they tell little of how possession of the TABP may promote occupational achievement. Because both the Global and J scales of the JAS correlated significantly with occupational level, this process was further explored by examining the effect on associations while controlling simultaneously for characteristics of the job; this information may be seen in Table 2.

Partial correlations showed that where job characteristics reflected a situation imposed by the occupational organization, associations remained essentially unaltered. The pathway through which TABP influences occupational achievement does not seem to lie, therefore, in any simple congruence of individual characteristics and the occupational environment. However, when the simultaneous operation of personal effort (expressed in terms of time commitment to the job) was explored, associations between the TABP and occupational level either disappeared or diminished markedly in significance. These data indicate, then, that Type A individuals not only work longer and more irregular hours than others but that the link between the TABP and occupational level is at least partially mediated by the practice of committing long hours to the job.

Howard, Cunningham, and Rechuitzer (1976) also reported that the TABP among individuals sampled from a managerial population was associated with

Table 2 Partial correlations between Jenkins Activity Survey Global Type A and Job Involvement scales and occupational level, controlling for job characteristics[a]

Job characteristic	Global Type A Scale with occupational level (simple r = .15**)	Job Involvement Scale with occupational level (simple r = .21***)
No. of people supervised	.12**	.19***
No. of years in present position	.15**	.21***
Time of arrival at work	.14**	.20***
Time of leaving work	.09	.12*
Length of training period required for present position	.15**	.21**
Perceived likelihood of promotion	.15**	.19***
Feelings about overtime	.13**	.16**
Frequency of weekend work	.05	.07
Standard working hours per week	.05	.13**
Excess working hours per week	.11*	.14**

[a]Because only the Global Type A Job Involvement scales of the Jenkins Activity Survey correlated significantly with occupational level, partial correlations are presented only for these scales.
**p < .01. ***p < .001.

more working weeks per year, more discretionary work hours per week, and more days per year spent on occupation-related travel than among individuals without the behavior pattern. These joint data underscore the importance of an occupational time commitment in excess of organizational expectations as a manifestation of the TABP. The present study extends these findings to suggest that this time commitment is instrument in facilitating occupational achievement among those with the TABP.

These results reveal a clear association between the TABP and occupational level, and one in which possession of the former might well facilitate advancement in the latter. It has been suggested that where the occupational environment allows unhindered expression of the TABP, the Type A individual enjoys job satisfaction and shows no elevations in risk factors for CHD. Where the nature of the job frustrates expression of the TABP, the resultant job dissatisfaction may well promote personal distress and, through well-established neuroendocrinological mechanisms, may lead to increases in levels of coronary risk factors.

TYPE A BEHAVIOR, OCCUPATION, AND CORONARY RISK FACTORS

In view of this reasoning, one might expect quite particular associations among occupation, the TABP, and accepted risk factors for CHD, the nature of which would not be simple but decidedly interactive. The list of identified risk factors for CHD is both long and diverse; at last count, some 246 individual factors were implicated in the genesis or precipitation of cardiovascular disease (Hopkins & Williams, 1981). Parsimony allows us to reduce this list to three factors (excluding the TABP itself): elevated levels of serum cholesterol, hypertension, and cigarette smoking (Frick et al., 1987). A number of major investigations, notably the Framingham Study (Truett, Cornfield, & Kannel, 1967) have resulted in the construction of weighted indices of coronary risk based on statistical combinations of known or hypothesized risk factors. Work by Byrne (1985) may be cited to illustrate the interactive ways in which the TABP, in combination with occupational measures, associates with assessments of these risk factors.

Subjects were 447 employed males occupying a broad range of positions, from unskilled manual workers to tertiary trained professionals and administrators, in a single government department. These individuals were participating in a longitudinal study of coronary risk factors and had been extensively assessed for serum lipids, blood pressure, and smoking status; in addition, each subject had been assessed for the TABP using the structured interview technique. A simple categorization of occupational level (unskilled manual work, unskilled clerical work, and tertiary trained professional or managerial work) was used as the measure of the occupational setting because, though this is a somewhat crude metric, it does indicate the degree of responsibility, power, and status held by each individual and therefore the potential for challenging interaction from the work environment.

Contrary to expectation, but of great interest, it was found that this simple categorization of occupation did not relate significantly to the interview measure of the TABP. It is worth noting that there are strong links between occupation and self-reported TABP (Byrne & Reinhart, 1989) though the nature of self-report measures may be such as to promote such relationships (Byrne et al., 1985).

Table 3 Coronary risk factors broken down by structured interview assessments of the Type A
behavior pattern (TABP)

Systolic blood pressure	No significant effect
Diastolic blood pressure	No significant effect
Serum cholesterol	Trend ($p = 0.06$): greater TABP, higher cholesterol
Serum triglyceride	Trend ($p = 0.09$): greater TABP, higher triglyceride
Smoking rates	Significant ($p = 0.007$): greater TABP, lower smoking rate
Framingham weighted risk index	No significant effect

Coronary risk factors did relate marginally to presence of the TABP (see Table 3). There was no evident relationship between the TABP and blood pressure, whether diastolic or systolic. Those with the TABP did appear to exhibit higher levels of serum lipids (both cholesterol and tri-glycerides) than Type Bs in the sample; however, smoking rates among cigarette smokers were inversely related to presence of the TABP. The use of a weighted index of coronary risk based on the predictive equation developed by the Framingham Study (Truett et al., 1967) revealed no simple relationship between coronary risk and the TABP.

Nor were simple associations abundantly evident when coronary risk factors were examined with occupational level. No single coronary risk factor related significantly to occupational level, though the Framingham weighted index did reveal a significant effect, with lower occupational level being associated with higher weighted coronary risk level. This is very much in accord with the contemporary view that blue collar workers, rather than their executive and managerial colleagues, are at greatest risk of CHD (Bolm-Audorff & Siegrist, 1983).

Examination of coronary risk factors by occupation and the TABP intractively did, however, suggest a relationship unique to this combination of variables; a summary of these associations is shown in Table 4. From Table 4 it can be seen that simple relationships with the TABP emerged much as they did for the structured interview, as shown in Table 3. Of far greater interest, however, was the finding that a combination of occupational level and the TABP produced a significant interaction effect on the Framingham weighted index of coronary risk: Highest levels of coronary risk were found among blue collar workers with the TABP.

The importance of this finding lies in the view that coronary risk endowed by occupational level or status, though questionable when examined in isolation, is enhanced when considered in combination with possession of the TABP. The results of this study are tentative and must be interpreted with some caution. Above all, these data are cross-sectional in nature and nothing can be said regarding the causal influence that either the TABP or occupation might have on coronary risk. Moreover, the dependent variables in the study were those of physiological or metabolic risk factors and not evidence of coronary artery pathology or

Table 4 Coronary risk factors broken down by the Type A behavior pattern and occupational level

Systolic blood pressure	No significant effect
Diastolic blood pressure	No significant effect
Serum cholesterol	Trend ($p = 0.08$) for main effect of structured interview
Serum triglyceride	No significant effect
Smoking rates	Significant main effect ($p = 0.008$) of structured interview
Framingham weighted risk index	Significant interaction ($p = 0.05$) of structured interview and occupational level

CHD. The extension of the data to comment on associations among the TABP, occupation, and CHD cannot, therefore, be presently made. Nonetheless, the emergence of an interactive relationship such as that found does encourage further exploration of the area.

TYPE A BEHAVIOR, OCCUPATION, AND CORONARY HEART DISEASE: MECHANISMS OF INFLUENCE

Although there is equivocal evidence relating aspects of occupation to risk of CHD and much firmer evidence linking CHD with possession of the TABP, there are as yet, no epidemiological data concerning coronary risk endowed by a combination of the two, at least so far as the end point of CHD is concerned. However, there are good reasons for believing that such a combination of variables may act to enhance epidemiological explanatory power in the quest to understand the pathogenesis of CHD.

It is clear from the multitude of evidence on risk factors for CHD that no single factor typically accounts for large proportions of coronary risk (Hopkins & Williams, 1981). Indeed, risk factors for most noncommunicable diseases rarely explain more than a small percentage of disease variance, perhaps reflecting the long recognized but often tacitly accepted dictum of epidemiology that possession of a risk factor does not inevitably lead to clinical episodes of the disease it has been statistically associated with. One possible solution to this apparent puzzle involves the notion that risk factors endow attributable risk only when activated by some characteristic endogenous within the individual or contained within the environment.

As discussed earlier, not only does the TABP appear to reflect attributes indicative of the work environment, but overt behavioral episodes of the pattern may be activated by occupational occurrences. Moreover, given the potentially interactive nature of this conception, it must be admitted that both adaptive and maladaptive combinations of the TABP and occupation are possible. The theoretical basis for this view may lie in the concept of frustration. Type A individuals are strongly goal oriented and are therefore likely to exhibit higher levels of frustration than their Type B colleagues when prevented from achieving their desired goals. There is evidence to suggest that those with the TABP respond with higher levels of cardiovascular reactivity to tasks involving goal frustration than do those in whom the TABP is absent (Manuck, Morrison, Bellack, & Polefrome, 1985). Occupational settings and the nature of occupations themselves vary considerably in the extent to which they permit the achievement of Type A goals or allow the expression of Type A behaviors. Overall, however, it is more likely that goal achievement will be frustrated in blue collar than in white collar occupations because the structure of occupations gives greater freedom for white collar workers to exercise personal initiative, formulate and carry out individual decisions, assume control of job-related tasks, and work toward sought-after goals.

The possible consequences of such occupation-based frustration will be both behavioral/affective and physiological. On the one hand, a degree of job dissatisfaction might be expected to emerge, leading to emotional distress and perhaps burnout. At another level, and not unrelated to the affective situation, a state of physiological arousal akin to the stress reaction is also likely. The translation of these states, by means of neuroendocrinological mechanisms, to elevations in levels of coronary risk factors (particularly those regulated by the autonomic nervous system) and to vulnerability to acute coronary events (most likely by means of thrombogenic enhancement), is not a far-fetched hypothesis.

The present evidence is tentative. The short-term biological consequences of this suggested situation must be confirmed in the laboratory and the long-term influences await confirmation by prospective studies of CHD incidence. Collection of these data may, however, further strengthen the increasing confidence in behavioral attributes as coronary risk factors.

SUMMARY

The notion of occupational stress has often been linked with risk of coronary heart disease, but close examination of the evidence shows this link to be tenuous. There is little to associate crude occupational structure to risk of coronary heart disease, and studies of stress arising from the work environment have been largely inconclusive. Much of the difficulty appears to be the methodological problems bound up in the measurement of occupational stress; simply, much of the evidence has been anecdotal and intuitional. The Type A behavior pattern (TABP), however, seems to offer a possible mechanism through which occupational factors might influence risk of coronary heart disease. The TABP has clear correlates with a number of aspects of the occupational setting, and there is developing evidence of an interactional effect among the TABP, occupation, and risk of coronary heart disease. It is this interactional possibility which seems most worthy of exploration in future studies of coronary risk in the workplace.

REFERENCES

Alfredson, L., Karasek, R., & Theorell, T. (1982). Myocardial infarction risk and psychosocial work environment: An analysis of the male Swedish working force. *Social Science and Medicine, 16,* 463–467.

Alfredson, L., & Theorell, T. (1983). Job characteristics of occupations and myocardial infarction risk: Effect of possible counfounding factors. *Social Science and Medicine, 17,* 1497–1503.

Bolm-Audorff, V., & Siegrist, J. (1983). Occupational morbidity data in myocardial infarction. *Journal of Occupational Medicine, 25,* 367–371.

Booth-Kewley, S., & Friedman, H. S. (1987). Psychological predictors of heart disease: A quantitative review. *Psychological Bulletin, 101,* 343–362.

Byrne, D. G. (1981). Type A behaviour, life-events and myocardial infarction: Independent or related risk factors? *British Journal of Medical Psychology, 54,* 371–377.

Byrne, D. G. (1985, July). *Type A behavior, occupation and risk factors for coronary heart disease.* Presented at the 8th World Congress of the International College of Psychosomatic Medicine, Chicago.

Byrne, D. G. (1987). Personality, life events and cardiovascular disease. *Journal of Psychosomatic Research, 31,* 661–671.

Byrne, D. G., & Reinhart, M. I. (1989a). Occupation, Type A behavior and self-reported angina pectoris. *Journal of Psychosomatic Research, 33,* 609–619.

Byrne, D. G., & Reinhart, M. I. (1989b). Work characteristics, occupational achievement and the Type A behaviour pattern. *Journal of Occupational Psychology, 62,* 123–134.

Byrne, D. G., Rosenman, R. H., Schiller, E., & Chesney, M. A. (1985). Consistency and variation among instruments purporting to measure the Type A behavior pattern. *Psychosomatic Medicine, 47,* 242–261.

Byrne, D. G., & Rosenman, R. H. (1989). *Anxiety and the heart.* Washington, DC: Hemisphere.

Chesney, M. A., & Rosenman, R. H. (1980). Type A behaviour in the work setting. In C. L. Cooper & R. Payne (Eds.), *Current concerns in occupational stress* (pp. 187–212). New York: Wiley.

Chesney, M. A., Sevelius, G., Black, G. W., Ward, M. M., Swan, G. E., & Rosenman, R. H. (1981). Work environment, Type A behavior, and coronary heart disease risk factors. *Journal of Occupational Medicine, 23,* 551–555.

Frank, F. D., & Weintraub, J. (1973). Job satisfaction and mortality from coronary heart disease: Critique of some of the research. *Journal of Chronic Diseases, 36,* 351–354.

French, J. R. P., & Caplan, R. D. (1970). Psychosocial factors in coronary heart disease. *Industrial Medicine and Surgery, 39,* 31–45.

Frick, M. H., Elo, O., Haapa, K., Heinonen, O. P., Heinsalmi, P. et al. (1987). Helsinki Heart Study: Primary prevention trial with Gemfibrogil in middle-aged men with dyslipidemia. *New England Journal of Medicine, 317,* 1237–1245.

Friedman, E. H., & Hellerstein, H. K. (1968). Occupational stress, law school hierarchy, and coronary artery disease in Cleveland attorneys. *Psychosomatic Medicine, 30,* 72–86.

Friedman, M. (1969). *Pathogenesis of coronary artery disease.* New York: McGraw-Hill.

Haw, M. A. (1982). Women, work and stress: A review and agenda for the future. *Journal of Health and Social Behavior, 23,* 132–144.

Haynes, S. G., & Feinleib, M. (1980). Women, work and coronary heart disease: Prospective findings from the Framingham heart study. *American Journal of Public Health, 70,* 133–141.

Haynes, S., Feinleib, M., & Kannel, W. (1980). The relationship of psychosocial factors to coronary heart disease in the Framingham study: III. Eight year incidence of CHD. *American Journal of Epidemiology, 3,* 37–58.

Haynes, S. G., Feinleib, M., Levine, S., Scotch, N., & Kannel, W. B. (1978). The relationship at psychosocial factors to coronary heart disease: II. Prevalence of coronary heart disease. *American Journal of Epidemiology, 107,* 384–402.

Herman, S., Blumenthal, J. A., Black, G. M., & Chesney, M. A. (1981). Self-ratings of Type A (coronary prone) adults: Do Type A's know they are Type A's? *Psychosomatic Medicine, 43,* 405–413.

Hopkins, P. M., & Williams, R. R. (1981). A survey of 246 suggested coronary risk factors. *Atherosclerosis, 40,* 1–52.

Howard, J. H., Cunningham, D. A., & Rechuitzer, P. A. (1976). Work patterns associated with Type A behavior: A managerial population. *Human Relations, 30,* 825–836.

Jenkins, C. D. (1971). Psychologic and social precursors of coronary disease. *New England Journal of Medicine, 284,* 244–255, 307–317.

Jenkins, C. D. (1976). Recent evidence supporting psychologic and social risk factors for coronary disease. *New England Journal of Medicine, 294,* 987–994, 1033–1038.

Jenkins, C. D. (1978). A comparative review of the interview and questionnaire methods in the assessment of the coronary prone behavior pattern. In T. M. Dembroski, S. M. Weiss, J. L. Shields, S. G. Haynes, & M. Feinleib (Eds.), *Coronary prone behavior* (pp. 71–86). New York: Springer Verlag.

Jenkins, C. D., Zyzanski, S. J., & Rosenman, R. H. (1979). *Jenkins Activity Survey manual: Form C.* New York: Psychological Corporation.

Karasek, R., Baker, D., Marxer, F., Ahlborn, A., & Theorell, T. (1981). Job decision latitude, job demands, and cardiovascular disease: A prospective study of Swedish men. *American Journal of Public Health, 71,* 694–705.

Kasl, S. V. (1978). Epidemilogical contribution to the study of work stress. In C. Cooper & R. Payne (Eds.), *Stress at work* (pp. 1–48). New York: Wiley.

Kittel, F., Kornitzer, M., & Dramaix, M. (1980). Coronary heart disease and job stress in two cohorts of bank clerks. *Psychotherapy and Psychosomatics, 34,* 110–123.

Kornitzer, M., Kittel, F., Debacker, G., & Dramaix, M. (1981). The Belgian heart disease prevention project: Type A behavior pattern and the prevalence of coronary heart disease. *Psychosomatic Medicine, 43,* 133–145.

Kornitzer, M., Thilly, C. H., Van Roux, A., & Balthazar, R. (1975). Incidence of ischemic heart disease in two cohorts of Belgian clerks. *British Journal of Preventive and Social Medicine, 29,* 91–97.

Langosch, W., Brodner, G., & Borcherding, H. (1983). Psychological and vocational long-term outcomes of cardiac rehabilitation with post-infarction patients under the age of forty. *Psychotherapy and Psychosomatics, 40,* 115–128.

Liljefors, I., & Rahe, R. H. (1970). An identical twin study of psychosocial factors in coronary heart disease in Sweden. *Psychosomatic Medicine, 32,* 523–542.

Magnus, K., Matroos, A. W., & Strackel, J. (1983). The self-employed and the self-driven: Two coronary prone sub-populations from the Zeist study. *American Journal of Epidemiology, 118,* 799–805.

Manuck, S. B., Morrison, R. L., Bellack, A. S., & Polefrome, J. M. (1985). Behavioral factors in hypertension: Cardio-vascular reactivity, anger and social competence. In M. A. Chesney & R. H. Rosenman (Eds.), *Anger and hostility in cardiovascular and behavioral disorders* (pp. 149–172). Washington, DC: Hemisphere.

Maschewsky, W. (1982). The relation between stress and myocardial infarction: A general analysis. *Social Science and Medicine, 16,* 455–462.

Mundal, R., Erikssen, J., & Rodahl, K. (1982). Latent ischemic heart disease in sea captains. *Scandinavian Journal of Work Environment and Health, 8,* 178–184.

National Heart Foundation of Australia. (1986). *Heart facts report.* Canberra, Australia: Author.

National Heart, Lung and Blood Institute. (1981). Coronary prone behavior and coronary heart disease: A critical review. *Circulation, 63,* 1199–1215.

Orth-Gomer, K. (1979). Ischemic heart disease and psychological stress in Stockholm and New York. *Journal of Psychosomatic Research, 23,* 165–173.

Rosenman, R. H., & Chesney, M. A. (1981). The relationship of Type A behavior pattern to coronary heart disease. *Activitas Nervosa Superieur, 22,* 1–45.

Russek, H. I. (1960). Emotional stress and coronary heart disease is American physicians. *American Journal of Medical Sciences, 240,* 711–721.

Russek, H. I. (1965). Stress, tobacco, and coronary disease in North American professional groups. *Journal of the American Medical Association, 192,* 89–94.

Sales, S. M., & House, J. (1971). Job dissatisfaction as a possible risk factor in coronary heart disease. *Journal of Chronic Diseases, 23,* 861–873.

Siegel, J. M. (1984). Type A behavior: Epidemiologic foundation and public health implications. *Annual Review of Public Health, 5,* 343–367.

Siegrist, J. (1984). Threat to social status and cardiovascular risk. *Psychotherapy and Psychosomatics, 42,* 90–96.

Theorell, T., & Floderus-Myrhed, B. (1977). 'Workload' and risk of myocardial infarction—a prospective psychosocial analysis. *International Journal of Epidemiology, 6,* 17–21.

Theorell, T., & Rahe, R. H. (1971). Psychosocial factors and myocardial infarction: I. An in-patient study in Sweden. *Journal of Psychosomatic Research, 15,* 25–31.

Truett, J., Cornfield, J., & Kannel, W. (1967). A multivariate analysis of the risk of coronary heart disease in Framingham. *Journal of Chronic Diseases, 20,* 511–524.

Willerson, J. D., Hillis, L. D., & Buja, L. M. (1982). *Ischemic heart disease: Clinical and pathophysiological aspects.* New York: Raven Press.

Zorn, E. W., Harrington, J. M., & Goethe, H. (1977). Ischemic heart disease and work stress in West German sea pilots. *Journal of Occupational Medicine, 19,* 762–765.

Zyzanski, S. J. (1978). Coronary prone behavior pattern and coronary heart disease: Epidemiological evidence. In T. M. Dembroski, S. M. Weiss, J. L. Shields, S. G. Haynes, & M. Feinleib (Eds.), *Coronary prone behavior* (pp. 25–40). New York: Springer-Verlag.

18

Type A Behavior and the Processing of Causal Attributions of Success and Failure

Michel Pierre Janisse, Cynthia Yerama, Emerald Yeh,
Cathy G. Moser, and Dennis G. Dyck
University of Manitoba, Canada

Researchers have become increasingly interested in providing a psychological conceptualization of Type A behavior (see Matthews, 1982, for a review). Perhaps the most comprehensive account of why Type A persons behave as they do is Glass's (1977) uncontrollability hypothesis. According to Glass, the Type A individual has a high need to control the environment that leads to a unique set of perceptual and behavioral reactions to experiences of uncontrollability (e.g., Krantz, Glass, & Snyder, 1974). In recent tests of this formulation several interesting findings have emerged. For example, Dembroski, MacDougall, and Musante (1984) have provided correlational evidence for a positive relationship between measures of Type A behavior and scores on Burger and Cooper's (1979) Desire for Control scale. In the same study Type A measures were inconsistently related to a general measure of expectancies of control (Rotter, 1966), and the desire for control and expectancy to control measures were unrelated.

This chapter describes two studies that were designed to compare Type A and Type B college students on measures of attributional processing. According to the reformulated model of learned helplessness (Abramson, Seligman, & Teasdale, 1978), the attributions people make for their helplessness are assumed to affect subsequent coping by mediating expectancies of control and self-esteem changes. For example, Abramson et al. (1978) predicted that uncontrollable, negative outcomes will have negative self-esteem implications only if the individual makes internal attributions. In a similar vein, a number of researchers have argued that internalizing success but not failure reflects a cognitive strategy that is designed to boost self-esteem (Bradley, 1978; Zuckerman, 1979).

Thus a considerable amount of research suggests that Type A persons are likely to be more self-serving than Type B persons. Known relationships between attributions and several components of Type A behavior suggest that Type A persons should be more "self-serving" than Type B persons. In particular, cognitive medi-

This research was supported by the Natural Sciences and Engineering Research Council and the University of Manitoba/SSHRCC Fund Committee of the University of Manitoba to Dennis Dyck. Study 2 was conducted by Cynthia Yerama in partial fulfillment of the requirements for the honors bachelor's degree. We wish to thank Linda Wilson for her substantive contribution to this project.

ation models of achievement (Weiner, 1974, 1979) suggest that individuals who are high in achievement motivation make internal and stable attributions for success and external and unstable attributions for failure (see Weiner et al., 1972) and it is well established that Type A persons are highly motivated to achieve success (e.g., Gastorf & Teevan, 1980; Matthews & Saal, 1978). The relationship between external attributions of blame and aggression measures is also fairly well established. For example, in a representative study Kulik and Brown (1979) found that participants who made external attributions of blame for their inability to persuade a confederate to donate to a charity became more angry and aggressive toward the confederate than did participants who were led to make other kinds of attributions. Because evidence from both Structured Interview (SI) ratings of hostility (Matthews, Glass, Rosenman, & Bortner, 1977) and recent behavioral measures (Check & Dyck, 1986; Strube, Turner, Cerro, Stevens, & Hinchey, 1984) indicates that Type A individuals are more hostile and aggressive than Type B individuals, it seems probable that external attributions of blame could mediate this difference.

Although prior theory and evidence are consistent with the prediction that Type A persons should be more self-serving in their attributions than Type B persons, there have also been reports suggesting that Type A persons self-attribute outcomes even when they are negative. For example, Brunson and Matthews (1981), adopting a procedure from Diener and Dweck (1978), assessed subjects' problem-solving strategies and concurrent attributions for failure on Levine discrimination problems. It was found that when the cues signaling noncontingent failure were salient, Type A subjects used more primitive problem-solving strategies and tended to attribute failure to lack of ability—an internal–stable attribution. Type B subjects also began to use somewhat more primitive problem-solving strategies than they had under "success," but unlike Type A subjects, tended to regard their failure as due to an external factor, task difficulty. These results were interpreted to mean that Type A subjects made more internal attributions for failure than did Type B subjects. Findings reported by Rhodewalt (1984) using the Attributional Style Questionnaire led to a similar conclusion. It was reported that both Type A and Type B subjects made internal attributions for hypothetical positive events, but only Type A subjects made internal attributions for negative events. It was also found that in describing the causes of all events, Type A subjects made a greater number of self-referencing statements than did Type B subjects. Rhodewalt interpreted the self-attributional and self-referential differences as evidence that Type A individuals are more self-involved than Type B individuals. It was further speculated that the salience of the control dimension for Type A individuals is mediated by the activation of a self-as-causal-entity schema.

Using the Attributional Style Questionnaire (ASQ) to compare the attributional tendencies of Type A and Type B subjects, Strube (1985) observed a somewhat different pattern of results. He found that Type A subjects were more self-serving than Type B subjects in their attributions for hypothetical positive and negative events, although this effect was more consistently observed among male than among female subjects. It may be important that success and failure situations are clearly defined by the ASQ. In contrast, in the studies cited above success and failure were not clearly defined for the participants; nor were the participants' perceptions of success and failure clearly measured. It is possible, therefore, that the internal attributions made by Type A subjects in these studies under experimenter-defined failure simply reflect a greater reluctance to admit failure under the circumstances. In the present studies we circumvented this definitional problem by having subjects either believe they performed very much above or below stated norms (Study 1) or label their own performance as a "success" or a "failure." Thus, as in the Strube (1985) study, the definition of success and failure was clear; however, in the present study the outcomes were real rather than hypothetical.

STUDY 1

Female Type A and Type B college students were exposed to success and failure on a laboratory task and then given the opportunity to provide attributional ratings. It was predicted that Type A subjects would attribute their "success" more to internal and stable causes than would Type Bs, and would attribute the "failure" more to external unstable causes than would Type Bs.

Method

Subjects

Fifty-six female subjects were selected from 400 introductory psychology students who had completed a battery of tests including Form T of the Jenkins Activity Survey (JAS; Jenkins, Zyzanski, & Rosenman, 1971). From the larger pool, subjects were selected from the upper and lower quartiles of the JAS range. There were 28 Type A and 28 Type B subjects. Of the Type A subjects, 13 were assigned to the success condition and 15 were assigned to the failure condition. Similarly, 16 Type B subjects were in the success group and 12 Type B subjects were in the failure group. The experimenter was blind as to the Type A or Type B status of the subjects.

Procedure

Subjects were tested individually, with all instructions presented via a tape recorder. Subjects were asked to complete two word-naming tasks in which they named as many words as possible, in a 30-s period, beginning with a specific letter, B, for which the mean number of words named was 11.40. The second task was more difficult, using a less frequently occurring initial letter K. The mean number of responses was 5.36.

Before beginning the second task, the subjects were informed that the average response rate for a person of *high intelligence* and *above average ability* was 20 responses per 30 s. Following their performance on the second task, we randomly provided subjects with either success or failure feedback by telling them that their performance was either very much above or below the average of other students *in the study*. Subjects then filled out a questionnaire for either "success" or "failure" attributions. The questionnaire provided a description of each of four potential causes that could influence performance outcomes. The causes were easy task, effort, skill and ability, and luck for success and difficult test, lack of effort, lack of skill and ability, and bad luck for failure. The subjects responded by making a vertical mark on a 5-in. horizontal line that was labeled "not a cause" and "very much a cause" at the end points and "somewhat of a cause" at the midpoint.

Attributional scores could range from 1 to 5, with higher values reflecting greater weight assigned to the factor.

Results

The attributional data were analyzed in two ways. First, an analysis was performed to assess the effects of behavior type and outcome on the ratings provided to the individually listed causes. Second, the ratings given to the individual causes were combined to form dimensional scores such as internal–external and stable–unstable and were analyzed separately. The latter measure provides a more powerful test of the self-serving bias hypothesis. Thus, ability and effort were combined to form an "internal" score, whereas task difficulty and luck were combined to form an "external" score. Similarly, task difficulty and ability were combined to form a "stable" score, whereas effort and luck were combined to yield an "unstable" score.

The analysis of the individual factors began with a multivariate analysis of variance (MANOVA). Where appropriate this was followed up with univariate analyses and specific contrasts using Dunn's procedure (Dunn, 1961; alpha = .05). The subjects in the success condition generally provided higher ratings on the internal attributional factors, $F(4, 50) = 15.25, p < .001$. Specifically, subjects in the success condition provided higher ratings for effort, $F(1, 53) = 53.88, p < .001$, and skill and ability, $F(1, 53) = 12.96, p < .001$, than subjects in the failure condition.

The results relevant to the effects of behavior type on success and failure attributions are presented in Figure 1. Specific comparisons using Dunn's procedure revealed that Type A subjects attributed success significantly more to internal than to external factors ($p < .05$). Type B subjects showed a similar pattern ($p < .05$), but their ratings of internal factors under success were significantly lower than those of Type A subjects ($p < .05$). Thus both Type A and Type B subjects attributed success to internal factors, but the former did so to a significantly greater degree. In contrast, in the failure condition it was found that Type A subjects attributed their performance significantly more to external than to internal factors ($p < .05$) whereas Type B subjects did not differentially weight their attributions to internal or external causes. None of the stable versus unstable comparisons produced differences between or within groups. Collectively, the results of this study suggest that Type A females tended to attribute causality in a self-serving manner. This tendency was not a powerful one, but it is consistent with predictions.

Discussion

Both Type A and Type B females made self-serving attributions in the success condition; that is, internal causes were rated significantly higher than external ones. But, consistent with the prediction of a greater self-serving bias, Type A subjects made significantly greater internal attributions for success than did the Type B subjects. Again, consistent with the hypothesis, Type A subjects displayed a self-serving bias in the failure condition by making significantly greater external attributions than internal ones.

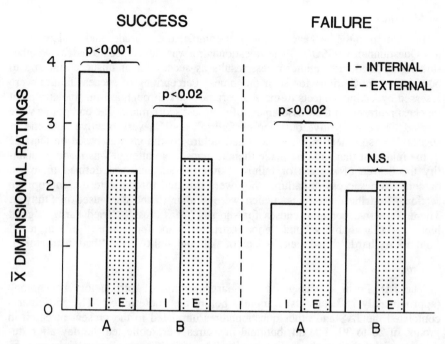

Figure 1   Mean dimensional ratings for female subjects as a function of success and failure in
Study 1.

STUDY 2

We assessed the attributions of Type A and Type B college students for performance on the midterm examination in an introductory psychology course. It was
predicted that Type A students who self-defined their academic performance as a
"success" would make more internal and stable attributions than would Type B
subjects. In contrast, Type A subjects were expected to make more external and
unstable attributions for self-defined "failure" relative to Type B subjects. These
effects were predicted to be more pronounced among males than among females,
because males tend to make more self-serving attributions than females in achievement settings (Frieze, Parsons, Johnson, Ruble, & Zellerman, 1978).

Method

Subjects

The subjects were a class of 87 introductory psychology students from a large
class that had completed the JAS Form T (Jenkins et al., 1971). There were 20
Type A males, 19 Type B males, 26 Type A females and 22 Type B females who
participated. Subjects who had scores of 8 or higher on the JAS were designated as
Type A while those with scores of 5 and lower were categorized as Type B. The
subjects received partial course credit for their participation.

Materials

In addition to the JAS each participant completed the Grades and Student Opinion Questionnaire (GSOQ). The questionnaire was developed to assess whether students defined their midterm test results as successful or unsuccessful and to obtain their attributions for such outcomes. Perceptions of success/failure were assessed by asking subjects to make a vertical mark through a 5-in. line at a point that best represented their assessment of their test score mark. The end points were labeled "a very negative outcome or failure" and "a very positive outcome or success." Assignment to the success and failure conditions was based on the side of the midpoint that subjects made their response. No attempt was made to quantify the degree of success or failure. After the subjects had defined their test outcome as a success or failure, they were directed to complete the appropriate section of attribution ratings, which were similar to the ones used in Study 1. There were five potential causes for success ("easy test," "tried hard," "good luck," "skill and ability," and "good instructor") and for failure ("difficult test," "did not try hard," "bad luck," "lack of skill and ability," and "bad instructor").

Procedure

The JAS Form T was given to a large section of introductory psychology (approximately 250 students) 2 months before the midterm test. The participants completed the JAS and other questionnaires unrelated to the present research in groups of 20 to 30. The attributional measures were collected the day after students received their midterm test results. The experimenter who administered the GSOQ was not the same person who had earlier administered the JAS and was unaware of the subjects' A/B classification. In addition, subjects were unaware of the connection between the two data collection situations. Data linkage was accomplished through matching ID numbers on the two data sets. Following the attributional ratings the subjects were briefed and given experimental credit.

Results

The attributional data were analyzed in two ways, as in Study 1. First, an analysis was performed to assess the effects of behavior type, gender, and outcome on the ratings provided to the individually listed causes. Second, the ratings given to the individual causes were then combined to form the dimensional scores of internal–external and stable–unstable and were analyzed separately. The ratings assigned to the instructor factor were not included in the dimensional analyses.

Again a MANOVA was used for the individual factors and, where appropriate, followed up with univariate analyses and specific contrasts using Dunn's procedure. The MANOVA yielded a significant main effect for outcome, $F(5, 75) = 27.99$, $p < .001$, that when broken down indicated that "success" subjects made higher ratings for ability, $F(1, 79) = 62.64$, $p < .001$; effort, $F(1, 79) = 3.78$, $p < .05$; and the instructor, $F(1, 79) = 92.86$, $p < .001$ relative to "failure" subjects.

Univariate analyses also indicated a significant interaction between behavior type and outcome on ability ratings, $F(1, 79) = 5.30$, $p < .05$; an interaction between behavior type and gender on task difficulty ratings, $F(1, 79) = 4.69$, $p < .05$; and an interaction between gender and outcome on luck ratings $F(1,$

79) = 5.95, $p < .01$. Although somewhat isolated, these univariate interactions were generally in accord with the hypotheses and are graphically shown in Figure 2. The left panel of Figure 2 shows that although both Type A and Type B subjects rated skill and ability higher under perceived success than under failure, this effect was more pronounced among Type A participants. This difference was reflected by the fact that Type A subjects made lower ratings for these internal causes under perceived failure than did Type B subjects ($p < .05$). A second result, shown in the middle panel, was that Type B males made higher ratings for the task factor than did Type B females. The theoretical import of this effect is obscure because task attributions have different self-esteem implications, depending on whether they refer to success or to failure. Finally, as shown in the right panel, females used luck to a greater extent to explain success ($p < .05$) and to a less extent to explain failure ($p < .05$), relative to males. This finding is consistent with previous research that has found females to be less self-serving than males in attributing achievement outcomes (e.g., Frieze et al., 1978).

The prediction that Type A subjects would attribute academic outcomes in a more self-serving fashion than Type B subjects received support with the male participants. Figure 3 presents the dimensional scores for the male subjects. It may be seen that Type A males under perceived success made higher ratings for internal causes than for external ones ($p < .01$) and for stable causes relative to unstable ones ($p < .01$). In contrast, under perceived failure Type A males made higher ratings to unstable causes than to stable ones ($p < .05$). Thus, Type A males clearly took credit for success but not for failure outcomes. Although Type B males generally tended toward a self-serving pattern, in no case did they make significantly different ratings for the internality and stability dimensions under success and failure.

The results with females did not reveal any Type A/B differences. Under success, both Type A and Type B females provided higher ratings for the internal causes than the external ones ($p < .05$ in both cases), but no other comparisons

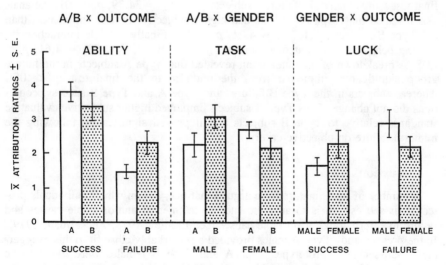

Figure 2 Mean attribution ratings for significant interactions in Study 2.

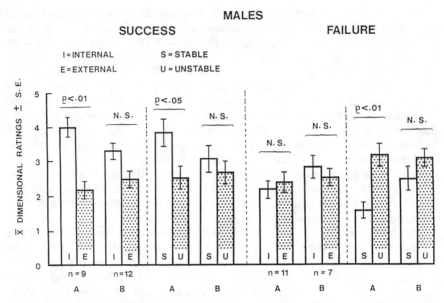

Figure 3   Mean dimensional ratings for male subjects as a function of success and failure in
Study 2.

were significant. Taken together the results suggest that (a) Type A males were the
most self-serving in the present study, (b) Type B males were the most evenhanded
in their attributions, and (c) females in the present study were intermediate in their
attributions, attributing success in a self-serving manner and failure evenhandedly.

To assess whether Type A and Type B participants defined success and failure
differentially, we analyzed the midterm and final test scores for the various groups.
In addition to showing that "success" subjects indeed had higher midterm and
final test scores than did "failure" subjects $F(1, 78) = 34.39, p < .01$, the analysis revealed that Type A subjects had higher subjective criteria for success than
did Type B subjects, $F(1, 78) = 4.21, p < .05$. Finally, a triple interaction involving behavior type, outcome, and test was observed, $F(1, 78) = 4.61, p <
.05$. A breakdown of this interaction revealed that Type A subjects in the failure
group significantly improved from the midterm to the final test ($p < .05$),
whereas subjects in the Type B failure, and Type A and Type B success, conditions did not change. Thus Type A subjects employed higher subjective evaluative
standards relative to Type B subjects and improved significantly following the
midterm failure on objective criteria.

Discussion

A number of investigators have argued that one way in which individuals pro-
tect their self-esteem is to attribute success to internal and/or stable causes and
failure to external and/or unstable causes (see Bradley, 1978; Zuckerman, 1979).
In the present study Type A males provided a remarkably close fit to this exagger-
ated "self-serving" prototype. Type A and Type B females were found to be
somewhat more evenhanded in their attributions.

This is consistent with Weidner's (1980) finding that following failure, Type A subjects were more likely to adopt handicapping strategies than were Type B subjects. Of course, making external attributions for failure is a form of cognitive handicapping that other investigators have identified as an ego protective strategy (cf. Frankel & Snyder, 1978). Finally, as indicated in the introduction to this chapter the attributional profile seen here is also consistent with known linkages between attributions and some of the defining features of the Type A behavior pattern (i.e., achievement striving and hostility and aggression components).

It should also be noted that the significant improvement of the Type A subjects who "failed" their midterm examination would be predicted from existing literature. Schwartz, Burish, O'Rourke, and Holmes (1986) have shown that following failure on a task that is not impossible, Type A individuals devote more effort to subsequent tasks than do Type B individuals, and Holmes, McGilley, and Houston (1984) have argued that Type A persons respond with arousal to all challenging situations. Also, Lulofs, van Diest, and van der Molen (1986) found that after a failure experience, Type A relative to Type B persons experienced greater sympathetic arousal and exerted greater effort to perform well. Given the above, in the present study it is likely that Type A subjects were energized to exert greater effort following the midterm examination results (a failure that could be overcome) and that this greater effort resulted in improved performance on a subsequent task (the final examination).

GENERAL DISCUSSION

The two studies reported here indicate that Type A individuals process both laboratory and naturally occurring outcomes differently than do Type B individuals. Type A subjects demonstrate a greater self-serving bias than Type B subjects under conditions of both success and failure.

The results of these studies are consistent with the literature noted in the introduction that links attributions to Type A characteristics such as achievement striving and aggressiveness. In addition, the results are consonant with Strube's (1985) finding that Type A and Type B subjects differ in their attribution of outcomes. For both positive and negative hypothetical outcomes, he observed Type A subjects to be more self-serving than Type B subjects. The present data replicate Strube's finding and extends it to more veridical success and failure outcome situations, that is, a laboratory experiment where success and failure are spelled out for the subjects, and a classroom situation in which success and failure are rated by the subjects themselves.

However, the A/B differences observed are at variance with the conclusions reached in several other recent reports (e.g., Musante, MacDougall, & Dembrowski, 1984; Rhodewalt, 1984). As noted in the introduction, there are several methodological differences that may account for some of the discrepant findings. It is perhaps important that in both Strube's (1985) research and in the present studies success and failure were "subject" defined (Study 2) and these labels were likely made after subjects had viewed their test scores in the context of the class distribution (the scores were posted in the classroom along with the means and standard deviations). Thus there was ample opportunity for the subjects to evaluate their performance "relative to others" in Study 2. In contrast, in other research (e.g., Brunson & Matthews, 1981), subjects experienced objectively noncontingent laboratory failure in a context that did not readily afford the opportunity for social comparison. Because of the self-esteem implications of these contextual factors (see Abramson et al., 1978; Bandura, 1977), it is not surprising that different attributional patterns were observed in these studies. Strube and Werner (1985) have found that Type A individuals are more reluctant to attribute a partner's success to his or her ability than are Type B individuals, indicating the importance of social comparison in the attribution process of Type A persons. Finally, other factors such as the duration of failure, importance of the outcomes, and the use of different attribution measures doubtlessly varied in the two studies, and these differences may have also contributed to the different pattern of results.

Many of the studies mentioned above conceptualized the Type A individual in much the same way as depressed persons with regard to attribution of outcomes. For example, in a recent review, Peterson and Seligman (1984) characterized depressive subjects as attributing success to external, unstable, and specific causes, but attributing failure to internal, stable, and global causes. Kammer (1984) summarized evidence that depressed persons also tend to focus more of their attention on negative stimuli, at the expense of positive stimuli, and has shown that depressed, compared with nondepressed, persons spend more time considering the causes of their failure than the causes of their success. The present results do not support such a view and indeed suggest that Type A and depressive individuals may have quite different attributional profiles. Further, other evidence suggests that Type A individuals are unlikely to spend a disproportionate amount of time reflecting on their failures. In fact, the opposite may be the case—that Type A persons deny the salience of failure by denying the possibility of control in failure situations. There is generally little consistent evidence that Type A behavior and depression are associated. In one study of Canadian military personnel (Janisse, Dyck, & Malcolm, 1986), depression was *negatively* correlated with the hard-driving component of the JAS, and unrelated to the global Type A measure. This is consistent with Chesney and Rosenman's (1980) review, which concluded that Type A persons generally do not report greater depression than Type B persons.

Another context in which to put these results is in relation to perceptions of control. Dembroski et al. (1984) made a distinction between desirability of control and expectancy or locus of control, that is, counterpoising the desire to control outcomes versus beliefs about the control of outcomes. A significant positive relationship was found between the desire to control and the Type A behavior pattern, as well as those speech stylistics associated with Type A. A question for the present research is to what extent the desire for control versus the belief in control may differentially influence attributions for positive and negative outcomes. Clearly, if Type As are invested in control, then when the situation permits the possibility of success, attributions may reflect the desired level of control (internal attributions). On the other hand, when a person has clearly failed in a situation, attributions for negative outcomes may represent a more veridical belief of how little control was objectively possible (external attributions). Viewed in this way, the Type A person may tend to behave as an idealist in response to positive outcomes but as a realist following negative outcomes. This interpretation has received support in an investigation of perceived control in recalled situations (Dyck, Moser, & Janisse, 1987). For a moderately pleasant recalled experience (competition), but not for an unpleasant one (time pressure), Type A subjects made higher ratings of perceived control than did Type B subjects.

Quite possibly, in discussing control and the Type A subject, it has been a mistake not to distinguish between the two aspects of control—desire and belief. Taken together, the motivational and cognitive/perceptual aspects of control likely interact with each other and situational variables to affect how Type A and Type B individuals perceive their commerce with the environment. Kelley's (1971) description of attribution processes would seem to be particularly apt for the Type A individual: "Attributional processes are to be understood not only as a means of providing the individual with a veridical view of his world, but as a means of encouraging and maintaining his effective exercise of control in that world" (Kelley, 1971, p. 22).

Finally, some mention should be made of the measurement format used to assess Type A behavior. The preferred format seems to be the SI (Rosenman, 1978), yet the majority of studies have used some sort of paper-and-pencil measure (most often the JAS). It seems clear, at this point, that the SI measures something different than does the JAS (cf. Matthews, 1982). With regard to control, these issues were concisely presented by Dembroski et al. (1984), who found a stronger relationship between desire for control and JAS-defined, rather than SI-defined, Type A. They emphasized differences in assessment methodologies between the JAS and SI, pointing to the latter's reliance on speech stylistics as a major determinant of the Type A behavior pattern. It is implied in their discussion that the SI may be the best assessment technique to use when focusing on differences in physiological responsivity. Alternatively, the JAS (or other paper-and-pencil measures), may be a better assessment tool when the focus of the research is on cognitive variables. Similarly, Musante et al. (1984) found attributional differences between Type A and Type B subjects only when they were defined by the JAS and not when defined by the SI. They argued that in the literature, SI Type A subjects tend to be described as action oriented and dominant, with a heavy emphasis on content-free speech stylistics, whereas JAS Type A subjects tend to be described in terms of an achievement orientation. There are many questions yet to be addressed about these two assessment techniques, particularly those revolving around their relationship to coronary heart disease. For the present, however, we feel that the use of the JAS is not inappropriate when the focus is on the psychological dimensions of the behavior pattern.

SUMMARY

The attributions for success and failure of Type A and Type B individuals, as classified by Form T of the Jenkins Activity Survey, were examined in two studies. In the first study, students provided success–failure attributions for a laboratory task. In the second study, students evaluated their midterm test performance and gave attributional ratings for self-defined success or failure. Type A subjects generally made more self-serving attributions than did Type B subjects in both the experimental and naturally occurring situation. Type A and Type B participants both tended to make internal and stable attributions for success, but the former did so to a greater extent. For failure, Type A subjects tended to make attributions to external and unstable factors, whereas Type B subjects were more evenhanded. The results are discussed within the framework of David Glass's (1977) uncontrollability hypothesis, and the egotism hypothesis of Frankel and Snyder (1978).

REFERENCES

Abramson, J. Y., Seligman, M. E. P., & Teasdale, J. (1978). Learned helplessness in humans: Critique and reformulation. *Journal of Abnormal Psychology, 87,* 49–74.

Bandura, A. (1977). Self-efficacy: Toward a unifying theory of behavioral change. *Psychological Review, 84,* 191–215.

Bradley, G. W. (1978). Self-serving biases in the attribution process: A reexamination of the fact or fiction question. *Journal of Personality and Social Psychology, 36,* 56–71.

Brunson, B. I., & Matthews, K. A. (1981). The type of coronary-prone behavior pattern and reactions to uncontrollable stress: An analysis of performance strategies, affect, and attributions during failure. *Journal of Personality and Social Psychology, 40,* 906–918.

Burger, J. M., & Cooper, C. (1979). The desirability of control. *Motivation and Emotion, 3,* 381–393.

Check, J. V., & Dyck, D. G. (1986). Hostile aggression and Type A behavior. *Personality and Individual Differences, 7,* 819–827.

Chesney, M. A., & Rosenman, R. H. (1980). Type A behavior in the work setting. In C. L. Cooper & R. Payne (Eds.), *Current concerns in occupational stress* (pp. 188–212). New York: Wiley.

Dembroski, T. M., MacDougall, J. M., & Musante, L. (1984). Desirability of control versus locus of control: Relationship to paralinguistics in the Type A interview. *Health Psychology, 3*(1), 15–26.

Diener, C. I., & Dweck, C. S. (1978). An analysis of learned helplessness: Continuous changes in performance, strategy, and achievement cognitions following failure. *Journal of Personality and Social Psychology, 36,* 451–462.

Dunn, O. J. (1961). Multiple comparisons among means. *Journal of the American Statistical Association, 56,* 52–64.

Dyck, D. G., Moser, C., & Janisse, M. P. (1987). Type A behavior and situation-specific perceptions of control. *Psychological Reports, 60,* 991–999.

Frankel, A., & Snyder, M. L. (1978). Poor performance following unsolvable problems: Learned helplessness or egotism? *Journal of Personality and Social Psychology, 36,* 1415–1423.

Frieze, I. H., Parsons, J. E., Johnson, P. B., Ruble, D. N., & Zellerman, G. L. (1978). *Women and sex roles: A social psychological perspective.* New York: W. W. Norton.

Gastorf, W. W., & Teevan, R. C. (1980). Type A coronary-prone behavior pattern and fear of failure. *Motivation and Emotion, 4,* 71–76.

Glass, D. D. (1977). *Behavior patterns, stress, and coronary disease.* Hillsdale, NJ: Erlbaum.

Holmes, D. S., McGilley, B. M., & Houston, B. K. (1984). Task-related arousal of Type A and B persons: Level of challenge and response specificity. *Journal of Personality and Social Psychology, 46,* 1322–1327.

Janisse, M. P., Dyck, D. G., & Malcolm, A. T. (1986). *Personality, control and the Type A behavior pattern.* Unpublished manuscript, Department of Psychology, University of Manitoba, Winnipeg.

Jenkins, C. D., Zyzanski, S. T., & Rosenman, R. H. (1971). Progress toward validation of a computer-scored test for the Type A coronary-prone behavior pattern. *Psychosomatic Medicine, 33,* 193–202.

Kammer, D. (1964). Attributional processing style differences in depressed and nondepressed individuals. *Motivation and Emotion, 8,* 211–220.

Kelley, H. H. (1971). *Attribution in social interaction.* Morristown, NJ: General Learning Corporation.

Krantz, D. S., Glass, D. C., & Snyder, M. L. (1974). Helplessness, stress level, and the coronary-prone behavior pattern. *Journal of Experimental and Social Psychology, 10,* 284–300.

Kulik, J. A., & Brown, R. (1979). Frustration, attribution of blame, and aggression. *Journal of Experimental and Social Psychology, 15,* 183–194.

Lulofs, R., van Diest, R., & van der Molen, G. M. (1986). Differential reactions of Type A and Type B males to negative feedback about performance. *Journal of Psychosomatic Research, 30,* 35–40.

Matthews, K. A. (1982). Psychological perspectives on the Type A coronary-prone behavior pattern to achievement, power, and affiliation motives. *Psychosomatic Medicine, 40,* 631–636.

Matthews, K. A., Glass, D. C., Rosenman, R. H., & Bortner, R. W. (1977). Competitive drive, pattern A, and coronary heart disease: A further analysis of some data from the collaborative group study. *Journal of Chronic Diseases, 30,* 489–498.

Matthews, K. A., & Saal, F. E. (1978). The relationship of the Type A coronary prone behavior pattern to achievement, power and affiliation motives. *Psychosomatic Medicine, 40,* 631–636.

Musante, L., MacDougall, J. M., & Dembrowski, T. M. (1984). The Type A behavior pattern and attributions of success and failure. *Personality and Social Psychology Bulletin, 10,* 544–553.

Peterson, C., & Seligman, M. E. P. (1984). Causal explanations as a risk factor for depression: Theory and evidence. *Psychological Review, 91,* 347–374.

Rhodewalt, F. (1984). Self-involvement, self-attribution, and the Type A behavior pattern. *Journal of Personality and Social Psychology, 47,* 662–670.

Rosenman, R. H. (1978). The interview method of assessment of the coronary-prone behavior pattern. In T. M. Dembroski, S. M. Weiss, J. L. Shields, S. G. Haynes, & M. Feinleib (Eds.), *Coronary-prone behavior* (pp. 55–69). New York: Springer.

Rotter, J. B. (1966). Generalized expectancies for internal control of reinforcements. *Psychological Monographs, 80*(Whole No. 609).

Schwartz, D. P., Burish, T. G., O'Rouke, D. F., & Holmes, D. S. (1986). Influence of personal and universal failures on the subsequent performance of persons with Type A and Type B behavior patterns. *Journal of Personality and Social Psychology, 51,* 459–462.

Strube, M. J. (1985). Attributional style and the Type A.coronary-prone behavior pattern. *Journal of Personality and Social Psychology, 49,* 500–509.

Strube, M. J., Turner, C. W., Cerro, D., Stevens, J., & Hinchey, F. (1984). Interpersonal aggression and the Type A coronary-prone behavior pattern: A theoretical distinction and practical implications. *Journal of Personality and Social Psychology, 47,* 839–847.

Strube, M. J., & Werner, C. (1985). Relinquishment of control and the Type A behavior pattern. *Journal of Personality and Social Psychology, 48,* 688–701.

Weidner, G. (1980). Self-handicapping following learned helpless treatment and the Type A coronary-prone behavior pattern. *Journal of Psychosomatic Research, 24,* 319–325.

Weiner, B. (1974). *Achievement motivation and attribution theory.* Morristown, NJ: General Learning Press.

Weiner, B. (1979). A theory of motivation for some classroom experience. *Journal of Educational Psychology, 71,* 3–25.

Weiner, B., Frieze, I., Kukla, A., Reed, L., Rest, S., & Rosenbaum, R. H. (1972). Perceiving the causes of success and failure. In E. E. Jones, D. E. Kanouse, H. H. Kelley, R. E. Nisbett, S. Valins, & B. Weiner (Eds.), *Attribution: Perceiving the causes of behavior.* Morristown, NJ: General Learning Press.

Zuckerman, M. (1979). Attribution of success and failure revisited, or: The motivational bias is alive and well in attribution theory. *Journal of Personality, 47,* 245–287.

19

Attributions of Type A Individuals in an Experimental Academic Stress Situation

Anja Leppin and Ralf Schwarzer
Freie Universität Berlin, Germany

The Type A behavior pattern is usually described in terms of ambition, excessively high performance standards, hard-driving behavior, competitiveness, time urgency, impatience, aggressiveness, hostility, certain speech and motor characteristics related to speed, and a constant need for control over the environment (Friedman & Rosenman, 1974; Matthews, 1982; Price, 1982). Glass (1977) conceived of the Type A pattern as a set of coping behaviors specifically developed in order to maintain control. Seen in this light, time urgency, hard-driving behavior, and aggressiveness would reflect a general mastery orientation meant to gain and keep control over one's life.

At first sight, this conception of the Type A behavior pattern suggests a rather straightforward, expansive, self-confident person with strong achievement motivation and a basically positive attitude toward his or her job who has little dependence on the approval of others. In fact, much empirical work has shown that the attribute "Type A" is positively related to self-esteem and self-confidence (Glass, 1977), that there is no relation to trait anxiety (Glass, 1977; Lovallo & Pishkin, 1980), that Type B individuals believe in an active mastery style of coping rather than a passive-avoidant style (Lohr & Bonge, 1980; Smith & Brehm, 1981), that there is no relationship between the Type A behavior pattern and fear of failure (Glass, 1977), and that Type A individuals are not socially anxious (Smith & Brehm, 1981) and do not seek the approval of others (Lohr & Bonge, 1980; Smith & Brehm, 1981; Smith, Houston, & Zurawski, 1983).

Research results, however, are not that unanimous. When measured by the Framingham Scale (Haynes, Feinleib, & Kannel, 1980) instead of by the Jenkins Activity Scale (JAS: Jenkins, Rosenman, & Zyzanski, 1974), as in the aforementioned studies, it seems that Type A behavior pattern is significantly related to trait anxiety (Chesney, Black, Chadwick, & Rosenman, 1981; Haynes, Levine, Scotch, Feinleib, & Kannel, 1978), less self-control, overreaction to frustration, and anxious overconcern (Smith et al., 1983). Hamberger and Hastings (1986) also detected positive correlations between the JAS-measured Type A and anxious overconcern. Pittner and Houston (1980) found that Type A subjects responded with higher systolic and diastolic blood pressure to threatened self-esteem than did Type B subjects, and that they also employed more cognitive coping strategies such as denial and suppression, which might suggest a specific vulnerability of Type A individuals' self-esteem.

The explicit view that the Type A behavior pattern is much more likely to reflect a secretly defensive rather than an offensive attitude toward life has been taken by Price (1982), who has undertaken one of the rare attempts at explaining the Type A behavior pattern from a comprehensive theoretical background. In a social–cognitive learning model of the Type A behavior pattern, Price indeed suggested that at the core of this pattern there might be a basic feeling of insecurity about one's self-worth. Type A individuals may be dominated by a set of irrational beliefs, among them the conviction that one must constantly prove oneself—to others and, thereby, to oneself. Self-esteem is thus a direct function of observable accomplishments: Because these fluctuate, the individual's sense of self-worth does too.

According to Price (1982), the Type A behavior pattern is a complex system of observable characteristics, typical behaviors, and interrelated core beliefs and fear. Because of the instability of the self-concept, Type A behavior might partly be interpreted as defense of the self. Price also points to the fact that these cognitive sets probably lead an unconscious existence and thus might be difficult to tap by self-report measures. The negative relationship between Type A measures and a need for approval by others, as reported above, might thus be due to the circumstance that this feature would not fit into the self-image or schema Type A individuals have developed over time. Because they conceive of themselves as being strong, dynamic, and independent, Type A individuals cannot afford to admit to being so "weak" that they need the acceptance and praise of others. Herman, Blumenthal, Black, and Chesney (1981) investigated the self-image of Type A subjects in comparison to interview-based ratings and found that they indeed described themselves as dynamic, assertive, extraverted, action oriented, quick, self-confident, and individualistic. They seemed less willing to admit to socially less positive attributes such as hostility, bossiness, hastiness, restlessness, self-centeredness, and so forth, all of which were ascribed to them by means of the interviews. In a similar vein, Type A individuals might be prone to deny or ignore any deeper roots for their behavior, that is, their need for recognition. In addition, Price points to the fact that up to the present day the conception of Friedman and Rosenman (1974), from which fears and anxiety have been excluded by definition, has dominated all research in this area.

In an attempt to test the hypotheses put forward by Price, Burke (1984) found some modest support for the proposed link between beliefs and fears and the Type A behavior pattern as measured by the JAS, especially for the speed and impatience subscales. In a more recent study, Matteson, Ivancevich, and Gamble (1987) similarly found empirical evidence for this model.

One area of research that might provide some valuable insight into the cognitive–emotional processes of Type A and Type B individuals might be the field of attributional behavior in achievement situations. If the "defensive model"—as it has been proposed by Price—is valid, then Type A persons should be very vulnerable to any threat to their self-esteem and thus react more defensively, that is, attribute in a more self-serving manner than Type B persons. At first glance, however, the empirical evidence does not seem to favor this notion.

Several of the studies that have tackled the issue of Type A behavior pattern and attribution of negative and positive performance outcomes have come up with findings that would fit much better into a "control theory" approach. For instance, Brunson and Matthews (1981) found that when they exposed both types of subjects to uncontrollable events, Type A subjects were more likely to attribute their poor performance internally, that is, to lack of effort or to their own inability. Similarly, Rhodewalt (1984); Musante, MacDougall, and Dembroski (1984); Rhodewalt and Strube (1985); and Furnham, Hillard, and Brewin (1985) found Type A subjects to assume more responsibility for negative outcomes than did Type B subjects, whereas there was no significant difference for positive outcomes. Rhodewalt and Strube (1985), discussing these results, concluded that the self-attributions of Type A persons in certain situations might not necessarily reflect self-blame, but much rather enhance their perceptions of the potential for control over the aversive event. Thus, they construct causal explanations that logically allow for additional effort in order to regain control. Indeed, several experiments have shown that Type A subjects reacted with additional effort to salient cues, which signals loss of control, whereas Type B subjects seemed to distract themselves from the task. However, after continuous and prolonged exposure to uncontrollable conditions, the performance of Type A subjects decreased, they blamed themselves as being incapable, and they expressed anger at themselves (see Brunson & Matthews, 1981; Glass, 1977; Glass & Carver, 1980).

Whereas reactance seems to dominate the short-term response of Type A individuals, the learned-helplessness paradigm may be applicable for the long-term response. On the other hand, Strube (1985) suggested that withholding effort might just as well be interpreted in terms of self-esteem protection. Lack of effort is definitely a more modifiable and less self-detrimental attributional factor than lack of ability, and thus might be chosen to explain a negative result while preserving one's own self-image at the same time.

In contrast to the preceding findings, recent studies by Strube (1985) and Strube and Boland (1986) came up with results supporting the case of a self-esteem approach. Type A subjects turned out to be more self-serving; that is, they took more credit for success than for failure compared with Type B subjects. This would suggest that a self-esteem approach might be more helpful than a control-at-any-cost explanation for understanding the attributional behavior of Type A persons. However, it is not necessary to construe a contradiction between two positions that might just as well be combined. A sense of control thus could perhaps be conceptualized as one important component of the need to maintain self-esteem.

According to the Type A behavior pattern model presented by Price (1982), such a strategy might not only serve to maintain self-esteem, but might also be due to self-presentational needs. If it is true that Type A individuals need approval of others in order to approve of themselves, they should be expected to try modeling their image according to situational circumstances. One study has provided some evidence for this notion: Weidner (1980) found Type A subjects to engage in more self-handicapping than Type B subjects after a failure experience. Some indirect support has also been provided by Harris and Snyder (1986), who found self-handicapping tendencies in male subjects with an uncertain self-esteem facing a threatening evaluative task. According to these results, if Type A individuals do have an uncertain self-esteem, they should be expected to engage in self-presentation, too, especially because the Type A behavior pattern seems to be strongly associated with a stereotyped male sex-role orientation. Recently, a great deal of research has been directed to further explore self-related cognitions in Type

A individuals (Ivancevich & Matteson, 1988; Janisse, 1988; Krantz & Raisen, 1988; Rhodewalt, Strube, & Wysocki, 1988).

METHOD

Design

The present study was designed to investigate this issue further. Type A and Type B subjects were exposed to a laboratory-induced stress situation in which they had to perform a series of tasks purported to measure "theoretical intelligence" (in contrast to "practical intelligence"). Following the rationale of Kelley's (1967, 1972) cube model of attribution, we presented *consistency information*, that is, either continuous success feedback or continuous failure feedback, to each subject. All feedback was given in terms of *consensus information*, that is, on a social comparison basis. Subjects were told that their results were either considerably above or below the average result of their peers. After each task unit they were asked to name the main cause for their performance results. Type A subjects were expected to engage in more self-serving attributional behavior, mainly trying to externalize failure, than Type B subjects. In an additional treatment condition, subjects performed the same tasks, but they were confronted not only with a video camera and a television monitor, but also with the presence of the experimenter. The intention was to induce a state of public self-awareness that was expected to influence attributional behavior by moderating any tendency for a self-serving bias. The experiment was planned and conducted as a $2 \times 2 \times 2$ factorial design. The three predictor variables were treatment (success vs. failure), personality traits (Type A vs. Type B), and public self-awareness (presence or absence of camera and television).

Subjects

A total of 207 persons participated in the experiment (101 male, 106 female), with a mean age of 29. They had been recruited by newspaper advertisements that stipulated that they should not be students. In the end, about half of the total sample consisted of people who were unemployed, and the other half came from a variety of professional and nonprofessional vocations, such as teachers, nurses, housewives, clerks, hairdressers, and shop assistants. Each participant was paid DM 30 (about $16).

One hundred two persons were randomly assigned to the success condition, and 105 to the failure condition. Fourteen subjects in the success group were identified as Type A and 25 as Type B (see below). In the failure group, 20 subjects could be classified as Type A and 21 as Type B.

Procedure

After arriving at the laboratory for individual sessions, each participant was greeted by the experimenter and was asked to fill out a series of personality questionnaires, among them one for measuring components of the Type A behavior pattern (see below). After giving instructions, the experimenter left the room. Completing the questionnaire took about 1 hr. Following a 10-min break, the task section began, for which an additional treatment factor was introduced: Half of the subjects were left completely alone while working on a series of computer tasks, whereas the other half were confronted with a video recorder and a television screen that showed them at work on the tasks. In addition, the experimenter sat at a desk about 4 m away, facing the person's profile.

Except for this differential condition, all the subjects were confronted with six action episodes, each consisting of (a) anagrams, (b) performance feedback, and (c) self-report items. First, subjects were to work on tasks consisting of 15 anagram items presented on a computer screen. The introductory information was provided by the computer program. The tasks were described as being cognitive problem-solving tasks, designed to measure a certain aspect of intellectual ability and to be performed under time pressure. Each anagram was presented individually on the screen with a number shown below each letter. Subjects were to type the correct sequence of numbers in the order of the letters forming the word which was looked for. The time was limited to 40 s for solving each anagram. Subjects were instructed to call the next item by pressing a certain key if they had found the solution before the time was up. If they did not succeed in the allotted time, a tone was heard, and the next anagram appeared automatically. The anagrams varied according to the length of the word and the degree of difficulty, becoming more complicated from the 1st to the 15th in each unit. All but the last one were actually solvable. After each of the anagram episodes, fictitious success feedback was given to one group and fictitious failure feedback to the other group. The feedback was partly related to the actual performance by means of a computer algorithm in order to make the outcome seem more credible. The feedback was presented in a way that considered actual individual performance (number of points achieved) as well as (fictitious) performance of students in the same age group (social comparison). After the achievement feedback was given, the program presented 22 verbal items reflecting various self-related cognitions and causal attributions for performance. This cycle (anagrams, feedback, and self-report) was repeated six times. The whole procedure took about 2½ hr.

Instruments

In order to measure components of Type A behavior pattern, scores on three different scales were compiled to form a profile. The first scale was called work involvement and consisted of four items (e.g., "It happens often that I wake up thinking about work problems" and "When I have finished one task I immediately start on the next one"), with a Cronbach's alpha of .91. Next was a 12-item Social Comparison Scale (Jerusalem, 1986) as a measure of competitive drive (Cronbach's alpha = .85). Examples of the items are "For me, to be successful means to outperform others" and "I am proud if others envy my success." In addition, there was a German adaptation of the Anger subscale of the State–Trait Personality Inventory (STPI; Spielberger, 1979) containing 10 items, for example, "I get angry when I'm slowed down by mistakes made by others" and "I feel annoyed when I am not given recognition for doing good work." This trait anger scale deals with the general tendency to react angrily and nervously in a variety of situations. This scale yielded a Cronbach's alpha of .82. The frequency distribution of each of these three variables was split at the median. Those subjects whose scores exceeded median values in involvement, competition, and anger were classified as

Type A, and those scoring below as Type B. Using this diagnostic strategy, extreme groups of 34 Type A and 46 Type B subjects were established. Attributions were tapped by seven items, with a 4-point answer format ranging from *does not apply at all* (1) to *applies completely* (4). Subjects were asked, "Which of the following causes could have been decisive for your personal achievement result in the task group you have just completed?: 1. Ability/talent. 2. Concentration. 3. Effort. 4. Chance. 5. Momentary mood. 6. Task difficulty. 7. Computer."

Data Analysis

The data were analyzed to explore whether different attributional patterns for Type A and Type B persons existed. Performance feedback (success vs. failure), personality (Type A and Type B), and induced self-consciousness conditions (camera vs. no camera) served as the independent variables, and the seven attributions served as the dependent variables. A series of repeated measurement analyses of variance were computed for the 6 points in time in order to include a consistency perspective. A three-factorial design, using Type A/B (two levels), time (six levels), and self-awareness (two levels), was computed separately for the success and failure conditions.

RESULTS

Attributional Differences Between Type A and Type B Individuals During the Six Anagram Episodes

As had been expected, Type A persons were definitely reluctant to accept failure as their own product. Especially remarkable was a significant main effect for behavior type on inability attribution under failure conditions: $F(1, 39) = 6.43$, $p = .015$. Whereas those with a Type B behavior pattern were willing to admit some lack of ability for the negative outcome experienced, those classified as Type A tended to reject this possibility over the whole time span. Further, a significant time effect, $F(5, 195) = 2.70, p = 0.22$, indicated that Type B subjects increased their inability attributions with each consistent failure feedback, and only dropped somewhat inexplicably toward the end. Type A subjects, in contrast, seemed almost imperturbed by any consistency influences, continuing to deny inability as an influential factor (see Figure 1). There were no significant differences between the two groups under the success conditions. Over the whole time span both groups attributed some of their success on ability, the Type B group only slightly more so than the Type A group.

Further comparisons showed that Type A subjects seemed to ascribe more causality to the external and specific factor of computer equipment and to the internal, but unstable, specific factor of bad mood. Persons with a Type A behavior pattern attributed significantly more to the computer monitor in case of failure than did those with a Type B pattern, $F(1, 39) = 4.45, p = 0.41$, while there was no such difference under success conditions (see Figure 2). As for attribution to bad mood, repeated measurement analyses brought about a significant main effect for behavior type, $F(1, 39) = 6.04, p = .018$, and a borderline significant interaction effect between behavior type and time, $F(1, 195) = 2.19, p = .057$. Thus,

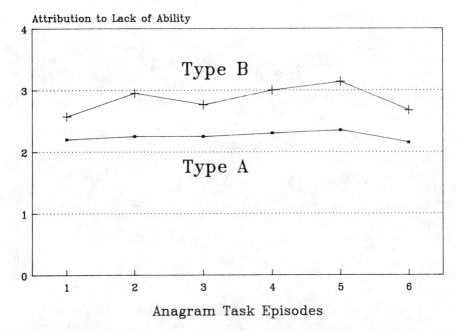

Figure 1 Inability attributions of Type A and Type B subjects under conditions of continuous failure.

Type A subjects were more willing to attribute at least a moderate amount of responsibility to bad mood, whereas Type B subjects rather distinctly denied any influence of this factor on their negative performance outcome. Under the success condition there was a highly significant Behavior Type × Time interaction, $F(5, 185) = 3.54, p = .004$, indicating a very erratic attributional behavior of Type A subjects, who irresolutely oscillated between moderately high and very low attribution to mood. Type B subjects also oscillated, but to a much lesser degree (see Figure 3). There were no significant intergroup differences for attribution to effort, concentration, and chance.

Attribution Under the Public Self-Awareness Condition

An interesting change in the aforementioned results occurred when the subjects were confronted with the video camera, the television screen, and the presence of the experimenter during the six anagram episodes. Although Type A persons denied a causal effect of inability for failure under the noncamera condition, the presence of such devices, which were intended to raise public self-awareness, caused them to increase the internal responsibility ascription to a considerable degree. While in the public self-awareness condition there was no longer any overall significant difference between the two types, a moderately significant effect for self-awareness arose for the intragroup (Type A) comparison, $F(1, 18) = 3.73, p = .07$ (see Figure 4). There was no such intragroup difference for

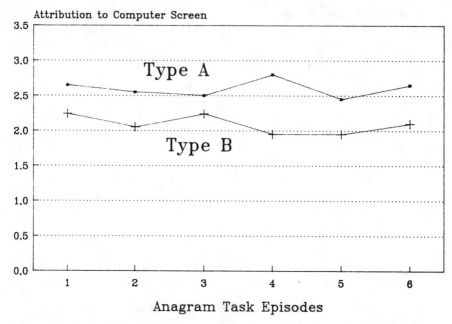

Figure 2 External attributions of Type A and Type B subjects under conditions of continuous failure.

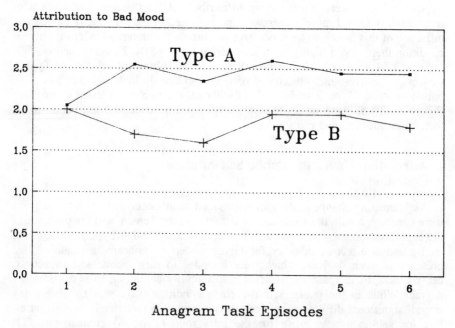

Figure 3 Mood attributions of Type A and Type B subjects under conditions of continuous failure.

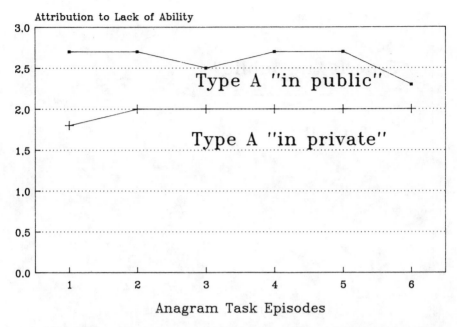

Figure 4 Inability attributions of Type A subjects under two conditions of self-awareness.

the Type B group: Their attributions were fairly independent of presence or absence of camera (see Figure 5).

In the case of success, there was again no notable intragroup difference in terms of self-awareness effects for Type B subjects, whereas for Type A subjects there was a slight, however nonsignificant, tendency, $F(5, 60) = 1.89, p = .11$, for a Self-Awareness × Time interaction. This indicated that whereas Type A subjects were very erratic in their success attribution over time when they were alone, the attributional trend steadied remarkably toward a moderate increase over time with each consistent positive feedback when the camera was present.

DISCUSSION

In accordance with the hypotheses, the present results showed that Type A individuals attributed their failures in a more self-serving way (i.e., less internally) than did Type B persons. Especially remarkable is that they did so in a very definite and decided manner, ignoring the consistent negative feedback. Type B individuals, on the other hand, seem to have taken in the consistency information, continuously increasing their inability attributions in a rational manner. The only drop, which occurred at the end, might have been due either to a reactance effect or to boredom. Type A subjects seem to have settled for an external factor as a causal agent (i.e., having had to work at a computer screen) and an internal but unstable element independent of intellectual capacity (i.e., bad mood). Because there were no differences between the attributions of both behavior types under the success condition, one might assume that Type A individuals are perhaps more concerned with defend-

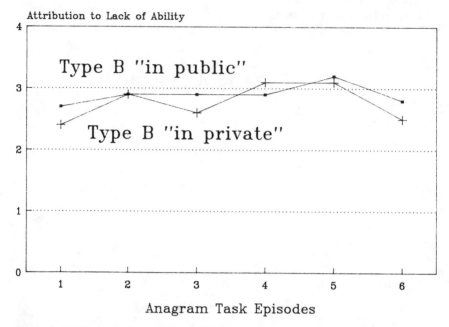

Figure 5 Inability attributions of Type B subjects under two conditions of self-awareness.

ing their self-esteem against the threat of failure than enhancing it under conditions of success. This finding would be consistent with those of other researchers, such as Rhodewalt (1984), Strube (1985), and Strube and Boland (1986).

The most interesting finding, however, is that the attributional behavior of Type A persons was remarkably different when the setting was changed from private to public. When the video camera and the experimenter were monitoring their performance, Type A subjects no longer denied the influence of their own capacity—or lack of it—on the outcome. Type B subjects, however, were not influenced that much by the introduction of a factor designed to arouse public self-awareness. When they reacted at all, it was in terms of a slightly lesser amount of inability attributions. One might assume that, as they were already willing to admit to a considerable degree of responsibility, the camera would incite them to limit their frankness. Thus, there is evidence for not only self-serving impulses, but also for self-presentational ones in both Type A and Type B individuals. However, these two kinds of reactions seem to follow different patterns. One might assume that the presence of the camera and the experimenter witnessing the subject's poor performance helped restrict Type A subjects in their attempt to disclaim responsibility, which they did so extravagantly when these conditions were not present. Under these public conditions it might have seemed advisable for them to make more modest statements and to take some of the blame. This suggests that Type A subjects are not completely immune to thoughts about how others evaluate them, but take into account how they appear to others.

For Type B subjects, the process worked the other way around. Over a long period of time they were willing to state their own responsibility independent of the situation, that is, whether they were being observed or not. The general tendency of these results is consistent with findings reported by Weidner (1980), Strube (1985), and Strube and Boland (1986), but is contradictory to those conveyed by Brunson and Matthews (1981), Furnham et al. (1985), Glass (1977), and Rhodewalt (1984). The following reflections might shed some light on these discrepancies.

In view of the present findings on the influence of public self-awareness, the results of the study by Brunson and Matthews (1981) could be reinterpreted in the light of a public self-awareness perspective. In fact, Brunson and Matthews made their subjects verbalize their thoughts during task performance while an experimenter was listening. This might have involuntarily caused their subjects to experience a state of self-awareness that kept them from engaging in self-serving attributions. All the other studies in which the results were in line with the learned helplessness approach used the Attributional Style Questionnaire (Peterson et al., 1982), which deals with hypothetical situations for attribution. It seems possible that this material is not self-relevant enough to threaten self-esteem. In this case the need for environmental control, which is inherent in the Type A personality, may have dominated any tendency for maintaining self-esteem. A similar argument might hold for the Glass (1977) study, in which subjects were asked to manipulate the occurrence of unpleasant sounds. Here, too, the threat to self-esteem might not have been intense enough.

Recently, Strube, Boland, Manfredo, and Al-Falaij (1987) suggested yet another theoretical approach rather than control or self-esteem. Developing a self-appraisal model, they hypothesized and found some empirical evidence that Type A behavior primarily reflects active attempts to generate diagnostic information about abilities. Although a self-esteem protection perspective would have to maintain that this diagnostic interest is motivated by a need to confirm a high ability appraisal, the design of the present study did not allow for a comparison between the two approaches, because the feedback given was not uncertain or ambivalent at all, as in the experiments of Strube et al. Certainty or uncertainty of feedback would therefore be an important moderator variable to be included in further studies on Type A and attribution.

A critical point in the present study may be the specificity of Type A assessment. Because there is no German adaptation of the JAS, a different measure was used, whereas the JAS has been employed in most of the other studies on the topic of Type A and attribution. By measuring only certain components of Type A, that is, competitiveness, anger, and work involvement, the current results are not directly comparable to findings based on the use of the JAS, and therefore do not provide more than certain hints that deserve further attention. It is important to note, however, that the JAS itself is far from being the "gold standard" of measurement. Though not an element of the JAS, the "anger–hostility–aggression" syndrome has turned out to be the most important Type A characteristic with respect to coronary incidents (Rosenman & Chesney, 1985; Spielberger et al., 1985), and thus seems vital for any instrument claiming to link psychological constructs with medical and behavioral outcomes.

Future research should aim specifically at identifying those components that constitute Type A behavior—those core beliefs and fears that make up this very specific style of coping with environmental demands. Causal attributions in face of challenging demands may serve to identify such components and to construct valid diagnostic measures to tap these dimensions. Multiple test scores that allow for a

Type A profile and process measures in addition, as proposed in the present study, may contribute to theory and assessment as well.

SUMMARY

The present study examined the core beliefs and fears that constitute the Type A behavior pattern. One substrate of this pattern may be a basic feeling of insecurity about one's self-worth. Judgments about own accomplishments, therefore, could be distorted by a self-serving bias that helps to maintain self-esteem. A computerized stress experiment was designed to assess causal attributions of 34 Type A and 46 Type B individuals. Subjects had to solve 90 anagrams of increasing complexity under time pressure. They received fictitious feedback of either continuous success or continuous failure at 6 points in time. After each feedback subjects were requested to respond to causal attribution items. Type A individuals did not attribute as much to inability as a possible causal factor as Type B subjects did. However, an experimental self-awareness condition yielded a moderator effect, indicating the presence of self-presentation strategies. The presumed self-serving bias appeared to be valid only for the non-self-awareness condition.

REFERENCES

Brunson, B. I., & Matthews, K. A. (1981). The Type A coronary-prone behavior pattern and reactions to uncontrollable stress: An analysis of performance strategies, affect, and attributions during failure. *Journal of Personality and Social Psychology, 40,* 906–918.

Burke, R. J. (1984) Beliefs and fears underlying Type A behavior: What makes Sammy run—so fast and aggressively? *Journal of Human Stress, 10,* 174–182.

Chesney, M. A., Black, G. W., Chadwick, J. H. & Rosenman, R. H. (1981). Psychological correlates of the coronary-prone behavior pattern. *Journal of Behavioral Medicine, 4,* 217–230.

Friedman, M., & Rosenman, R. H. (1974), *Type A behavior and your heart.* New York: Knopf.

Furnham, A., Hillard, A., & Brewin, C. R. (1985). Type A behavior pattern and attributions of responsibility. *Motivation and Emotion, 9,* 39–51.

Glass, D. C. (1977). *Behavior patterns, stress, and coronary disease.* Hillsdale, NJ: Erlbaum.

Glass, D. C., & Carver, C. S. (1980). Helplessness and the coronary-prone personality. In J. Garber & M. E. P. Seligman (Eds.), *Human helplessness: Theory and applications* (pp. 223–243). New York: Academic Press.

Hamberger, K., & Hastings, J. E. (1986). Irrational beliefs underlying Type A behavior: Evidence for a cautious approach. *Psychological Reports, 59,* 19–25.

Harris, R. N., & Snyder, C. R. (1986). The role of uncertain self-esteem in self-handicapping. *Journal of Personality and Social Psychology, 51,* 451–458.

Haynes, S. G., Feinleib, M., & Kannel, W. B. (1980). The relationship of psychosocial factors of coronary heart disease in the Framingham Study: III. Eight-year incidence of coronary heart disease. *American Journal of Epidemiology, 111,* 37–58.

Haynes, S. G., Levine, S., Scotch, N., Feinleib, M., & Kannel, W. B. (1978). The relationship of psychosocial factors to coronary heart disease in the Framingham Study: Vol 1. Methods and risk factors. *American Journal of Epidemiology, 107,* 362–383.

Herman, S., Blumenthal, J. A., Black, G. M., & Chesney, M. A. (1981). Self-ratings of Type A (coronary-prone) adults: Do Type A's know they are Type A's? *Psychosomatic Medicine, 43,* 405–413.

Ivancevich, J. M., & Matteson, M. T. (1988). Type A behavior and the healthy individual. *British Journal of Medical Psychology, 61,* 37–56.

Janisse, P. M. (1988, September). *Individual differences in anger and control: Type A behavior, hostility, and self-schema.* Paper presented at the 24th International Congress of Psychology, Sydney, Australia.

Jenkins, C. D., Rosenman, R., & Zyzanski, S. J. (1974). Prediction of clinical coronary heart disease by test for the coronary-prone behavior pattern. *New England Journal of Medicine, 23,* 1271–1275.

Jerusalem, M. (1986). Fragebogen zur Sozialen Vergleichstendenz [Social Comparison Tendency Questionnaire]. In R. Schwarzer (Ed.), *Skalen zur Befindlichkeit und Persönlichkeit (Forschungsbericht 5)* (pp. 229–234). Berlin: Freie Universität, Institut für Psychologie.

Kelley, H. H. (1967). Attribution theory in social psychology. In D. Levine (Ed.), *Nebraska Symposium on Motivation* (Vol. 15, pp. 192–238). Lincoln, NE: University of Nebraska Press.

Kelley, H. H. (1972). Causal schemata and the attribution process. In E. E. Jones, D. Kanouse, H. H. Kelley, R. E. Nisbett, S. Valins, & B. Weiner (Eds.), *Attribution: Perceiving the causes of behavior* (pp. 151–174). Morristown, NJ: General Learning Press.

Krantz, D. S., & Raisen, S. E. (1988). Environmental stress, reactivity and ischaemic heart disease. *British Journal of Medical Psychology, 61*, 3–16.

Lohr, J. M., & Bonge, D. (1980). Relationship of coronary-prone behavior and irrational beliefs in college-age and older men. *Psychological Reports, 47*, 1274.

Lovallo, W. R., & Pishkin, V. (1980). Performance of Type A (coronary-prone) men during and after exposure to uncontrollable noise and task failure. *Journal of Personality and Social Psychology, 38*, 963–971.

Matteson, M. T., Ivancevich, J. M., & Gamble, G. O. (1987). A test of the cognitive social learning model of Type A behavior. *Journal of Human Stress, 13*, 23–31.

Matthews, K. A. (1982). Psychological perspectives on the Type A behavior pattern. *Psychological Bulletin, 91*, 293–323.

Musante, L., MacDougall, J. M., & Dembroski, T. M. (1984). The Type A behavior pattern and attributions for success and failure. *Personality and Social Psychology Bulletin, 10*, 544–553.

Peterson, C., Semmel, A., von Baeyer, C., Abramson, L. Y., Metalsky, C. I., & Seligman, M. E. P. (1982). The Attributional Style Questionnaire. *Cognitive Therapy and Research, 6*, 387–300.

Pittner, M. S., & Houston, B. K. (1980). Response to stress, cognitive coping strategies, and Type A behavior pattern. *Journal of Personality and Social Psychology, 39*, 147–157.

Price, V. A. (1982). *Type A behavior pattern. A model for research and practice.* New York: Academic Press.

Rhodewalt, F. (1984). Self-involvement, self-attribution, and the Type A coronary-prone behavior pattern. *Journal of Personality and Social Psychology, 47*, 662–670.

Rhodewalt, F., & Strube, M. J. (1985). A self-attribution reactance model of recovery from injury in Type A individuals. *Journal of Applied Social Psychology, 15*, 330–344.

Rhodewalt, F., Strube, M. J., & Wysocki, J. (1988). The Type A behavior pattern, induced mood, and the illusion of control. *European Journal of Personality, 2*, 231–237.

Rosenman, R. H., & Chesney, M. A. (1985). Type A behavior and coronary heart disease: Review of theory and findings. In C. D. Spielberger, I. G. Sarason, & P. B. Defares (Eds.), *Stress and anxiety* (Vol. 9, pp. 212–229). Washington, DC: Hemisphere.

Smith, T. W., & Brehm, S. S. (1981). Cognitive correlates of the Type A coronary-prone behavior pattern. *Motivation and Emotion, 5*, 215–223.

Smith, T. W., Houston, B. K., & Zurawski, R. M. (1983). The Framingham Type A Scale and anxiety, irrational beliefs, and self-control. *Journal of Human Stress, 9*, 32–37.

Spielberger, C. D. (1979). *Preliminary manual of the State–Trait Personality Inventory.* Unpublished manuscript.

Spielberger, C. D., Johnson, E. H., Russell, S. F., Crane, R. J., Jacobs, G. A., & Worden, T. J. (1985). The experience and expression of anger: Construction and validation of an Anger Expression Scale. In M. A. Chesney & R. H. Rosenman (Eds.), *Anger and hostility in cardiovascular and behavioral disorders* (pp. 5–30). New York: Hemisphere/McGraw-Hill.

Strube, M. J. (1985). Attributional style and the Type A coronary-prone behavior pattern. *Journal of Personality and Social Psychology, 49*, 500–509.

Strube, M. J., & Boland, S. M. (1986). Postperformance attributions and task persistence among Type A and Type B individuals: A clarification. *Journal of Personality and Social Psychology, 50*, 413–420.

Strube, M. J., Boland, S. M., Manfredo, P. A., & Al-Falaij, A. (1987). Type A behavior pattern and the self-evaluation of abilities: Empirical tests of the self-appraisal model. *Journal of Personality and Social Psychology, 52*, 956–974.

Weidner, G. (1980). Self-handicapping following learned helplessness treatment and the Type A coronary-prone behavior pattern. *Journal of Psychosomatic Medicine, 24*, 319–325.

20

Two Kinds of Type A Behavior Pattern

Andrzej Eliasz
Polish Academy of Sciences, Warsaw, Poland

Kazimierz Wrześniewski
Warsaw Academy of Medicine, Poland

HETEROGENEITY OF TYPE A PERSONS

Research on the connection between Type A behavior pattern (TABP) and coronary heart disease (CHD) has been conducted for more than 30 years. According to Meyer Friedman and Ray Rosenman (1959), most patients with CHD are characterized by TABP. This pattern has been identified as coronary-prone behavior. Individuals classified as Type A are

> *in chronic struggle to achieve poorly defined goals or to obtain excessive number of things from their environment and to be in habitual conflict with others and with time. (Rosenman, Swan, & Carmelli, 1988, p. 8)*

The theoretical definition of TABP usually encompasses such behaviors as ambitiousness, competitiveness, impatience, time urgency, and job involvement. The Jenkins Activity Survey (JAS; Jenkins, Zyzanski, & Rosenman, 1979) covers such behaviors, with subscales such as Speed and Impatience, Job Involvement, and Hard-Driving Competitiveness. A lot of data, however, indicate that JAS TABP relates much more weakly to CHD than TABP assessed by the Structured Interview (SI; Rosenman, 1978). There are marked differences, however, between the TABP conceptual definition and the operational definition used in the SI (cf. Dembroski & MacDougall, 1985; see also Byrne, Rosenman, Schiller, & Chesney, 1985). The SI operational definition of TABP is confined mainly to speech mannerisms (loudness, explosiveness, rapidity, and quickness of response) displayed in situations that potentially elicit reactions of impatience, competitiveness, and hostility. The interviewer not only asks subjects in what way they react in such situations but also provokes such reactions in subjects. Rosenman's (1978) descriptions used to categorize (on the basis of the SI) individual patterns of behavior (i.e., A-1, A-2, X and B) refer almost exclusively to formal behavior characteristics observable during interviews.

The SI and JAS are the most well-known techniques for assessing TABP. Thus differences between them and the apparent superiority of SI have caused great

This work was supported by the Polish Ministry of Science and Higher Education, Research Grant RPBP.III-25.

confusion among researchers and, after 30 years of research on TABP, have led to the formulation of the rather unusual question, What exactly is the TABP (O'Rourke, Houston, Harris, & Snyder, 1988)?

Data gathered before 1978 were very promising but later data were ambiguous. Booth-Kewley and Friedman (1987) compared results before 1977 with those after 1977. After 1977, results were definitely less promising as regards a TABP–CHD relationship. Methodological flaws of recent studies and societal changes over time concerning manifestations of TABP have been offered as explanations of this phenomenon (O'Rourke et al., 1988). Also, it is pointed out that enormous changes in health behavior and the treatment of CHD in the United States may have affected the TABP–CHD relationship. For example, physicians aware of TABP as a risk factor of CHD can pay much more attention to patients displaying this pattern of behavior.

Scherwitz (1988) described changes over time in the style of administering of the SI. According to him, TABP ratings derived by "facilitative" interviewers correlate with CHD. A facilitative interviewer speaks slowly, does not interrupt or hurry the subject, and waits for some time after the subject has finished speaking before resuming the interview. In contrast, TABP ratings derived by a disruptive interviewer are probably not associated with CHD. Characteristically, the disruptive style was recommended after 1977, which is when the number of studies showing clear and positive TABP–CHD relationships started to decrease.

The discouraging results of studies carried out in recent years have prompted researchers of TABP to pose dramatic questions: "Has the Type A construct outlived its usefulness? Is Type A dead?" (O'Rourke et al., 1988, p. 313). Researchers try to overcome these difficulties in various ways. First, TABP and the coronary-prone behavior pattern are not treated now as synonymous concepts. It appears that some variables that lie outside of TABP, such as anxiety and depression, can contribute to the development of CHD (Booth-Kewley & Friedman, 1987; Friedman & Booth-Kewley, 1987, 1988; Matthews, 1988).

Second, some data actually undermine the usefulness of the TABP concept. Some researchers contend that hostility is the only "toxic" element of TABP (i.e., contributes to the development of CHD) (Dembroski & Costa, 1988; Williams, Barefoot, & Shekelle, 1985; Williams et al., 1980). According to Williams and Barefoot (1988), these elements of TABP that constitute the hostility complex are manifested in "a cynical, mistrusting attitude toward others and willingness to express openly the anger and contempt" (p. 206). Dembroski and Costa (1988) pointed out that antagonistic hostility expressed in cynical, manipulative, arrogant, selfish, and antagonistic attitudes and behaviors is an important risk factor. This constitutes hostile style, whereas neurotic hostility (irritation, resentment, annoyance, and rage) is not a risk factor for CHD. Dembroski and Costa presented data that indicated that global TABP (measured by SI) is completely unrelated to CHD.

However, some data still support the idea of TABP (cf. Haynes & Matthews, 1988). An especially important contribution to this discussion is Houston's work (1988) on cluster analysis for identifying individuals who have similar combinations of TABP characteristics. Using this cluster analysis, Houston questioned the assumption concerning the equivalence of each particular element of TABP. When the same value is ascribed to each element of TABP, then the group of people classified as having TABP are in fact heterogeneous; they can be differentiated as regards the internal structure of TABP, although they can receive the same global indices of TABP. Houston found that males classified by cluster analysis as TABP had significantly higher systolic blood pressure than males in the non-TABP group. Houston argued for the superiority of grouping subjects into Type A or B on the grounds of cluster analysis but, unfortunately, he did not present the relations of each element of TABP with the physiological reactivity of subjects.

Third, Friedman, Hall, and Harris (1985) undertook the task of refining the Type A–B classification. They hypothesized that a group of people classified as TABP is heterogeneous in other than the aforementioned respects. On the basis of accepted measurement techniques, they maintained that TABP persons can also be described as confident, dominant, vigorous, and active in their expressive style. These persons can be quite healthy. In contrast, some Type B persons can be quiet, slow to speak, and unaggressive because they may have repressed hostility and ambition. This Type B pattern of behavior is likely a risk factor in CHD. This hypothesis has been confirmed by Friedman and Booth-Kewley (1987), who also presented data suggesting that emotional expressiveness is taken into account in classifying subjects as Type A or B on the basis of SI.

We present below a hypothesis concerning the heterogeneity of persons labeled as having TABP. We maintain that an expressive style is a by-product of the relationship between various individuals' potentials determined by the biological bases of temperament. Simply put, persons can be forced by social milieu to behave in TABP manner or they can spontaneously acquire TABP because it reflects their biological determinants of temperament. We hypothesize that mainly TABP acquired under social pressure can be a risk factor of CHD.

TEMPERAMENT AND THE TYPE A BEHAVIOR PATTERN

To recapitulate the above-mentioned material: Scholars do not entirely agree about the essential element of TABP; there is no consistency between operational and theoretical definitions or between most commonly used techniques. Because those techniques frequently constitute the basis for assessing the validity of newly constructed scales, without basic theoretical analysis concerning the very nature of TABP, any subsequent TABP scales will be no more coherent than their most popular predecessors.

In our opinion, the presented discrepancies result partly from the belief that TABP is a CHD predictor. Detailed theoretical assumptions have been adjusted to fit this basic general assumption. Moreover, the validity of TABP diagnostic methods depended on the capacity for predicting CHD. Later data which contradicted this assumption led only to additional correcting assumptions.

Our own collected data along with that provided by the literature allow us to question the general nature of the TABP–CHD relation. Such a conclusion arises from studies that reveal that the origin of TABP and its health consequences depend to a considerable extent on one basic temperament dimension, namely, reactivity (Eliasz & Wrześniewski, 1986, 1988).

High-reactivity persons are characterized by high dynamics of respondent behavior that results from their high sensitivity to weak stimuli and low resistance to strong stimuli. On the other hand, low-reactivity individuals demonstrate low dynamics of respondent behavior caused by low sensitivity to weak stimuli and correspondingly high resistance to strong stimuli (Strelau, 1983, 1985). The lower the reactivity, the higher the stimulation need. This is manifested in behavioral preferences and the development of personality according to this need (Eliasz, 1985; Klonowicz, 1985; Strelau, 1983, 1985).

It may be assumed that the TABP, providing considerable feedback stimulation connected with the subject's own activity (e.g., aggression or haste) and his or her participation in highly stimulating situations (e.g., competition), may be conducive to satisfying the high need for stimulation of low-reactivity subjects, and on the other hand may lead to overstimulation of high-reactivity subjects. In the first case, we would be dealing with coherence of acquired behaviors, and with the subject's potential being determined by the biological foundations of temperament. In the case of high-reactivity subjects, behaviors would be inconsistent with the subject's abilities.

The same may be said of behaviors typical of a strong need for achievement (Eliasz, 1973). It turns out that TABP as well as a strong need for achievement are acquired by both high- and low-reactivity subjects. This corresponds with data obtained by Svebak and Apter (1984), who discovered that both persons defined by Apter (1982) as being under "telic dominance" (avoiding threats) and those categorized as "paratelics" (striving for inner stimulation) are able to adopt TABP. These data are consistent with findings obtained by Maciejczyk and Terelak (1986). TABP persons were characterized by high indices of standard deviation with regard to the dimensions of temperament measured by Strelau's Temperament Inventory and the Guilford-Zimmerman Temperament Survey.

Proof can be found in the literature that TABP is formed in children under the impact of parental influence. Parents' values and educational practices play a great role in the formation of TABP. Matthews (1978) put forward the hypothesis that high parental demands, associated with frequent punishing and rewarding of continuously improving functioning, may cause the child to acquire a chronic need for achievement and a sense of time urgency. Price (1982) has found that such parental behaviors as increasing demands for exemplary activity as a condition of acceptance as well as severe criticism of a child's errors and of his or her expected behavior dominate the family climate of TABP persons.

MacCranie and Simpson (1986) have found that boys who score high on Scale A, and are in particular characterized by a high dynamics of behavior and a strong tendency toward competition, describe their parents as rigid, expecting competition in different areas, and prone to using physical punishment and other aggressive methods of control.

All this indicates that the behavior pattern is formed in the course of interaction with parents,[1] and may be learned regardless of innate possibilities and predispositions. Obviously, no one can ignore the role of innate predispositions in forming TABP (cf. Eysenck & Fulker, 1983). We assume that innate predispositions either facilitate or complicate the acquiring of behavior patterns.

The findings of our research (Eliasz & Wrześniewski, 1986) show that the

---

[1] Interpersonal relations are not only important in acquiring TABP, but it is very likely that the very consequences of TABP depend on social relations. For example, for TABP men (defined by SI), the indices of CHD depend on the characteristics of their wives. CHD is relatively frequent in the group of TABP men married to dominant and active women with at least 13 years of schooling (Carmelli, Swan, & Rosenman, 1985). These wives probably induce in their TABP husbands unhealthy behavior such as continual competition with the wife or with others.

environmental conditions that nurture a high need of achievement and TABP differ considerably depending on the reactivity of adolescent boys. When high-reactivity adolescents are brought up in an environment that

1. promotes ambitious educational goals (e.g., prestigious schools and mothers with a strong need for achievement in sons) and
2. at the same time "impels" the young to fulfill these goals (e.g., large, competition-inspiring schools [see Barker & Gump, 1964] and mothers exercising rigid control over their sons).

then the development of a high need for achievement and a more intense TABP correlating with anxiety are enhanced. Apart from this correlation, no connection between the TABP and the need for achieving distant life goals was found among the high-reactivity boys.

Low-reactivity adolescents brought up in an environment that sets ambitious goals but, at the same time, gives much freedom to pursue them (e.g., small schools and mothers bringing up their children with considerable freedom) probably encourages the development of a high need for achievement and high TABP intensity not correlated with anxiety. It has also turned out that, in the case of low-reactivity persons, TABP is correlated with the need for achievement referring to distant life goal.

One more thing should be added to the above relations: The lowest TABP indices were obtained among high-reactivity subjects brought up in an environment where much freedom was given and little was expected from them, that is, in conditions of low social pressure to maximize educational achievements (for details, see Eliasz & Wrześniewski, 1986, 1988).

The collected findings reveal that high-reactivity subjects manifest high TABP intensity connected with intensive stimulation only when they encounter pressure to maximize educational achievements. Under similar conditions, however, low-reactivity subjects resist social pressure. The phenomenon of "reactancy" (cf. Brehm, 1966) of low-reactivity subjects encountering such pressure is indicated by low TABP indices and low achievement need compared with those of low-reactivity subjects from environments promoting ambitious goals and the freedom with which to pursue them. Such conditions for the development of low-reactivity subjects stimulate a high need for achievement and high TABP intensity. Low-reactivity subjects' activity focused on accomplishing ambitious goals is then internally reinforced, because it allows for the satisfaction of a high stimulation need. In high-reactivity persons (i.e., those with low stimulation need), however, activity typical of the high intensity of achievement need or TABP most probably causes disturbances in the regulation of stimulation. Strong social pressure is then needed for this kind of activity to be assimilated. Activity typical of the high achievement need and high TABP intensity is externally reinforced by the social environment. This obviously refers to the phase in which such aspirations are being formed. After the aspirations have become autonomic, external reinforcements are replaced by internal ones related to reliance on success and control of the situation (cf. Glass, 1977).

A consequence of the inconsistency between stimulation need and TABP assimilated by high-reactivity persons is the relation between high TABP indices and increased anxiety.[2] Another effect of the above inconsistency is that high TABP

---

[2] Anxiety is a risk factor of CHD that lies outside TABP (see "Heterogeneity of Type A Persons").

intensity does not correspond with high achievement need concerning distant goals. Because for many scholars achievement need is the basic element of TABP, it can then be presumed that this element is not absent in TABP. Perhaps the high-reactivity subjects characterized by high TABP intensity concentrate on short-term goals. This would mean that such persons are characterized by high achievement need restricted to these kinds of goals.

Our data suggest different TABP origins depending on temperamental features. A hypothesis may also be formulated that health consequences associated with TABP depend, among other things, on the consistency of the relationship of TABP to temperament. We are then inclined to presume that the relationship between TABP and coronary heart disease refers only to the kind of TABP that is formed under the pressure of the social environment, against the subject's capabilities as defined by the biological foundations of temperament. In other words, we assume that a relation between TABP and CHD is to be found probably in the group of high-reactivity persons.

This hypothesis may be also derived from data concerning the relation between temperament and resistance to various stress situations: The higher the person's reactivity, the lower his or her general stress resistance (Strelau, 1983). Hence, persons low in stress resistance should be found among TABP high-reactivity subjects. The confirmation of this hypothesis may be found in the data collected by Kobasa, Maddi, and Zola (1983). According to them, of persons experiencing many stress situations, those with low stress resistance who are at the same time characterized by TABP, are usually in the worst state of health compared with TABP, stress-resistant persons and with Type B persons regardless of resistance. Also, the finding (Kobasa et al., 1983) of a lack of correlation between TABP and stress resistance appears consistent with data showing that TABP can be adopted by both high- and low-reactivity subjects.

We formulated above the hypothesis that TABP origin differs depending on the person's temperament and various health consequences connected with it. In addition, both our own research and other data provided in the literature seem to indicate that differences in TABP origin probably correspond to different internal structures of TABP. The following premises regarding the differentiation of the two kinds of TABP pattern can be tentatively formulated:

1. Instrumentality of given behaviors and their forms versus behaviors characterized by fear or hostility constituting a permanent emotional background for various behaviors;

2. Relation of the positive (achievement striving) to negative (hostility) TABP aspects;

3. Limitation of TABP characteristic behaviors to certain specific task situations, and the ensuing flexibility of behaviors in compliance with a situation versus their general character;

4. Ability to perform actions regulated by distant or near aims;

5. Treating difficult tasks as challenge versus threat.

The empirical research that would aim at verifying the presented hypothesis would be of considerable importance for the understanding of TABP origin. Data thus collected could also serve as the basis for preparing a new TABP measurement instrument of greater predictive value than hitherto obtained concerning the risk of CHD.

SUMMARY

On the basis of our research, we conclude that probably two kinds of Type A behavior pattern (TABP) exist. Recent research has suggested that people acquire behaviors typical of TABP, which are strongly self-stimulating, either spontaneously or because of social pressure according to temperament. High-reactivity persons, that is, those very susceptible to stimuli and consequently with a very low need for stimulation, acquire TABP by virtue of external reinforcements. On the contrary, their opposites, that is, low-reactivity persons, acquire TABP by way of internal reinforcements supporting the gratification of these persons' high need for stimulation. These two kinds of reinforcements lead to the formation of two kinds of TABP. Both the different internal structure and the apparently different health consequences of these TABPs are described.

REFERENCES

Apter, M. J. (1982). The experience of motivation: The theory of psychological reversals. London: Academic Press.

Barker, R. G., & Gump, P. V. (1964). Big school, small school. Stanford, CA: Stanford University Press.

Booth-Kewley, S., & Friedman, H. S. (1987). Psychological predictors of heart disease: A quantitative review. Psychological Bulletin, 101, 343–362.

Brehm, J. (1966). A theory of psychological reactance. New York: Academic Press.

Byrne, D. G., Rosenman, R. H., Schiller, E., & Chesney, M. A. (1985). Consistency and variation among instruments purporting to measure the Type A behavior pattern. Psychosomatic Medicine, 67, 242–261.

Carmelli, D., Swan, G. E., & Rosenman, R. H. (1985). The relationship between wives' social and psychological status and their husbands' coronary heart disease: A case-control family study from the Western Collaborative Group Study. American Journal of Epidemiology, 122, 90–100.

Dembroski, T. M., & Costa, P. T. (1988). Assessment of coronary-prone behavior: A current overview. Annals of Behavioral Medicine, 10, 60–63.

Dembroski, T. M., & MacDougall, J. M. (1985). Beyond global Type A: Relationships of paralinguistic attributes, hostility, and anger-in to coronary heart disease. In T. Field, P. McCabe, & N. Schneiderman (Eds.), Stress and coping (pp. 223–242). Hillsdale, NJ: Erlbaum.

Eliasz, A. (1973). Temperament traits and reaction preferences depending on stimulation load. Polish Psychological Bulletin, 4, 103–114.

Eliasz, A. (1985). Transactional model of temperament. In J. Strelau (Ed.), Temperamental bases of behavior: Warsaw studies on individual differences (pp. 41–78). Lisse: Swets and Zeitlinger.

Eliasz, A., & Wrześniewski, K. (1986). Type A behavior resulting from internal or external reinforcements. Polish Psychological Bulletin, 17, 39–53.

Eliasz, A., & Wrześniewski, K. (1988). Ryzyko chorób psychosomatycznych: Srodowisko i temperament a wzór zachowania A [A risk of psychosomatic diseases: Environment—Type A behavior pattern]. Wroclaw: Ossolineum.

Eysenck, H. J., & Fulker, D. (1983). The components of Type A behavior and its genetic determinants. Personality and Individual Differences, 4, 499–505.

Friedman, H. S., & Booth-Kewley, S. (1987). Personality, Type A behavior, and coronary heart disease: The role of emotional expression. Journal of Personality and Social Psychology, 53, 783–792.

Friedman, H. S., & Booth-Kewley, S. (1988). Validity of the Type A construct: A reprise. Psychological Bulletin, 104, 381–384.

Friedman, H. S., Hall, J. A., & Harris, M. J. (1985). Type A behavior, nonverbal expressive style, and health. Journal of Personality and Social Psychology, 48, 1299–1315.

Friedman, M., & Rosenman, R. H. (1959). Association of specific overt behavior pattern with blood and cardiovascular findings. *Journal of the American Medical Association, 169,* 1286-1296.

Glass, D. C. (1977). *Behavior patterns, stress and coronary disease.* Hillsdale, NJ: Erlbaum.

Haynes, S. G., & Mathews, K. A. (1988). The association of Type A behavior with cardiovascular disease—update and critical review. In B. K. Houston & C. R. Snyder (Eds.), *Type A behavior pattern: Research, theory, and intervention* (pp. 51–82). New York: Wiley.

Houston, B. K. (1988). Cardiovascular and neuroendocrine reactivity, global Type A, and components of Type A behavior. In B. K. Houston & C. R. Snyder (Eds.), *Type A behavior pattern: Research, theory, and intervention* (pp. 212–253). New York: Wiley.

Jenkins, C. D., Zyzanski, S. J., & Rosenman, R. H. (1979). *Jenkins Activity Survey.* New York: Psychological Corporation.

Klonowicz, T. (1985). Temperament and performance. In J. Strelau (Ed.), *Temperamental bases of behavior: Warsaw studies on individual differences* (pp. 79–115). Lisse: Swets and Zeitlinger.

Kobasa, S. C., Maddi, S. R., & Zola, M. (1983). Type A and hardiness. *Journal of Behavioral Medicine, 6,* 41–51.

MacCranie, E. W., & Simpson, M. E. (1986). Parental child-rearing antecedents of Type A behavior. *Personality and Social Personality Bulletin, 12,* 493–501.

Maciejczyk, J., & Terelak, J. (1986). Dependence between Type A behavior pattern and personality features. *Biology of Sport, 3,* 215–226.

Matthews, K. A. (1978). Assessment of developmental antecedents of coronary-prone behavior pattern in children. In T. M. Dembroski, S. M. Weiss, J. L. Shields, S. G. Haynes, & M. Feinleib (Eds.), *Coronary-prone behavior* (pp. 207–218). New York: Springer-Verlag.

Matthews, K. A. (1988). Coronary heart disease and Type A behaviors: Update on and alternative to the Booth-Kewley and Friedman (1987) quantitative review. *Psychological Bulletin, 104,* 373–380.

O'Rourke, D. F., Houston, B. K., Harris, J. K., & Snyder, C. R. (1988). The Type A behavior pattern: Summary, conclusions, and implications. In B. K. Houston & C. R. Snyder (Eds.), *Type A behavior pattern: Research, theory, and intervention* (pp. 312–334). New York: Wiley.

Price, V. A. (1982). *Type A behavior pattern. A model for research and practice.* New York: Academic Press.

Rosenman, R. H. (1978). The interview method of assessment of the coronary-prone behavior pattern. In T. M. Dembroski, S. M. Weiss, J. L. Shields, S. G., Haynes, & M. Feinleib (Eds.), *Coronary-prone behavior* (pp. 55–70). New York: Springer-Verlag.

Rosenman, R. H., Swan, G. E., & Carmelli, D. (1988). Definition, assessment, and evolution of the Type A behavior pattern. In B. K. Houston and C. R. Snyder (Eds.), *Type A behavior pattern: Research, theory, and intervention* (pp. 8–31). New York: Wiley.

Scherwitz, L. (1988). Interviewer behaviors in the Western Collaborative Group Study and the multiple risk factor, intervention trial structured interviews. In B. K. Houston & C. R. Snyder (Eds.), *Type A behavior pattern: Research, theory, and intervention* (pp. 32–50). New York: Wiley.

Strelau, J. (1983). *Temperament–personality–activity.* London: Academic Press.

Strelau, J. (1985). Pavlov's typology and the regulative theory of temperament. In J. Strelau (Ed.), *Temperamental bases of behavior: Warsaw studies on individual differences* (pp. 7–40). Lisse: Swets and Zeitlinger.

Svebak, S., & Apter, M. J. (1984). Type A behavior and its relation to serious-mindedness (telic dominance). *Scandinavian Journal of Psychology, 25,* 161–167.

Williams, R. B., & Barefoot, J. C. (1988). Coronary-prone behavior: The emerging role of the hostility complex. In B. K. Houston & C. R. Snyder (Eds.), *Type A behavior pattern: Research, theory, and intervention* (pp. 188–211). New York: Wiley.

Williams, R. B., Barefoot, J. C., & Shekelle, R. B. (1985). The health consequences of hostility. In M. A. Chesney & R. H. Rosenman (Eds.), *Anger and hostility in cardiovascular and behavioral disorders* (pp. 173–185). New York: Hemisphere.

Williams, R. B., Haney, M. A., Lee, K. L., Kong, Y., Blumenthal, J. A., & Whalen, R. (1980). Type A behavior, hostility and coronary atherosclerosis. *Psychosomatic Medicine, 42,* 539–549.

Author Index

Subject Index